STUDIA POST-BIBLICA

VOLUMEN TRICESIMUM

STUDIA POST-BIBLICA

INSTITUTA A P. A. H. DE BOER

ADIUVANTIBUS

L. R. A. VAN ROMPAY ET J. SMIT SIBINGA

EDIDIT

J. C. H. LEBRAM

VOLUMEN TRICESIMUM

LEIDEN
E. J. BRILL
1981

A SAMARITAN CHRONICLE

A Source-Critical Analysis of the Life and Times of the Great Samaritan Reformer, Baba Rabbah

BY

JEFFREY M. COHEN

LEIDEN
E. J. BRILL
1981

ISBN 90 04 06215 7

PRINTED IN THE NETHERLANDS

TO GLORIA

גמלתהו טוב ולא־רע כל ימי חייה.

TABLE OF CONTENTS

PREFACE

This book is the fruit of research undertaken in the Department of Hebrew and Semitic Languages of Glasgow University, under the supervision of Professor John Macdonald, during the period 1972–1977.

I should like to place on record my profound thanks to Professor Macdonald for having introduced me to the study of Samaritanism and for having made available to me the fruits of his great erudition in this field. His sincere interest and encouragement throughout the years of my research have been a source of profound satisfaction and academic stimulation.

I also thank my colleagues, Drs Robert Gordon, Berl Cutler and Alexander Broadie, whose academic companionship provided a reliable sounding-board for my theories and ideas.

This publication was made possible by several generous grants which I have pleasure in acknowledging:

The Arthur Davis Memorial Fund (Friends of the Hebrew Univ. of Jerusalem).
The Maurice And Joseph Bloch Trust.
The Chief Rabbi's Jewish Educational Development Trust.
The Goldberg Family Trust, Glasgow.
The Glasgow Jewish Community Trust.
The Isidore and David Walton Charitable Trust, Glasgow.
The Edith & Isaac Wolfson (Scotland) Trust.

I should also like to thank the Glasgow Jewish Educational Trust for administrative assistance, and my friend, Mr. Fred Hall, for help with certain problems of translation.

My greatest thanks are reserved for my wife, Gloria, for her love, patience and encouragement, as well as to my children, Harvey, Suzanne, Judith and Lewis, without whose sacrifice of long hours, which, otherwise, would have been devoted to them, this research could never have been undertaken.

Jeffrey M. Cohen

ABBREVIATIONS

(Biblical books are not listed here. They are referred to by their customary abbreviation)

AF	*Abu'l Fatḥ* (ed. Vilmar).
Akk	*Akkadian.*
Aram.	*Aramaic.*
Arab.	*Arabic.*
BDB	*Brown, Driver and Briggs (Hebrew and English Lexicon of the Old Testament).*
Ber. Rabb.	*Midrash Bereshith Rabbah.*
BH	*Biblical Hebrew.*
BH[3]	*Biblica Hebraica* (Kittel[3]).
b	*ben.*
BT	*Biblical Text* (Judaistic version).
CESC	*A Critical Edition of the Baba Rabbah Section of the Samaritan Chronicle No. II.* Glasgow University Thesis, 1977 (unpublished section only of present work).
Cf.	*Compare.* (Used, especially in our Commentary, to indicate biblical references where text differs from version of Chronicle. Otherwise "See" is used.)
Dittog.	*Dittography.*
DSS	*Dead Sea scrolls*
EJ	*Encyclopaedia Judaica.*
Ed.	*Edition.*
GK	*Gesenius-Kautzsch, Hebrew Grammar*
Gr.	*Greek.*
GRP	*Gazetteer of Roman Palestine,* (ed. M. Avi-Yonah).
Heb.	*Hebrew.*
Ibid.	*Ibidem.*
Inf	*Infinitive.*
KB	*Koehler and Baumgartner, Lexicon in Veteris Testamenti Libros.*
Lit.	*Literally.*
Loc. cit.	*Loco citato.*
LOTS	*The Literary and Oral Tradition of Hebrew and Aramaic among the Samaritans,* Z. Ben-Hayyim, Jerusalem, 1957.
LXX	*Septuagint version of the Old Testament.*
MT	*Masoretic Text.*
n.	*Note.*
NEB	*New English Bible.*
NH	*New (late) Hebrew.*
Op. cit.	*Opere citato.*
OT	*Old Testament.*
OTL	*Old Testament Library.*
pl.	*Plural.*
SH	*Samaritan Hebrew.*
Se. Ha.	Sepher Ha-Šômrônîm, I. Ben-Zevi (3rd ed.), Jerusalem, 1976.

sing.	*Singular.*
SP	*Samaritan Pentateuch.*
ST	*Samaritan Targum.*
Tal.	*Talmud.*
Targ.	*Targum.*
TSL	*The Samaritan Liturgy,* A.E. Cowley, Oxford, 1909.
Tol.	*Tolidah.*
v	*Verse.*
Vb	*Verb*

JOURNALS

AAJR	*American Academy for Jewish Research.*
AJBA	*Australian Journal of Biblical Archaeology.*
AJSL	*American Journal of Semitic Languages.*
ALUOS	*Annual of the Leeds University Oriental Society.*
BA	*The Biblical Archaeologist.*
BASOR	*Bulletin of the American School of Oriental Research.*
BJPES	*Bulletin of the Jewish Palestine Exploration Society.*
BS	*Bibliotheca Sacra.*
BZAW	*Beihefte zur Zeitschrift für die Alttestamentliche Wissenschaft.*
EI	*Eretz Israel.*
HTR	*Harvard Theological Review.*
HUCA	*Hebrew Union College Annual.*
IEJ	*Israel Exploration Journal.*
JA	*Journal Asiatique.*
JAOS	*Journal of the American Oriental Society.*
JNES	*Journal of Near Eastern Studies.*
JPOS	*Journal of the Palestine Oriental Society.*
JQR	*Jewish Quarterly Review.*
JThS	*Journal of Theological Studies.*
NTSt	*New Testament Studies*
OTS	*Oudtestamentische Studiën.*
PAAJR	*Proceedings of the American Academy for Jewish Research.*
PEFQSt	*Palestine Exploration Fund: Quarterly Statement.*
PSBA	*Proceedings of the Society of Biblical Archaeology.*
REJ	*Revue des Etudes Juives.*
RB	*Revue Biblique.*
SHi	*Scripta Hierosolymitana.*
TrGUOS	*Transactions of the Glasgow University Oriental Society.*
VT	*Vetus Testamentum.*
ZAW	*Zeitschrift für die Alttestamentiche Wissenschaft.*

A Folio of Chronicle II
(H2)

I. INTRODUCTION

The present study constitutes a critical edition, with commentary, of a hitherto unpublished section of the fullest extant Chronicle of Samaritan history. This Chronicle — Chronicle II — commences with the period of the biblical historical books (Joshua, Judges, Samuel and Kings/II Chronicles) and continues the Samaritan saga down until the beginning of the 20th century.

The publication of this section of the Chronicle fills an important gap in Samaritan studies, in that it treats of one of the most charismatic personalities in Samaritan tradition and of a period (3rd–4th cent. A.D.) which constitutes a high-water mark in Samaritan history.

The figure of Baba Rabbah looms large on the Samaritan canvas. Much has been said of him that is legendary, much that is true. Earlier and later traditions have been interwoven around his personality. No comprehensive, critical attempt has yet been made, however, to present a biography of his life based upon an analysis of the historicity of these traditions, and the social, religious and political reforms he is credited with having introduced in order to achieve a total reconstruction of Samaritan life.

The biblical section of this Chronicle has already been published by John Macdonald,[1] as has a small section on the Jesus period.[2] The present study focusses upon the lengthy section on the life and activity of Baba Rabbah; and we have attempted in our research to reconstruct the exact nature of the contribution of that great leader.

The scope of this study has inevitably been fairly wide, as the Chronicle possesses linguistic as well as historical significance. We have presented the major burden of our linguistic inquiry in Chapters II–IV, which comprise the text, translation and commentary, and in Chapter IX, which presents the main linguistic and syntactical characteristics of the Chronicle.

It should be noted that, apart from the work done by J. Macdonald, the Samaritan chronicles have been a neglected field from the point of view of critical textual inquiry. A critical edition of the type here offered has long been a *desideratum.*

---

[1] For works of scholars referred to in this introduction, see Bibliography.

[2] Published by J. Macdonald and A.J.B. Higgins.

A considerable amount of interest has been aroused, however, in recent decades, in other aspects of Samaritanism, with important works having been contributed in the fields of wider Samaritan linguistics (by Ben Hayyim, Kahle and Murtonen), grammar (by R. Macuch), hermeneutics (by S. Lowy[3]), Theology (J. Macdonald), Philosophy (A. Broadie[4]), history (Bowman, Coggins and Kippenberg) — not forgetting the pioneering contribution, in so many aspects of Samaritanism, made by scholars of a less recent period, notably A. Cowley, M. Gaster and J. Montgomery. The fruits of the present research will be of considerable importance, it is believed, in each of the above-mentioned aspects of Samaritanism, serving to offer a newly published source which can only help to extend the insights and results so far obtained by these scholars.

The text of the Chronicle is set out in the parallel versions of H1 and H2, two recensions, each possessing a totally different linguistic complexion. The former is written in a uniquely classical form of Samaritan Hebrew; the latter in a more colloquial and familiar Aramaic dialect. Both these recensions are of great importance. H1 offers a form of *Waw-Consecutive* Classical Hebrew which extends our knowledge of non-Masoretic forms, disclosing verbs which appear in other conjugations, and semantic shades of meaning, than those of biblical Hebrew, as well as a syntax which is not bound by rules as clearly defined as those of biblical Hebrew. H2, likewise, makes a significant contribution to our lexical knowledge of Samaritan Aramaic, providing interesting and new vocabulary to supplement that already gleaned. The parallel texts provide, we believe, the best method of demonstrating the varying stylistic approaches of both versions, as well as their undoubted interrelationship.

Among the intriguing problems raised by the Chronicle is that of the very liberal use made of the Judaistic book of Psalms. The significance of this employment of "external literature" by a Samaritan author is discussed in Chapter VI. The significant textual variations in the chronicler's version of these Psalms is monitored and discussed in our Commentary. These will be of special interest to the biblical scholar interested in non-Masoretic forms.

The 4th cent. period of Palestinian history is not well

[3] Lowy's contribution, *The Principles of Samaritan Bible Exegesis* (Leiden, 1977), was published too late to be considered by the present writer. Many problems raised by Lowy are elucidated however, by the material contained in Chronicle II.

[4] Details of Broadie's research are taken up by us in *CESC* 475–489.

documented, and our Chronicle provides an unexpectedly rich harvest of historical data and traditions which shed much light on the history of the community at that period, the inter-community relations between Samaritans and Jews, the intrigue, struggle and recriminations which characterized this relationship, as well as their mutual dealings with the Romans.

The Chronicle provides new slants on important issues which dogged attitudes of the rabbinic authorities toward the Samaritans. Especially interesting is the suggestion we offer that the Mishnaic charge that the Samaritans kindled beacons on the wrong night of the New Month, solely in order to frustrate the Jews' attempt to convey its date to their diaspora communities, may well have been a misrepresentation of fact based upon ignorance (real or pretended) of a Samaritan ritual of fire-purification, prescribed for *Rosh Ḥōdesh,* and not an act of mischief! (See Chapter VIII).

New slants are also provided on the familiar charge that the Samaritans worshipped a dove on the top of Mount Gerizim. We have related this charge to an episode described in our Chronicle, and have re-examined the rabbinic sources in the light of this new material, in order to determine the basis for such a charge (Chapter VII).

The personality of Baba Rabbah has hitherto been enigmatic, as has been the exact significance of his name and title. We have attempted to demonstrate, by the textual-critical approach, that a number of the generally-accepted traditions about him are, in fact, later accretions, intended to enhance his legendary mystique, and based upon unreliable evidence with little historical credibility. In this context we have highlighted the confusion surrounding the chronology of the period, and have been constrained, on the basis of a chronological reconstruction, to offer a new date for the life and activity of Baba Rabbah. We have also demonstrated that the generally-held view that he was a High Priest (see *Encycl. Judaica,* 4, 17) cannot be substantiated, and that the tradition that he ended his days in captivity in the city of Constantinople is a later tradition which has no basis in historical fact, and which cannot be harmonized with other traditions linking Baba with the period of the pre-Constantine emperors (Chapter X).

Baba is known to have been a great reformer, but the chronicles, other than Chronicle II, provide a rather sketchy description of the exact nature of these reforms. On the basis of the material contained in our Chronicle, we have analyzed these reforms, as well as the hierarchic re-structuring which Baba embarked upon. This has enabled us to determine a tripartite structure of leadership comprising — under Baba — a supreme council of seven leaders, eleven "pairs" of priestly administrators and fifty Synagogue administrators or *Šimmûrê Ha-Tôrāh.*

Baba's reforms were especially geared toward a spiritual re-construction of Samaritan life around the institution of the Synagogue; and to this end he re-opened Synagogues that had been closed by the Romans, and built many new ones. The locations of these Synagogues are carefully described in our Chronicle, although the significance of the overall siting of these Synagogues has hitherto remained unnoticed. We have discussed the various sites,[5] some of which are still a matter of archaeological conjecture, and we have detected a definite symmetry, whereby all the Synagogues lie around the circumference of a circle, with Shechem and 'Amartah at the epicentre. This arrangement served to further Baba's political aspiration of a centralized authority.

The question of Baba's Dositheanism has recently been re-opened in the light of the research into this sect by J. Isser.[6] Again our chronicle provides important insights into this question.

From a passage in our chronicle, referring to a rival 'family' that did not accept the authority of Baba Rabbah, but maintained their own political and religious autonomy, we were led to examine the origin, extent and significance of this opposition — referred to by the name of *Mišpaḥath Haššibh'îm* — and the manner in which Baba came to terms with it. This, inevitably, provides a new dimension from which to assess Baba's diplomatic achievements and his limitations.

An important period of cultural and spiritual activity was inaugurated by Baba Rabbah, a period which inspired men of the calibre of 'Amram Darah and Marqah who, in turn, laid the foundation for Samaritan theological speculation and liturgical development. The antecedents of a number of Marqah's ideas are also traced in our Chronicle.

Unfortunately, within the editorial limitations imposed upon the length of the present volume, it was not possible to present the full burden of our research into all the above aspects of our Chronicle. This is particularly so in the case of the final chapter, 'Baba Rabbah — His Life and Times', which heroically attempts to condense 130 pages of research into one small chapter. It will be appreciated, therefore, that a number of statements contained in that chapter might appear arbitrary, even mystifying, when

[5] See CESC 490–504.

[6] J. Isser, *The Dositheans,* Leiden, 1976.

presented as conclusions with no supportive argumentation and source treatment. The reader is respectfully directed to the original research volume[7] for full treatment of the individual topics referred to.

[7] Jeffrey M. Cohen, *A Critical Edition of the Baba Rabbah Section of the Samaritan Chronicle No. II: With Translation and Commentary,* Glasgow University Doctoral Thesis (1977).

II. HEBREW TEXT

§1

1 ויהי אחרי כן נתן יי׳ יתברך שמו לכהן הגדול נתנאל שלשה בנים.

2 ואלה שמותם האחד קרא את שמו בבא והשני קרא את שמו עקבון והשלישי קרא את שמו פינחס.

3 ופינחס היה ישב בקרית מחנה אשר היא בקצה המקום המבחר הר גרזים בית אל תחת ההר.

4 ובבא מנעריו היה איה איש מוסר בעל חכמה ובינה ויהי איש מצליח וכל אשר הוא עשה יי׳ מצליח בידו.

5 וקנאת יי׳ שכנת בלבו ותהי עליו רוח קדושה.

6 ויהי בימים ההם ויגדל בבא ויהי איש כבוד ואימה ופחד בין כל בני עמו בני ישראל השמרים על האמת וירא בסבלותם וירא את אשר היה עליהם מאת האויבים.

7 ויתחכם להסיר את הצרעה הזאת מעליהם וירא את שרי המסים אשר שמו עליהם למען ענותם וימררו את חייהם הארורים בני אדום.

8 ויאמר בבא הזוכיר בלבו ויעבר בענינו וכוח גדול היה ביצרו.

9 וייטב אלהים את מחשבו יגלי קנאה גדולה להראות את פני יי׳ אלהיו.

10 ואחרי כן הקהל בבא את כל אנשי דרו אשר היו שמעים לקולו ויאמר אלהים לאמר.

11 אחי האזינו כלכם לאמרתי רוח הקנאה דבר עם לבבי לאמר.

12 לנגלא את האימן הישראלי כי חזקת יד האויבים עליו וימחו מן הארץ את כל דגליו.

13 וידיק בבא הזוכיר את חניכו וינציר את יצרו על כן וירבי לפני יי׳ אלהיו את פלליו.

14 ויקרא את אנשיו אשר הקהל אתם מטרם והם בני דרו אשר זכרנו אתם ויאמר אליהם לאמר.

15 עד מתי הערלים האלה הכפורים ביי׳ אלהינו ואלהי אבותינו מפנינו עבודי אלהי זרה הצרים לתורת משה הקדושה

---

1 ואחר כן שת יהוה לכהן הגדול נתנאל שלשה בנים.

2 וזאת שמותם הראש יתקרי בבא והשני עקבון והשלישי פינחס.

3 וזה פינחס היה שכון בקרית מחנא אשר היא בתחתית ההר הקדש.

4 ובבא היה מן צעירו יקיר משתעבד.

5 ואגדל ושם יהוה בלבה קנאה על הדת ומלא אתו מן רוח החכמה ואציל עליו מן רוח הקדש.

6/7 וכד אגדל צפר איש מורם בעל אימה ומשלה בין עמו ומן רב חכמתו אתחכם ואתבונן ועמה מה בא על משפחתו ועל בני דתו מן חמס האדום שנאה אימנותו הכפורים ביהוה התמיד באלהותו.

8 ואתור בלבו ואתגדלת מדעותו.

9 ואתיטב ביצרותו כי יגלי ביהוה קנאתו לדת.

10 ואחל בראש למן היו בני דרה ומתיסרים אתו ואמר להם.

11 כי עתה חם לבבי אגלי קנאה לכוננת דת משה הנבי.

12 כי חלשו הכפור ומבקש לו יגויע והקשט צפר מתכבי ואכרת דכרניו אה אהבי.

13 ודק קנאתו ואנציר בזה יצרותו וגם אחל ביחדאות להתמיד ביחדאותו.

14 ונדב בני עמיתו וכל נשיאי עדתו ואמר להם.

15 עד מתי אהלין הערלים דלא בהם אחד הנמל בשר ערלתו הכפורים ביהוה ותורותו

ימררו את חיינו ואת חיי כל
השמרים אחינו.
16 עד מתי לעדה הרעה הזאת עד מתי
ינכרו צרינו ויאמרו ידינו רמה עד
מתי יהיה זה לנו למוקש.
17 עד מתי תשקע מעלינו זאת האש עד
מתי ימנעו לנו את משמר דרך יי׳
אלהינו להקים את מצוותיו.
18 עד מתי ימנעו לנו מן המקרא בקדוש
תורותיו ולשמר את משפטיו ועדתיו.
19 וישיבו אתו אנשי דרו דבר לאמר
20 שמענו אדני ראה את הגללים אשר
מנעת לנו לקום לפני אויבינו וכי
נלאים בזאת הימים הזינו.
21 ראה כי אזלת ידינו ותקומה אין
לנו בין ידי שנאינו.

מצררים לנו כל אחד הך
די ריחותו.
17 והם מבקשים ישמידו לנו
וימיתו וימאנו אתנו מן
משמר דרכי יהוה חקותו
ומשפטו ותורותו.
19/21 ואחלו עדתו לו יספרו
הגללות אשר תמאן אתם
במה מדרשו יעפלו ונלאותם
ומה להם אויביהם שפלו.

§2

1 ויען אתם בבא לאמר הלוא מבני יעקב
ישראל אנחנו אשר שנים אחים מבניו
קנאו ליי׳.
2 ויהרגו שניהם את כל אנשי עיר שכם
אשר אמר בעדם בתורותו הקדושה לאמר
ויקחו שני בני יעקב שמעון ולוי אחי
דינה איש חרבו ויבאו על העיר בטח
ויהרגו כל זכר ואת חמור ואת שכם
בנו הרג לפי חרב ויקחו את דינה
מבית שכם ויצאו.
3 הלוא ימצא בתוכנו אנשים משבט
לוי אשר קנאו ליי׳ אלהיהם לעת
העגל.
4 ואמר בעדם בתורותו הקדושה ויאספו
אליו כל בני לוי והרגו איש את
אחיו ואיש את רעהו ואיש את קריבו
וימחו את עבודי העגל בעצם היום
הזה לפי חרב.
5 ראו את הברכה אשר אשית יי׳
יתקדש שמו עליהם.
6 הלוא ימצא בתוכנו אנשים מבני
פינחס אבינו ונראה לו כי אז קנא
ליי׳ אלהיו מלבין כל בני ישראל
עמו איך נתן יי׳ לו יתר שאת ויתר
עז.
7 ואמר בעדו ופינחס בן אלעזר בן
אהרן הכהן הנני נתן לו את בריתי
שלום והיתה לו ולזרעו אחריו
ברית כהנת עולם תחת אשר קנא
לאלהיו יכפר על בני ישראל.
8 זכרו את אשר היה לשמעון ואל
לוי איך יי׳ יתברך שמו הפל

1 ואמר להם הלוא מבני ישראל
אנחנו דשנים מבניו קנאו
ליהוה.
2 ואתכוננו וחרבו מדינה
וכל מנון חרבו בימינו
ובזו כל מדלות דאמרו להם
והתחתנו אתנו.
3 הלוא ימצא בנו מן השבט
הלוי דקנאו ליהוה בהרגות
עבודי העגל.
4 ואתאמר בגללון בתורה הקדשה
ויאספו אליו כל בני לוי
למימרו והרגו איש את אחיו
ואיש את קריבו עד אחרה
ומחו עבודי העגל הקב בחרב.
5 ועמו מה היה להם מן
הברכה.
6 הלוא ימצא בנו מן זרע
פינחס אבינו איך קנא
לאלה בל עמו ישראל
ואיך יהוה נצחנה ונתן לו
מיתובה.
7 וכרת אתו ברית לעלם וכהנה
מתקוממה תמידה לו ולזרעו
עד עולם.
8 הלוא תזכרו מה היה לשמעון
ולוי ואיך יהוה אשקח אימה

חתת על הערים אשר היו סביבותיהם
ולא רדפו אחריהם.
9 ועתה חייב עלינו נאמץ את לבבינו
ונקנה ליי׳ אלהינו כקנאת אבותינו
על זאת המעשים אשר פגענו להם
מפני אויבינו.
10 ונתן את מאדינו לקוממית חקות
יי׳ אלהינו אשר מלבין כל העמים
בחר בנו ולו לעם סגולה לקחנו.
11 ועתה אין לנו בלתי השובה והתחנון
והצעקות לרם כבודו ולדרש את טובו
וחסדו ולעמל לפני גדלו בצלות
והציאם והתחנון והתפלות והנחמות
והדרישות.
12 ונתן את מאדנו לעשות את מצותיו
ולשמע בקולו ולהדבקה בו עד
ישים לנו עזרה ביכלותו וגאותו
על אויבינו ושנאינו הן קבלנו
הוא מן טובו וחסדו והן גרשנו
הוא מרעות מעשינו.
13 כי הוא יתברך שמו מקבל השובים
אשר ישובו לפני גדלו.
14 ועתה טוב לנו נהיה מן הקנאים
לתורותו הקדושה ונתן את כל
מאדינו לחדשות תלמודה כי היא
עתה אבדה ונקים את דגלי.
15 עתה נפילה ודרסה לנכרים
הארורים ונקם את ירכי האימון
לזאת הקנאה אולי נהיה כמו
אשר עברו לפנינו מן הישרים
והצדיקים אשר חפצו את דרך
יי׳ אלהיהם ודרשו את טובו
וחסדו ולשמר את כל מצותיו
אהבו לדרגי אשר לדרכיו השיגו.
16 הבו מעת והלאה נטהר את
לבבינו מן העונות והחטאות
ובנציר נשוב ליי׳ אלהינו
וננקי מכל הרעות ולא נטה משפט
ולא נכיר פנים.
17 ונרחק את נפשותינו מכל עשוי
העונים אשר כחשו את מצות
אדון האדונים וסר לרע דרך
דרכי הרשעים החטאים.
18 אחי דעו כי נעשה כה בנציר
היצרים וירא יי׳ כי אנחנו
עשים מעשה הצדקים הישרים
וטהורי היצרים בנגלאים
ונסתרים לא פג כי ישא את
פניו אלינו ויקבל את
שובתינו וישמע את נקעתנו
ומכל מצור ומצוק יוצאנו

ופחד על יושבי הערים
דסביבות שכם ולא רדפו אחריהם.
9 ועתה לאוי עלינו נתחזק
ונאמץ ונקנא על זאת הגללות
דקוממת עלינו מעם הזה
השותפים ביהוה.
10 ונקנא על קעמות התורה וככן
המשפטים והחקות דיהוה צוה
אתנו במשמרון.
11 ולא נשאר לנו בלתי השובה
והתפלה והצעקה והתהללות
והנחמה.
12 ובמאדנו נשתעבד ונתקוי
על שנאינו ביכלותו אן
היה כן הוא חסד ממנו
ואן אתריח ישגב רחמותו
מעלינו נהיה נפשותינו
בשבעדותו.
13 ויהוה לא יאבד אגר
החסדים.
14 ובזה עתה חיב עלינו
נקנא לתורה ונלמדה כי
עתה צפרת בעודות מתאבדה
ונקים את דגלי הקשט דבלת.
15 ונשיד ארכוני הדת בזאת
הקנאה דבלבבינו עתה הורידת
אולי נדמי למן אתקדמו
דחשקת נפשותם ודרגון אנשת
והכבדת ובקראת יהוה נמצא
מנינו חננות מן הביא
מימינו אש דת.
16 והבו מיום הזה והלאה
נטהר לבבינו מן כל תועבה
ונשוב שובה בלא שובה
וננקיא מכל מסה ומריבה.
17 ונרחק מעלינו עשוי
התועבה אשר הרעו בנו
וטמאו הארץ הטובה.
18 ודעו כי אנחנו עשינו כן
וידע יהוה טהרות יצרינו
בלא פג יראה לדלותינו
ובכוח והמצליח יעננו.

19 וירחיב את לחצנו ויעני את מדרשינו
וירא את ענינו ואת דלותינו ויתן
לנו מאתו יכולה על שנאינו ויצליח
את דרכינו ועבוטה יעביטנו ודבוקה
ידבקנו על רעצות הערלים האלה
בעלי הקללה הטמאים הרשעים החטאים
העשוי הפשעים עבודי הנכרים לפני
אלהי הרוחים אשר מן חסר ברא
הבוראים.
20 ונשמידם ונגלא אתם מזאת הארץ
הקדושה עד לא תראה בה נפש בישה
וילכו לארץ האחרית וראשם יקדית
לפני עדת השמרים על האמת.
21 קומו בנו נרגף אחריהם ובעזרת יי׳
אלהינו ונחלשם ונאבדם ונשא את
זאת המגפות הרעות מעלינו.

19/20 ועל זאת הערלים יעזר
אתנו כי טמאו הארץ
אחזתנו דנשבע בה
לאבותינו ותשאר
ראשם מתנדחים.
21 שם נרדף אחריהם ונשא
זאת האלות המרירה.

§3

1 ויכל הכהן בבא רבה מן הדברים
האלה עם מעיני עדת בני ישראל
השמרים ועם כל בני דרו.
2 ואחרי כן לחץ בבא רבה את ידיו
ואת פניו ואת רגליו ויתפלל
וישתחוה לפני יי׳ אלהיו.
3 ויצום ביום ההוא לחם לא אכל
ומים לא שתה.
4 ויהי ביום השני וישכם בבא רבה
בבקר ויעל אל הר הברכה הר הקדוש
המקום המבחר הר גרזים בית אל.
5 ויי׳ יתברך שמו הצליח את דרכו
עד השיג אל המקום ההוא ויחן
שם בראש ההר.
6 ויחל הכהן בבא רבה את פני יי׳
אלהיו ויתנפל לשלטניו ויתפלל
לגדלו ויתחנן לכבודו ויצליח
את צלותו ויקד ארצה וישתחוה.
7 ויתפלל בתפלות אדון הנביאים ויאמר
אם נא מצאתי חן בעיניך אדני ילך
נא אדני בקרבנו כי עם קשה ערף
אנחנו וסלחת לעונינו ולחטאתינו
ונחלתנו.
8 ואחרי כלותו מן צלותו קרא בזאת
התפלה ואלה הם הדברים אשר התפלל
בהם.
9 ויאמר אדני יי׳ אשאלך תעני את
שיאלי.
10 אה מן המצא הנמצאות בגאותו ותקנה
בחכמתו ונוע הנועות ביכלותו והשכן
השכינות בחפצו ואשר בחר את העם הזה
לו לעם סגולה לעבד את יחדאותו ואשר

1/2 ואחר זאת המוכחות והמגידות
דהוכיח בה בבא רבה עם אנשי
עמו ובני דרה קעם ורחץ במים.
2/3 וצלא וצעם בלב תמים.
4 וסלק להר הקדש הרגריזים
בית אל שער השמים.
5 ואכן יהוה לו הדרך
במובאו עליו.
6 וכד הניח שם אחל לעבדת
יהוה ואתפלל ואתנפל בין
ידיו.
8 ומן כליל מה אמר אחר
חסול צלותו.
9 אדני יהוה אשאלך.
10 אה מן מצאת הנמצאים
ביכלותך אה מן יתבת
אתם בחכמתך אה מן התנועת
אתנועו בריחותך ואשכנת

שב על מן שב אליו מחטאתו ורשעתו
ואשר כפר למן קראו בנציר יצרותו
ואשר ענה למי שב אליו בטהרות
חשבנותו ואשר הוליך אליו אשר סר
מדרך הישר בחננותו ואשר פתח למי
הכה את דלותו ופלטו מחזק דלותו
ידעיו.
11 חכם אשר אין חכמה כחכמתו ולא
בינה כבינתו אשאלך אדני תרחם את
עמך ועבדיך בני עבדיך אשר אין להם
מקלט בלעדי כבודיך ולא בטח אלא על
רחמיך וחסדיך ולא גאל להם בלעדיך.
12 אדני יי׳ מה רב צרינו רבים קמים
עלינו ואתה תדע את כל הקרות אשר
קראתנו מעם זאת העמים והמלכים
הרשעים החטאים אשר כחשו את שמעך
אשר חשכו ממשמרת חקות נוראך.
13 במקראנו עננו אלהינו בצר לנו
חננו ושמע תפלותינו.
14 עד מתי לכלמה יהיה כבודינו עד מה
מי יאהבון ריק ויבקשון כזב משלים
עלינו ומן התפשות בתורותך הקדושה
ימנעו לנו ולמיח זכרון את שמך
הקדש יכעסו לנו.
15 המשתחוים לכל תועבה לפנינו הדרשים
ממנו להסיר לנו מן הדרך אשר הוריתנו
המבקשים להשמידנו העבדים לבעלים
הנאמנים באלילים המתברכים במעשה
ידיהם אלהים עשו כפי חפצם להם
ומתברכים בם.
16 לאמירתי האזינה יי׳ אלהי בינה
להגגי ומקראוי הקשיבה לקול שועתי
מלכי ואלהי כי אליך אתפללתי.
17 כי לא תחפץ רשע אתה ולא תגור הרעים
ההלכים בדרך בישתה.
18 אדני יי׳ הן היו עונינו גדולים מנשא
לא תיסרנו באלה עם הרשע כי אם לקחנו
אליך בדרך המות פן ישמידו לנו אלה
הרשעים בצרעה הזאת.
19 ואם היו אשמינו מנעו את דביקותך ואת
ישועתך לנו לא תמשיל את צרי תורתך
עלינו.
20 אדני יי׳ אל באפך תוכיחנו ואל בחמתך
תיסרנו חננו יי׳ כי חלים אנחנו רפאנו
יי׳ כי נבהלה עצמינו ועד מאד נבהלה
נפשנו.
21 עד מתי ואתה יי׳ אלהינו שובה יי׳
והצלינו ולמען חסדך הושיענו.
22 אדני יי׳ אם היו אשמינו גלל להרים
את רחמיך מעלינו אתה אליך לקחנו ולא
ימשלו אלה הרשעים בנו ולא תשא עלינו

השכונות ביחדאותך אה מן
דבחרת זאת העדה למען יעבדו
אתך אה מן תכפר על מן ישוב
מאחטאו לאלהותך אה מן תסלח
למן התפלל לך בסליחתך אה
מקבל שובת התהבים אה שמור
הברית והחסד למן לגדלך
אהבים אה דבוק למן בך מדבק
אה רחוק מכל רחיק אה שמעיו
לכל צעק אה ידעיו.
11 אה חכום אשאלך תסלח לעמך
ועבדיך דלית להם בלעדיך
ולא מנוס אלא לתרח רחמיך
וחסדיך וגדלך.
12 ידעיו מה קם עליהם מן העמים
והמלכים הכפורים בך ובנביך
ובכתבך הסגודים למן תתעבם
תורותך דיעבדו לבעלים
הנדחים לגלולים והשקוצים
אשר בטמאות מתשבצים.
18 אלהינו אן היו חטאינו
אשר עשינו והם הגלל
להשמידנו אליך עתה
אקמצנו.
19 ואן היו פשעינו שגבו
עזרותך וישועתך מעלינו
לא תמשל בנו שנאינו ואן
היו רעותינו גלל נשאות
רחמיך ונשאת עלינו חמס
צרינו ..
22 לא תסבל אתנו

מי לא נוכל על משאו לעבד כעובד מדרך
האמת תעו ולזכרון את שמך הקדוש דרשים
לנו ימנעו.
23 יי׳ אלהינו בך בטחנו מכל הרדפים לנו
אושיענו פן יטרפו כאריה את נפשנו
פרק כי אין מציל בלעדיך לנו.
24 יי׳ אלהינו אם עשינו מום אם יש עול
בכפינו אם גמלנו רעה אתה סלחיו כל
חטאה.
25 לא תשים אויב ירדף נפשנו ולא ירמס
כארץ כבודינו.
26 יי׳ אתה אמרת לא תעזבנו כאמרך על
יד אדון הנביאים משה רבנו בתורה
הקדושה כתבך לא ירפך ולא יעזבך.
27 אדני יי׳ אתה אמרת בספרך בצר לך
ובקשת משם את יי׳ אלהיך ומצאתו.
28 יי׳ אלהינו מה אדיר שמך בכל הארץ
אשר תנה הודך על השמים לחפץ.
29 מפי עוללים ויונקים יסדת עז להשבית
אויב וצורר מתנקם ולגאיל ישר וצדיק
עשה שלם.
30 כי נראה שמיך מעשה גאיך ירח
וכוכבים אשר כוננת באצבעיך מה
אנוש רשע כי תמשילהו במעשה גאיך
לשום תחת רגליו אהבים ידרשו מן
גדלך רפאיך.
31 נודך יי׳ בכל לבבינו ונרנן בתהללותיך
ובמאדינו נספר כל נפלאותיך נשמח
תמיד ונתפא בעצמך ונזמרה עליון שמך
בשוב לאחור אויבינו יכשלו וייאבדו
מפנינו.
32 כי הסכנתך תגער גוים מפני עמך ותאבד
רשעים ותמיח את שמך מעולמך כי אתה
תמיד משגב למי אליך ברח מקלט הדל
לעתות בצרה.
33 ויבטחו בך יודעי שמך כי אל רחום
וחנון שמך ולא תעזב דרושיך ולא
תרף מבקשיך.
34 ועתה ראה לדלותינו וקבל בעמל משה
בן עמרם שיאלינו ולאשר זממנו עליו
השיגנו כי לדרך רצונך דרשים נלך
בטהרות לבבינו לתמימות לכתנו אחרי
דרך יחידותך.
35 ואתה יכול קנאה מבור הלחץ אריצנו
וחדש לנו ישועה והשקף עלין ברחמיך
וחסדיך כי אנחנו מזרע הצדיקם עבדיך.
36 עשה לנו בחסדך כמעשה כבודך עם
אבותינו בני ישראל וכאשר אגאלת
להם לנו גאל.
37 מופתים גדלים גלית בארץ מצרים

מה לן יכולה על משאו מן
הנקם בשמיע מעבדות בעלותם
ופשעותם ומאנותם לנו זכרון
רבותך ויכלותך.
26 ואתה נשבעת לנו כי
לא תעזב אתנו מן
רחמיך ורתותך כי נפלנו
בנגע שנאינו.
34 עתה עזר אתנו כפי
בצענו בקנאתך.
35 ואתה היכול המחלש
הצילנו מן הצרר דעלינו
חבש מן ההלכם אחרי המוקש,
והשקף עלינו בחסדך.
36 ועבד אתנו הך מה
עבדת עם אבותינו
והצלת אתם על יד
נביך הצדיק.

ואמרת על גדלך אלהי העברים.
38 ובגלל זה הדבר היו מצרים ברב צרר.
39 והים שמת לחרבה עד עברו בו על
רגליהם הלכים ביבשה בבלי תבה
ואת פרעה ועמו טבעו בתוך הים
ולעמך הצלת ממנו.
40 ויצאו בטוב שלום וערי הגבורים
להם נחלת ואימה ופחד על לב
אויביהם שמת.

37 הענו בסימנים ונפלאות
מעבדת מן בהם מכאו.
39 ובחילך נבקעת מימי
הים דבו באו והשמדת
פרעה ועמו וכעופרת
במים צללו ופלטנון
מן חמסם.
40 וערי הגבורים ירשת
אתם כאשר נשבעת לאבותם.

§4

1 ויכל הכהן בבא רבה מן תפלותו
ומקראו וצלותו ותהללותו ותשבחו
וישב אל אחיו ונדיבי קהלו אשר
לפניו בעצם היום הזה הקהלו.
2 ויאמר אליהם מה תאמרו ולמה
ראיתם בעין לבבכם באזני דברו
מה עיצותיכם עתה עד אפני פני
אליה לעשותה.
3 ויענו כלם יחדו כל אשר תאמר
אלינו נשמע ונעשה בטוב לבב
ושלומה אנחנו עתה תחת מצוך.
4 צוה לנו כחפץ לבבך ולא נמרי
את פייך ולא נעזב לקולך וייטב
בעינינו ובעיני כל אחינו הדבר
אשר דברת לנו ועיצותך אשר אעצת
בה.
5 אכן כי היא טובה אין בה מום
ולא תועבה.
6 כל הישר בעיניך עשה כי כל אשר
תצוה לנו בו עלינו לא יקשה.
7 אך אנחנו לכל מצותך שמועים בנציר
הנפשות והרוחים.
8 לכל מקום תחפץ נלך כי לבבינו
טהרנו לשמע ולעשות את כל קולך
ואכן לא נמרי את פייך.
9 ויהי אחר הדברים האלה וילכו הכהן
בבא רבה ואת כל אחיו ונדיבי העם
עמו ויעברו בכל מושבי בני ישראל
השמרים על האמת ויפתחו את כל בתי
הכנשיות אשר הסגירו להם אויביהם.
10 ויאסף בהם ראשונה הוא ואחיו ויקראו
בתחילה את ספר התורה הקדושה באזני
כל קהל עדת בני ישראל השמרים על
האמת מאיש ועד אשה ויוסיפו מן
השירות והתפלות והתהללות והתנחנות
והרוממות לאלהי הרוחות יי׳ אל
צבאות בקולות עליונים גדלות.
11 וישלח הכהן בבא רבה ויאסף אליו את
כל חכמי התורה הקדושה ואת כל

1 וכד כלה תפלותו שב
לאחיו ומעיני עדתו.
2 ואמר להם מה תאמרו ומה
מדעיכם לכם אורו.
3 ויענו אתו כהלון ואמרו
החזי לך ואנחנו תחת
דברך.
4 וממללך דדברת אלינו הוא
טוב החזי ראינו ואנחנו
לא נימיר במה תאמר לנו.
8 והמכון אשר תצוה עליו
לנו נלך אליו כי בך
לא נמרי ושמעים כלנו.
9 ואחר כן יצא בבא רבה
ואחיו ומעיני עמו אתו
ובא בכל מכון היו
שכונים בני ישראל בהם
דמן עדת השמרים ולכד
הכנשנות אשר היו שנאיהם
מסגרים אתם.
10 ואתקבץ הוא ואחיו בהם
וקראו ספר התורה באזני
כל עמה ואוסיפו מן
התשבחות והמודאות והתהללות
לאלהי השמים וארעות בקולות
עלות.
11 ושלח בבא רבה והביא כל

הכהנים ואת כל הזקנים מכל המכונים
ולא מצא הכהן בבא רבה מחכמי עדת
בני ישראל השמרים ומן הזקנים בלתי
מעט מן המספר כי נשמדו ביד הזידנים
האדומים בגלל לא הקריבו לאלהיהם
ויעבדום ויעזבו את מעבד יי׳ אלהיהם
ואלהי אבותם.
12 ויאמר הכהן בבא רבה לאשר מצאו מהם
לאמר קומו לכו כל איש מכם למקומו
ושמרו והשמרו ובינו את מאדכם תנו
בעבור תלמוד כל עדת בני ישראל השמרים
אנשים ונשים וכל הטף את התורה הקדושה
לשמרה ולעשות את כל חקותה ומשפטה עד
תמם כאשר היו אבותיכם יעשו.
13 וגם את מאדכם תנו לשמר את מקרת
התורה הקדושה ולהטיב את מקראתה
בבטא שפתיכם בטא ישר כאשר אתם
עתיקים על אשר היו מפניכם.
14 ולא תפלו בתרדימה והלכו דרך תמימה
וגם שימו את כל מאדכם לשרת את כל
בתי הכנשיות עם כל הדרישות אשר
תדרש מכם.
15 לכו לשלום משתמרים מכל מום.
16 לכו נא הגברים מאת יי׳ מברכים.
17 יי׳ אלהי אבותיכם יסף עליכם ככם
אלף פעמים ויברך אתכם כאשר דבר לכם.
18 ויכחשו לכם איביכם ואתם על במתם
תדרכו ולכל ממשלותם אמן תמשלו.
19 רק דעו כי כל איש מכם לא ישמר
ויעשה לעשות את המצוה הזאת אשר
אנכי מצוה אתכם היום אני מכה
אתו להמיתו.
20 ואלה היא זאת הטרחה אשר היתה
על עדת בני ישראל השמרים מאת
בבא רבה כי חזק מאד על הגדלים
והקטנים הנערים והילדים לתלמוד
את מקרת ספר התורה הקדושה ואת
מקרת ספרי החכמים והנבונים.
21 ויתעצב לעיניהם הדבר בעת ההיא
וישמחו עדת בני ישראל השמרים
על האמת שמחה גדולה ויראו כי
מצילם מן אויביהם קרוב ותסור
המגיפים מעליהם וכי חן ורחמים
וחסד תבוא עליהם בגלל זה המעשה.

שמורי התורה הקדושה וכל
הכהנים מכל מכון ולא מצא
מן האנשים אשר שמורים התורה
הקדושה אלא מעט למשמרה חמישים
כי הרב מנון הכו אתם האדומים
דפניון כושים בגלל הם לא
ארשו יזבחו לאלהיהם ויעזבו
את יהוה אלהי השמים והארץ
הים וכל אשר בם.
12 ואמר בבא רבה לאשר מצא אתם
כל איש מכם ילך וישוב לביתו
ושמרו ואתבוננו ולמדו כל בני
ישראל השמרים האנשים והנשים
והטף תורת יהוה וחקותה ומצוותה
ומשפטה הך מה היו אבותיכם יעשו.
13 ובכל מאדיכם במשמרה אתקדשו
ועל קשיטות מקראה לא תמושו
הך מה אתם עתקים מן ארשיכם
אשר למשמרה צדיקה רשו.
14 ולא תהונו מן השלים
ובכל מאדיכם הכנשנות
שמשו.
15 לכו מברכים והוו
בדת משה סמיכים.
16 וביכלות יהוה בנזר
הנצען מתנזרים.
18 ושנאיכם לכם תכים.
19 וכי כל אנש מכם דלא
ישמר ויעשה על פי אלה
המצוה אשר אני מצוה
אתכם הכה אתו בלא פג.
20 וזאת עקה דפגעו אתה
בני ישראל השמירים
מן בבא רבה כי הוא
אבם הקטנים והגדלים
והזקינים עד יתלמדו.
21 וזה היה מריר עליהם
בזה עת דצוה בו להם
ושמחו השמירים
ואתבסרו בפשורון מן
שנאיהם ונשא הלחצות
והעקות מעליהם ובא
עליהם השש והנפוש
המתרבי מזה המעשה
דלו צפר ענן הרצון עבי.

§5

1 ויקח הכהן בבא רבה שבעה אנושים
מראשי בני ישראל השמרים אנשי

1 ולקח בבא רבה שבעת אנשים
מזקיני בני ישראל החמישים

	חיל יראי אלהים אנשי אמת שנאי בצע חכמי התורה כמו האנשים אשר צוה יי׳ את משה כאשר יאמר בתורה הקדושה ואתה תחזה מכל העם אנשי חיל יראה אלהים (עד כלה).		אנשי חיל יראי אלהים אנשי אמת שנאי בצע שמורי התורה על פי מימר יהוה בתורותו בגלל האנשיאים והפוקדים.
2	ויפלא אתם הכהן בבא רבה בקראו את שמותם חכמים.	2	ואגדיל אתם במקרא שמותם חכומים.
3	והחכמים השבעה הזוכירים היו שלשה מן הכהנים וארבע מן השמירים משבט יוסף הצדיק.	3	והשבעה הזוכירים היה מנון שלשה כהנים וארבע אנשים מן העם מן הזקינים.
4	והכהנים היו מפני העת ההוא כל איש בעל אימה וכבוד מהם יקראו את העם שמו כהן.	4	והיו הכהנים קדם זה זבן כל מן היה איש יקיר ישתמה כהן בישראל.
5	ומיום הכהן בבא רבה נקראו חכמים ויחלף שם הכהנה מעל אנשים רבים מן הכהנים.	5	ומן בבא רבה והלאה יתקראו שופטים והמיר שם הכהנים על קרב כהנים.
6	ויסר לאנשים רבים מהם מעל חנותם.	6	ונשא אנשים מנון מן מיתובותם
7	והגלל לדבר הזה לעת בא הכהן בבא רבה לבשן הכהנים אשר היו שם לא יצאו לקראתו ולא עשו כאשר הוא חייב עליהם להכבידו ולאיקרו.	7	בגלל כי לא צאו לקראתו כד בא לבשן ולא עשו הך מה חיב עליהם למוקרא.
8	רק כי כאשר בא העיר ויחן במקום אשר הנכון לו בא שמה וישלמו עליו כפי הסכנתם עם כל האנושים.	8	רק כי במובאו למדינה באו ושלמו עליו כפי אמנותם עם האנשים דלית הם נגישים.
9	בגלל הדבר הזה אשר עשו הסירם מעל מקום חנותיהם כי לא יצאו הם לקראתו למחוץ לעיר.		
10	ואנשים מן אנשי העם שם תחתיהם ישרתו את משמרתיהם בלתי משא הספר הקדוש.	10	ושם מן העם תחתם ישרתו מלבד משאות המכתב הקדש.
11	ובני ישראל השמרים על האמת היו יעשו בימי הכהן בבא רבה ומאחריו את חקת הנמלה; כי מפני ימי הכהן בבא רבה לא היה מבני ישראל השמרים ימול את ערלת יליד מבני ישראל כי אם הכהנים היו הם אשר ימילו את ערלת כל יליד יוליד לכל העם.	11	והיו בני ישראל בימי בבא רבה ובתרו יעשו ברית הנמילה; כי קדם כן לא היה להם עשותה רק אל הכהנים והיא מן כליל מיתובתם.
12	ויהיו גם הכהנים אמרים מלי רבואתה ומלי סליחתה וגם משרתים לעבד את כל עבדה בבתי הכנשיות.	12	ויאמרו בכנשנות מלי רבואתה ומלי סליחתא וכל עבדת הכנשנות היו ישרתו אתה. ומשם אתכסת תולדות הכוהנים ושמו תולדותם למן גשו פניהם כי לא נשאר דאג לאחד מהם בשמירות תולדותו
13	ויצו הכהן בבא רבה את כל העם לאמר לא יקרא שם חכמים אלא על כל איש חכום ונבון מן הכהנים הוא היה או היה מן העם.	13	כי בבא רבה לא שלח שם אלא על החכומים אך היו מן הכהנים או מן בני ישראל.
14	ואשר היה איננו נבון וחכום מן הכהנים לא יקרא לו לא בשם חכם ולא בשם כהן.	14	והסוכילים מן הכהנים לא היה ישלח עליהם לא שם חכום ולא שם כהן.

15 רק שם הכהנים וזרעם רק היה משתמר
בתולידה (פלאן אבן פלאן).
16 וישם הכהן בבא רבה אל החכמים
השבעה אשר שמם ראשים על כל העם
כנות וילבישם חליפות שמלות וישם
לכל אחד מהם מיתובה משתמרה ליקרו
וליקר את זרעיו מאחריו לא תשבת
ולא תכלה.
17 ויתבם לפניו כל אנוש מהם בכנותו
עד ידע כל אחד מהם את מקומו.
18 ויהיו אלה השבעה ראשים על כל
עדת בני ישראל השמרים על האמת
לשמר כל אנוש מהם את גבולו ויורי
את כל עדתו ויבדיל אליהם בין
הטמא ובין הטהור ובין הקדש ובין
החל.
19 ויצגם על תלמוד מקרת התורה הקדושה.
20 ואלה שמותם רחמות יי׳ תטלל עליהם:—
הראש
שמו פרובעי ומפתרו פרי מדרשי והוא
חבתה מזרע איתמר בן אהרן הכהן
עליהם השלום.
21 וגבולו היה מציל האלון הגדול ולו
המקום הראישון עד יהיה ראש
הפתורים לפניו.
22 השני
שמו יוצבי ישראלי והוא מן ישבי
קרית כופר יסלה ולו המקום השני
והפתרון באחרנית.
23 השלישי
שמו אלינאה סרפין ולו המקרא השנית.
24 הרביעי
כהן לוי מקרית זיתה ולו המקראה
הראשונית ויזכר את שמות אשר
הרימו תרומות ואשר נתנו מתנות
בכל עת.
25 החמישי
ישראלי מקרית כפור מרות ולו הפתרון
החמישי.
26 הששי
שמו עמרם והוא כהן לוי מקרית
כופר ספאסה ולו מקום הפתרון השני.
27 ויאמר כי זה הוא עמרם אבי מרקה
בעל החכמים והמדעים; ויאמר עוד כי
הוא עמרם דרה אשר הלף בתי הדראן
אשר יתבם על ימי הבריה ששת הימים
שנים עשר בתים וליום השבת ששה
ולראש כל חדש אחד ולחדש הראישון
אחד ולחדש השביעי אחד וליום הכפור
אחד ואלף.
28 חמשה בתים מרקה יתאמרו בצלות

15 רק תולדת הכהנים נשאר
משתמר בשמירות השלשלה והיו
תולדו פלוני בן פלוני.
והסוכילים מהם היו מתנגדים
בכך הך מה קדמנו.
16 ושם בבא רבה על החכומים
השבעה מיתובות ואלביש אתם
בגדים ושם לכל אחד דרגה
משתמרה איקר לו ולזרעו
אחריו לא תבטל ולא תתכלה.
17 ושב אתם בין ידיו כל אנש
בחנותו עד ידע כל אחד מכונו.
18 והיו אלה השבעה נשיאים על
כל עדת השמרים למשמר כל
איש מהם גבולו ויאעץ עדתו
ויבדיל להם בין הטמא ובין
הטהור.
19 ויעמד אתם על מקרא התורה
הקדושה התמימה.
20 ואלה שמותם רחמות יהוה עליהם: —
החכום הראש
פרובעי והוא מן זרע איתמר
21 חבתה. וגבולו מן האלון הגדול
ולו המשרית הראישונה למען
יהיה בין ידי הפתור הראש.
22 השני
יצובי מן כפר סילה ולו
המשרית השנית המפתר באחרת.
23 השלישי
אלינאה סרפין ולו המקרא השני.
24 הרביע
כהן לוי מן קרית זיתא ולו
המקרא הראישונה ובזכרון
שמות אשר משאות שאו ונתן
לו מתנות בכל דר.
25 החכום החמישי
ישראלי מן קרית כפר מאורות
והוא הפתור החמישי.
26 החכום הששי
עמרם כהן לוי מן קרית כפר
ספאסה ולו מכון המפתר השני.
27 והמימר עליו כי הוא אב מרקה
פרוט החכמות; ואתאמר כי הוא
עמרם דרה.

יום השבת בבקר ובית אחד יתאמרו הן
פגע בחדש שבת חמישי מפני מקרת
הפרשה אשר תאמר בעוד צלות צהרים
אשר היא תחת המנחה.
29 ולו עוד שירה תאמר בלילת הכפור
ושירה שנית תאמר ביום הכפור וכן
שירה תאמר ביום מודע מעמד הר סיני
בצלות הבקר.
30 זאת נשארו מאשר אלפו החכם הזוכיר
עד היום הזה.
31 השביעי
ישראלי רק לא מצאנו בספר הימים
זכרון למקומו ואף למושבו.

31 החכום השביעי
ישראלי. לא מצאנו לו שם בספרים
ולא למכונו ולא לתמונו ויהוה
היעדו.

§6

1 על פי היתוב ההוא יתבם הכהן בבא
רבה ויאמר להם לאמר.
2 אתם תהיו מצוים לכל העם הקהל הזה
ותחשכו להם והייתם פנים לכל עדת
השמרים מנער ועד זקן והייתם עליהם
שופטים ושפטתם בין איש ובין רעהו.
3 לא תכירו פנים במשפט כקטן כגדול
תשמעון לא תגורו מפני איש כי
המשפט לאלהים הוא.
4 והאיש אשר יעמד לפניכם והמיר
אתכם בכל דבר אשר תדברונו אליו
ותצוו אתו אנכי אדרש מעמו.
5 ובקרב שבעת האנשים האלה הקים הכהן
בבא רבה ארבעה אנושים מהם אנשי שם
פקדים עליהם.
6 וזה היתוב לא היה בימי הרצון
כי אם היו בימי הרצון שבעים זקן
בחורים חכמי הקהל ובתוכם שנים עשר
איש ראשי השבטים ואיש אחד מתוך את
שנים עשר איש הנשיא על הכל.
7 שמו גדול השבטים עזר לגדול מהם
במשפט כי אם אין לו ממשלה על
הכהנים ולא ישפט עליהם לא בכל
עון ולא בכל משפט ולא בדין.
8 רק את כל דבריהם תשוב את הכהן
הגדול המשיח אשר מלא ידו לכהן או
אחד מאת הכהנים הגדולים והם זרע
אדונינו פינחס בן אלעזר עליהם
השלום לעולם.
9 והמיתובה לא תהיה מורשה לבן
מאביו ולא מן הבן לאביו רק כי
ימות אחד מהם יבחרו אחד תחתיו.
10 יהיה בעל מדע וחכמה ובינה מן
הקהל על יד הכהן הגדול בעתו
ועל יד זקני העם וראשיהם ושטריהם.

1 ועל כמו זה יתבון בבא
רבה ואמר אליהם.
2 אתם תצוו ותכלאו ותהיו
הנגישים על כל קהל
ישראל השמירים מן הגדולים
והקטנים וגם תהיו השופטים
עליהם.
4 וכל מן עמד פניכם ואומיר
אתכם בכל דבר תצוהו בו
אני אדרש מעמו.
5 ובקרב אהלין האנשים השבעה
קעם בבא רבה ארבע אנשים
מהם מראים עליהם.
6 ולא היה זה היתוב בימי
הרצון רק היה בימי הרצון
שבעים זקן מתבחרים על
הקהל ואתם שנים עשר והם
נשיאי השבטים ואחד מן
האלין השנים עשר נשיא
עליהם.
7 ישתמה גדול השבטים יעזר
לגדול במשפט רק לא היה
לו משלה על הכהנים ולא
ישפט עליהם לא בחטא ולא
במשפט.
8 רק היה דברון מושבו לכהן
הגדול המתמשיח לכהנה
הגדלה או המתפקיד תחתיו
מן הכהנים הגדולים אחד
מן זרע פינחס.
9 ומיתובית לא הות תנחל מן
אב לבנו ולא מן הבן לאביו,
10 רק אן מת אחת יתחזה תחתיו

11 אלה הוא יתוב ימי הרצון.

מן הידועים והנבונים
במראה הכהן הגדול והזקינים.
11 וזה היה היתוב בימי הרצון.

§7

1 בעת ההיא היה בתוך בני ישראל משפחה
ושמה משפחת השבעים.
2 ואנשי המשפחה הזאת לא אבו לשמע אל
הכהן בבא רבה בגלל היתוב הזה אשר
יתבו ואשר בחר בו ולא באו תחת משפט
החכמים אשר הפקידם על כל קהל ישראל
השמרים הכהן בבא רבה הזוכיר.
3 רק הם אקימו להם במקומותם ובכל
עריהם אשר היא תחת אחזתם כהנים בני
לוי ישפטו בם.
4 ושבעת החכמים אשר בחר בם הכהן בבא
רבה הזוכירים מטרם היו יסובבו
בסביב כל הערים או ישלחו פקידים
בעלי מדע וחכמה ובינה עד יראו בכל
מקום.
5 וכי ימצא כהן היתה ממנו שגגה
בחקות התורה או במשפט או בדין מן
כהני משפחת השביעים אשר אתקדם
להם הזכרון
6 ימהרו ויגישו את דבריהם אל
הכהן הגדול אשר להם ויהיו אלה
השביעים מסעדים את הכהן בבא רבה בכל
מלחמה וישאו לו את המשביר ויתנו
לו מתנות גדולות לא תמני במספר
עד כי חדל לספר וגם יגישו לו את
כל מחסורו.

1 ובקהל ישראל השמרים אשר
הם השמירים עמה יתקרו.
2 ואהלין הזוכירים לא קבלו
מן בבא רבה זה היתוב ולא
שמעו למן להם בחר ולא באו
בשמיע השופטים דיתבון בבא
רבה.
3 רק היו ישפטו במכרתיהם
ועריהם הכהנים דמבני קהת.
4 והחכומים השבעה דהגישם
בבא רבה היו ילכו לכל
הקריות או ישלחו תחתיהם
אנשים ידועים ובוננים
ויגלו בכל מכון.
5 ואן מצאו כהן עשה שגגה
בתורת או בחקות או במשפט
מן הכהנים השביעית דאתקדם
זכרונם.
6 יגישו דבריו לכהן הגדול
דלהם והיו אהלין השבעה
יעזרו בבא רבה בכל מלחמה
וישאו לו הטמונים וישיגו
אתו במתנות הפחרות ובכל
מה ימך עליו.

§8

1 והחכמים אשר בחר בם הכהן בבא רבה
ויפקדו על כל קהל בני ישראל השמרים
על האמת אשר היה בכל עת יצוה אתם
לאמר.
2 ראו והביטו ושמרו והבינו את כל
אשר תעשון וגם שמרו את כל אשר אנכי
מצוה אתכם והשמרו פן תשכחו את מצותי
... ולא תעשון את כל חפצותי ומן כלילה
משמר מקרת התורה הקדושה על מקרת
העשרה כי זה הוא הדבר הראש הגדול
אשר אני דרוש מכם.
3 ובכל עת שימו זכרון בינכם ובין
המלמדים ונסיתם את התלמודים עד
תעמדו על האמת דבר בעבור מקרת
התורה הקדושה על מקרת העשרה אשר
אתעתקת מאת השבעים זקני קהל ישראל
ועל הכהנים אשר היו בימי אדון

1/2 והשופטים דקעם אתם בבא רבה
היה יצוה אתם ממן יהיו
שמעין מסתכלים מתבוננים
בכל מה הם ידעים לו וישמרו
מן השגגות והמגרעות...

.. ויהיו ממן בפקדות
מקרא התורה הקדושה קדוש
כל התורות כי זה הוא רב
דבר.
3 ויזכרו היעדים בכן עד
יהיה בטב פג מהם במשמר
התורה הקדושה על העשרות
האקרים אשר היא מתעתקה
מן השבעים הזקינים המתוקרים
ומן הכהנים אשר היו בימי

הנביאים הנבי הגדול משה בן עמרם
עליו השלום התם.
4 ויהי אחר הדברים האלה ויבן הכהן
בבא רבה בגבול המקום המבחר הר
גרזים בית אל הר הנחלה והשכינה
מקוה מים לטהרה כי הוו יטהרו בו
לעת עתות כל צלות לאשר ידרש מעדת
בני ישראל השמרים על האמת יצלי
על ההר הזה.
5 והם שתי צלות תחת קרבן התמיד;
הראשית היא צלות ערב מאז תבוא השמש
והשנית היא צלות בקר מאז עלות
השחר עד הן תזרח השמש על הארץ.
6 ויבן עוד בקצה המקום המבחר הר
גרזים בית אל בית כנשה עד יצלו
בו העם מול זה הר הקדש.
7 וישארו זה המקוה וזה בית הכנשה
עד הן מלכו (הפרנג); ובית הכנשה
אשר בנאו הכהן בבא רבה על מדי
הבית אשר בנאו אתו בעיר (בצרה)
בימי הרצון.
8 וישימהו על תבנתו וישם את ארצו
מעפר כאשר ראה בעיר (בצרה) ויקח
בבא רבה אבנים מאבֿנים̈ (ההיכל)
אשר הריסו אתו אנשי שאול בימי
שאול מלך בני ישראל בעתו מלבד
עדת בני ישראל השמרים על האמת
כי הרסו את (ההיכל) הזה שנאה בהם.
9 וישם את שבעת האבנים האלה שבעה
מיתובים לחכמים השבעה וגם לקח אבן
אחד גדול לנפשו עד ישב עליו.
10 ויבן גם הכהן בבא רבה בתי כנשיות שבעה
בשבעה קריתים וישם את ארצות כלם עפר.
11 ואלה שמותם:–
הראשית
כנשת קרית כופר עמרתה הנקברים בה
הכהנים הגדולים בני אהרן הכהן והם
אלעזר ואחיו איתמר ופינחס בן אלעזר
עליהם השלום ואת שבעים הזקנים וגם
כהנים גדולים רבים
והיא ממזרח עיר שכם.
12 השנית
כנשת בית נמרה.
13 השלישית
כנשת קרית חגה והיא נגלאה עד היום הזה
לא נפלאה והיא מפאת נגבה אשר היא לעמת
קרית (עסכור); ואולם קרית (עסכור) אשר
היא בית ההיא חרבה רק את מקומותם ואת
הברכה נמצאים עד היום הזה.
14 הרביעית
כנשת קרית (טירה) והקריה הזוכירה היא

אדונן משה בן עמרם דמע
הספרים של׳ יה׳ על׳.
4 ובנה בבא רבה בגבול
ההר הקדש מקוה מים לטהרה
בזבני הצלואן למן יבקש
הצלות עליו.
5 והם צלות הערב אשר היא
מן מובא השמש והשנית
צלות הבקר והיא מן עלות
הבקר למזרח השמש.
6 וככן בנה בתחתית ההר
מקום לצלות עד יצלו בו
המתעבדים ממול ההר הקדש.
7 ונשארו המקוה והמעבד
לעת מלכו הריפתים; ובית
המעבד דבנה אתו בבא רבה
על מדד בית הצלות אשר
קעמו אתו בבצרה.
8 ולקח בבא רבה אבנים מאבני
המשכן דאבדו אתו אנשי
שאול.
9 ושם אתם מיתובות לשבעת
השופטים וככן לקח אבן גדול
ושם אתו לנפשו למען ישב
עליו.
10 וגם בנא בבא רבה שמנה
כנשנות בשמנה קריות ושם
כל ארצם עפר.
11 ואלה שמותם: –
הראישונה
כנשת קרית עבורתה היא
הקריה המטמונים בה הכהנים
הגדולים אדונינן אלעזר
ואיתמר ופינחס עליהם
השלום וככן השבעים הזקינים
ורב מן הכהנים רצון יה׳
עליהם.
12 והכנשה השנית
בבית נמארה.
13 השלישית
בקרית חגה והיא מתגליה
עד עתה מנגב שכם לפאת
צפונה המיתיגרה למחנים;
ומחנים עתה חרבה וצרבותה

עד היום הזה.
15 החמישית
כנשת (צבארין) והקריה הזוכירה שוכנה
עד היום הזה והיא בערי השפלה.
16 הששית
כנשת קרית (שלם) והקריה הזוכירה שוכנה
עד היום הזה והיא באצל שכם מפאת קדמה
וגם היא מול המקום המבחר הר גרזים בית
אל ממזרחה לפאת צפונה.
17 השביעית
כנשת קרית (בית דגן) והקריה הזוכירה
שכונה עד היום הזה וגם היא מקדם המקום
המבחר הר גרזים בית אל לפאת צפונה.
18 השמינית
לא ידענו מקומה ולא מצאנו לו
זכרון בספר הימים רק יאמר הן
היא כנשת אבנתה אשר היא היתה
בין אלון מורא ובין הר גרזים
בית אל אשר בנה בה שלש מאות
וששים חדרה על מספר יום השנה
ומקומה מתודע עד היום הזה אשר
הוא מנגב קבר אדונינו יוסף
הצדיק עליו השלום.
19 אלה הם את שמנה הכנשיות
אשר בנה אתם הכהן בבא רבה
כלם בנא אתם באבן אין באחת
מהם עץ.

וצרבת מקוה מימותה
נמצאים עד עתה.
14 הרביעית
כנשת קרית אלטירה והקריה
מתכוננה עד עתה.
15 החמישית
כנשת צבארין והקריה
הזוכירה מתכוננה עד עתה.
16 הששית
כנשת שלם והקריה הזוכירה
מתכוננה עד עתה והיא
מקדם ההר הקדש לפאת צפונה.
17 השביעית
כנשת קרית בית דגן והיא
מקדם ההר הקדש לפאת צפונה.
18 השמינית
לא ידענו מכונה ולא מצאנו לה
שם בספרים ויהוה היעדיו כי
היא כנשת המעבד דאתקדם זכרו.
19 אלה הם שמונת הכנשנות
דבנה אתם בבא רבה כל כנשה
מהם בבניאן אבן אין בהם
עץ.

§9

1 ויבן עוד הכהן בבא רבה מקוה
רחב וישמו מקוה המקרא והפתרון
ולשמע את כל שיאל.
2 ויקמו מנכח בית הצלות אשר בנה
אתו בתחתית המקום המבחר הר
הברכה מקום הקדשה הר הנחלה
והשכינה הר גרזים בית אל למען
כל איש מבני ישראל השמרים לו
שיאל יבוא שמה וישאל בשיאלו
את החכמים אשר היו שם ויגידו
לו את פתרון שיאלו על דבר האמת.
3 ולמען כל איש מהם יקרא את נפשו
חכום בעת ההיא יביאו אתו בראש
החדשים או בימי המועדים ויציגו
אתו לפני המלך (הכהן) הגדול בעת
ההיא ולפני החכמים לנסותו.
4 ויתן את הנסות לפני הכהן הגדול
ולפני החכמים וכי ימצאו אתו בעל
חכמה ומדע ובינה יקראו את נקיבו חכם.

1 וגם בנה מקוה רחב ושמו
במחוקק המקרא והמפתר
ומשמע השאלות.
2 וקעם אתו ממול בית הצלות
דקעמו בתחתית ההר הקדש
עד כל מן היה לו שיאלה
יבוא שם ויעלים שיאלתו
על החכמים ויגידו לו על
דבר משפטה הקשיט.
3 והוה כל מן אתריח כי יקרי
חכום יביאו אתו בימי המועדים
ובזבני ראש החד׳ ויעמידו
אתו פני הכהן הגדול והשופטים.
4 וינסו אתו אן מצאהו נבון
וידעיו יקרא אתו חכום.

5 והגלל ליתוב הכהן בבא רבה היתוב
הזה ולבנות את בתי הכנשיות ואת
מקוה החכמה עד לא יאמרו מלכי הארץ
עליו לאמר הכהן בבא רבה לא פנה
פניו לדבר מדברי המלכים אשר ישמו
את עצמם במלאכות תרחקם מן תהללות
שם יי׳ הקדוש יתקדש שמו ואת עשות
מצותיו וחקותו לעשות התועבות.
6 ויחלק הכהן בבא רבה את הכהנים
על כל עמו עדת בני ישראל השמרים
על האמת ויתן להם נחלה.
7 ואלה שמותם כאשר מצאנו אתם כתובים
בתולידה והם אנשי עם בני ישראל
השמרים ונשיאי בתי אבותם אשר היו
פקידים עליהם על פי הכהן בבא
רבה הזוכיר.
8 הראש
הנקרא שמו ישמעאל נתן לו הכהן בבא
רבה ולכל אנשי משפחתיו אחזת נחלה
מן עיר לוזה עד מקום (הגליל) אשר
על הים וישם עמו הכהן נערה.
9 השני
הנקרא שמו יעקב מקרית (עסכור) נתן
לו הכהן בבא רבה ולכל אנשי משפחותיו
אחזת נחלה (מעסכור) אל (טרבלוס)
והאמת (מעסכור) לטבריה וישם עמו
הכהן נתן אל.
10 השלישי
הנקרא שמו זית בן תהם נתן לו הכהן
בבא רבה אחזת נחלה מקדם המקום
המבחר הר הקדש הר גרזים בית אל
עד הירדן ויתן עמו כהן אלעזר
בן פלח.
11 הרביעי
יהושע בן ברק בן עדן נתן לו אחזת
נחלה (מכופר חלול לבית השבט) וישם
עמו כהו עמרם בן סרד והוה נקיב
שמו (טוטה).
12 ויאמר כי זה הוא אבי הכהן מרקה
החכם הגדול בעל החכמה ומיתב
דברי על מדע ובינה רצון יי׳
וסליחתו עליו אמן.
13 החמישי
הנקרא שמו אברהם בן שמעלעימה
בן אור בן פרת נתן לו אחזת
נחלה מגבול ים וין לפלשתים
ויתן עמו כהן חכומה.
14 הששי
ישראל בן מכיר נתן לו אחזת
נחלה מעיר עזה עד נהר מצרים
ואת הכהן שלום נתן עמו.

5 והגלל ביתוב בבא רבה
זה היתוב ובניאנו
הכנשות ומקוה המדע
למען לא יתורו מלכי
הארץ כי הוא אתפני
למאום מן העודות עלמה
והודות המלכים אשר היו
יתפנו לה ויעזבו עבדת אלה.
6 ופלג בבא רבה
הכהנים על עמו דמצא אתם
ונתן להם נחלה.
7 ואלה שמותם הך מה מצאנו
אתם מתכתבים בתולידה והם
אנשי העם השמרים ונשיאי
משפחתם אשר היו מתפקדים
על כרני הדת העברים החסדים.
8 הראישון
יתקרי ישמעאל נתן לו בבא
רבה ואל משפחתו אחזת לוזה
אל הגלגל אשר על הים ושם
אתו הכהן נענה.
9 השני
יתקרי יעקב מן מחנים נתן
לו ואל משפחתו אחזת מחנים
ואל כנרת ושם אתו הכהן
נתנאל.
10 השלישי
זית בן תהם נתן לו אחזה
מקדם הר הקדש אל הירדן
ושם אתו הכהן אלעזר בן
פלח.
11 הרביעי
יהושע בן ברק בן עדו נתן
לו אחזה מן כפר חלול לביט
שבט ושם אתו הכהן עמרם בן
סרד המתנקב בשם טוטה.
12 והוא בקשט אבי הכהן מרקה
החכום הגדול בעל החכמה
ומיתיב החכמות רצון יהוה
על רוחו הקדושה.
13 החמישי
אברהם בן שמטעימה בן אור
בן פרת נתן לו אחזה מים
דין לפלשתים ושם אתו הכהן
הכומה.
14 הששי
ישראל בן מכיר נתן לו אחזה
מן עזה לנהר מצרים ושם אתו
הכהן שלום.

15 השביעי
הנקרא שמו יוסף בן שותלח
נתן לו אחזת נחלה מן גבול
הר הנחלה והשכינה הר הברכה
הרגרזים בית אל (לקיסיריה)
וישם עמו כהן את אהרן בן זהר.

15 השביעי
יוסף בן שותלח נתן לו אחזה
מן הרגריזים טורה טבה לקיסאריה
ושם אתו כהן אהרן בן זהר.

16 השמיני
הנקרא שמו לאל בן בכר נתן לו
נחלה מגבול מקדם הכרמים אל
עיר (עכה) וישם עמו כהן את
יוסף בן צנינה.

16 השמיני
לאל בן בכר נתן לו אחזה מן
תהוות הכרמל אל עכה ואתו
כהן יוסף בן צפינה

17 התשיעי
הנקרא שמו בכר בן אור אשר
שם את גבולו מהר (נקורה) עד
(צור) וזאת (צור) אשר בנה
אדונינו ירד בן מהלאלל וישב
בה וימת (בכופר מרואן) וישם
עמו כהן את אהרן בן זבד.

17 התשיעי
בכר בן אור שם גבולו מן טור
אלנאקורה אל צור; וזאת העיר
דבנה אתה ירד ושכן בה ומת
בכפר מרואן. ושם אתו כהן אהרן
בן זבד.

18 העשירי
הנקרא שמו שפט בן צבו בן
מכיר נתן לו אחזת נחלה מנחל
(ליטה); ויאמר כי הוא נחל
(טבריה) וממנו אל (צידון)
סביב וישם עמו כהן את זריז
בן מניר אשר היה בעל חכמה
ודעת בינה עד מאד.

18 העשירי
שפט בן צפו בן מכיר נתן לו
אחזה מן נהר כנרת מנה לצידון
סביב; והוא היה נבון וחכום.
ושם אתו כהן זריז בן מניר.

19 אחד עשר
הנקרא שמו ברד בן שריאן בן עמד
נתן לו אחזת נחלה מהר גליל עד
הנחל עד לבנון ואת כל בנתיה אשר
סביבתיה מן ההרים ושפילים וישם
עמו כהן את זית בן לוי אשר היה
איש יקיר ומגידו נשמע בכל מקום
מלבין כל הכהנים כי היה ראשון
לכל חכמה ובינה ומדע ודעת ופתרון
רצון יי׳ וסליחתו עליו אמן.

19 העשתי עשר
ברד בן שיראן בן עמד נתן לו
אחזה מן טור גליל לנהר לבנון
וכל כפורה אשר סביבותיה מן
ההרים וככרות ושם אתו כהן
זית בן לוי; וזה לוי היה
מתודע בין הכהנים בעל מימרים
טבים.

§10

1 אלה הם ראשי עדת בני ישראל
השמרים על האמת אשר מצא אתם הכהן
הנכבד בבא רבה ויחלק עליהם את כל
ארץ כנען כל הערים אשר היו ישבים
בה כל עדת בני ישראל השמרים.

1 אלה הם נשיאי בני ישראל
השמירים דאמצאם בבא רבה ופלג
להם ארץ כנען וזה היה על פיהו.

2 ובבא רבה הזוכיר נגלא בין עמו
לעשות את כל המעשים האלה בשנת
ארבע אלפים ושש מאות לבריאת העולם
אשר היא שנת אלף ושמנה מאות ושש
שנים לעבר בני ישראל ארץ כנען.

2 והוא נגלי בשנת ארבע אלפים
וששה מאות לבריאת עלמה
היא שנת אלף ושמנה מאות
וששה וששים למובא בני ישראל
ארץ כנען.

3 אשר היא שנת אלף וחמש מאות וחמשה
וארבעים שנה למן נסתר המשכן הקדש

3 היא שנת אלף וחמשה מאות וחמשה
וארבעים שנה להסתרות המשכן.

אשר עשו אתו במדבר כאשר צוה יי׳
את משה.
4 אשר היא שנת אחד אלף ושלשה מאות
וששה ועשרים שנה לבנות את שלמה
בן דוד המלך בית מקדש בעיר ירושלם
במקום אשר קנהו את אביו מן היבוסי
והוא מקום הגרן.
5 אשר היא שנת אחת אלף וחמשים שנה
לגלות בני ישראל אשורה בימי כהנת
הכהן הגדול עקביה.
6 אשר היא שנת אחת אלף שנה וחמש שנים
למובא בני ישראל השמרים על האמת
מן הגלות הראשונית בימי כהנת
הכהן הגדול שריה; וזאת הגלות
היא גלות נבוך דנצר.
7 אשר היא שנת שבע מאות וחמשה
ותשעים שנה למבוא בני ישראל
השמרים על האמת מן גלות השנית;
וזאת הגלות היא גלות מלך היונים
אשר מובאם בימי כהנת הכהן הגדול
עבדאל בן הכהן הגדול עזריה בשנת
חמשה ושלשים שנה לכהנתו.
8 אשר היא שנת חמשה וחמשים שנה
ושבע מאות שנה לעמיר את עדת
יהודים את בית מקדשם בעיר ירשלם
שנית על יד זרובבל ונחמיה ועזרא
הכהן; כי הביאו להם צו מן מלך
בבל ויעמירו את (ההיכל) ואת העיר.
9 אשר היא שנת חמשה וחמשים ושש
מאות למלך אסכנדר אשר מלך את כל
הגוים.
10 אשר היא שמנה ושלש מאות שנה
אחרי נגלאות ישו בן מרים אשת
יוסף החרש עץ אשר מזרע דוד
המלך אשר קם מן היהודיים ויצלבו
אתו.
11 ויהי בימי הטובים ההם
המצא יי׳ יתקדש שמו את האיש
הגדול הזה וימלך על כל עדת בני
ישראל השמרים הארץ כנען ארבעים
שנה.
12 גם עדת בני יהודה היו תחת משפטו
ויגלי את אימנות ישראל ויבן את
בתי הכנשיות ויתן את מאדו בתלמוד
עדת בני ישראל השמרים על האמת
את מקרת התורה הקדושה בתקון מקרא
על האמת המתעתק בין דורות ישראל
מן השבעים הזקנים זקני ישראל
אשר היו בדור אדון הנביאים משה בן
עמרם עליו השלום.
13 ויכן את בתי המקוה בטב יתוב וישיב

6 היא שנת אלף וחמש שנים למובא
בני ישראל השמרים מן הנסחת
הראישונה.
וזאת הנסחת היא נסחת נבוך
דנצר היא שנת שבע מאות וחמש
ותשעים שנה למובא בני ישראל
מן הנסחת השנית; וזאת הנסחת
היא נסחת מלך תובל.
9 היא שנת ששה מאות וחמשה
וחמשים שנה לגלות המלך
אסכנדר דמלך על כל עלמה.
10 היא שנת שלשה מאות ושמנה
שנה לגלות ישוע בן מרים
אשת יוסף החרש דקעם מן
היהודאים.
11 בזה הספר אמצא יהוה זה
האיש הרם ומלך ארבעים
שנה.
12 ואגלי האימן המתקומם
ובנה הכנשנות ובמאדו
דאג בתלמוד מקרא התורה
הקדשה על המתעתק הקשט
המתעתק בין דרי ישראל
השמירים מן השבעים הזקנים
ומן הכהנים הקדושים דאמצאו
בימי אדון הראישונים והאחרונים.
13 ויתיב בתי המדרשות והשיב

את כל בני ישראל איש למקומו.
14 ויחלק את הכהנים בני אהרן עליו
השלום על כל ערי עדת בני ישראל
השמירים ומהם הכהנים החבתים והם
אשר מזרע אדונינו איתמר עליו
השלום.
15 ואלה שמותם הבכור עבדי
השני מלך
השלישי צדקיאל
הרביעי שבע
החמישי אור
הששי עז.
16 אלה הם אשר פרו וישרצו וירבו
ויעצמו בארץ כנען.
17 ויהי כאשר חלק הכהן הנכבד בבא
רבה את ארץ כנען על משפחות עדת
בני ישראל השמרים ויחלק עליהם
את הכהנים ויאמר אליהם לכו לשלום
חזקו ואמצו אל תיראו ואל תערצו
מפני איש כל ימי חיי.
18 פחדכם ומראכם יתן יי׳ אלהיכם על
כל העמים אשר סיבותיכם ואתם אל
תיראו בלתי מיי׳ אלהיכם ואלהי
אבותיכם אשר הוציא להם מכור
הברזל.
19 ותנו את כל מאדכם לשמר משמרתו
חקותיו ומצותיו ומשפטיו כל הימים
למען תחיון.
20 ויצאו חכמי בני ישראל וראשיהם
והכהנים מפני הכהן הנכבד בבא רבה
בקהל בני ישראל השמרים בכח גדול
ובשמח יתר.
21 בעת ההיא מצאו עדת בני ישראל השמר׳
על האמת חן בעיני יי׳ אלהיהם וירבי
השמח ביניהם ויפרק עול הברזל מעל
צואריהם וישבר את מטות עולם
ויוליכם קוממית.
22 ויהי כאשר באו החכמים אל הערים
אשר חלק הכהן הנכבד בבא רבה אליהם
עפלו ישבי הערים לנגלאות השמחות
ולהרים הקולות בשירות ותהללות
ורוממות אלהיהם ואלהי אבותיהם
אשר מלבין כל הגוים בחר בהם ומזאת
הצרעה הציל אתם.
23 ויעשו בני ישראל השמרים על האמת
את כל זה המעשה על פי החכמים
והזקנים על פי המלך הנכבד הכהן
בבא רבה רצון יי׳ וסליחתו עליו אמן.
24 ויוסיפו מן השמחות ויגלו את
אימנות דת משה בן עמרם עליו השלום.

עדתו בני ישראל כל איש למכונו.
14 ופלג הכהנים בני אדונן אהרן
עליו השלום על השמרים
בקריהתם והיו הכהנים החבתה
הם המתשלשלים מן אדונן
איתמר עליו השלום.
15 ובניו היו ששה הבכור עבדי
ושני מלך
והשלישי צדיקאל
והרביע שבע
והחמישי אור
והששי עז.
16 אהלין פרו ורבו ואתרבת
פרותון בארץ כנען.
17 וכד פלג בבא רבה ארץ כנען
על משפחות בני ישראל השמרים
ופלג עליהם הכהנים
ואמר להם לכו בשלום
וחזקו ואמצו ואל תיראו
מן אחד.
18 מלבד דברא לכם אלהיכם ואלהי
אבותיכם.
19 ושמרו על קעמות החקים
והמשפטים דבתורותו
דהסגיל בה לכם למען תחיו
בשני עלמות נפשותיכם.
20 ויצאו השופטים והאנשיאים
והכהנים בהעם ישראל השמירים
מן בין ידי בבא רבה בגאות
גדלה ושמח רב עדף.
21 ויהוה נתן להם נצענות אחר
עקות ולחצות.
22 וכד באו השופטים לערות
עפלו שכוני הקריות בשמחות
וקולות התשבחות והתהללות
אל אלהי הרוח׳ וגלו בקעמות
הדת.
23 ועשו בני ישראל השמירים
כן על פי מצות השופטים
כפי מצות בבא רבה.
24 ואוסיפו מן השמחות ונשאו
עמודי הדת בטב נשאות על
כעסות מן אלהותם נלאות.

§11

1 ויבאו הראשים אשר היו פקדים עליהם
מאת מלכי הגוים הנכרים למנע אתם
מעשות את חקות התורה הקדשה כאשר
היו ימנעו להם מתמול.
2 ויקמו כל אנשי עדת בני ישראל
השמרים עליהם וימהרו להרגם וישרפו
אתם באש בכל עיר ובכל קריה ובכל
מקום עת אחד.
3 היה זה המעשה לכל ראשי הגוים
הנכבדים בכל ערי עדת בני ישראל
והוא לילת תמול ראש חדש השביעי
וישמו בני ישראל השמרים זכרון
למודע הזה.
4 ויהי כי הרגו אנשי עדת בני ישראל
השמרים על האמת את הראשים אשר היו
עליהם מאת מלך אדום וישרפו אתם
באש וישמעו נגישי המלך ושוטריו
בדבר הזה.
5 וישלחו מאתם מלאכים עד יתפשו
על כל נגישי עדת בני ישראל
ללכת בהם אל מלך אדום.
6 וישמע המלך הנכבד הכהן בבא רבה
בדבר הזה ויצא לקראתם הוא והאנשים
אשר היו עמו ויך מהם אנשים רבים
על המספר והנשארים מהם הלכו אחור.
7 וינסו מפניהם אל מלכיהם ברע דבר
ויספרו להם את כל אשר יעשה להם
ואיך הכהן הנכבד בבא רבה אשר
הקים אשר הקימו אתו עדת בני
ישראל השמרים מלך חדש עליהם
הכה מספר רב מהם.

1 ובאו פוקידי הרפתים עליהם
עד ימנעו אתם מן מעשה
מצות הדת הך די אמנותם.
2 וקעמו אנשי השמרים וחליצו
להם והכו אתם ושרפום באש
ומחו צרבותם.
3 וזה היה בלילת ראש החדש
השביעי וקעמו זכרון לזה
המעשה.
3a (ופרט יאמר כי מן כליל
המעשה דיעשו אתו בני ישראל
השמירים לזאת העודה כי
הילדים ישרפו מן טף דיעשו
אתו סכות בלילת מפוק מועד
השמיני.
3b וגם אתאמר כי זה זכרון
לזאת העודה ונשאר זה
ליומינו בלילת מפוק
המועד הזוכיר יעבירו
מן אש טף הסכות
3c ואנחנו נאמר זאת אמנותה
חיב עשותה בעדנה חיב
עשותה על אביה ובניה
וילדתה מן סדר עדתה
דמבני השמרים דהלכים על
טף אימנותה ביהוה ובמשה
ובתורה והרגריזים וביום
דבו יבאו לגנתה.
4 ונשוב למה ההינו בו)
ונאמר כד השמרים הכו
הפוקדים אשר היו מתפקדים
עליהם מן הרפיתים ושרפו אתם
באש ושמעו נגישי המלך כי
נגישי ישראל השמירים הכו
המחוקקים אשר היו מתפקדים
עליהם.
5 ושלחו יקמצו על נגישי בני
ישראל.
6 אתשיג הדבר אל בבא רבה צא
לקראתם והכה אנשים רבים
מהם והניס הנשארים.
7 וישבו למלכיהם ברעות עדפה
והגידו להם מה קם עליהם
מן המכות והמריבה ואיך
הכה הרב מהם בבא רבה.

8 והכהן הנכבד בבא רבה אתיקץ לכל
אשר עשה עם נגישי המלכים וידע
את כל אשר יתחדש עליו מאת המלכים
וכי יאספו להם מחנה רב ויבאו למלחמתו.
9 ויבחר לו אנשים מבחורי אנשי עמו עדת
בני ישראל השמרים אנשי מלחמה ויכן
אתם לקראת ולמלחמות את מלכי הגוים.
10 ויהי כאשר שמעו מלכי הגוים
במעשה המלך בבא רבה אשר עשה בנגשים
ויאספו אנשים רבים מן מחניהם וישלחו
אתם למלחמות המלך בבא רבה ביד חזקה.
11 ויצא בבא רבה לקראתם ביד חזקה ובזרוע
נטויה ויתן יי׳ את המחנה הזה ביד
המלך בבא רבה ויך מהם אנשים רבים על
המספר ודכה אתם במדכה.
12 וימלא את כל הר (עסכר) אשר מול הר
הקדש הר הברכה הר גרזים בית אל מן
נבילותם והנשארים מהם נסו.
13 וימהרו ויבאו על מלכיהם ויגדו להם
באשר עשה עמהם המלך הנכבד בבא רבה
הוא ועמו ואיך שחטו את רב אנשיהם
ויתן יי׳ אתם בידו וביד עדת בני
ישראל השמרים עמו.
14 ויהי כאשר שמעו המלכים את הדברים
האלה ויחר להם מאד ויקצפו על המלך
הנכבד בבא רבה ועל כל השמרים עמו.
15 ויקם מלך (קסטנטיניה) ויסף אנשים
רבים עד מאד אלפים ורבבות לשלח אתם
למלחמה את בבא רבה ואת כל עמו.
16 ויגד לבבא רבה את הדבר הזה וישלח
לכל מקומות בני ישראל השמרים על
האמת יביאו אליו את כל אנשי המלחמה.
17 ויבאו אליו מכל פא מכל ההר וככר
ומחוף הים ומכל אלון עשרת אלפים איש
מלחמה בכלי מלחמתם בחרחים ובחצים
וברחמים נכנונים לקראת איביהם בחזקת
לב.
18 ויירא המלך הנכבד הכהן בבא רבה כי
מספר אנשי הצוה רב. וכי יצרכו למזון
רב ויצא ביד החזקה ובזרועה נטויה.
19 ויכרש אכתל הנכרים מן הערים אשר
סביבו כי אויבי עדת בני ישראל
השמרים וירשו אתם מהם.
20 ויהי כי בה המגיד למלך הצדיק
בבא רבה הכה מנון אנשים רבים
והנשארים מהם נצו מפני בבא רבה
וידגד את הערים האלה ויורשים
וישכן בהם את אנשי הצבה אשר
הקלו אליו למלחמות את אויבו.

8 ובבא רבה היה מתיקץ למה
עשהו ומה יתשפע מן מעשהו
ואתחכם כי המלכים אלא עליו
יצבאו ויבאו ובמלחמה לו ימכאו.
9 בבחר לו אנשים מן אנשי
עמו בני ישראל השמירים
אנשי שם רגלאים למלחמה
חמישים ואתכינן לקראת
ומלחמות מלכי התרפים
אשר להשמידו מבקשים.
10 כי כד שמעו במה עשהו
בקשו מלחמתו בלבבים קשים.
11 וצא לקראתם ונתן לו
יהוה נצען עליהם והכה
אנשים רבים מהם.
12 ואמלא ההר מחנים דאצל
ההר הקדש מן נבלותם
ואשר נשארו נסו למלכיהם.
13 והגידו להם מה היה
עליהם ואיך הוא חלש
אתם וכחשם.
14 ואתגדלו המלכים ואתגברו
ואתחזקו ואתאמצו ואתפוררו
ואתחילו.
15 ואתאמץ מלך אלקסטנטיניה
אפו על המלך הצדיק בבא
רבה ואסף עליו עסכרים
רבים.
16 וכד אתשיג הדבר אל בבא
רבה שלח לבני ישראל
השמרים הנמצאים בכל
האתרים ישלחו לו אנשי
מלחמה.
17 ובאו עליו מכל פאת מן שפעת
הים וההרים והככרים עשרת
אלף מן הגברים בכלי המלחמה
מחגרים.
18 ובעת עמה בבא רבה רבות
העסכרים אתכיר כי ימך לסגי
המדלים וצא ביד חזקה.
19/20 וגרש הנכרים דמקדם בקריות
שרים והכה מהם אנשים רבים
ואשר נותרו נס כל מנון
מן מישרו ולקח זאת הקריות
והביאו העסכרים דבאו
לעזורותו בה.

21 ויקח מעדת בני ישראל השמרים
את המוס אשר היו יתנו אתו
למלכי אדום ויקנא בו .....
וכלי מלחמה לאנשי הצבא ויתן
לאנשי הצבא כל אשר יצרכו אליו
יום ביומ(יו).
22 ויצו המלך הצדיק בבא רבה
ויעבירו ... בכל ערי עדת בני
ישראל השמרים לא יתנו מיום
והלאה מומס למלכי אדום ולא ..
ולא לחם למלכי אדום כאשר היו
מית... עליהם למחניהם.
23 ויכרת את אלה למנ......... הזה
והלאה כי היה יקחו לצב.. ישראל
השמרים.
24 וישם המלך הצי. .ב. רבה את
מקום מושבו בעיר עמרתה ......
בה אדונינו ארשי הכהנים הגדולים
אלעזר ואיתמר ופינחס עליהם
השלום לעולם.
25 וכן יש בה קברים רבים לנביאים
ולזקנים ולזכאים ולצדקים רבים.
26 ובגלל הדבר הזה נקרא שמה קרית
עמרתה כי אתעמרת בקברי אלה
הצדקים הנכבדים; וישם המלך
הצדיק בבא רבה את מחנהו בתוכה..

21 ולקח מן עדתו מה היו
יביאו ל. כראותו וגאה
בו גאות האנשים דקנאו
בקנאתו.
22 וצוה לא אחד יתן המוס
מן עדתו אל הרפתים
דהוו יביאו אתו מכל
הפאתים.
24 ואחר כן שם בקריאת
עבורתה מקוהו אשר היא
קברת אבהתיו דבכהנים
ידיהם אמלאו אלעזר ואיתמר
ופינחס דבשמן המשחה אמשחו
עליהם השלום.

§12

1 ויהי אחרי כן ויבא המגיד אל המלך
הצדיק בבא רבה ויגד לו לאמר.
2 אויביך באו במספר רב עד מאד עד
כי חדל לספר כי אין מספר.
3 ויעמדו בבא רבה וכל חכמי עם
השמרים בין ידי יי׳ אלהיהם
וישתחוו על פניהם ארצה ואמרו
לאמר.
4 יי׳ אל ..חק את פניך ממנו אל
תעלים לעת הצוק בגאו ....
...... יעבדו בני ......
תרח........... בעני.......
....
את אלהיך .... בלבו לא תדרש ...
כעסנו תביט לתת בידך .... את
דבריהם.
5 אתה ההית מגן ועזר לעמך שבר
זרוע הרשעים וכל רע ידרש ולא
ימצא.
6 יי׳ מלך עולם ועד אבדו גוים
נכרים מארצו תאות ענוים שמעת
יי׳ תכן לבם תתן אזנך לשמע את

1 ואחר כן אתת אל בבא רבה
המגידים במובא שנאיו
ברב עסכרון ומה לון
מן הקדקדים ובכלי
המלחמה מתיסדים.
3 שם עמד בבא רבה הוא ועמו
בין ידי יהוה וקולותם ארימו
בתפלה בטהרות הלב ובנצירות
יצר לית כמו.

שיאלם לא יוסף עוד יערצם אנוש
מן הארץ.
7 הושיע יי׳ את עמך כי נשמדו
חסידים כי ספו אמונים מבני אדם.
8 עד אנה יי׳ תשכחנו עד מתי תסיר
פניך ממנו עד אנה נשית עצות
בנפשנו ויגון כל יום בלבבינו
עד מתי ירום אויבינו עלינו.
9 ראה ועננו יי׳ אלינו אניר את
עינינו פן נישון למות פן יאמרו
אויבינו יוכלנו עליהם פן יאמרו
כי נמוט ואנחנו בחסדך בטחנו
נשיר לשמך לטוב לנו.
10 ויהי כאשר כלו בבא רבה ואת
כל זקני העם מתפלותם זאת ויתקעו
בחצצרות תרועה לזכרון ולעשות את
מצות יי׳ אשר צוה על יד אדון
הנביאים עבדו משה בן עמרם עליו
השלום לעולם.
11 וכי תבאו מלחמה בארצכם על הצר
הצרר אתכם והרעתם בחצצרות
ונזכרתם לפני יי׳ לפני יי׳
אלהיכם ונועשתם מאיביכם
12 ויצעקו צעקה גדלה עד מאד קול
אחד לאמר השקף ממעון קדשך מן
השמים והציל את עמך את ישראל
מידי איביהם.
13 וישמע יי׳ את קול צעקותם
ביום ההוא ויתן את אויביהם בידיהם
ויכו את עדת בני ישראל השמרים
על האמת מספר רב מן אויביהם
והמלחמה הזאת היתה בהר אשר
הוא נכח עיר שכם הקדשה ויזרקו
בני ישראל את דם אויב במקום ההוא.
14 וירד הדם מן ההר ההו וילך הך
המים ויקרא את שם המקום ההוא
דרך דם הטמאה עד היום הזה.

10 ותקעו בשופרים בתרועה וכן זכרון
השבועה דנשבע בה ישתבח שמו
בתורותו הקדושה כמימרו ..
11 .. כי תבוא מלחמה בארצכם על הצר
הצרר אתכם והרעתם בחצצרות
ונזכרתם לפני יהוה אלהיכם
ונושעתם מאיביכם.
12 וצעקו צעקה גדלה בקול אחד
אמרים השקף ממעון קדשך מן
השמים והציל את עמך את
ישראל מידי דבביהם.
13 ויהי ככלותם זאת תפלותם יהוה
ביכלותו שמע אליהם ומן זאת
הצרעה נפש להם ונצען אתם על
איביהם ועל פי חרב השמידו אתם
ונפלת זאת המלחמה בגלגל דממול
שכם.
14 ואטמא המכון ואשתמי אבן
הטמא עד היום הזה מרב
הדם דנשפך מן שנאיהם בו.

§13

1 ויהי אחרי כן ויבאו את המלך הצדיק בבא רבה
ואת כל זקני העם וישתחוו ארצה לפני יי׳
אלהיהם ויאמרו לאמר.
2 נודך יי׳ בכל כוחינו צור ישוענו ומגנו
ומפלטנו.
3 מהללים נקרא את יי׳ ומאבינו נושע.
4 אפפו אתנו חבלי מות ונחלי בליעל
יבעתונו.
5 חבלי שאול סבבו לנו מוקשי המות תפשו בנו.
6 בצר לנו קראנו ליי׳ ואל אלהינו צעקנו וישמע יי׳
את קולנו ואת קול צעקותינו.

7 ותחרד הארץ ומוסדי ההרים ירגזו ויחרדו כי חרה לו.
8 כי אש קדחה אוקדת באפו ויט שמים וירד וישלח חציו
על צרינו ויפצם וגם ברקים רבים ויחרדם.
9 מאיבינו הצלינו ומשנאינו כי אמצו ממנו ואל מרחב
הוציאנו ויחלצנו כי חפץ בנו.
10 יגמלנו יי׳ חסד כגדל חסדו ונהיה תמים עמו ונשתמר
מעונינו.
11 כי הוא עם חסיד יתחסד ועם התמים יתמם עם טהור
יתטהר ועם עקש יתפתל ועם עני יושיע ועיניהם
רמות ישפיל.
12 הוא יאיר נורותינו ויגל את חשכותינו.
13 כי בך רעצנו צבא ושור דלגנו.
14 דרכי יי׳ תמימה ואמירתו צדיקה מגן הוא לכל
הבטחים בו.
15 כי מי הוא האל מבלעדי יי׳ ומי הוא צור זולתי
אלהינו.
16 נפרד אויבינו ונשיגם ולא נשוב עד כלותם.
17 יצעקו ואין מושיע יושיעם ונשחקם מעפר על פני
רוח כחרש חוצות נשליכם.
18 תפלטנו מריבי העמים תשימנו עליונים לכל הגוים
גויים לא ידענו יעבדו לנו.
19 לשמע אזן ישמעו אלינו בני נכר יכחשו אלינו
בני זרים יפלו ויחרגו מחדריהם.
20 חי הוא אלהינו יי׳ ומברך צורנו ורם אל ישענו.
21 האל הנותן נקמות בגללנו ויכחשו העמים לנו ועל
במתם נדרך אנחנו.
22 מפלטנו מאבינו אף מן הקמים עלינו מאנשי חמס מגאלנו.
23 לכן נודך בין הגוים אלהינו ולשמך נרנן בכל כוחינו.
24 מגדל ישועה לנו ועשה חסד לבן אהביו.

ושם יהוה ישתבח שמו
בזה היום נפוש רב.
והכירו כי יכלות יהוה
דנצעתם ומיד איביהם
הצילת אתם כי היו
מתכוננים מן עסכרים
וכלי מלחמה לא תזכר
בממול העסכרים וכלי
מלחמות עבודי אלהי
נכר.
ואוסיפו מן התשבחן
והמודאה והתהללות
והרבואן והורמת
השמחות ביניהם
ונתנו ליהוה שכר.

§14

1 בעת ההיא קם בפני מלך כשדים עשות
מלחמה עם מלך (אסכנדרה) ויעש עמו
מלחמה ביניהם ויקח מלך כשדים את
הערים מן המלך (אסכנדרה) ויהי כן

1 בעת ההיא שם יהוה ישתבח שמו
בנפש המלך אשור כי ילחם
אלאסכנדרה ולחמו ולקח הערים
מנו והורמת המלחמה ואתחזק

גלל למנע אתו מן מלחמות המלך
הצדיק בבא רבה.
2 ויהי בימים ההם ויבאו הערבים
בני ישמעאל אל עיר (דאריה) ויבזו
אתה ויהרסו לה.
3 כי עיר גדלה היתה זאת העיר ואנשים
רבים מעדת בני ישראל השמרים היו
ישבים בה.
4 וישמע המלך הצדיק בבא רבה במובאם
ויצא לקראתם ויכם וישברם וירדפם
עד מעבר הירדן.
5 ויהרג מהם אנשים רבים על המספר
ויבזו בני ישראל השמרים על האמת
מן הערבים מקנה צאן ומקנה בקר
ובהם השמלות וכסף וזהב וכלי מלחמה
רבים עד מאד לא ימנו במספר.
6 וישמעו המלכים במוצא המלך הצדיק
הכהן בבא רבה לקראת הערבים בני
ישמעאל ויעש עמהם מלחמה ויכם וישברם
וירדפם עד מעבר הירדן גונבים נחשים
עלי דרך שפפון ועלי ארח נושכים עקבי
סוס זידנים יכלים על הכל וממשלם
היתה בעת ההיא חזקה ויחד כל המלכים
בגלל הדבר הזה וישמחו שמח גדול.
7 וישלחו למלך הצדיק בבא רבה לחם
ומזון היה דים לעשרת אלפים אנשי
צבאו וגם שלחו אליו כסף וזהב
ושמלות וידברו עמו ויהללו אתו
בגלל זה המעשה אשר עשה בהערבים.
8 אז ישיר המלך הצדיק בבא רבה
את השירה הזאת ליי׳ ויאמר לאמר.

עם אלאסכנדרה ועזב מלחמות
גדלות בבא רבה.
2 ושם יהוה ככן בזאת הימים
בנפשות הערבים הישמעאליה
המובא לארץ כנען ובזותה
וחרבותה.
3 כי הות ערים מתכוננה ורחבה
ורב שכוניה מבני ישראל השמירים.
4 ושמע בבא רבה במובאם וצא
ולחם אתם ורדפם אל ערבת
הירדן.
5 ושברם והכה אנשים רבים מהם
ובזו השמרים טובות רבות
מצאן ובקר ובהמה ובגדים
וכסף וזהב ומה מדמי לזה
מקנה לא יספר.
6 וכד שמעו פרט המלכים כי יצא
בבא רבה לקראת הישמעאלים
ולחמם ושבר אתם במה הם
ככן היו באזים וכרתים
הדרך וזודים על הכל כי הות
קוצותם גאות ושמחו המלכים
בכן שמח תמים.
7 ושלחו אל בבא רבה
מטעמים יכלכל לעשרת
אלף פרש ושלחו לו מדל
רב ושמלות טובות ודברו
אתו ושכרו לו על זה המעשה.

9 אשירך יי׳ אלהי עזי וזמרתי אנוהיך וארוממך.
10 יי׳ גיבור במלחמה יי׳ שמו.
11 יי׳ בגאותך ישמח המלך ואיך בישועתך לא יחד.
12 ימינך יי׳ נאדרי בכח ימינך יי׳ תרעץ אויב.
13 תאות לבי נתתה לי כל מבטא שפתי לא מאנת ממני.
14 כי תקדמני ברכות טוב תשית על ראשי נצר חסד.
15 מי כמוך באילים יי׳ מי כמוך נאדרי בקדש נורא תהלת עשה פלאה.
16 גדל כבודי בישועתך הוד והדר שמת עלי.
17 כי המלך בטח ביי׳ ובחסד אל עליון לא ימוט.
18 תמצא ידך לכל איביך תרעץ לכל שנאיך.
19 פריהם מארץ תאבד וזרעם מבני אדם.
20 רומה יי׳ בעזך נשירה ונהלל ונרומם גבורתך.

21 וישלח המלך הצדיק הכהן בבא רבה לקרת
לזקני העם ולראשיו ולשטריו ויבאו
לפניו ויאמר אליהם לאמר.
22 עתה חייב עלינו כלנו נתן רב שירות
ותהללות ואודות לאלהינו ואלהי
אבותינו אשר צדק ברחמיו היתרה
עלינו ואושיענו בזאת הישועה ונתן
את אויבינו בידנו וירעץ אלה אשר

21 ואודה בבא רבה יהוה
על כן ואמר.
22 עתה חיב עלינו נתן
ליהוה אודאות כי
עתה הטיב לנו מן
טבהתו דלא תספר
והציל אתנו מיד איבינו

באו בגלל לקחתנו ובגלל לקחות את
בנינו ולשביות את נשינו ויתנם יי׳
בידנו ונקח את כל מקניהם ואת כל רכושם.
23 עתה ידעו אויבינו כי מאת יי׳ אלהינו
היה זה המצליח לנו כי להם רעצנו ובגלל
הדבר הזה שלחהו מנחה טובה לנו ויקרו
את נפשותינו בכבוד הזה.
24 אין זה כי אם מחסד אלהינו ומכוננו
ואדונינו עלינו אשר כחש את שנאינו
אלינו וישלחו בזה היקר הרב אלינו
מאחרי כי היינו נלאים לקום פניהם
יראים מחמסם אבדים מגברותם.
25 ויקם אלהינו לנו את אשר בארו על
יד אדון הנביאים בן עמרם רבנו
בקדוש התורה ספרינו ויכחשו איביך
לך ואתה על במתם תדרך.

ונתנם בידנו וחלש
אהלין דבאו עד יקחו
אתנו ובנינו ונשינו
וישבו לנו וביכלותו
לקחנו אתם ואת מקניהם
ואת רכושם.
23/24 ועתה אויבינו כד אכירו
נצענו על מן לחמו אתנו
שלחו מנחות לנו
אחר מה ההינו מתחלשים
מן שנאי.
25 דבחר וחשק באבותינו וקומם
לנו מה ביאר בספרו דבא
משה בו בימינו והוא
מימרו המתברך ויכחשו
איביך לך ואתה על במתם תדרך.

§15

1 ויהי אחר הדברים האלה הקהל המלך
הנכבד הכהן בבא רבה את כל עמו
לפניו ויאמר אליהם לאמר.
2 לכו עתה בשלום כל איש אל עירו
ואל מקומו והיה כי יש לי צריכה
אליכם אשלח ואקרא אתכם.
3 אך יעמד מכם אצלי שלשת אלפים איש
לי היה מושבם קרוב מפני בכל עת
אמצא אתם עמדים נכחי.
4 את אלה ישבו בחצרים אשר הם סביב
קרית עמרתה אשר אני שכן בה אין
להם רחיקה מעלי.
5 וייטב הדבר בעיני זקני עם בני
ישראל השמרים וראשיו ושטריו
ויענו ויאמרו טוב הדבר אשר דברת
לעשות.
6 ויעשו כן כאשר צום ויקמו שלשת
אלפים איש צבא בחצרים אשר הם
מסביב לקרית עמרתה.
7 ויברך המלך הצדיק הכהן בבא רבה
את כל עמו וישבו ברב שמח ושלום
איש למקומו מהללים משירים את
יי׳ אלהיהם יתקדש שמו הגדול.
8 ויהיו זקני עדת בני ישראל השמרים
על האמת בכל לילת חדה ראש כל
שבוע יבאו מן הקריתים הקרובים
לעיר שכם הקדושה ויקהלו בזקני
העיר ההיא וילכו יחדו אל קרית
עמרתה למען יקהלו במלך הצדיק
בבא רבה רצון יי׳ וסליחתו עליו אמן.
9 בעת ההיא היה וכל עדת בני

1 ואחר כן אתאסף בבא רבה עם עמו
ואיטיב להם ואמר אליהם.
2 עתה הלכו אל ארצכם ומקומיכם
בבטח כל איש למכונו עד כי
אתצריך לכם.
3 רק חיב ישאר אתי שלשת אלף
איש יהיו קרובים מני בכל
עת אמצאון.
4 ואשימם באלכפור אשר הם סביב
כפר עמרתה אשר אני שכן בה
עד יהיו תחת דברי לבר יחדש.
5 וראו כל זקיני בני ישראל
השמירים כי זה הדבר חסיד.
6 ועשו כאשר דבר אליהם וקעמו
שלשת אלף איש פרש בקריות
דקרובים לקרית עבורתה.
7 וגדלות בבא רבה קרא לעמו
וברך אתם ונשק להם וישבו
למכוניהם שלשים בשמח וזהו
ושש וכל איש הלך למקומו.
8 והיו נגישי בני ישראל
השמירים הקרובים אל
שכם בכל לילת חדה
יתאספו וכהלון ילכו
לקרית עבורתה למען
יתקבצו עם בבא רבה.
9 והם היו בזאת הימים

ישראל השמרים על האמת בכבוד ואיקר
ועז יתר שמחים בנגלאות אימנותם
ששונים כי יי׳ יתברך שמו הסיר את חמס
אויביהם מעליהם והוו יחנו איש את
רעהו ויהיו עדת בני ישראל השמרים
על האמת בכל לילת חדה יקהלו
במקוה בשמח יתר; וישאר זה המעשה
ביניהם עד היום הזה.
10 והמלך הצדיק בבא רבה רצון יי׳ עליו
אמן המקום אשר על שמו לא היה יפתחו
כי אם על פי הכהנים וישאר על כן
אחד ימים.
11 ויהי אחר הדברים האלה מת המלך
(אסכנדרה) והמלך הזוכיר באחר ימיו
לא יכל יצא על עדת בני ישראל השמרים
להלחם אתם כי פחדם ויראתם נתן יי׳
יתברך שמו.
12 והמלכים אז נלאו לקחת המוס מעדת
בני ישראל השמרים ולא יכלו לעשות
עמהם מלחמה שלחו לקרא את זקני ושטרי
עדת היהודים אליהם לאמר.
13 כי תוכלו על הכות המלך הצדיק בבא
רבה והכיתם אתו נתן לכם צו לבנות
את בית מקדשכם אשר בעיר ירושלם.
14 ויאספו אחרי כן זקני עדת היהודים
ויאמרו איש אל רעהו איך נעשה למלך
בבא רבה עד נוכל על הכותו ונבני את
בית מקדשנו.
15 ויענו אנשים מהם לאמר למה נשלם
בבא רבה רעה תחת טובה כי מאז
הגדלת ממלכת בבא רבה הנשאת
מעלינו את כל משאי וטרחי המלכים
האלה ולא יוכלו לעשות עמנו רעה.
16 ועתה כי נעשה דבר עם המלך בבא רבה
ולא נשיג למדרשנו נהיה עשינו גלל
להביא עלינו רעות רבות מאת בבא
רבה ומאת כל עמו עדת בני ישראל
השמרים וגם נהיה שנאים למלך בבא
רבה ולכל מלכי הגוים.
17 ואנשים אחרים מהם אמרו כי נוכל על
עשות רעה עם המלך בבא רבה להכות
אתו נכהו ולא נחדל מעשות הדבר הזה
אולי נבני את בית מקדשנו; הלוא
ידעתם אחינו כי המלך בבא רבה וכל
עמו עדת בני ישראל ימנעו אתנו
מלבנות את בית מקדשנו ויאמרו אלינו
כי עיר ירושלם איננה עיר הקדש ולא
המקום המבחר, אך יאמרו המקום המבחר
הוא הרגריזים בית אל.
18 והמלך הצדיק בבא רבה לא היה מחשבו
בדברים כאלה רק היתה כל מחשבות לבו

בטוב רב ועז וכח זהים
בנצען הדת ואנשמה מן
חמס טרחון מעליהם האבדת
והם תמיד כל איש יחני
לחברה בחסדות דנועדת.
10 ובבא רבה לא היה ילכד
בכל עת המכון דחתוקק
לו וככן לא היה ילכדו
אלא על פי הכהנים ואמצא
זה ימים מן השנים.
11 ואחר כן מת המלך אסכנדרה
ולא ישב יוכל יצא לבני
ישראל השמרים בארך יומי
חייו למען ילחם אתם כי
פחדתם נפלה יהוה בלבה.
12 וכד נלאו המלכים בלקחתם
המוס מבני ישראל השמרים
ולא שבו יוכלו למלחמותם
ואמרו אל עדת היהודאים.
13 אן יכלתם על בבא רבה
והכיתו אתו נטשנו אתכם
בבניאן מקדשכם.
14 ונפל בנפש היהוד׳ למבקשון
בבניאן מקדשון.

ובבא רבה כד נצענה
יהוה על המלכים שאו
חמסם אשר היה על
היהודאים במשפטים
ובלעדה עד לא יבאו
תחת משפט בבא רבה..
18 וגדלות בבא רבה איננו
מבקש כן ומבקשו היה

נגלאות אימנות דת משה הקדושה ולרב
את השירות והתהללות לאלהי השמים
והארץ יתברך שמו הקדוש ולתקון
מקרת התורה הקדושה ולעשות את חקותה
ומצותה על האמת.

פשאת הדת הקשט ונגלאות
הצלואן והתה׳ והרוממות
וגם נגלאות התורה.

19 ויהי בעת ההיא ואנשים רבים מעדת
היהודים היו ישבים בקרית (נמרה)
ויבאו אנשים מזקני היהודים לקריה
ההיא ויעשו עיצות כסות ביניהם
ויתנו לו למלך הצדיק בבא רבה להמיתו
בצע מהם הן ישיגו מן המלכים הנכרים
לקחת מהם צו לבנות את בית מקדשם
בעיר ירושלם.

19 ובימים ההם היה יהודאים
רבים שכונים בקרית נמארה
ועבדו להם נכליה ונכלו בה;
וזה היה ברז ביניהם בצע
עד יתשגו למדרשון.

§16

1 ויהי בימים ההם וילך המלך הצדיק
הכהן בבא רבה לקרית (נמרה) הזוכירה
והלכותו אליה היתה ביום הששי מן
השבוע עד יעשה השבת בקריה ההיא כפי
הסכנתו.

1 ובפרט הימים הלך בבא רבה
לקרית כפר נמארה וזה היה
ביום הששי למען יעשה השבת
בכנשת הקריה הזוכירה כפי
אמנותו.

2 וישבת בכנשתה כי בכל מקום היה בבא
רבה יבוא לילת השבת בבית הכנשה ולא
יצא ממנו עד כלות השבת.

2 והוא ביום השבת לא יצא
מן המקדש דישבת בו.

3 והיהודים דרשו יבאו על המלך הצדיק
בבא רבה ועל כל אנשיו בלילת השבת
כי בעת ההיא לא יוכלו עדת בני ישראל
השמרים לשאת את כלי מלחמה והם יבאו
עליהם בתוך בית הכנשה והם קעצים
בצלותם ויכו אתם שם.

3 ואתנכלו היהודאים למען
יבאו עליו ועל אחיו
בלילת השבת ויכו אתם והם
קעמים בצלות כי שם לא יכלו
על שאת כלי מלחמה עד ינשאו
על נפשותם בה.

4 ולא אבה יי׳ יתברך שמו ישיגם למדרשם
כי אם בחכמתו גלא את כסות עיצתם
מיום החמישי מפני מובא המלך בבא רבה
לקרית (נמרה).

4 וחכמת יהוה לא נטשת אתם על
התלתםִ רק חנן ברחמותו ואגלי
מים הששי נכלותם ואתאמר
מיום החמישי היה מובא בבא
רבה לכפר נמארה.

5 היה ביום השביעי מן השבוע ויי׳
יתקדש שמו גלא את כסות עיצת עדת
היהודים לעדת בני ישראל השמרים על
האמת ביום החמישי מן השבוע.

6 וגלא נגלאות זה הדבר כי אשה מעדת
היהודים לה חברה מנשי עדת בני ישראל
השמרים ומאהבה גדלה היתה בין האשה
הישראלית ובין האשה היהודית ויהי
ביום החמישי מימי השבוע ותאמר האשה
היהודית לאחותה האשה הישראלית אחותי
אדרש אני ממניך לא תלכי לילת השבת
לבית הכנשה.

6 וגלל זה כי אשה מן היהודאים
הות לה אשה תאהבה מן האנשים
השמירות והיא חברותה ואמרת
לה אחמד מניך אה אחותי
כי לא תבאי לכנשה בלילת
השבת אתי.

7 ותען האשה הישראלית את אחותה היהודית
לאמר מדוע אחותי תמנעי אתי מלכתי
לבית הכנשה ומה הגלל.

7 וענתה ואמרת לה למה תמנעי
אתי אה מן ביך דביקה
מאהבותי ומה הגלל כי לא
אבוא לכנשה עד אצלי צלותי.

8 ותען האשה היהודית למה תפצרי בי
להגיד ליך עתה את הגלל ואנכי אירא

8 ואמרת לה היהודאיה אן ליך

מאד כי אז אגלי ליך את הגלל תגידי בו על לשני ואהיה אני הגלל לנפל את נפשי בלחץ רב ובמגפה גדלה.

9 ותען האשה הישראלית לאמר כי תגלי נא לי את הגלל לא אדבר בו לאחד מבני אדם על פיך אחותי.

10 ותאמר אליה היהודית לאמר דעי נא אחותי.

11 ותאמר אליה היהוד׳ עשו בינם עיצות על הכות את המלך בבא רבה ואת כל אנשיו בלילת השבת והם עמדים בצלות יבאו עליהם בכסי ויכו אתם שם.

12 הנה נא הגדתי ליך כסי את הדבר הזה ולא תדברי בו.

13 ויהי כאשר שמעת האשה הישראלית אשר מעדת בני ישראל השמרים את הדבר הזה מחברתה היהודית ויקם גיד הקנאה בפניה.

14 ותמהר ותלך אל המלך הצדיק בבא רבה ותגיד לו בדבר הזה ואת שם האשה היהוד׳ לא זכרת לו כאשר אמרת אליה.

15 ויהי כאשר שמע המלך הצדיק בבא רבה את הדברים האלה יחר אפו על עדת היהודים.

16 ויגלי אליהם כי ילין לילת השבת בבית הכנשה מיום הששי.

17 ויהי בערב ויבא המלך בבא רבה לבית הכנשה והוא לבוש בגדים בדים ויהי השמש באה ועלטה היה ויפשיט המלך הצדיק בבא רבה את בגדי הבד אשר עליו אשר היא מלבש השבת הקדש ויצא מבית הכנשה ולא ידע איש במוצאו.

18 ויהי השמש לאביו ויאספו אנשים רבים מעדת היהודים לא ימנו במספר ויבאו אל בית הכנשה וימששו שם על המלך הצדיק הכהן בבא רבה כי הוא מדרשם.

19 ויסגרו את הדלתים ויביערו כי ידעים הם הן המלך בבא רבה יש בבית הכנשה.

20 ויהי כי ראה המלך בבא רבה רצון יי׳ וסליחתו עליו אמן מעדת היהודים את המעשה הזה ויצעק עליהם בקול גדול ויצעקו גם כל אנשיו קול אחד על היהודים אוי מזה באתו ואנה תלכו.

21 ויבהלו אנשי היהודים מקול צעקותם כי היה גדול מאד ותפל עליהם אימה ופחד וירגזו ויאחזמם רעד ונמגו את

ידעתי הדבר אשר שמעתי אירא אהיה לרעה לנפשי בקשתי.

9 ואשבעת לה האשה אמרה אה אחותי מה תאמרי לי עליו לא אדברו אל אחד במוצא שפתי.

10/11 וענת לה ואמרת כי היהודאים שנאות בבא רבה ואחיו בלבביהם נכמרת וחרוצים בלילת השבת והם קעמים בצלות יעברו עליהם ויכו אתם למען זכרון וכרת.

12 ועתה הגדתי אליך מה אלי נודע הסתירי דברי עד לא תמושני חרדה.

13 שם פשת הקנאה קנאת הדת בלב האשה השמרה.

14 והלכת אל האדון בבא רבה והגידת לו במהרה על מה שמעת אתו מן היהודיה עד לא יפל הוא ואחיו בצררה ולא הגידת לו על שם היהודאה ולא על אקרה הך מה אשבעת לה בטהרות יצרה.

15/16 וכד שמע בבא רבה זה הדבר אתבצר ואגלי כי הוא משנתן בכנשה מיום הששי.

17 והוא היה במובאו לכנשה לבוש בגדים בד המתכוננה לשבת דמקדם לה היה עשה; ויהי במחשכת העין פשט מה היה עליו מן הבגדים דלה זכרנו וצא מן הכנשה ולא אחד ידע במה היה ממנו.

18 והיהודים כד בא הליל הקהל כל מנון דלקדשות השבת מחלל ובאו לחצר הכנשה ועברו בקשות לב ופשע ואחפשו על בבא רבה כי היה רב עפלון בהכותו

19 והסגירו התרחים והבעירו האש אהלין הרעים כי היו מסתכלים בבא רבה בכנשה קעם.

20 וכד עמה בבא רבה מנון זה המעשה צעק עליהם הוא ועדתו בקול רב עד מאד לא שמעו כותו.

21 וכד שמעו קולו אתשברת צלעם ונבהלו והשליכו כלי מלחמותם ונסו ואתעורת עיניהם ואתכשלו.

לבביהם וישליכו את כלי המלחמה
מידיהם וינסו מפני המלך הצדיק בבא
רבה ומפני כל אנשיו.
22 ויצאו בבא רבה וכל אנשיו וירדפו
אחריהם וישיגום וישיבום אל המלך
הצדיק הכהן בבא רבה ויגשו אנשים
מהם ויפלו לפניו ארצה.
23 ויאמרו לו בי אדני אנחנו עבדיך
חטאינו ליי׳ אלהיך ולך כי דרשנו
את דמך ואתה לא עשית עמנו רעה כי
אם כל טוב עשית לנו וגם כי אתה
הוא הגלל להסיר את עול הברזל אשר
מעם המלכים הנכרים מעלינו.
24 ויצו המלך הצדיק בבא רבה את אנשיו
ויתפשו את כלם ויאמר אליהם למה
שלמתם רעה תחת טובה הלוא ידעתם
כי אנכי כל מדרשי לחזק את אימנות
דת ישראל ולהסיר את חמס כל המלכים
מעליהם ועשית עמם מלחמות גדולות.
25 ויתן יי׳ את כלם בידי והוצאתי את
כל שבטי בני ישראל מתחת ידם עד
יגלו את אימנות ישראל ויהללו
וישירו את יי׳ אלהיהם ויצלו ויקרו
בספר תורת משה הקדושה בקול גדול
ואין מי ימנע אתם אחרי לא יוכלו
לעשות דבר מאלה.
26 בגלל הדבר הזה באתם אלי לשפך את
דמי ולשרף אתי ואת כל אחי באש.
27 אוי לכם אוי לכם הלוא ידעתם כי יי׳
יתן אתכם בידי ועתה אין לכם ישועה.
28 ויצו המלך בבא רבה ויוציאו את אנשי
היהודים מעלי ויניחו אתן במשמר עד
מחרת יום השבת ויציגום לפניו לשפט
עליהם משפט צדק.
29 ויאמר בבא רבה עתי אין חייב תשארו
חיים אחרי מדרשכם את נפשי ואת נפש
אנשי להמיתן בלילת השבת הקדוש
ואנחנו עמדים נצלי ונהלל ונגדל
ונרומם ליי׳ אלהינו ואלהי אבותינו.
30 ויהרגם וישרפם באש ויעש להם כאשר
אמר יי׳ בתורותו הקדושה ועשית לו
כאשר זמם לעשות לאחיו ויקח גם מן
היהודים את הגבעה אשר היא מול המגדל
ויהרג את יושביה.
31 ולא נשאר מהם איש או אשה בלעדי
האשה אשר הגידת לחבירתה הישראלית
בדבר הזה כי באת תחת קורת חברתה
הישראלית הזוכירה ותבוא בעדת בני
ישראל השמרים על האמת כי יראת על
נפשה מעדת היהודים.
32 וישלח המלך הצדיק הכהן בבא רבה

22 ומנון מן באו אליו ותכו
לרגלו ועמדו הך עבדים ממלו,
בצע בנחמו דיהוה הנחילו.
23 ואמרו לו אנחנו עבדיך
וחטאינו נכמרת ועתה באנו
בין ידיך וגדלך לא ארע בנו
ובקשנו דמך מרעות עמלינו
ואתה כל חסד עשית עמנו ונשאת
חמס עבודי הבעלים מעלינו
ומן ערינו ומה ייטב בעיניך
אעשה לנו.
28 ותמכם כהלון אחרי רדפו
עדתו מן ברחו ואשיגו
אתם ולפניו בהם באו
ואסרם בבית הסהר ואחר
אזלת שבתה עמד אתם תחת
המשפט.
29 ואמר להם לא יישר השיר
אתכם נשמת חיים בכם
אחר מה בקשתם תשמידו
אתי בכלי מלחמותיכם
ולו בו תמכם אתי הכיתם
ולמלכים פגרי שלמתם
ובזה אשבעו לכם ינטשו
לכם בבניאן בית מקדשכם.
30 שם שפט עליהם והכו אתם
ושרפום ולקח הגבעה דממול
המגדל מידיהם; וקדם הזה
לא היה ישטנם.
31/32 והוה לקחתו אתה אחר
הכותו שכוניה ולא נשאר
מהם מלבד האשה אשר בכן

לקרא את האשה זאת מתוך חברתה
וייטב לה.

הגידת להם; ולקח אתה אחר
מובאה תחת קורת האשה
השמרה חברתה; ואיטיב לה
והביאה בדת כי נשארת היא
יראה על נפשה מן היהודאים.

§17

1 ויהי אחרי כן וישמעו כל בני יהודה את
כל אשר עשה המלך הצדיק בבא רבה
לאחיהם היהודים ישבי קרית (נמרה)
ויבאו אנשים מהם וישרפו את כל זרע
עדת בני ישראל השמרים על
האמת אשר בשדה.
2 וישמע המלך בבא רבה ויצא אחריהם הוא
וכל אנשיו ויכום ולא נשאר מהם כי אם
מספר מעט.
3 ויהי כאשר שמע המלך (גורדיאנוס)
במעשה אשר עשו לעדת בני ישראל
השמרים על האמת ולכהן בבא רבה וישלח
להם צו לבנות את בית מקדשם בעיר ירושלם
כי דרש בכן לגדלות השנאה בין עדת
היהודים ובין עדת בני ישראל השמרים
על האמת ועד תהיה מריבות ביניהם.
4 והמלך הצדיק בבא רבה לא מנע את
היהודים מלבנות את בית מקדשם בעיר
ירושלם; ויאספו עדת היהודים את
צריכות הבית בגלל בניאנו ולעת
דרשו יחלו ויעש יי׳ בעת ההיא מופת
גדול מן השמים.
5 וזה המופת הוא סופה גדלה עד מאד
נשאת את כל אשר הכינו ואת כל אשר
אספו עדת היהודים לניאן ותזרע
אתו על פני כל הארץ.
6 ויחדלו עדת בני יהודה מלבנות את
בית מקדשם ואחרי כן יצא את הבית
הזה מיד היהודים עד היום הזה ולא
יכלו לבנות אתו.
7 אז ישר בבא רבה ובני ישראל השמרים
על האמת את השירה הזאת ליי׳ ויאמר לאמר: –
8 אליך יי׳ נרים את ידינו בך בטחנו אלהינו לא נבושה.
9 ואל יעלצו איבינו בנו כי קויך לא יטרף כי אם
יטרפו הבוגדים לנו.
10 דרכים אלהינו אודיענו ארחיך חכמנו.
11 הדרכינו באמתך ולמדנו כי אתה אל ישוענו.
12 רחמיך וחסדיך מעולם המה זכרם עתה לנו.
13 אל תפן אל קשהנו ואל רשענו למען טובך יי׳
כחסדך זכר לנו.
14 צדיק וישר אתה ועשוי החטאים אנחנו.
15 כל ארחות יי׳ חסד ואמת לשמרי חקותיו ומצותיו.

1 ואחר כן באו עדת היהודאים
כד ידעו במה עשהו בבא
רבה באחיהם ושרפו התבואתים
דלשמרים בשדה.
2 וצא עליהם בבא רבה והכה
אתם ולא נשאר אלא מעט מהם.
3/4 וכד בא ארשות ליהודאים
מן המלך גורדיאנוס בבניאן
מקדשם קבצו כלים הבניאן
וארשו יעפלו בבניאן משכן
מקדשם גלה יהוה ישתבח
שמו מופת מן השמים.
5 והיא רוחות מנשבה גדלה
נשאת כל מה הקהלו אתו
לבניאן ונדחתו והפיצתו.
6 ולכן שבתו מן בניאן
מקדשם באורשלים ולזה
היום לא ישבו יעלימו
לבניאנו.

16 למען קדוש שמך הקדוש יי׳ כפר את עונינו.
17 מי הוא האנש הירא מיי׳ עד הדרך אשר בחר יורינו.
18 נפשו תלין בטוב וזרעו את הארץ יירשו.
19 סוד יי׳ ליראיו ובריתו לשמורי אמת ספר קדשו.
20 שירו ליי׳ בנים אתם ליי׳ והבו כבוד ועז ליי׳
אלהינו והבו גדל ליי׳ אלהינו.
21 השתחוו ליי׳ בהר גריזי הר קדשו ולבלעדיו לא
תתפנו.
22 יי׳ יתן עז לשמרים עמו יי׳ יברך את עמו
השמרים בשלום.

§18

1 ויהי כי חזקת יד מלכי אדום על הכהן
הצדיק בבא רבה רצון יי׳ וסליחתו עליו
אמן אסף אליו את כל זקני עמו עדת בני
ישראל השמרים על האמת ויאמר אליהם לאמר
2 ראו ראיתי לעשות את הדבר הזה אשר אדבר
אליכם עתה לטובה והוא מדרשי אשלח את
לוי בן אחי לערי (הרומים) עד יעבד
ביניהם וישם את נפשו כאחד מהם ויתלמד
את כל מעשה אימן.
3 וישוב לאנה כמו (קסיס) לא ידעו את
שרשו ומה הוא למען יעלה על הר גרזים
בית אל המקום המבחר ויתן כל לשבר את
העוף הנמצא שם.
4 וכי יעשה כן נוכל לעלות הר גרזים בית
אל ונדרש את יי׳ אלהינו יתקדש שמו
עליו אולי יקבלנו ויתן את איבינו
בידנו.
5 כי היה נמצא על הר הקדש ההוא הרגרזים
בית אל עוף כמו עוף היונה מעשות
הנחשים והמחשפים אשר מן כושפי (הרומים).
6 והעוף ההוא מן נחשת וכל איש מבני ישראל
היה יעל להר גרזים בית יקרא עליו העוף
ההוא אשר עשו (עבריוס) וכאשר ישמעו
אנשי (הרומים) את קול העוף הזה יקומו
וימששו על האיש הישראלי עד יתפשו בו
וירגוהו וימיתו אתו; ובגלל הדבר הזה לא
יכלו עדת בני ישראל השמרים לעלות הר
גרזים בית אל.
7 ויהי כאשר שמעו זקני העם ושטריו
מן המלך הצדיק הכהן בבא רבה את
הדבר הזה ויענו אתו יחדו אדונינו
כל הישר בעיניך עשה כי כל אשר
תצונו נשמע ונעשה.
8 ויען בבא רבה אתם לאמר אם אתם
תחפצו לעשות את הדבר הזה תנו לי
את מכתב ידיכם כי אחרי מובא בן
אחי משם לא תגעל נפשכם מן מובאו
ולהשיבו אל דתו כיום הזה.

1 ונמצא בספר הימים דלארשינו
אשר הוא בכיר העברי
הקדש יזכר בו דברא עודה
על גדלות המלך בבא רבה
ארשנו נספר אתו בזה
הספר והיא כי בבא רבה
רצון יהוה עליו אמר
לעדתו השמרים עתה ראיתי
שלח לדבר אשר עתה העודה
מימכה עליו והיא כי
אשלח בן אחי לוי לערי
האדום בבקוש במעשהו
באימנותון ויתלמד כל
יסידותון.
3 וישוב לאנה בדמות קסם
ולא ידעו אקרה ומה הוא
למען יסק להר הקדש
הר גרזים בדמות קסם ויבא
לכנשה אשר אל האדום
ויתנכל על שברות זה
העוף דעשו אתו בנחשם
הנמצא שם.
4 ואן עשה כן ננטש לעלות
ההר הקדש ונבקש מיהוה
עליו אולי ישים לנו
נצען עליהם.
5/6 כי היה על ההר הקדש עוף
מטלסם מן עשות האדומים
במעשה הקסמים וכל מן יעל
אל ההר הקדש מן השמרים
יצעק עליו זה העוף עבריוס;
ויחפשו עליו השנאים ויתפשו
בו ויכו אתו; ומזה הדבר לא
יתנטשו בני ישראל להעלות
ההר הקדש.
7 ונשוב למה ההינו בו ונאמר
כי כד שמעו העם מן גדלות
בבא רבה זה הדבר ענו אתו

9 ויעשו כאשר צוה אתם ויתנו אליו
את מכתב ידיהם.
10 ויהי אחר הדברים האלה הביא בבא
רבה את לוי בן אחיו לפניו ויאסף
את כל זקני העם וראשיו ושטריו
ויצו את בני אחיו לעיניהם
בדברים האלה.
11 בן אחי דע נא כי צריכים אנחנו
לשלחך לערי (הרומים) הכופרים
עבודי הבעלים עשוי התועבות
ההלכים על רע דרך; השמר לך פן
תנקש אחריהם ושים בלך לתלמוד
כל דבר מן מיני אימנותם.
12 בן אחי השמר ושמור את משמרת אימנך
ולא תט מן הדרך הטובה זאת למען
תחיה בה בכל ימי חייך ובאחריתך.
13 בן אחי השמר לך פן תעזב את
מקרת התורה הקדושה בכל יום
ובכל לילה.
14 בן אחי אתיקץ לשמר משמרת את כל
חקות ומצות התורה הזאת.
15 בן אחי השמר לך פן יסיתך את
אשר הלך במדרשו כי אם בכל עת
זכר את כל אשר בראך יי׳ אלהיך
אליו ואת אשר לך בו טוב גדול
בימיך ובאחריתך.
16 ויי׳ יתקדש שמו יסעדך בכל
מעשיך אשר אנחנו דרשים עשותם
מעמך.
17 ויודיענו את המעשה אשר
יעשנו שמה; וישלח בבא
רבה בן אחיו לוי ואנשים
רבים מזקני העם וישובו
למקומם וילך לוי דרוש
את עיר (קסטנטינה).
18 ויהי לוי איש נבון וחכום
ידעיו ריטור צדיק בין
כל בני דרו וכל אשר
הוא עשה יי׳ מצליח בידו.
19 ובגלל הדבר הזה שלחו דדו
המלך הצדיק בבא רבה על
ארץ בני אדום היא ארץ
(הרומים) בלי זולתו.
20 ולוי בן שבע עשרה שנה
לעת לכתו למדינת (קסטנטינה)
ויהי כמובאו לעיר ההיא
הסתיר את נפשו ודרש את
התלמוד.
21 ויתן את כל מאדו בתלמוד
את כל הסכנת (הרומים)
וישיג את כל מדרשו במספר

כהלון ואמרו אה אדונן
ודמעינן ומצנפת ראשינן
אעשה כל מה ייטב בעיניך
ואנחנו שמעין לדברך.
8 ואמר להם אן ההיתם עמין
כי חסד זה הדבר דלו עתה
אני לכם בו נחי תנו לי
מכתב מתכתב בכיר ידיכם
בגלל כן עד אשמרו אשמרו
במקוהי לאחר ישוב משם בן
אחי עד לא תחמד נפשותיכם
מנו ותאמרו כי צפר מן
דרך הקשט תעי.
9 ועשו מה אמר ונתנו לו
מכתב ידיהם ולו שמר.
10 ואחר כן נגש בבא רבה לבן
אחיו לוי והעמידו בין ידיו
וכל נשיא מן העם אתו מתקוי,
ואחל לו יצוה ויוכיח לו
וישמרו.
11 ומן פרט הממלל דמללו לו
והוא אה בן אחי עתה ה׳ מ׳ כ׳
הדבר לשלחך לערי אדום
הכפורים הבישים עבודי
הצלמים ההלכים אחרי הנחשים;
השמר לך פן תנקש אחריהם
ושים תורותך בתלמוד כל אקרי
אימנותם.
12 ודבק באימנותך ביהוה ובמשה
ובתורותו התמימה כי בזה חיותך
בעלמה וביום נקמה.
13 ולא תעזב המקרא בתורה בחשך הליל
וביום מאז יזרח אורה.
15 והשמר כי יסיתך מה את הלך במדרשו
אפס בכל זבנך זכור מה אמצאת
בגללו דבו טוב לך בעלמה וביום
דבו הבוראים יקח כל מנון אגרה
מה אדבקת בו בעלמה נפשו.
16 ויהוה עבודך הוא יסעדך אן אהבת
אתו בכל מאדך.
17 והודיע אתו בגלל הלכותו והלך מאתו
מבקש אלקסטנט׳.
18 ולוי היה איש חכום ונבון ידעיו
זכי ברוח החכמה מתדכי ולו לא
הוא מן אחכמה.
19 ממלא היה דודו בלעדיו שלח.
20 ובעת הלכותו ללקסטנ׳ היו ימי שני
חייו שבע עשר שנה וכד אתשיג לזאת
מדינה הזוכיר אסתיר נפשה והואל

עשרה שנים עד היה פריד
בין אנשי (הרומים) אין
ימצא אנש מהם ידעיו בכל
הסכנת ובכל דברי (הרומים)
כמהו.
22 ותעל מתוביתו ביניהם מעט
מעט עד הן השיג למיתובה
גדלה וירימו את מחנהו
וישרתו אתו ויתברכו ממנו
וינשקו כל עת את ידו.
23 ולרבות המדעות אשר גלא
להם קראו את שמו (אסקף)
גדול וישימו אתו בחנות
עליונה עד מאד עד היו
כל מלכי (הרומים) לא יוכל אחד מהם
ישב על כסא ממלכתו אלא על פיו
והוא אשר היה ילבישם את נזר
הממלכה ואת בגדיה.

בטהרה ובקש המדע.
21 ובכל מאדו כל יסוד אימנות האדום
ידע ובעשרה שנה לא אמצא בין זאת
העדה ואתעלי אתם במדע עד היה
נבון.
22 והיו כל האדומים ישרתו לו.
23 ומרב מה אגלי להם מן החכמות
קראו שמה הסקף הרב
ושמו דרגותו במעלה
עד היו כל מלוכי
האדום ילכו לדלתו ולא
יוכל אחד מנון יתפקיד
על כסא המלוך אלא
בארשותו ועל פיהו והוא
היה דיצניף המלך בנזר המלוך.

§19

1 ויהי מקץ שלשה עשר שנת מלכת
לוי הזוכיר והוא בעת ההיא בן
שלשים שנה ויאמר לגדול מלכי
(הרומים) מדרשי אלך אל ארץ פלשתים
אל עיר שכם אשר בארץ ההיא להראות
את בתי הכנשיות אשר שם.
2 ויכן המלך את כל אנשי הצבא אשר
היו במדינת (קסטנטינה) ללכת עם
לוי וילך לו ויצא מן מדינת (קסטנט׳).
3 וילכו עמו את כל ראשי עם (הרומים)
ואת כל שטריו ומן המלכים ואת כל
אנשי הצבא לשרתו ולעשות את כל אשר
יצוה להם ויצא במספר רב עד מאד לא ימני.
4 ויהי כקרב לוי ואת כל אשר עמו מעיר
שכם הקדושה וישלח המלך הגדול אשר
היה עמו צו מאתו לכל הגוים לאמר
קומו צאו כלכם לקראת את (האסקוף)
הגדול אשר עמי.
5 ויהי כאשר שמע המלך הצדיק בבא רבה
את הדבר הזה ויירא מאד ויצר לו
וישלח ויאסף את כל זקני עדת בני
ישראל השמרים על האמת ואת כל
ראשיהם ואת כל שטריהם אליו.
6 ויאמר אליהם לאמר לא טוב עשינו
בשלחנו את לוי בן אחי לארץ בני אדום
כי זה שלשה עשר שנה מלכתו עד היום
הזה לא שמענו במגידו ועוד בכל אשר
יעשה לו בארץ ההיא ולא יפג לבי כי
בן אחי הזוכיר מת בארץ בני אדום.

1 ומקץ שלשה עשר שנה
מן מהלכותו היו ימי שני
חייו שלשים שנה ואחר כן
אמר למלך הגדול דמהם עתה
אחמד הלך אנשק הכנשנות
דבשכם.
2 ואתכוננת כל העסכרים אשר
היו באלקסטנטיניה.
3 והלכו פרט הנביאם ופרט
המלכים אשר אתו וכל
העסכרים בשרתו והלכו
במחנה כבד.
4 וכד אתשגו להקרוב מן
שכם שלח המלך דברו את
פרט נעריו לכל העמים כי
תצא לקראת הסקוף הרם
אשר אתו.
5 וכד שמע בבא רבה
בדבר הזה ירא ודחל
וארתת וקבץ דמעי עמו.
6 ואמר אליהם אנחנו
ארענו בהחזי בבן אחי לוי
דשלחנו אתו ולא שבנו
נשמע לו דבר וזאת שלשה
עשר שנה והוא הלוך מעמנו
ובלא פג כי הוא מת.

7 ואני שמעתי את מגיד (האסקף) הזה כי
איש חמס הוא וכי בא לארצינו להכיתנו
כלנו ועתה לא נוכל אלא נצא לקראתו
נירא על נפשותינו ממנו פן יקצף
עלינו ומספר רב מצבא הרומים בין
ידיו וכי יצוה אתם להכיתנו יכו
את כלנו.
8 ואנחנו עתה מה נוכל נעשה לו כי
איננו נכונים למלחמה ולא להכות וגם
אין עמנו כלי מלחמה נדקר בה את
איבינו ונפלט את נפשותינו מהם ועם
זה אנשי צבא רבים עד מאד הם בין
ידיו כי יצוה להם להכיתנו יכו לנו
עד כלנו כי לא ימנו במספר.
9 ויהי כאשר שמעו את כל הזקנים
והראשים והשטרים את הדבר הזה וייראו
העם מאד ויאמרו להמלך הצדיק בבא רבה
אנחנו בטחנו על יי׳ אלהינו יתקדש
שמו הוא ידבקנו והוא יסעדנו והוא
מזאת הרשעי האלה יצילנו.
10 ואחרי כן השיג לוי בן אחי בבא
רבה הנקרא שמו (אסקוף) לשער עיר שכם
הקדושה ויצאו כל עדת בני ישראל
השמרים לקראתו והמלך הצדיק הכהן בבא
רבה הלך לפניהם.
11 ויהי כי קרבו ממנו שא את עיניו וירא
והנה דדו הכהן בבא רבה וכל עדת בני
ישראל עמו והיראה נגלאות בפניהם
וטטפות בין עיניהם והם יצעקו ויקראו
לו טוב מקרא בקול גדול עד מאד.
12 ויהי כשמעו את קול צעקותם
ויחמל עליהם.
13 והמלך הצדיק בבא רבה וכל העם לא
הכירהו והוא הכירם כי לעת לכתו
מאצלם אל ארץ בני אדום היה נער אין
שער ולא זקנה בפניו וישב בעת ההיא
ומספר ימי חייו שלשים שנה והוא בעל
שיבה גדלה ארכה לבש עליו בגדים מכל
שחרים.
14 ועם כל זה בא בזאת המיתובה
הגדלה כי לא הביטו בני עדתו
הן ישיג לזאת המיתובה.
15 ויפן לוי אל המלך אשר היה
הלך אצלו ויאמר לו מי הם את
האנשים האלה אשר לא ראיתי כהם
בכל דרכי.
16 ויען המלך ויאמר אליו אדני אלה
עם ממרים ויאמרו אן הם מבני
ישראל השמרים אל האמת והם
נקיבים בעדת השמרים.
17 ויען ויאמר לו מה מעבדם ויענו

7 וזה הסקוף הרם שמעתי עליו
כי הוא גבור קשה ועתה
בא לערינו עד ישמידנו
ומכן לא יתנטש לנו אלא
נצא לקראתו ואן עזבנו
כן ולא יצאנו לקראתו
לא נאמן על נפשותינו
מן רעותו ויתל בנו ועם
זה כל עסכרי האדום תחת
משל ריחותו אן צוה אתם
להכותנו יכו אתנו ולנו
ימיתו.
8 ואנחנו מה נעשה ולינן
מתכוננים למלחמה ולא
אתנו חיל ולא כלים
תמימה עד ננשא מעלינו
גבורותון בתקומה.
9 וכד שמע העם מן בבא
רבה זה הממלל פחד
ואירא ודחלה בלבו שרא
ואמרו אל בבא רבה
בנצירות לבבה עתה
שמנו רחצונן על יהובה
יצובה דלאבותינו נשבע
ולישועתו קוינו והוא
בחסדו ינחמנו וירא
את ענינו ואת עמלנו
ואת לחצנו.
10 ואחר כן אתשיג לוי
המשתמה בסקוף הרה אל
שכמה וצאו לקראתו כל
עדת השמרים אשר שם,
וגדלות בבא רבה הלוך
פניהם.
11 וכד אתקרבו לה לקראתו
שא עיניו ועמה עביבו
וכל עדתו אשר אתו והכל
מנון מתרקף ובעין עיניו
ט׳טף היראה מטפטף
והם צעקים במקראם ודחלים
מנה לון ינגף שם רדת
הדמעות מן עיניו על
גבות פניו.
13 וגדלות עביבו וכרניו אינם
ידעים לה מן גדלות זקניו
כי מקדם עזבו אותו נער
לית בפניו שער ושב עליהם
והות בן שלשים שנה תמימה
ומתחלפה אימתו ובגדיו שחר
בגדותו.
14 ואינם מסתכלים משיגותה

ויאמרו יעבדו אלהים אשר לא
יוכל אנש לראותו וע׳ זה יאמרו
אן הות אלהי האלהים ואדון האדונים
אלהי השמים והארץ וכל המתבראים.
18 ויאמר לו האסקוף ואיך לא יעבדו
הצלמים והבעלים ויעזבו מאמנם
הזה אשר לא נאמר בה אנחנו אה
עדת הרום.
19 ויענו המלך ויאמר אה אדוני דברנו
עמך בעבור זה דברים רבים דרשנו
מהם את הדבר הזה מימים ימימה ועד
היום הזה ולא שמעו אלינו ולא עבדו
את הבעלים ולא הצלמים ולא עזבו את
מקראם בעד אלהיהם כי הוא אלהי
האלהים ואדון האדונים אשר ברא כל
המינים.
20 ויען (האסקף) את המלך לאמר כי לא
ישמעו אלינו ולא יעשו את אשר אנחנו
נצום ולא יעזבו את אימנם זה ויעבדו
את הבעלים כמונו לא ישארו חיים כלם.
21 והדבר הזה נשמע בין הכל בגלל
עדת בני ישראל השמרים כי דבר (האסקף)
עליהם.
22 ואחרי כן הלך האסקף והוא לוי בן אחי
המלך הצדיק בבא רבה ויעל אל המקום
המבחר הר גרזים בית אל ויעל
בתשמישותיו המלך.
23 ויהי כבאם לראש ההר ויצעק
עוף הנחשת אשר ההוא ממע׳
הנחשים (עבריוס) כהסכנתו
לעת ימצא בהר ההוא איש מעדת
בני ישראל יצעק (עבריוס)
ומפתרה בלשון הקדש עברי
בי אדני.
24 ויאמר (האסקף) הגדול והוא
לוי מה זה ויאמרו לו זה
עוף מן נחשת ממעשה הנחשים
הניחו אתו במק׳ הזה אחינו
ראשי (הרומים) על אדות עדת
בני ישראל השמרים כי לעת
ימצא מהם איש בהר הזה יצעק
(עבריוס).
25 ויען (האסקף) אתם לאמר
אראנו עתה לא ישבית מן
הצעקה לכו ראו ומששו את כל
ההר הזה וכי תמצאו איש מעדת
בני ישראל השמרים הכו אתו
עד ננח מקול צעקות זה העוף.
26 וישלחו אנשים רבים לרגל
את כל ההר על איש מעדת בני
ישראל השמרים וילכו וימששו

לזאת הענינה.
15 ואתפני לוי בפניו למלך
אשא אתו ואמר לו בשפתו
אהלין האנשים מה הם ומה
יהיו ומה יתקרא עליהם.
16 ויען לו המלך העדה האלה
אה אדני כפורים יקראו כי
הם בני ישראל השמירים
ובדת הקשט מתוקרים.
17 ואמר לו מה יעשו ומה יעבדו
אמר לו אלהים לא יראה
יעבדו ולו ישתחוו ויקרו
ויאמרו עליו כי הוא אלהי
האלהים מלוך כל הרוחים
ואדון האדונים אלהי השמים
והארץ וכל מה בעלאי וארעי
מברי ומקבץ.
18 ויען אתו ואמר איך לא יעבדו
הגלולות והתמונות וישבקו
עבדת דלא תחזי לה העינות
דלית נתפני לו בכל המכונות
אנחנו האדום דגלולים
במכונינו מתכונות.
19 אגיבו אה אדני מקדם אנחנו
ענינו נפשותינו ולהם צרינו עד
באלהותינו יאמנו ולא אחד מהם
שמע למימרינו.

20 ויענו אותו ואמר אן לא ישמעו
אלינו ויעזבו אלהיהם וישתחוו
וינדחו לאלהינו הך מה נעשה
אנחנו לא נאשיר בהם נשמת חיים
פן באלהיהם יכעסו אתנו.
21 ונודע זה הדבר לעיני השמרים
ואזדזעת בהם אברים וצפרת
לבביהם משתברים.
22 ואחר כן הלך לוי והמלך בשרתו
להר הקדש הרגרזים הר יהוה
ומכון שבתו.
23 וכד אתשיג לראש ההר צעק העוף
עבריוס כפי אמנותא ומפתרה
עברי אה אדני.
24 ואמר להם הסקוף הרב מה הוא זה
ואתא מר לו זה עוף נחשת במובא
שמרי לזה ההר יצעק עבריוס.
25 ואמר להם אראה אתו יצעק ולא
יעזב הצעקה ראו פן יהיה ממצא
בזה ההר איש שמרי הכו אתו ואנחו
אתנו מקול זה העוף.
26 ושלחו אנשים יחפשו בההר ובקצתיו
ולא מצאו אחד מן השמרים.

את כל פאתי ההר ההוא ולא
מצאו איש עברי בו.
27 ויבאו אל המלך ואל כל
אנשיו ויאמרו אליהם מששנו
את כל ההר ולא מצאנו בו
איש עברי.
28 ויבא אחרי כן (האסקף) אל
בית הכנשה אשר על ראש ההר
וישב שם וכל הזקנים וכל
הראשים עמדו לפניו ועוד
הנחשת מצעק בקול גדול ורע
(עבריוס) ולא ישבית מן צעקותו
רגע אחת ארך הלילה ההוא עד
היות הבקר.
29 ויפן לוי ויאמר אל הנערים אשר
מששו בכל ההר המששתם את כל
פאתי ההר זה ולא ראיתם בו איש
עברי מן השמרים.
30 ויענו ויאמרו בי אדני מששנו את
כל פאתי ההר כאשר צויתנו ולא
מצאנו בו איש עברי מעדת בני
ישראל לא קטן ולא גדול.
31 ויאמר לוי אכן העוף הזה בא
עליו שגיעון כי בעלו נחסר ממנו
ועתה לא נשאר בו לנו צריכה בלתי
רעות רוח ומכאוב לראשינו יהיה
מאת קול צעקו הרע ובליל תמול
חסרנו מן הנושן.
32 ויאמר לו המלך ועתה אדני מה
תחפץ נעשה בו ויאמר לו שברו אתו
והשליכו את בחוץ.
33 וימהרו וישברו את ההעוף ההוא
וישליכו אתו בחוץ כאשר צוה
ויפגע זה בלילת ראש חדש השביעי.
34 ויהי מקץ שלשית הלילה ההיא כארבע
שעות מראש הלילה ויישנו כל הפקדים
וכל הזקנים והראשים וגם המלך
ואנשיו אשר היו עמו כי השקיהם מן
היין והשכר ויפצר בם עד כי שתו
משתה רב וישכרו ויישנו.
35 וירא לוי כי משל המשתה בם מאד עד
כל איש מהם היה לא ידע הימין מן
השמאל ויצום עד הן ישכבו ויקמו
וישכבו ותרדימה נפלת עליהם עד
מאד.
36 בשעה ההיא עמד לוי על רגליו ויקח
את חרבו בידו וילך וירד מן
הרגרזים בית אל דרוש את דדו המלך
הצדיק הכהן בבא רבה בקרית עמרתה
כי ידע הוא כי מושב דדו הזוכיר
שם.

28 ויבא הסקוף הרב לוי אל הכנשה
דבהר אל האדום ושבו כל השופטים
והפוקדים בין ידיו והעוף
הנחשת יצעק בקולות תועבות
עבריוס ולא עזב הצעקה
בארך זאת הלילה עד
בקר.
29 ואמר לוי אל הנערים
דהלכו יחפישו הלוא
חפשתם בהר ובאצליו.
30 וענו ואמרו אחפשנו
ולא אחד מן השמרים
מצאנו.
31 ואמר בלא פג כי זה
העוף הנחשת חרף ולא
נשאר לנו בו צריכה
כי חרטמיו אתחסר ולא
יתרון בו אלא יגר
לראשינו בצעקו ובלילה
דאזלת חסך אתנו טוב השנתן.
32 ואמר לו המלך אשר אתו
אה אדונן איך תתריח
נעשה בו ואמר להם שברו
אתו והשליכו אתו בחוץ מעלינו.
33 שם שברו אתו והשליכו אתו
וזה היה בלילת ראש
החדש השביעי.
34 וכד אזל שלשית הליל הראש
ונגע יאכל הפקודים אשר
אתו והמלך והעסכר' והקסמים
ובלעדם והגמי אתם מן המשתה
ופצר עליהם בכן.
35 והם לא יכלו לו ימירו ושתו
רב ושכרו ואסתולל עליהם
השכר וצוה אתם בישן.
36 וקעם לוי בזאת השעה ולקח
חרבו בידו וירד מן ההר
הקדש דרש דדו בבא רבה
בקרית עבורתה למודעה
כי הוא שם.

37 והמלך הצדיק בבא רבה כשמעו
את הדבר אשר דבר בו (האסקף)
הגדול והוא בן אחיו לוי הקהל
את כל ראשי וזקני עדת בני ישראל
השמרים על האמת אליו לקרית עמרתה.
38 והם פחדים הלבב יראים נביכים לא
ידעו איך יעשו באיש הזה אשר הוא
(האסקף) אשר נחם בהכותם ואיך
ישיגו לפאתו ויתנצלו מן רעתו.
39 והנה כי הם נביכים בגלל הדבר הזה
ולוי עמד על הדלת ויכה אתו במעט
מעט ותרבה יראתם ופחדם גדל מאד
ולא יוכל אחד מהם יפתח את הדלת
ויראה מי הוא המכה.
40 ויקם המלך הצדיק בבא רבה בנפשו
ויקומו עמו כל הנשיאים וילכו
לראות את אשר על הדלת.
41 ויהי כי פתחו אל הדלת וייראו
והנה הוא (האסקף) הגדול עמד על
הדלת בנפשו ולא יוכלו ידברו עמו
דבר כי נבהלו מפניו לעת ראיתם
אתו.
42 וימהר לוי ויפל על רגלי דדו המלך
הצדיק הכהן בבא רבה וינשק אתם
ויקח גם את ידיו בידיו וינשק אתם
ויפל כן על צוארו ויבך.
43 ויאמר בלשון הקדש לשון העברי
אמותה הפעם אחרי ראיתי פניך כי
עודך חי.
44 וידע המלך הצדיק בבא רבה (כי האסקף)
הגדול הוא לוי וכי בן אחיו הוא.
45 בעת ההיא צעקת שמחה גדלה היתה
במקום ההוא בין בבא רבה ובין כל
הנאספים מעת בני ישראל השמרים.
46 וימהר בבא רבה ויקח ביד בן אחיו
ויבא בו למבית המקום וישבו על
ימינו.
47 ויחל בבא רבה וישאל את בן אחיו
על כל אשר עשה בימי גירתו בארץ
(הרומים).
48 ויספר (האסקף) לוי לבבא רבה את
כל הדברים אשר עשה באזני כל
הנאספים שם ושמחתם תונף ותורם
מהללים ומשירים ומודים בקול
גדול רם ליי׳ אשר פלטם מכל
מגפה ומכל נקם.
49 ויהי כאשר כלה לוי לדבר אל דדו
אל בבא רבה ויסף עוד לדבר אליו
לאמר והיה בלילת מחר כחצית
הלילה חליצו אנשים נשאים את

37 וגדלות בבא רבה כד שמע
הממלל דמללו הסקוף הרב
אסף השמרים אתו.
38 והם יראים נביכים איך
יהיה עובדם בזה הסקוף
דשפט בהכותם ואיך יהיה
משיגותם אליו ומצילותם
מן רעותו וגברותו.
39 ובין מה הם בזה הדבר
ואלא הדלת ידכה דך מעט
ואתרבי דחלון מכן ונפל
בלבביהם פחד יתר ולא
יכל אחד מן הנמצאים
יקום ויראה מן הוא
ידכה על הדלת.
40 שם קעם בבא רבה בנפשו
וקעמו לקעמיו כל נשיאי
העם ויצאו למען יראו
מן הוא אשר ידכה על הדלת.
41 וכד אתפתח הדלת ועמו והנה
עמד על הדלת הסקוף הרב
וכד עמו אתו אזדעו
וארתתו.
42 ולוי מהר ונגש ועקד
בין רגלי עביביו בבא רבה
ואחר נשקותו רגליו עקד
על צואריו.
43 ואמר אמותה הפעם אחרי
ראיתי פניך כי עודך חי.
44 שם אתקשט בבא רבה כי
זה הסקוף הוא בן אחיו לוי.
45 מה רב השמח דשרא בשעה
ההיא בלב בבא רבה ובלב
מן היה מתשקח אתו מן
עמו.
46 שם לקח בבא רבה ביד
בן אחיו לוי ויבא בו
למקום אשר היו מתאספים
בו ועל ימינו השיבו.
47 ואחל ישאלו על מה היה
לו בזאת הלכותו.
48 ויען אתו ואגיד מה היה
לו במשמע הנמצאים מן
קהלו מיום הלך ליום
מעמדו על הדלת ובנשוקו
אתברך וצפרו דדו
ומשפחתו שמחים וחדים
וככן הנמצאים אשר היה
לבב כל מנון מרך.

חרבותם.
50 יהיו קרובים ממני שמעים את
מקראתי אליהם והיה כי יישנו העם
אמהר אני ואקום והכה את כל ערפם
בחרב קנאה ליי׳ יתקדש שמו ונכה
אתם ונשמידם ונמחה את שמם מתחת
השמים ועזרה מעם יי׳ אלהינו
תחת לנו ומן רעתם ישמרנו.
51 ויהי אחר כן ויקם לוי
ויעל אל ההר במהרה וימצא את כל
אנשי (הרומים) ישנים כלם ולא
ידעו ברדתו ולא בעלותו לראש ההר.
52 ויהי בלילת מוצא מועד חדש השביעי
ואמר עוד כי היא לילת מוצא מועד
השמיני עצרת.
53 וישלח המלך הצדיק בבא רבה אל
כל הערים אשר סביביו הישבים
בהם אנשים מעדת בני ישראל השמרים
על האמת ויאמר אליהם.
54 הוו חלוצים חמישים למלחמה והוו
נכונים עד חצי הלילה והיה
כראותם את האש להבה על ראש
הגבעה אשר היא בראש המקום
המבחר הרגרזים בית אל והכיתם
הראשים והפקידים אשר עליכם
מאנשי (הרומים) לא תשירו מהם
שריד.
55 ואבדתם את כל פוקד עליכם מהם
ואת כל אשר ימנעו אתכם מן
קוממית אימנותכם ואת כל אשר
הם סביבתכם הכו אתם בחרב עד
כלותם עד תפגעו את אחיכם
ותאספו כלכם יחדו באלון מורא
אשר הוא אצל המק׳ במבחר הר
גרזים בית אל.
56 ויהי כחצית הלילה ויצבאו את
כל צבא המלך הצדיק בבא רבה
רצון יי׳ וסליחתו עליו אמן.
57 ויעלו כלם אל הר הקדש הקדש
הרגרזים בית אל והמלך הצדיק
הכהן בבא רבה היה הלך לפניהם
ויהי כמטוחי קשת בינם ובין
ראש הר הברכה הר גרזים בית
אל וידע לוי כי קרובים היו
ממנו ויקם בקנאה גדולה
ויקח את חרבו בידו ועזרה
מאת יי׳ יתקדש שמו היתה לו.
58 ויוקר בחרבו את המלך ואת
אנשיו ואת כל (קסיס) אשר
היו נמצאים בהר ההוא.
59 ויצעק לוי בקול גדול יי׳

49 ואחר כן אמר לדדו בבא
רבה בלילת מחר בחצי
הליל חלוץ אנשי המלחמה
בחרביהם.
50 ויהיו קרובים מני
ונכונים לצעקותי ואני
בעת ישכבו הנכרים אמהר
ואתקוי על מן בישועתו
קויתי והכה צואר הנכרים
אשר אתי קנאה ליהוה
הרחום הרתי ונכם לפי
חרב ונמחה צרבתם ויהוה
בכן בישועתו וביכלתו
יהי לנו עזר בברכת
ארשינו דלא קרבון זר.
51 וכד אתכלה החזי ביניהם
וקוממו על מה יעשו
בנגיפות שנאיהם קעם לוי
ועלה במהר להרגריזים
ומצאם שכבים ולא ידעו
ברדתו ולא במובאו.
52 ובזאת הלילה לילת מפוק מועד
החדש השני׳ ואתאמר כי זה היה
בלילת מפוק מועד השמיני.
53 שלח בבא רבה לקריות דבהם
השמרים ואמר להם.
54 היו חלוצים מתכוננים למלחמה
לחצי הליל וכד תראו האש
אוקדת על ראש הגבעה דבהר
הקדש הכו הפוקדים אשר עמכם
דמן האדומים ולא תותירו מהם
אחד.
55 והמיתו מן היה מתפקד עליכם
והוה ימאן אתכם על קעמות
דגלי אימנותיכם וכל אשר
סביבותיכם ועל פי חרב כבסו
אתם על אחריתם עד תתקראו
באחיכם ותהיו מתקבצים כלכם
באלון מורא אצל ההר הקדש.
56/57 ויהי בחצי הליל הקהלו עסכרי
בבא רבה ועלו להר הקדש ובבא
רבה היה פניהם וכד קרבו מן
ההר ומש לוי בקרבון מנה רץ
בקנאה וגברות ואצלחות מן אל
58 אלהי הרוחות. ונשל חרבו והכה
בו כל המלכים והקסמים וכל
מן לגלולים ישתחוו.
59 וצעק בקול עלי לא היה כמו

גיבור במלחמה יי׳ שמו.

60 וישמעו את קול צעקותו כל מחנה בני ישראל השמרים ויענו אתו יחדו קול אחד יי׳ גיבור במלחמה יי׳ שמו.

61 ותחרד מקול צעקותם כל הארץ ובשעה ההיא לא נשאר בהם מן חית השדה רבץ בקנו כי אם כלם כשמעם את קול העם נסו לקולם כי אמרו זאת הקולות לא שמענו כמוה מימים ימימה.

62 ואחרי כן קם לוי ודדו המלך הצדיק בבא רבה ואת כל האנשים אשר היו עמהם ויוקדו את האיש על ראש הגבעה אשר היא בראש הר הנחלה הר גרזים בית אל עד יראו אתה את כל עדת בני ישראל השמרים הישבים בערים ויעשו ככל אשר צוה אתם המלך הצדיק בבא רבה.

63 ויהי כראות העם היושבים בערים ובחצר ובכל מקום את להבות האש ויקמו ויכו את כל הראשים ואת כל הפקידים אשר היו פוקדים עליהם מעדת (הרומים) לא השאירו מהם שריד.

64 ויקמו עדת בני ישראל בלילה ההוא ויהרסו את כל בתי כנשיות (הרומים) ואת כל מקומותיהם וימחו את שמם מן הר השכינה הרגרזים בית אל.

65 למן היום אשר עשו עדת בני ישראל השמרים על האמת את הדבר הזה באנשי (הרומים) היו ילידי השמרים יוקדו את עץ הסכות בלילת מוצא מועד השמיני עצרת אשר הוא חתמת מוע׳ יי׳ ונשאר זה המעשה זכרון בינם עד היום הזה.

66 ואחרי כן אשיר המלך הצדיק בבא רבה ואת כל זקני העם את השירה הזאת: –

67 יי׳ אלהינו רעינו לא נחסר דבר.

68 ליי׳ הארץ ומלואה השכינה וכל היושבים בה.

69 כי הוא על ימים יסדה ועל נהרים כוננה.

70 אליך יי׳ אלהינו נשא את פנינו.

71 אלהינו בך בטחנו ולא תרפנו ולא יצחקו אויבינו עלינו.

72 כי כל קויך לא יטרפו
יטרפו הבוגדים חנם.

73 כי יי׳ ישוענו ממה נירה
כי יי׳ בידו חיות נפשותינו
ממה נפחד.

74 ויהי כי קרבו הרשעים לאכל את בשרנו

יהוה גבור במלחמה יהוה שמו.

60 ושמעו קולו עסכרי השמרים וענו אתו בזאת המימרים בקול אחד.

61 וככן ענו אתם בה כל השמרים אשר שמעו קולותם בצעקה אחדה גדלה חזקה ולא נשאר בזאת השעה עוף והחיה אשר בקיניהם בהר ובבקע אלא אתחרקו ברחוקה מרב קולותם דנבקע.

62 ואף גם זאת לוי ודודו בבא רבה והעסכרים אשר אתם אוקידו האש על ראש הגבעה אשר בהר הקדש למען יראוה השמרים השכונים בקריות ויעשו כאשר צוה אתם בבא רבה.

63 וכד עמו שכוני הקריות האש רצו וכל הפוקידים הכו אשר מן האדום ולא נשאר מהם אחד אלא לו הרגו.

64 ונשארו השמרים ארך זאת הלילה והם בכנשתון ישרפו ומחו אתם מחוץ ומבית ולא נשאר לאדומים צרבת.

צרינו ואיבינו כשלו ונפלו.
75 כי יחן עלינו מחנה רב לא יירא לבב׳
אם תקום עלינו מלחמה לא נפחד;
כי הוא מפלטנו.
76 שאלה מאת יי׳ אתה נבקש
שובתינו במקומו הר הברכה
הר הקדשה הר הנחלה והשכ׳
המקום המבחר הרגרזים בית אל.
77 וירום את ראשינו על אויבינו
אשר סביבותינו ויקום את רצונו
ויראה את משכנו לעינינו
ונזבח על מזבחו את קרבנינו.
78 ונראה לכן ולא עתה
נשורנו ולא קרוב
דרך כוכב מיעקב וקם שבט ישראל
ומחץ פאתי מואב וקדקד כל בני שת.
79 והיה אדום ירשה ואחר הדבר
וישראל עשה חיל.
80 וברוך אלהינו לעולם וברוך שמו לעולם ועד.

§20

1 ויהי אחר הדברים האלה וישמעו אנשי
(הרומים) אשר הם ישבים בערי (המוצל)
בכל אשר עשו עדת בני ישראל השמרים
על האמת באנשיהם.
2 ויקצפו קצף גדול ויחר אפם עד
מאד ויאספו אנשים רבים על
הספר ויבאו דרשים את המלך
הצדיק בבא רבה ואת כל עמו
השמרים.
3 ויגד אל בבא רבה בעבורם ולא
רץ ממקומו עד השיגו לאצל עיר
שכם הקדשה.
4 וירץ המלך בבא רבה ויצא
לקראתם למקום ההוא ויעש
עמם מלחמה.
5 ויתן יי׳ אתם בידו ויך אנשים
רבים מהם והנשארים נסו מפניו
וירדף אחריהם דרך יום אחד.
6 וישב למקומו משיר ומהלל את
יי׳ אלהיו יתברך שמו לעולם ועד.
7 ויהי אחר הדברים האלה
ויאמר אל מלך רומה ואל כל עמו
אנשי (הרומים) הישבים בערי
(המוצל) עשו מלחמה עם המלך
הצדיק בבא רבה ויכם הוא וכל
עמו והנשארים מהם נסו מפניהם
וירדפו אחריהם דרך יום אחד
ואשר המיתו אתו מאנשי הרומים
לא יספרו כי רבים הם.

1 ואחר כן שמעו האדומים
אשר באשורה מה קם על
חבריהם מן בבא רבה.
2 ויחר אפם עליו ואספו
בוראים גדולים ובאו
דרשים לבבא רבה
ואתגיד לו דבריהם.
3 ולא פג לבו מהם
עד אתשגו
בקרוב שכם.
4 שם צא לקראתם
ונפלת המלחמה ביניהם.
5 ושם לו יהוה נצחן
עליהם ושבר אספם ומשל
בהם והכה הרב מאתם
והנשארים נסו מנוסת חרב.
6 ובבא רבה שב למקומה וליהוה
ישתבח שמו עלת התמיד הקריב.
7/8 ואחר זאת המלחמה
אתשיג הדבר אל אסכנדריה –
וזאת אסכנדריה היא העיר
דבנה אתה אסכנדר פקד רומיה
ומלך רומיה הוא המלך הגדול –
וקצפו מזה הדבר.

8 ויהי כשמע מלך רומה את הדבר
הזה וכי כן עשה המלך הצדיק
בבא רבה הוא ועמו באנשי
(המוצל) ויקצף קצף גדול ויחר
אפו.
9 וישלח ויאסף אנשים למלחמה
רבים על המספר עד כי חדל
לספר וישלחם להלחם עם המלך
הצדיק בבא רבה ועמו השמרים.
10 ויהי כשמע בבא רבה במובאם ויצא
לקראתם ותפל המלחמה ביניהם.
11 ויתפלל ליי׳ לאמר אדני יי׳
כהסכנתם עמי אתן את אלה האנשים
הרשעים בידי.
12 ויעתר לו יי׳ ויתנם בידו ותהי
המלחמה בין מחנה המלך הצדיק
בבא רבה ובין מחנה (הרומים) בעיר
(עסכור) ויתן יי׳ ביד מחנה
השמרים ויכום עד לא נשאר מהם
בלתי מספר מעט.
13 וימהרו וינסו מפני עדת בני ישראל
השמרים וילכו עד באו על מלכיהם
ויגידו להם את כל אשר עשה בהם
המלך הצדיק בבא רבה הוא ועמו
השמרים.
14 ויאמרו אליהם הכו מכה רב ממנו
וחולל בהם לא ראינו.
15 ויחר אף מלכי (הרומים) על המלך
הצדיק הכהן בבא רבה ועל כל השמרים
עמו.
16 וימהרו ויאספו מחנה רב עד מאד רבים
על המספר עד כי חדל לספר כי אין
מספר.
17 ויאמר אל המלך בבא רבה דע כי
מחנה רב הבאים אליך מאת מלכי הרומים
אלפים ורבבות.
18 ויאסף המלך בבא רבה אליו את כל
זקני וראשי ושטרי עמו ויגד להם
בדבר הזה.
19 ויכתבו ספרים מאתם אל כל ערי עדת
בני ישראל השמרים ויגדו אליהם
במובא מחנה הרומים במספר רב לא
ימני להלחם עם עדת בני ישראל
השמרים.
20 וישלחו אליהם את כל איש מלחמה
ויאספו כלם בעיר המלך בבא רבה
והיא קרית עמרתה ומספרם עשרת
אלפים איש נשא כלי מלחמה מבן
עשרים שנה ועד בן ארבעים שנה.
21 וינח אתם בבא רבה בערים אשר
סביב לקרית עמרתה.

9 ואספו עסכרי המלחמה רבים
לא תספר מרב ושלחו
אתם למלחמות בבא רבה.
10 וצא בבא רבה לקראתם
ואפיל החרב בהם.
11 ובקש מיהוה יתן לו
נצען עליהם.
12 ושמע יהוה ישתבח שמו
נקעתו ונפלת המלחמה
ביניהם בקרית מחנים
ואסתולל עליהם והכה
הרב מהם.
13 והנשארים נסו עד אתשגו
למלכיהם ואמרו על מה
היה לחבריהם מן בבא
רבה דנגף אתם.
14 והגידו להם כי עסכרי
בבא רבה לא נפקד איש מהם.
15 ואתוסיף חרונם.
16 ומהרו וקבצו עסכרים
אלפים ורבבות מתכמרים
כחול הים דלא יוכלו
יספרו אתו הספרים.
19 וכד שמע בבא רבה ומעיני
עמו השמרים במה עשו המלכים
כתבו לעדת השמירים
הנשארים עד יבאו מכל
מכון לסעדותם על מלחמות
דבביהם הממרים.
20 שם רצו ובפני בבא רבה
אתקבצו ומספרם היה
עשרת אלף אנשי מלחמה
מתחגר כל מנון בכלי
מלחמתו התמימה.
21 ושלח להם בבא רבה
הקריות מכרתים.

22 ויבא המגיד ויגד למלך בבא רבה
דע כי אויביך באו אליך במספר
רב לא ימני.
23 ויירא המלך הצדיק בבא רבה מאד
ויצר לו ויעתר ליי׳ בזאת
התפלה והוא מתפני למקום המבחר
הר גרזים בית אל ויאמר: –
24 אדני יי׳ עליך בטחתי לא תרפני
ובצדקתך פלטני.
25 אהיה במהר מזה הלחץ הצילני
והיה לי ולכל קהלי לצור
ופלטם ופלטני כי צור לי אתה
וחרב גאותי ומגני.
26 בסוד שמך הקדוש תנחני ותנהלני
אלהי הוציאני וגם כל עמי מן
הרשת אשר טמנו לנו אויבי
כי אתה צור לנו.
27 בידך נפקיד את רוחינו פדי אתנו
אל רחום וחנון ארך אפים ורב
חסד ואמת.
28 אלהינו שנאנו השמרים הבלי שוא
ועליך בטחנו נשמחה בחסדך.
29 כי תראה את דלותינו
וביד אויב לא תסגירנו.
30 מכוננו רחמנו, רחמנו מכוננו
כי צר לנו כי כלו ביגון ימי חיינו
וימי חיי אבותינו מפנינו.
31 כשל בעונינו את כחינו
ונמסו את עצמינו.
32 חרפה לכל אויבינו היינו
נשכחנו כמת מלב
והיינו ככלי ריק.
33 עליך בטחנו כי אתה אלהינו ואלהי
אבותינו.
34 בידך רוחינו
הצילנו מיד אויבינו ורודפינו.
35 האירה פניך אלינו
ובחסד אושיענו.
36 אדני לא נבוש כי אליך אתפללנו
ואויבינו בחפצך בשאול ישכנו.
37 מה רב טובך אדני
אשר הצפנת ליראיך.
38 ועשית אתו לקוים את ישועתך
תסתירם בנסתרתך מכעסות הרשעים
תצפנם בסכות מקנאת החטאים.
39 ברוך יי׳ אשר על כל העמים הפלאנו.
40 אהבו את יי׳ בני אהביו
אמונים נצרם יי׳
כי הלכו בדרכיו.
41 חזקו ואמצו לבבכם
כל ההלכים על שביל תורותיו.

22 ואחר כן אתשיג הדבר אל
בבא רבה כי שנאיך הלכו
לך רבבות ואלפים נעותים
לא ימני מספרון מסתובבים
מן הפאתים.
23 ועמד בבא רבה בין ידי יהוה
ישתבח שמו ואתנפל אליו
ובקש מנה ואתפני להר הקדש
וסגד בתם לבבו ונפשו ישים
לו נצען על שנאיו דמבקשים
לו יכחשו; ואוריך מן
התשבחות והתהללות.

§21

1 ויהי כאשר כלה המלך בבא רבה מן
תפלותו ומקראתו הלך אל המקום
הקרוב אל מכון המלחמה אשר ידע
כי שם תהיה המלחמה בינו ובין
אויביו ויצפן שם בקברים אנשים
מאנשי הצבא.
2 ויצו אתם לאמר והיה כי תראו
המלחמה נפלת בינגו ובין אויבינו
במכון המלחמה וצעקתי עליכם בקול
גדול ואמרתי ישבי הקברים עקרוני
ודבקוני ויצאתם מן הקברים ואמרתם
אל תירא באנו אליך אל תירא ונתתם
את החרב בכל האויבים.
3 ויהי מספר האנשים אשר הצפנם
המלך בבא רבה בקברים חמשה אלפים
איש.
4 ויהי כקרב המלך בבא רבה ואנשי
צבאים מן האויבים ויתקעו הכהנים
בחציצרות וישאו כל העם את קולם
ויצעקו קול אחד בקול גדול יי׳
גיבור במלחמה יי׳ שמו ותחרד הארץ
מקול צעקותם.
5 והמלחמה נפלת ביניהם ובין אויביהם
ומלחמה גדלה היתה בעצם היום הזה
אשר כמוה לא נהיתה בימים ההם.
6 שם צעק המלך בבא רבה בקול גדול
בתוך המח׳ לאמר ישבי הקברים
עזרוני ודבקוני ותדם אנשי (הרומים)
מקול צעקותו.
7 וימהרו האנשים אשר הצפנם בתוך
הקברים ויצאו ויאמרו בקול גדול
אל תירא בבא רבה באנו אליך כלנו;
אל תירא בבא רבה וכל המיתים יבאו
אחרינו מכל מקום.
8 ויהי כראות את אנשי צבא (הרומים)
את הדבר הזה חשבו כי אמת היה הדבר
ותפל עליהם אימה ופחד וירגזו וינסו
מפני המלך בבא רבה ומפני אנשי
המחנה אשר היו עמו.
9 ויתנם יי׳ ביום ההוא ביד המלך
בבא רבה ויכם וירדפם עד סוף ארץ
עדת בני ישראל השמרים על האמת.

10 וזאת המלחמות אשר זכרנו אתם מטרם
עם זאת המלחמה כלם היו מאחרי הן בא
לוי בן אחי המלך בבא רבה מערי
(הרומים).
11 כי מטרם הלכות לוי לערי (הרומים)
לא היה מלחמות בין עדת בני ישראל

1 ובכלות צלותו ותפלותו
הלך למקום הקרוב מן
המכון אשר ידע תהיה
המלחמה בו, ושם לו
מן עסכריו אורב בקברות.
2 ואמר להם אן ראיתם המלחמה
נפלת בינגו שם וצעקתי
עליכם בעלאות קולי ואמר
אה מן בקברים שכוני עתה
קומו ועל שנאי עזרוני.

6 שם עסכרי האדום אדמו מן
קול בבא רבה דלית שמעו
כמו.
7 וכד אמר כן צאו האנשים
האורבים אמרים אה מלך
עדת העברים אל תירא ואל
תחת מן אלין הממרים עתה
באנו לעזרך ואשר נשארו
מן המיתים הם באים עליך
אחרינו מכל מכון.
8 וכד עמו עסכרי האדום כן
אתותרו כי זה הדבר קשט
ונפלת עליהם הרעה ודחלו
דחלה גדלה ואזדזעת אברון
ואתשברת צלעון ממה חזו;
ושמעו מן עזרות המיתים
הך מה אתותרו ונסו לחצרות
ונפלת עליהם אימה ופחד.
9 ונצען יהוה ארשינו בני
ישראל השמירים נצען רב,
ויהוה היעדיו.
10 כי זאת הנפילה והנפילות
השנים דאתקדם זכרונם הם

השמרים ובין מלכי (הרומים).
12 כי בבא רבה שלח בן אחי לוי לערי
הרומים מפני הן הגלא דברו.
13 כי לוי הזוכיר הוא אשר שבר את עוף
הנחשת אשר הוא ממעשה הנחשים.
14 כי מפני כן לא יוכלו איש מבני
ישראל השמרים לעלות אל ראש הרגרזים
בית אל הר הברכה המקום המבחר כי
העוף הזה היה שם בראש ההר ההוא
וכי ימצא איש שמרי בגבול ההר
יצעק העוף ההוא (עבריוס).
15 והמלחמות כלם אשר היו בין בבא
רבה ובין מלכי (הרומים) על אדות
הדבר אשר עשה אתו המלך הצדיק בבא
רבה ולוי בן אחיו כי הרסו את בית
כנשת הרומים אשר היתה בראש הר
הקדש הר הברכה המקום המבחר הר
גרזים בית אל ויכו כל (קסים)
אשר היה שם וגם כל ראשי (הרומים)
אשר היו משלים על כל עדת בני
ישראל השמרים וגם המלך אשר בא
עם לוי מן מדינת (קסטנטינה).

Rest of folio 438 (תלח) is illegible

17

..... על יד נאמן
ביתו אדון הנביאים משה בן
עמרם עליו השלום לעולם עד כל
מלכי (הרומים) יעו כי המלך
בבא רבה יוכל על מלחמותם חזיק
הלב ואמץ לבב עתיד לכל מלחמה
לא ילא מקראתם.
18 כי שנים רבים עשה עמם מלחמות
ויתן יי׳ את כלם בידו.

החל המלחמה דנפלת מן בבא
רבה עם האדום והות שלחותו
בן אחיו לוי לערי האדום
באחלת דבר עודה.
13 כי לוי אשר שבר העוף
הנחשת אשר היה בכלי
הכשף.
14 כי קדם זה הדבר לא אתנטש
אחד מן השמרים לעלות אל
ההר הקדש מן זה העוף כי
הוא היה בממצא אחד מן
השמרים על ההר הקדש או
בקצההו יצעק עברי יוס.
15 וגלל המלחמות דנפלו בין
בבא רבה ובין האדום היא
הנפלה דעשה אתה בבא רבה
ובן אחיו לוי הזוכיר
היא אבדת הכנשה דבנו
אתה האדום בהר הקדש
והכותם הקסמים ובלעדם
אשר היו שם וככן הכות
הפוקידים והשופטים והמלך
ופגתם כי הסקוף הרב
אתמכה עם אשר אתמכו.
16 ובבא רבה כד עשה כן
ועם הכותו כל הפוקידים
דהוו מסים על בני ישראל
השמירים למען ימנעו אתם
מעבדת אלהיהים והצלואן
והמקרא בתורה החסידה
ועשות מצותו ואגדיל
אסונו ולכד הכנשנות
ואתנטשו השמרים מן משיגותם
אל ההר הקדש וכונון כל
הכוננות דאתקדם דכרנו.
17 ובגלל זה אחלת המלחמות
והמריבות בינו ובין
האדומים ונשאר בבא רבה
יעשה עשות מן מכר נפשו
ואבד כל עמו בשביל אלה
עד אתקשטו מלכי האדום
כי בבא רבה אסונו חזק
מתנכון למלחמותם ואיננו
ילא מן שלטנותם וגברותם.
18 כי שנים רבים הצר עליהם
ועזרו יהוה ישתבח שמו
על נגיפותם רצון יהוה
וסליחתו עליו ועל אבהתו
דקעם מן זרעם.

§22

1 ויהי אחר הדברים האלה וייטב בעיני
מלך עיר (קסטנטינה) ידרש מן המלך
הצדיק בבא רבה שלום וידרש ממו
יבא אליו אל עיר (קסטנטינה) עיר
כסא ממלכתו.

2 והדבר הזה היה בעיצות מלך הרומים
אשר בעיר (קסטנטינה) ובעיצות את
כל אנשי ממלכתו על אדות שלשה
מאומים.

3 (הראש) כי דרשו ידעו את כח המלך בבא
רבה היש עמו יכולה לעשות עמם מלחמות
רב מזה כי הם נלאה מפניו ועם זה כי
שמעו כי גרש את (הערבים) הישמעאלים
וירדפם ויבז את כל אשר עמם מצאן
ובקר וגמלים וחמורים וכסף וזהב
מקנה כבד מאד לא יספר או לא יוכל
לעש׳ מלחמה אחרי כן כי נלא.

4 (השני) דרשו יכרתו את זאת השנאה
אשר היתה בינם ובין המלך הצדיק
בבא רבה ובין כל עמו עדת בני ישראל
השמרים על האמת כי לא יכלו עוד
יכינו אנשי צבא למלחמה בכל עת
לשלח אתם למלך בבא רבה כי אויבים
רבים מן אנשי צבאות המלחמה אשר

5 (השלישי) אמרו אולי נמשל על המלך
בבא רבה אשר הוא הגלל להקים את
כל המלחמות האלה ולהרוג את אנשים
רבים מן אנשי צבאות המלחמה אשר
שלחו עליו מאתם.

6 ושם מלך (קסטנטינה) אשר היה בעת
ההיא (פילפוס) ויכתבו הוא וכל
אנשיו למלך בבא רבה.

7 וישלח לו מלאכים מן ראשי ממלכתם
ובידם ספר מן מכתב יד המלך (פילפוס)
וזה אשר כתב לו בספר הזה: –

8 שלום לך אדוני המלך בבא רבה אנכי
דרוש מן אדוני המלך הגדול הנכבד
בבא רבה יתן את שיאלך משרתו מלך
קסטנטנה בעת ההיא ויכבדו וילך
ויבא אליו אל העיר הזאת וישב אתנו
ימים עד נראה את כבודו ואחרי כן
ישוב בשלום למקומו.

9 ויהי כבוא את ספר המלך
(פילפוס) עם ראשי המלך ויתנו אתו
ביד המלך בבא רבה ויקרא את הספר
וידע את כל הדברים האלה.

1 ואחר כן אתחסד את מלך
אלקסטנ׳ כי יעלים על
בבא רבה הצדיק והמובא
אליו.

2 וזה החזי היה קעום על
שלשה החזות וכן
בתדבירותו ובתדבירות
נביאתו ואנשי ממלכתו
דמן עדתו.

3 הראש
למען יראו גאות בבא רבה
הל הוא ימצא אתו קוממה
למלחמות רב מכן אם לא
כי נלאם ממה עשה בהם
ועם זה עת אתשיג הדבר
להם כי גרש הישמעאלים
ושבר אתם ואשבי מהם
טובות רבות וכי הוא נלא
מן רבות המלחמות דנפלת לו.

4 השני
מדרשו בכן חדלות השנאה
דביניהם ובין בבא רבה
ועמו ועמו כל נשאר
בנטשם הנכונות בכל עת
לעסכרים וחלוצותם על
בבא רבה.

5 השלישי
אולי ימשלו על בבא רבה
אשר הוא היה גלל זה חמות
האף והכות הרב מן
העסכרים.

6 ומלך אלקסטנטיניה היה
יתקרי שמה פילפוס וכד
קעם חזוה והחזי אנשי
משפטו כי יכתבו לבבא
רבה ויעלימו עליו
המובא אתם.

7 שלח המלך הזוכיר שרים
לבבא רבה מן השרים
הנגישים וכתב בכיר ידו
מכתב לבבא רבה ונתן
אתו להם למען במובאם
יתנהו לו; וזה מה בו
מתכתב: –

8 תחמדותי מן אדונן המלך
הגדול בבא רבה יטיב על
המלכים בקדשיו וילך
אלינו אל אלקסטנטיניה

10 ויאמר המלך בבא רבה למלאכי המלך
(פילפוס) אני יש עמי יכולה להלחם
עם מלך (קסטנטינה) ארך ימי חיי
וכן עמי עדת בני ישראל השמרים רבים
על המספר ואנשי הצבא הנמצאים תחת
ידי כלם חזיקי הלב.
11 וייראו המלאכים מאשר ראו אתו
ממעשה בבא רבה.

12 ובבא רבה הזוכיר אסף את כל
זקני וראשי עמו וגם אביו
ובנו ואת כל בני משפחתו
ויקרא אליהם את ספר המלך
(קסטנטינה) ויספר להם את רזו.
13 ויאמר אליהם אני מדרשי אלך
לאצל המלך פילפוס מלך
(קסטנטינה).
14 ויענו אתו אביו הכהן הגדול
נתן אל וזקני העם וראשיו
ושטריו וכל הנאספים לפניו
מה זה הדבר אשר זממת לעשות
אתו ואיך תחפץ עתה תלך
ותעזב העם אחריך כילדים
רכים הרף מהם אביהם ויעזבם
נביכים לא ידעו מה יעשו
ועם זה כי יי׳ יתקדש שמו
הרחיב לנו על ידך.
15 ויגשו זקני העם ושטריו
ויאמרו אליו לאמר קוינו
אדונינו מן כבודך לא תעשה
את הדבר הזה אשר דברת לפנינו
כי נירא אנחנו נשוב אחרי
הלכותך לדלותינו ולחצנו
ונלאותינו ומסכינותינו
ומצוקנו ומוצרנו הראשנים.
16 כי אתה תדע כי כבדה עתה
השנאה והאויבה בינגו ובין
(הרומים) בגלל המלחמות אשר
עשינו עמך ומכות אנשיהם.
17 קוינו ממך אדונינו הן תעמד
ולא תרחק את נפשך ממנו ולא
תרף את עצמך מעלינו ולא
תעזבנו פן ילעגו בנו אויבינו.
18 ויען אתם המלך בבא רבה לא
שמעוני אני עתה אלך אל עיר
(קסטנטינה).
19 וידעתם אתם כי אני אשלמתי את
דברי ליי׳ לבדו יתקדש שמו.
20 אולי תהיה הלכותי אל מלך
(קסטנטינה) הגלל להסיר את
השנאה אשר היא בינגו ובין

ויהיה קעם אתנו ימים
מעטים עד נתמלי בחזותה
ואחר כן ישוב למקומו בשלום.
9 וזה היה בכנע מן מלך
האדום ואנשיו הך מה
קדמנו ולקחו השרים
המכתב והלכו והשיגו
למקום גדלות בבא רבה
הרב ונתנו לו המכתב.
10 וקראו וידע מה בו מתכתב
ופני השרים אגלי גאות הלב
וכי לו יכולה על מלחמות
כל אויב בארך ימי חיותו
במדינת אלקסטנטינה ובלעדה
וימחה מה לו מן צרב ועמו
בני ישראל הכני מספרו לא
ימני כוחו מתודע בין כל
הכרני.
11 ואזדזעו השרים ממה חזו
מנה ומן ממלליו הרביאני.
12 וכד אתשיג לידה המכתב
וקרא אתו אסף אביו וילידו
וכל סדר משפחתו ואנשיאי
ישראל עדתו והודיע אתם מה
מתכתב במכתב דהתשיג אל
ידו מן המלך.
13 והחל ידבר אתם עתה זממתי
הלך למלך הזוכיר ולא
אתאחר מכן.
14 וענו כהלון ואמרו מה הדבר
דזממת עליו ואיך יתנטש עמך
תלך ותעזב משפחתך ועמך וישארו
אחריך כטפלים קטנים עזב
אתם אביהם וכל מנון לו ימך
ויצפרו נביכים ולא ימצאו
מן לידיהם יסמך ויהוה נפש
לחצון מיום קדומך.
15 ונגשו אל בין ידיו ראשי העם
ודמעיו וממלו אתו והוא ישב
במקוהיו ואמרו נבקש מן
כבודך אה אדונן בחסר מהלכך
וחרקותך מפנינן ונירא מזה
הרעות תקראנן.
16 ויראו בנו דבבינן דעדפת
השנאה בינם ובינן.
17 נדרש מן איקרך חסר מפומך
מן אתרך כי בפרקנך
לבבותינו תרך ויסתולל
עלינו הפרך.
18 ויען להם גדלות בבא רבה

הגוים האלה ותכבי האש אשר
בינגו ובינם עד היום הזה.
21 ואני עתה אחפץ הלכת לאצל המלך
(פילפוס) לעשות עמו שלום
ולכרת עמו ברית.
22 אחי לא יכסי עליכם כי הדבר
ארך עלינו ולא נשאר בנו כוח
לעשות עוד מלחמה עם אויבינו
כי זאת המלחמות ילאו מנון
המלכים הגדולים ואנחנו עתה
מה בלתי מספר מעט לא נוכל
לקום לעמד לפני המלחמות האלה.
23 ואנכי ברצון יי׳ יתברך שמו
אשוב אליכם קרוב והן התהפך
הדבר ויעשה לי דבר לא אדעו
או שפטו עלי בחסרן שובתי אל
מקומי ואל ארצי או יהרגוני
להמית אתי אצוה אתכם על בני
לוי.
24 וזה לוי בנו מלבד בן אחיו לוי.
25 ויענו אתו קול אחד לאמר
כי תדרש עתה תלך אל עיר
(קסטנטינה) כאשר דברת קח
אתך אנשים מן העם לשרתך
ולקום לפניך בארץ איביך עד
ידעו את כבודך ויק מיתוביך.
26 ויען המלך בבא רבה את ראשי
העם לאמר לא אעשה כן כי אגור
מעשות דבר לא נדעו אין לנו
בו שמחה וכי יהיה הדבר עלי
לבדי טוב מעשותו באנשים רבים
מן העם.
27 רק עתה אנכי מצוה אתכם מצוה
יהיה לכם רב שמח בזה העולם וחייה
תמידה בעולם השני והוא תהיה שמרים
את מצות יי׳ יתקדש שמו בתורותו
הקדושה ולא תשביתו מן המקרא בתורו׳
הקדושה בכל עת ולמדתם אתה אל
בניכם ולבנות׳ ולבני בניכם.
28 ואצוה אתכם אן תהיו אמצים וחזיקים
ולא תיראו ולא תחתו ולא תערצו כי
יי׳ אלהיכם יתקדש שמו לא יעזבכם
ולא ירפ׳ ולא ינזפכם ולא יפיר את
בריתו אשר כרת את אבותיכם ונביכם
הנני הגדול משה בן עמרם עליו
השלום לעולם.
29 והשמרו פן יסורו לבבכם מן דרכיו
ולשמר את חקיו ומצותיו.
30 וידעתם כי את כל אשר יעשה יי׳ לעמו
בני ישראל השמ׳ על האמת הוא נסות
מאתו להטיבם באחריתם.

ואמר דעו את העם הישר
אלא הלך למכון זה המלך
המתגבר.
19 ועתה משלם דברי לאלה
הצדיק והישר.
20 אולי זה יישר ותסור השנאה
דבינגו ובין עבודי אלהי
נכר ותשקע זאת אש המריבה
בכל מישר.
21 ואכרת את המלך ברית ונצפר
בבטח מתקשר.
22 כי לא נסתר עליכם אה דמע
הצבאות עתה צפרנו ברב
נלאות ואין נשאר בידנו
האות מלאות וזה דבר ילא
מנה מן באסמו המדלות
נסתרות ונגלאות מן המלכים
דישקו על פיהם הבוראות.
23 ובארשות אל אלהי הרוחות
קרוב אשוב עליכם ותקראנכון
השמחות ואן היה אה אחי הדבר
מלבד כן ואתקומם עלי דבר
איננו מתודע ושפט עלי
בחסר שובתי הזמן ושטני או
מבקש להכני ולא שבתי בשלום
לבית אבי ועל ילידי לוי;
ועליכם אה מן כל מכם מאהבותו
מלוא לבי עתה לכם אצוה
(על ילידי לוי).
25 וענו אתו ואמרו אה אדונן
דנודעת לנו בינתו וחכמתו
וטהרות לבבו ורבות קנאתו
על הדת פרו ורבו אן
ההית איננך לנו שמיע
ותלך מן מכונך הרמי
ותעזב זימונך ותחסך
יתן חננך עתה כלנו נלך
עמך למען כל מנון יהיה
משרתך ויקום במה הוא
לאוי לך ולא ישבק יתך
כי את הלך להערים דבי
הנכרים שרים לא ימצא
בה אחד מן עדת העברים
ובממצאנו אתך ידע כל
מנון רבות גליגותך
ועלות דרגותך.

26 ויען גדלות בבא רבה אל
ראשי העם לא אעשה כן
ואירא מן דבר איננו לטוב
מכין אן היה עלי טב מה

31 אשרי לאשר שמר
ואוי לאשר סר מדרך האמת.

יהיה על מספר רב מן קהלי.
27 אפס אצוה אתכם מצוה בי
נשמה תהיה לכם בזאת חצר
עלמה דלית מתקוממים בה אני
ואתם, ומצוותי היא אתכם
משמר מצוות יהוה בכל מאדיכם
אשר בתורותו הקדושה צוה
בה לכם עם משמר החקים
והמשפטים בטהרות לבביכם
ולא תעזבו המקרא בה כי
הוא חייכם ולמדו אתה
לבניכם.
28 וככן אל תיראו ואל תערצו
ואל תחפזו מפני איביכם
כי יהוה אלהיכם לא ירף
אתכם ולא יעזבכם ולא יפיר
הברית דכרתו את אבותיכם
על יד רום נביכם אדונן
משה בן עמרם עליו הצלות
והשלם.
29 והשמרו פן תסורו מן הדרך
אשר הראכם.
30/31 ודעו כי כל מה יבא עליכם
הוא נסות מיהוה דבחר בכם
וחשק באבותיכם עד יתקומם
מה נשבע בו יען בזאת חצר
עלמה וטוב מן בכם על
הנסות לו קוממה.

§23

1 ויהי כאשר כלה המלך הצדיק בבא
רבה ממצות את השמרים עמו תפש
ביד בנו לוי ודמעיו ירדים מעיניו
על לוחו כמטר.
2 ויגש בו לפני אביו הכהן הגדול
נתנאל וינשק את ידי אביו ויאמר
בי אדני זה בני לוי קח אתו מידי
כי אני מפקדך אתו.
3 ויפל עוד לפניו וינשק את רגליו
ויאמר בי אדני אשר יי׳ יתקדש
שמו הגלל לממצאי שמר את בני פרי
בטני והוי מרצה עליו בכל עת.
4 ויפן אל אחיו הכהן עקבון ויאמר
לו אחי אני מצוך היום בגלל בני
לוי להורי אתו את הדרך הישרה

1 ובכלות בבא רבה מצוותו אל
העם תפש ביד ילידו לוי
ודמעיו רדת מן עיניו בזה
הפעם.
2 ושלם אתו אל אביו הכהן
נתנאל ואגיע לרגליו ונשק
אתם ואמר לו אה אבי זה
פקדנותי כי הוא כבד לבבי.
3 וגם גשה אליו שנית ונשק
רגליו השמאלת והימינית
ואמר לו אה אדני ומלמדי
אה מן שמך יהוה לי נחי
ומעלצך הוה ממצאי שמר זה
ילידי והוי מתפלל בעבורו
לגדלות האלהים הרעי וארצה
עליו כי ברצונך יקום
שמחיו ושמחי.
4 ואתפני לכהן עקבון אחיו
וצוה אתו בגלל בנו קדם
מסעיו.

5	ויפן אל כל זקני העם ויאמר אליהם שמרו את בני זה עד יקום לכם הטוב.	וככן צוה עליו הזקינים וראשי העם ודמעיו ואמר להם אחי ומאהבים לבי שמרו ילידי אה זקיני העם למען יתקומם לכם הטוב והנחם.
6	ויהי הדבר ממנו אליהם על שביל הרומז.	והוה זה מנה על שביל הרז.
7	וישכם המלך הצדיק בבא רבה ויקם וילך עם מלאכי המלך פילפוס מלך (קסטנטינה) ויקמו את כל אחיו ואת כל בני דדו ואת כל קריבו ואת כל בני משפחתו ואת כל זקני העם ואת כל ראשי העם ואת כל שטריו וגם מן העם מספר רב ויצאו למחוץ לעיר וישלחו אתו וישבו איש למקומו.	ואחר כן רץ וקעם והלך עם שרי המלך דלחזותו לבו חם וצאו אחיו ובני דודו הטבים ככל סדר קריביו הלוים והזקינים ומן עדת השמרים אנשים רבים ובמחוץ העיר לו נשקו וישבו למקומיהם.
8	ויבך בנו לוי ואחיו הכהן עקבון והכהן פינחס; אז שלחו אתו וישבו העירה שבירי הלב.	והם בבכות יצעקו מתעכרים מן רחקו.
9	והמלך הצדיק בבא רבה הלך עד השיג לגבול ארץ עיר (קסטנטינה) וימהר איש אחד מן המלאכים וירץ ויגד להמלך (פילפוס) במובא המלך הצדיק מלך בני ישראל השמרים בבא רבה אליו.	וילך בבא רבה את שרי המלך וכד אתקרב למדינת אלקסטנטיניה הלך אחד מן השרים והגיד אל המלך פילפוס במובא גדלות בבא רבה.
10	ויצו המלך (פילפוס) ויעבירו קול בין עם הרומים יצאו כלם יחדו לקראת המלך בבא רבה.	שם שלח המלך מצעק יצעק במשמע יושבי העיר במוצאון כהלון לקראתו.
11	ויהי כמעט ויאספו כל אנשי צוה המלך וכל ראשי עמו וכל (קסיס) וכל העם נשאים בידיהם (את הצלבים) ואת הבעלים ויצאו לקראת המלך בבא רבה למחוץ לעיר והם מרננים בצלותם.	ברגע אחת אתאספת העסכרים והקסמים והאנשים והנערים בגלולאן והזמיראן והצלואן וצאו לקראת בבא רבה.
12	ובעת ההיא היו כל מלכי (הרומים) אשר הם תחת ידו נמצאים (בעיר קסטנטינה) ויצאו כלם עם המלך פילפוס לקראת המלך בבא רבה.	וככן המלכים אשר תחת פוקידת המלך יצאו כל מלך מנון וצבאו.
13	ויהי כאשר ראו את המלך בבא רבה ירדו כלם מעל רכבם ולא נשאר רכב על מרכבו בלתי המלך בבא רבה לבדו.	ובעת אתקרבו לה אנסע המלך פילפוס מעל מרכבתו ומן אתו אנסעו וגדלות בבא רבה מעל מרכבו נשאר תארו מזרח הך צהר.
14	כי דרש יעשה כאשר עשו ירד מעל רכבו וימנעו אתו ויאמרו לא אדני עבדיך אנחנו עשינו את כה להכבידך כי חייב הוא עלינו.	כי לא נטשו המלך ירד ובעלאי על כל האנשים אתפרד.
15	ויהי יום גדול (לרומים) היום הזה אשר בו בא המלך הצדיק בבא רבה למדינת (קסטנטינה) לא היה לפניו כמהו לכל המלכים.	והוה זה היום יום גדול אצל המלך פילפוס ואנשיו במקדום בבא רבה אל העיר דבה מתנצב ערשיו בהדר רב והכל עמד לשמשיו.

§24

1 ויהי כאשר בא המלך בבא רבה לעיר
(קסטנטינה) ויבא בתוך הגבעה ויאמר
המלך פילפוס אל ראשי ממלכתו עתה
המלך בבא רבה בידנו ותחת ממשלותינו
אעיצו נא אלי מה נעשה.
2 ויפרדו האנשים האלה לשתי פרקים
פרקה אחת אמרת נכה אתו ונמיתהו
ופרקה אחת אמרת לא טוב הדבר לא
נכנו.
3 ויגשו לפני המלך ויאמרו אליו דע
כי בבא רבה מלך גדול ואתה תדע כן
מפני מובאו אליך ותדע את כל אשר
עשה ואת כל אשר הכה מן אנשי צבעינו
בפעמים רבים.
4 ועם זה וזה אנחנו נשבענו לו לא
נעשה בו רעה.
5 ואלא הוא יכול עלינו ולא ילא מן
מעמדו לפנינו למלחמה רק הוא בטח
בשבועתינו אליו ולא בא אלינו וישלם
את נפשו בידנו אלא כי ידע כי לא
יגע בו אסון מפנינו.
6 ועתה כי בטח הוא בשבועתינו ויבא
תחת צל קורתינו אין טוב ממנו נמיתו.
7 והמלך כי יעשה בו רע תהיה חרפה על
המלך ועל כל עמו וידברו בגלל הדבר
הזה האנשים בכל דר ודור ויכתבו
אתו בספרי הימים וחרפה רעה תהיה
לנו תמיד בכל הימ׳.
8 רק כי יצוה המלך נעזבו אתנו כל
ימי חייו ולא יצא מן העיר הזאת
ולא פרקן בין הכותו ובין עצרו כל
ימי חייו בזאת העיר עד יום מותו.
9 ולא יכסי ממדע אדונינו המלך כי
המלך בבא רבה יחפץ הן נכהו ונמיתו
ולא ישאר עצור אתנו בזאת העיר.
10 וייטב הדבר בעיני המלך (פילפוס)
וישלח ויקרא את המלך הצדיק בבא
רבה רצון יי׳ וסליחתו עליו אמן
וידבר עמו דבר טוב ויתן לו כסף
וזהב וכלי כסף וכלי זהב וכלי
נחשת ושמלות רבות.
11 ויאמר אליו אחרי כן אדני בבא
רבה על פיך ישק כל עמי.
12 ויצו המלך (פילפוס) את כל אשר
על שעירי העיר כי ידרש המלך
בבא רבה יצא מחוץ לעיר ומנעתם
אתו ואמרתם אליו לא יוכל אחד יצא
למחוץ לעיר בלתי על פי המלך
(פילפוס).

1 וכד בא בבא רבה במובא
הגבעי צוֹה המלך פילפוס *אמר
לנשיאי ממשלתו עתה שוה
בבא רבה בקמצת ידינו
ותחת פקידותינו ועתה מה
אתכם מן החזי עד נעשה בו
למען אנשם מן חסר ממצאו
רוחינו וביכלות יהוה
אתנדח חזיהם מהם.
2 מן מללו בהכותו ומנון
הדמעים לא ארשו בכן ובו
יסיתו.
3 ונגשו לפני המלך ואמרו
אה מן אתרבי אתנו איקרו
זה האיש בבא רבה מלך רב
אקרו ומתודע בין המלכים
פחרו וכל מה עשה כל מנן
יכירו בהכותו אנשים מן
עסכרך בעדרו בחרב עסכרו.
4 ואנחנו אשבענו לו לא נרע
בו ולא נמכאו במכאנו.
5 והוא יוכל ירע בנו ולא
הוא ילאו נגיפותינו
ואצתדק אתו שבועתינו דנשבענו
לו בה אנחנו ולא בא עלינו
ושלם נפשה לנו אלא כד
הכיר כי לא יקראנו אסון
בחצרינו.
6 ועתה איננו חסד במובאו
למקומינו נרע בו ולו היה
ראש אויבינו.
7 ואן עשינו בו רעה תהיה
בעיני העמים איננה הדירה
וימללו בה האנשים וכל מנון
יחריפו אתנו בספירה.
8 והטוב לנו נאשיר אתו לימי
מותו ובמוצאו מזאת העיר
לא נטשהו ארך הימים הנשארים
מן ימי חיותו.
9 וזה החזי חסד הוא לנו ובו
נתשיג למה לו בקשנו טוב
מן מוקדות אש הדבות; ולא
פרק אצלנו בין הכותו
ונותרותו.
10 ואיטב בעין המלך מה מללו
ושלח אחר גדלות בבא רבה
ואכבדו ואיקרו איקר עדף
ונתן לו זהב וכסף והלביש
אתו בגדים כבדון מרחף

13 כי פקידים היו על שערי עיר
(קסטנטינה) ולא יוכל אחד יבא
לעיר ההיא ולא יצא ממנה בלתי
על פי אנשי המלך.
14 ויהי מקץ ימים רבים ויגש
המלך הצדיק בבא רבה לפני המלך
(פילפוס) ויאמר אליו לבי יחפץ
לשוב אל ארצי ואל מולדותי ועתה
אדרש מן המלך יצוה לי אלכה
ואשובה אל ארצי ואל בית אבי כי
נכסף נכספת אל אבי אשר הוא מביט
שובתי אליו וגם את אחי ואת בני
ואת כל קריבי.
15 ויען המלך (פילפוס) את המלך
הצדיק בבא רבה לאמר תשב אתנו כל
ימי חייך.
16 וידע המלך הצדיק בבא רבה כי עצר
עצר המלך (פילפוס) אתו ואחרי כן
לא יוכל יצא מעיר (קסטנטינה)
וידם המלך הצדיק בבא רבה ולא
דבר עם המלך בגלל הדבר הזה עוד.

ושם דבר המלוך מושבו אליו
ואתנאשת מפניו הקצף.
12 וצוה השמירים על תרחי העיר
לא ינטשו אתו לציאתו אתו
מן העיר למען לא ירף.
14 וקעם גדלות בבא רבה
במדינת אלקסטנטיניה ימים
רבים אצל המלך פילפוס ואחר
כן בקש מנה ינטש אתו עד
ילך לעריו ולבית אביו ועמיתו
ואמר לו לאמר עתה אה המלך
אחמד מן גדלך תנטש יתי
בשובתי לבית אבי וארץ מולדתי
כי עתה לראותם נכספתי.
15 ויען אתו המלך קעם עמדי
ולא תסור מן נגדי.
16 וידע גדלות בבא רבה כי המלך
מסגיר עליו ואיננו מנטשו
מן אלקסטנטיניה ישא רגליו
וילך לחצרו ולקהליו ועזב
בזה ממלליו ואתרחץ על הצור
והתמים בפעליו.

§25

1 והכהן הגדול נתנאל כי ידע כי בנו
הצדיק בבא רבה עצרו המלך (פילפוס)
אתו בעיר (קסטנטינה) וישלח אחרי
בנו עקבון ויאמר לו תנה את בתך
רבקה לאשה אל לוי בן אחיך בבא
רבה.
2 ויתנה לו לאשה כאשר צוהו אביו
ויעשו לו שמח שבעת ימים כהסכנת
חתני הישראלים.
3 ויהי אחר הדברים האלה ויגוע הכהן
הגדול נתנאל וימת ויאסף אל עמו
זקן ושבע ימים רצון יי׳ וסליחתו
עליו אמן.
4 ויהי אחרי מות הכהן הגדול
נתנאל נכסף לוי בן המלך הצדיק
בבא רבה אל אביו וילך אל עיר
(קסטנטינה) וישב את אביו ימים
אחדים.
5 בעת ההיא פגע המלך הצדיק בבא רבה
מחץ חזק ויגע בבא רבה כי קרבו
ימיו למות.
6 ולו היה חבר יהודי מעדת היהודים
וישלח המלך הצד׳ בבא רבה אחריו
ויאמר לו אחי שים נא ידך תחת
ירכי ואשביעך ביי׳ אלה השמים
ואלהי הארץ תקח את בני זה אתך

1 וכד אתגיד הכהן נתנאל
בחסר שובת ילידו לארץ
מולדתו והמלך איננו
מנטשו בכן זבג ילידו לוי
בבת דודו רבקה בת גדלות
הכהן עקבון.
3 ואחר כן מת הכהן נתנאל
לרחמות יהוה וסליחתו.
4 והכהן לוי נכסף לבה לראות
גדלות אביו הכהן בבא רבה
והלך אליו וקעם אצלו מעט
מן הימים.
5/6 ואתמחץ גדלות בבא רבה מחץ
חזק וכד פג בחסר רפאה שלח
אחרי איש יהודאי היה מאהב
לה ועבר עליו.

	אל ארצי ולמו׳ ותתנו אל קריבו ולא תחלילו בטמאה.		
7	וישם את חברו היהודי את ידו תחת ירך המלך הצדיק בבא רבה וישבע לו על הדבר הזה.	8	שם תפש ביד ילידו לוי ושלם אתו לו ואמר לה אדרש מנך אה חברי תשיג ילידי הזה לעביביו וקריביו אל ארץ מושביו ולא תחללו בטמא ותשמרו הך ילידך ותחן עליו בכל מאדך.
8	ואחרי כן תפש בבא רבה ביד בנו לוי וישלמו אל חברו היהודי ויאמר לו חברי השמו׳ לך פן תחליף את מצותי אשר צויתך.		
9	ויאמר לו חברו היהודי ככל מצותיך אשר צויתני אעשה.	9	וכרת אתו ברית על כן.
10	ויאמר לו המלך הצדיק בבא רבה אלהים עד ביני ובינך.		
11	ויהי אחרי כן מת המלך הצדיק בבא רבה ויאסף אל עמו רצון יי׳ וסליחתו עליו אמן.	11	ואחר כן אתעתק גדלות בבא רבה במות לרחמות יהוה.
12	ויקמו בנו לוי וחברו האיש היהודי וירחצו אתו כחקת בני ישראל וילבישו אתו בגדי המות בגדים לבנים.	12	ואתפקיד בכבסו ומלבשו ילידו לוי וסעדו על כן האיש היהודאי דאתקדם דכרנה.
13	וימת המלך הצדיק בעיר (קסטנטינה) ויום מותו יום גדול לישבי עיר (קסטנטינה).	13	והוה מותו באלקסטנטיניה ויום מתו היה יום גדול את יושבי זאת העיר.
14	ויבכו אתו מלך (קסטנטינה) ואת כל עמו וילכו מקטן ועד גדול אחריו לקבר אתו.	14/15	והוה לו מחנה לא היה כמהו דמי ליום אשר היה לה מובאו ואקבר בקבר טב ברחמות יהוה מסתובב.
15	ויעשו לו בעצם היום הזה כאשר עשו לו ביום מובאו לעיר (קסטנטינה) ויקברו אתו בקבר רחב וטוב.		
16	ויבנו אחרי כן (הרומים) על קברו בית כנשה.	16	ואחר הימים האלה בנו האדום על קברו כנשה.

III. TRANSLATION

§1

1 After that, the Lord, may His name be blessed, gave to the
2 High Priest, Nethan'ēl, three sons. Now these are their names:
the name of the first he called Baba; the name of the second
he called 'Aqbôn and the name of the third he called Pinḥās.
3 Now Pinḥās dwelt in the town of Maḥăneh, which is hard by
the Chosen Place, Mount Gerizim, Beth-El, at the foot of the
4 mountain. From his youth, Baba was a man of discretion,
wisdom and understanding; a prosperous man, for the Lord
5 made all his undertakings to succeed. Zeal for the Lord was
continuously in his heart, and he was endowed with holy
spirit.

6 During that time, Baba grew up to become a man of renown,
inspiring awe and fear among all his people, the Samaritan-
Israelites. He was cognizant of their burdens, seeing what was
7 happening to them at the hands of the enemy. He devised
means to remove this scourge from them, and he took note of
the task masters who had been appointed over them to afflict
them, and how the accursed Edomites were embittering their
lives.

8 Now this Baba gave thought, and cogitated over the matter
9 with great strength of purpose. God gave His approval to his
plan, because he revealed great zeal in communing with the
Lord his God.

10 After that, Baba assembled all the men of his generation,
who were subject to his authority, and he addressed them:
11/12 'My brethren, listen attentively to what I have to say. My
heart has been moved to act with zeal, to restore the Israelite
faith, for the enemy are tightly repressing it and have blotted
out every outward sign of it from the land.'

13 Baba mustered his trained men, and he gave spiritual
expression to his inner thoughts by uttering many prayers
14 before the Lord his God. He summoned his men, whom he
had previously assembled — namely, the men of his
generation, whom we have referred to — and he spoke to
15 them thus: 'How long will these uncircumcised, who deny
that the Lord our God is in our midst, who worship alien

gods and repress the Holy Law of Moses, embitter our lives
16 and the lives of our brethren, the Samaritans? How long
shall this wicked community prevail? How long shall our
repressers deny, saying that it is we who are provocative?
17 How long shall this be our ensnarement? How long before
this fire is quenched for us? For how long will they prevent
us from observing the way of the Lord our God, and executing
18 His commandments? For how long will they prevent us
reading His holy laws and observing His ordinances and
testimonies?'
19,20 The men of his generation made answer, saying: 'We agree,
master. Consider the causes that have prevented us from
rising up in the face of our enemies, and how weary we are
21 these days. Consider how our power is spent, and that we
have no standing among our enemies'.

§2

1 Baba answered them, saying, 'Are we not descended from
Jacob-Israel, from among whose sons two brothers displayed
zeal for the Lord by killing all the men of the town of
2 Shechem? It is said of them in the Holy Law, "The two sons
of Jacob, Simeon and Levi, Dinah's brothers, took each man
his sword and entered the town and killed every male. They
cut down Hamor and his son Shechem, and they took Dinah
from Shechem's house and went off".
3 Are there not to be found among us men of the tribe of
Levi, who displayed zeal for the Lord their God at the time
4 of the Calf? About them it is said in the holy Law, "And all
the sons of Levi gathered themselves together unto him, and
they killed, every man his brother and every man his
companion and every man his neighbour. And they blotted
out the Calf-worshippers on that very day with the edge of
5 the sword". Consider the blessing which the Lord, may His
name be sanctified, conferred upon them.
6 Are there not to be found among us men from the sons of
Pinḥās our father, of whom it is seen that once he had
displayed zeal for the Lord his God among all the Israelites,
his people, the Lord bestowed upon him a superabundance
7 of exaltation and power? Of him, He said, "Pinḥās, son of
Eleazar, son of Aaron the priest, behold I give unto him My
covenant of peace; and there shall be unto him and to his
seed after him the covenant of an everlasting priesthood,

because he was zealous for the Lord his God, and made
atonement for the Children of Israel".

8 Remember what occurred in the case of Simeon and Levi;
how the Lord, may His name be blessed, caused terror to fall
upon the cities round about them, so that they did not pursue
after them.

9 So now we have an obligation to take courage and to be
zealous for the Lord our God, as our forefathers were zealous,
on account of these deeds encountered by us from our
10 enemies. Let us direct all our might to the establishment of the
statutes of the Lord our God, who has chosen us from among
all peoples and has taken us to be unto Him a chosen people.
11 Now, therefore, nought will avail us other than repentance,
supplication and appeal to His exalted Glory, also to seek His
goodness and mercy and diligently to offer the prayers, fasting,
supplication, devotions, consolations and petitions before His
12 Greatness. Let us direct our might to fulfil His commandments
and to obey Him, and to cleave to Him that He may grant us
aid, in His majestic power, against our enemies and adver-
13 saries. For whether He receives us out of His goodness and
lovingkindness, or whether He banishes us for our evil deeds,
yet He, may His name be blessed, does accept the repentant
who return toward His greatness.

14 Now then, it is good for us that we should be among them
that display zeal for His holy Law, and that we direct all our
energies to the renewal of its study, which is now extinct,
15 and to the raising of its banner. Let us now overthrow and
tread down the accursed aliens, and let us strengthen the
faith with a zeal such as this. Perchance we might become
like our upright and righteous ancestors who desired the
way of the Lord their God, and who sought His goodness
and lovingkindness and kept all His commandments, loving
the paths of those who achieved His ways.

16 Come, from now onwards, let us purify our hearts from
iniquity and sin, and let us return wholeheartedly to the
Lord our God; let us render ourselves innocent of all evil
practices, neither perverting justice nor displaying partiality.
17 Let us keep our distance from the commission of such sins as
conflict with the commands of the Lord of Lords, and refrain
from the evil that is the way of wicked sinners.

18 My brethren, know that if we do this wholeheartedly, then
the Lord will see that we are acting as the righteous, the
upright and the pure in spirit do, both openly and in

private. He will not hesitate to show us favour, he will accept
our repentance, hear our cry and deliver us from our dire
19 straits. He will grant us full release from our oppression and
answer our requests. He will see our affliction and poverty
and will enable us to achieve power over our enemies. He
will make our ways to prosper and pledge His support for
us. He will cleave to us closely in order to crush those
uncircumcised, accursed, impure, wicked sinners, perpetrators
of transgression, worshippers of strange (gods) in the presence
of the Lord of the spirits who, from nothing, made all
creatures.

20 Therefore, let us destroy them and banish them from this
holy land, so that no shameful person will be seen in it. Let
them move off to another land, with their head bowed
before the community of the Samaritans. Arise, my sons, let
us pursue them and, with the help of the Lord our God, we
will defeat them and destroy them, and lift these evil
scourges from upon us.'

§3

1 The priest Baba Rabbah concluded these words in the
presence of the assembly of Samaritan-Israelites and of all
2 the children of his generation. After this, Baba Rabbah washed
his hands, face and feet, and he prayed, prostrating himself
3 before the Lord His God. He fasted on that day, eating no
bread and drinking no water.

4 On the following day Baba Rabbah rose early in the
morning and ascended the Mountain of Blessing, the holy
5 mountain, the chosen place, Mount Gerizim Beth-El. The
Lord God, may His name be blessed, led him safely until he
had reached that place and encamped there upon the top of
the mountain.

6 The priest Baba Rabbah entreated the Lord his God,
abasing himself before His sovereignty, addressing himself in
prayer to His Greatness, making supplication to His Glory
and making efficacious his prayer, bowing low and prostrating
7 himself. He prayed the prayers of the lord of the prophets,
saying, 'If I have indeed won thy favour, O Lord, then may the
Lord go in our company. However stubborn a people we are,
forgive our iniquity and our sin and take us as thine own
possession.'

8 After completing this (part of the prayer), he called out
further; and these are the words with which he prayed:
9 'Lord God, when I make a request of you, answer my
10 request. The Lord, through whose majesty all existence came
into being, and by whose wisdom it is controlled, who set all
things in motion by His power and made His presence to
dwell where He so desired, who has chosen this people to be
His special possession, to serve His Oneness; He responds to
those who repent of their sin and wickedness and grants
atonement to them that call upon Him with wholeheartedness;
He answers them that call upon Him with a pure intention, and
He graciously leads back to Him those who have strayed from
the way of uprightness; He opens His doors to all who knock,
and they that know Him find deliverance by way of His strong
11 door. O Wise One, unique in wisdom and understanding, I
now put my request before You: O Lord, have mercy upon
your people and your servants, the children of your servants,
who have no refuge without Your Glory and no security other
than through Your mercy and lovingkindness, and no
12 redeemer other than You. O my Lord God, how numerous are
our adversaries; many rise up against us, and You know full
well all that we have suffered from these peoples and from the
wicked and sinful kings who have denied all the reports of
You, and who are in such darkness that they cannot keep Your
wonderful statutes.

13 When we call, answer us O our God; in our distress be
14 gracious unto us and hear our prayers. How long will our
glory be turned to humiliation? How long will they that love
vanity and seek out falsehood rule over us and prevent us
from upholding Your holy laws, provoking us to blot out the
15 memory of Your Holy name? They bow before every
detestable thing in our presence, and request us to depart
from the way which You have instructed us, in their desire
to destroy us. They worship the Baals and put their trust in
idols, boasting of the work of their own hands, of gods that
they have made according to their own desire and through
whom they bless themselves.

16 Give ear to my speech, O Lord God, consider my inmost
thoughts; heed my cry for help, my King and my God, for
17 to You do I pray. For you will not welcome wickedness,
neither can the evil ones, who walk the path of evil, be Your
guests.

18 Lord God, if our iniquities are too great for You to bear,

do not chastise us for them with the wicked, but let us rather
be taken into Your presence by the agency of death, rather
than that those wicked ones should brutally achieve our
19 destruction. If it were our guilt that prevented Your being
close to us and Your salvation from reaching us, let not the
enemies of Your Law have dominion over us.

20 O Lord, Lord, do not condemn us in Your anger nor
chasten us in Your fury. Be merciful unto us, O Lord, for
we are sick. Heal us, O Lord, for our very bones are in
21 confusion; our very soul quivers in great consternation. How
long before You, O Lord, come back, O Lord, to deliver and
save us for Your lovingkindness' sake?

22 O Lord, our God, if our guilt has been the cause of Your
removing Your mercy from us, take us into Your presence
and let not these wicked ones rule over us, and do not raise
over us those whose grievous yoke we cannot servilely bear,
those who have strayed from the way of truth and who
demand of us that we refrain from making mention of Your
holy name.

23 O Lord our God, in You we trust; save us from all who
pursue us, lest they tear our soul like a lion. Redeem, for we
have no deliverer besides You.

24 O Lord our God, if our actions are blemished, if there is
injustice in our hands and if we have recompensed with evil,
25 forgive every sin. Do not permit an enemy to pursue us or to
tread our glory down like earth.

26 O Lord God, You said that You would not forsake us,
according to Your word, written through the master of the
prophets, our teacher, Moses. In the holy Law You wrote,
"The Lord God will not fail you nor forsake you." Further-
27 more, You said in Your book, "When you are in distress you
shall seek out from there the Lord your God, and shall find
Him."

28 O Lord our God, how mighty is Your name through all
the earth, and Your majesty which is praised high as the
29 heavens. Out of the mouths of babes and infants at the
breast You have founded strength, that You might still the
enemy and the avenging foe, and redeem the upright and
the righteous who promote peace.

30 When we behold Your heaven, Your exalted work, the
moon and the stars which You have established with Your
fingers — What is the wicked man that You should give him
dominion over Your exalted work, to place beneath his feet

those who love You, and seek Your greatness and healing
comfort.
31 We will give thanks to You, O Lord, with all our heart and
we will sing in praise of You, relating all Your wonders with
all our might. We will rejoice continually and we will be
glorified in You, singing, "Your name is exalted", when our
enemies are turned backwards, they stumble and perish
before us.
32 For it is Your wont to rebuke the nations before Your
people; for You will destroy the wicked and blot out their
name from Your world. For You are forever a high tower to
them that flee to You, a refuge to the poor in times of
33 trouble. All who know Your name will trust in You, for
Merciful and Gracious God is Your name. You do not
forsake them that seek You, and You do not fail them that
petition You.
34 Now, therefore, look upon our lowliness, and by the merit
of Moses, the son of Amram accept our requests, enabling us
to attain our desired goal. For, seeking to walk according to
Your will, we will go with pure hearts, and following the way
of Your Oneness, we will pefectly go.
35 O You who are in zeal (all-) powerful, from the pit of
oppression liberate us. Grant us a new redemption, and look
down upon us in Your mercy and lovingkindness, for we are
36 descended from Your righteous servants. As You dealt
gloriously with our forefathers, the Israelites, deal with us in
Your lovingkindness, and as You redeemed them, so redeem
37 us. You manifested great wonders in the land of Egypt, and
on account of Your greatness You declared Yourself "God of
38 the Hebrews." Because of this, the Egyptians suffered great
39 distress. Then You turned the sea into dry land until they
had passed over on foot, walking upon dry land without an
ark. Then were Pharoah and his people drowned in the
midst of the sea, and You delivered Your own people from
40 him. Then they went out, happy and safe; the cities of the
mighty You gave to them as a possession, and You put fear
and trembling into the heart of their enemies.'

§4

1 When the priest Baba Rabbah had concluded his prayer,
his address and his devotions, his praise and lauding, he

returned to his brethren and the leaders of his community
2 who had assembled before him that day. He said to them,
'What do you think and what are your considered opinions?
Declare now in my hearing what you advise, so that I might
give consideration to implementing it.'

3 They all answered together, 'Whatsoever you say to us we
will carry out. We are subject to your instructions wholeheart-
4 edly; command us as you will; we will not rebel against your
command, neither will we disregard your instructions. That
which you have declared to us, and the counsel you have given
us, is acceptable to both us and all our brethren. It is most
5 certainly good (advice), without flaw and unobjectionable. Do
6 whatever seems right to you, for whatever you command us
7 will be no hardship to us. To all your commands we shall be
obedient, with the sincerity of our whole being. We will go
8 wherever you desire, for we have dedicated our hearts to be
attentive to, and to obey, all you say. Therefore we will
certainly not disobey you.'

9 After this, the priest Baba Rabbah and all his brethren and
the leaders of his people went around visiting wherever the
Samaritan-Israelites were living, re-opening all the
10 Synagogues which their enemies had closed. At the very first
assembly, he and his brethren started with the reading of the
Book of the Holy Law in the hearing of the whole assembly
of the Samaritan-Israelite congregation, including both men
and women. They further augmented with hymns, prayers,
laudations, supplications and exaltations to the God of the
spirits, the Lord God of Hosts, with great utterances of high
exaltation.

11 The priest Baba Rabbah sent word that all the Sages of the
holy Torah and all the Priests and the Elders from all the
communities should assemble to him. The priest Baba Rabbah
could locate but a small number of the sages and Elders of the
Samaritan-Israelite community, for all the rest had been
blotted out by the Edomite fanatics, because they would not
offer sacrifices to their gods or worship them, neither would
they forsake the service of the Lord their God, the God of their
fathers.

12 The Priest Baba Rabbah addressed those whom he had
located in these words: 'Arise and go, each of you, to his
place. Observe, be obedient and consider carefully, and
direct your energies to teaching the Holy Torah to the whole
congregation of Samaritan-Israelites, men, women and all the

children; that they might keep it and perform all its statutes
and ordinances in their entirety, just as your forefathers used
13 to do. You shall also direct your energies towards maintaining
the (practice of) reading from the holy Law, and towards
improving (the standard of) such reading through your own
pronunciation — an accurate pronunciation — as you have had
it transmitted to you from those who came before you.
14 Fall not into lethargy, but walk perfectly; also direct all
your energies to the service of all the Synagogues, as well as
to attending to whatever requirements are found necessary.
15 16 Go in peace, being on your guard against any blemish. On
17 your way now, O men blessed of the Lord. May the Lord,
the God of your fathers, make you a thousand times more
18 than you are, and bless you as He has promised. May your
enemies dwindle away before you, and may you tread upon
their high places and rule faithfully over all their (former)
19 dominions. Know, however, that any man among you who
does not observe and fulfil the command that I give you this
day, I shall strike him dead.'
20 Now this was the obligation that devolved upon the
congregation of Samaritan-Israelites from Baba Rabbah.
Very heavily (did it weigh) upon the old and young alike, the
youths as well as the children, to learn to read the Book of
the Holy Law, as well as the books of the Sages and scholars.
21 At that time this matter was a source of anxiety to them
though the community of Samaritan-Israelites soon greatly
rejoiced when they realised that, on account of this act, their
deliverer from their enemies would come soon, suffering
would leave them and they would be the recipients of grace,
mercy and lovingkindness.

§5

1 The priest Baba Rabbah then took seven men from among
the leaders of the Samaritan-Israelites, brave men who
feared the Lord, truthful men who hated unjust gain, Sages
in the Law, exactly like the men about whom the Lord
commanded Moses, when He said in in the holy Torah,
2 "And you shall select from all the people men of valour who
fear the Lord (etc.)." So the priest Baba Rabbah set them
apart by designating them *Ḥākhām* (Wise Man).
3 Now these seven *Ḥăkhāmîm* comprised three priests and

four Samaritans of the tribe of Joseph the righteous.
4 Concerning the priests — before this time any man who
inspired awe and respect was called "priest" by the people.
5 With the advent of Baba Rabbah, the priest, they were
merely called "Sages" *(Ḥăkhāmîm)*; and the priestly title was
6 removed from many priests. He likewise removed many
7 people from their priestly rank. The cause of this was that
when the priest Baba Rabbah came to Bashan the priests
who were there did not come forth to meet him, neither did
they fulfil their obligation to accord him honour and glory.
8 However, when he arrived at the city and assumed his
rightful position then they came to greet him in their
9 customary manner with all the people. Because of this act he
removed them from their positions, because they did not
10 journey out of the city to meet him. In their place he
appointed ordinary individuals to discharge their supervisory
functions, with the exception of the responsibility (to teach)
Holy Scripture.

11 And so, during the days of the priest Baba Rabbah and
afterwards, the ordinary Samaritan-Israelites could perform
the ceremony of circumcision. For, before the days of the
priest Baba Rabbah, no Samaritan-Israelite could circumcise
the foreskin of any Israelite child. It was only the priests who
could circumcise the foreskins of every child born to the
12 people. Similarly, it was the priests alone who said the 'Praise'
and the 'Forgiveness', and they would have oversight of all
that was done in the Synagogues.

13 The priest Baba Rabbah commanded all the people as
follows: 'The title "Sage" *(Ḥākhām)* shall only be conferred
upon those who are sages and scholars, whether they be of
14 priestly stock or of the general community. Any priest who is
neither a sage nor a scholar shall not be entitled to be called
15 either "Sage" or "Priest".' However, the names and descendants of the priests have been preserved in the *Tolidah,* in the
form 'so-and-so begat so-and-so'.

16 The priest Baba Rabbah alloted specific ranks to the seven Sages whom he had appointed as leaders of all the people, and he gave them changes of robes to wear. He conferred upon every one of them, in the order of supervisory role, his honourable status and that of his descendants to be permanent and unending.

17 He then positioned them before him, each man in accordance with his rank, so that they would each know their

18 particular order of seniority. These seven were to be the
leaders of the whole community of Samaritan-Israelites, each
one supervising his own territory, teaching his own community, making a distinction within it between the impure and the
19 pure, the holy and the profane, and establishing it on the basis
of the study of the text of the Holy Law.

20 Now these are their names — May the mercy of the Lord
protect them:

THE FIRST

The name of the first was *Srwb'y*, which means 'the fruit of
my desire'. He was a *Ḥabtah*, a descendant of Ithamar, son
21 of Aaron the priest, peace be upon them. His territory commenced from the shade of the great plane, and he occupied the foremost rank as Chief *Pater*.

22 THE SECOND

His name was *Ywẓby Ysr'ly*, an inhabitant of the town of
Kwfr Yslh. He occupied the second rank, and patronage over
the rest.

23 THE THIRD

His name was *'lyn'h Srpyn*, and his task was that of second
convener.

24 THE FOURTH

He was a Levite Priest from the town of *Zyth*, and his task
was that of first convener. He had to record the names of
those who had made contributions and other gifts at any
time.

25 THE FIFTH

He was an Israelite from the town of *Kfwr Mrwt*, and he
had the fifth patronage.

26 THE SIXTH

His name was 'Amram, and he was a Levite Priest from
27 the town of *Kwfr Sp'sh*. He had the second patronage. It is
said that this was the same 'Amram who was the father of
Marqah, the master of scholars and scholarship. It is further
said that he is the same 'Amram Darah who composed the
Durrân Chapters. He composed twelve for the six days of
Creation, six for the Sabbath, one for the beginning of every
month, one for the first month (of the year), one for the
28 seventh month and one for the Day of Atonement. Five of
Marqah's compositions are recited during the Sabbath
morning prayers. Should a fifth Sabbath occur in the month,
another of his compositions is recited before the Scriptural

29 reading during the course of the Midday Service which
replaces the Afternoon Service. He has another hymn which
is recited on the Atonement eve, and a further one which is
said on the Day of Atonement, as well as one hymn for
recitation on the day of the Commemoration of the Standing
30 on Mount Sinai, during the Morning Service. Of that sage's
compositions, the above are extant to the present day.

31 THE SEVENTH

An Israelite. However, we have found no reference to his
place or his office in the Book of Chronicles.

§6

1 The Priest Baba Rabbah arranged them according to the
above order of rank, and addressed them thus:
2 'You are to instruct the whole assembly of this people.
Plan for them and display leadership of the whole
community of Samaritan-Israelites, both young and old alike.
Be their judges, and decide between one man and another.
3 Show no partiality in passing judgement; listen equally to the
small and the great. Be not in awe of any man, for justice
4 proceeds from the Lord. If any man, standing before you,
shall contradict you on any matter which you tell him or
command him, I shall make enquiry of him.'
5 Among these seven men, the priest Baba Rabbah appointed
four of them, men of renown, as overseers.
6 Now the above arrangement did not operate during the Era
of Favour. During the Era of Favour seventy elected Elders
constituted the "Sages of the Community". Among them were
the twelve "Heads of the Tribes", one from among these twelve
7 being the "Supreme Prince". He bore the title, "Supremo of
the Tribes", and he assisted the senior man on judicial matters.
However, he had no authority over the priests and could not
judge them for transgressions, in any case of dispute or
8 litigation. Any matter affecting them would be referred to the
annointed High Priest who was consecrated to that office, or to
one of the senior priests, descendants of our master Pinḥās son
of Eleazar, peace upon them forever.
9 Now such status was not to be an inheritance from father
to son, or from a son to his father; but if one of them died
10 they were to choose one in his place. He had to be a man of
culture, wisdom and discretion, belonging to the community

and acceptable to the High Priest of the day and to the
11 Elders of the people, their leaders and officials. This was the
arrangement during the Era of Favour.

§7

1 At that period there was an Israelite family by the name of
2 "The Family of the Seventy". The men of that family refused
to obey the priest Baba Rabbah, because of the administration
which he had introduced and the choice which he had made;
neither did they submit to the jurisdiction of the sages whom
the priest Baba Rabbah had appointed over the entire
3 Samaritan-Israelite community. Instead, they appointed Levite
Priests to judge them in all the areas and cities under their
control.
4 For this reason those seventy sages whom the priest Baba
Rabbah had previously chosen had to make a regular circuit
of all those cities or they had to send overseers of requisite
knowledge, wisdom and discretion to investigate every place.
5 Whenever they came across a priest from among those
priests of the "Family of Seventy" who erred in religious law,
in administering justice or in civil affairs, they would hasten
6 to consult their own High Priest. These "Seventy" also gave
the priest Baba Rabbah all manner of military assitance; they
turned over to him the revenue, as well as innumerable
substantial gifts, and supplied all his other requirements.

§8

1 Now the sages whom the priest Baba Rabbah had chosen,
and who had been appointed over the community of the
2 Samaritan-Israelites for all time, he commanded thus: 'Look
well to, regard and understand whatever you do. Fulfil also
whatever I command you, and be careful not to forget my
instructions nor to neglect my wishes, nor, during Divine
worship, the observance of the Reading of the Holy Torah,
according to the ten principles of the reading; for this is the
3 most important thing that I require of you. Confer regularly
among yourselves and among the teachers, and search the
learned literature so that you may base everything on truth,
by reason of the reading of the holy Torah, according to the
ten principles of the reading, as transmitted by the Seventy
Elders of the Israelite community and by the priests who

lived in the days of the Master of the Prophets, the great
prophet Moses son of 'Amram, perfect peace unto him.'
4 Later, the priest Baba Rabbah built a ritual bath for
purification on the boundary of the chosen place, Mount
Gerizim Beth-El, the Mountain of Inheritance and Divine
Presence, so that any members of the Samaritan-Israelite
community who wished to pray upon this mountain would
(first) purify themselves in it when the time for any Prayers
5 approached. Two Prayers replaced the continual offering: the
first was the Evening Prayer at sunset; the second was the
Morning Prayer, recited from dawn until sunrise.
6 He further built a Synagogue, adjoining the Chosen Place,
Mount Gerizim Beth-El, so that the people could pray in it
7 opposite this holy mountain. This ritual bath and this Synagogue remained until the advent of the Frankish King-
8 dom. The Synagogue that the priest Baba Rabbah built followed the dimensions of the one they had built in the town
of Bāṣrāh during the Era of Favour. He erected it on the same
pattern, with its floor made of earth, as he had seen in the town
of Bāṣrāh. Furthermore, the priest Baba Rabbah took some of
the stones of the Temple that Saul's men had destroyed in the
days of Saul, king of the Israelites — excluding the
Samaritan-Israelite community — for his destruction of that
9 Temple was an act of hatred against them. He set up those
seven stones, as seven seats for the seven Sages, and he took
10 one great stone for himself to sit on. The priest Baba Rabbah
also built seven synagogues in the seven towns, all having floors
made of earth.
11 Now these are the Synagogues' names:
THE FIRST: The Synagogue of the town of Kwfr 'Amartāh,
where the High Priests, sons of Aaron the Priest, are buried.
They include Eleazar, his brother Ithāmār and Pinḥās son of
Eleazar. Peace be upon them, on the Seventy Elders and on
many other High Priests. It is situated to the east of the city
of Shechem.
12 THE SECOND: The Synagogue of Bêth-Nimrāh.
13 THE THIRD: The Synagogue of Qryth Ḥāgāh. It is still visible
to this day, though it has no special features. It is in the
southern direction, opposite the town of 'Skôr. The town of
'Skôr, where that house was, is, however, in ruins. Only the
site (of both towns) and the pool still exist today.
14 THE FOURTH: The Synagogue of Qryth Ṭîrāh. That town
exists to the present day.

15 THE FIFTH: The Synagogue of Ṣabā'rîn. That town is still inhabited today, and is among the towns of the Shephelah.

16 THE SIXTH: The Synagogue of the town of Šālēm. That town is still inhabited today, and is near Shechem in an eastward direction. It is also opposite the Chosen Place, Mount Gerizim Beth-El, in a north-east direction.

17 THE SEVENTH: The Synagogue of the town of Bêth Dāgān. That town is still inhabited to this day. It is east of the Chosen Place, Mount Gerizim Beth-El, in the northern direction.

18 THE EIGHTH: We do not know its location, neither have we found any mention of it in the Chronicle. It is said, however, that it was the Synagogue of The Stone, which was situated between 'Ēlôn Môre' and Mount Gerizim Beth-El. Three hundred and sixty chambers were built in it, according to the number of the days of the year. Its site is acknowledged to this day as being south of the sepulchre of our master Joseph the righteous, peace be upon him.

19 These are the eight Synagogues which the priest Baba Rabbah built. He built them all of stone; not one of them was of wood.

§9

1 The priest Baba Rabbah built also a spacious hall which
he established as the Hall for Meeting and Decision, as well
2 as for hearing all petitions. He erected it opposite the House
of Prayer which he had built at the foot of the Chosen Place,
the Mountain of Blessing, the Place of Sanctity, the Mountain
of Inheritance and Divine Presence, Mount Gerizim Beth-El,
in order that any Samaritan-Israelite who had a problem might
come there and put his problem to the Sages who were there,
so that they could tell him the authentic decision on his
3 problem. Likewise, any man who used the title "sage" at that
time was brought, on the New Moon or a Festival day, and set
before the great (priest) king of the time, and before the sages,
4 in order that they might test him. The tests having been
administered in the presence of the High Priest and the Sages,
if he was found to have been endowed with wisdom, discretion
and understanding, they conferred upon him the title "Sage".
5 The reason why the Priest Baba Rabbah introduced this
procedure, namely to build Synagogues and the Hall of
Wisdom, was that the rulers of the land would not say of
him thus: 'Does not the Priest Baba Rabbah pay heed to the

affairs of those rulers who involve themselves in deeds which estrange them from the praise of the holy name of God, may His name be sanctified, and from the fulfilment of His commands and statutes, by doing abominable things?'

6 The Priest Baba Rabbah then alloted the priests to all his
people of the community of Samaritan-Israelites, apportioning
7 to them specific territory. These are their names as we find
them written in the *Tolidah,* all Samaritan-Israelite people,
princes of their ancestral clans, who were appointed overseers
according to the direction of Baba Rabbah:

8 THE FIRST

His name was Yišmā‘’ēl. The Priest Baba Rabbah gave to him and to all the men of his family a permanent possession from the town of Lûz up to the coastal part of Galilee. He appointed as his 'aide' the Priest Na‘ărāh.

9 THE SECOND

His name was Jacob from the town of ‘Askôr. The Priest Baba Rabbah gave him and all the men of his family a permanent possession from ‘Askôr to Tarblos (This is actually from ‘Askôr to Tiberias.) He appointed as his 'aide' the Priest N^{e}than'ēl.

10 THE THIRD

His name was Zayyith son of Tēhām. The Priest Baba Rabbah gave him a permanent possession from east of the Chosen Place, the Sacred Mountain, Mount Gerizim Beth-El as far as the Jordan. He appointed as his 'aide' the Priest Eleazar son of P^{e}lāḥ.

11 THE FOURTH

— Joshua son of Barak, son of ‘Eden. He gave him a
permanent possession from Kwfr Ḥalûl until Bêth ha-
Šēbhet. He appointed as his 'aide' the Priest ‘Amram son of
12 Sered, who is known as Ṭôṭāh. It is said that he is the father
of the Priest Marqah, the great sage, the master of wisdom,
who answered all matters with discretion and understanding.
May the favour and forgiveness of the Lord be upon him,
Amen.

13 THE FIFTH

His name was Abraham son of Š^{e}m‘al‘îmāh, son of 'Ôr, son of P^{e}rāth. He gave him a permanent possession from the coast to the territory of the Philistines. He appointed as his 'aide' the Priest Ḥakûmāh.

14 THE SIXTH

— Israel son of Mākhîr. He gave him a permanent possession

from the town of Gaza up to the River of Egypt. He appointed as his 'aide' the Priest Šalôm.

15 THE SEVENTH

His name was Yosef son of Šûthelaḥ. He gave him a permanent possession from the boundary of the Mountain of Inheritance and Divine Presence, the Mountain of Blessing, Mount Gerizim Beth-El as far as Caesarea. He appointed as his 'aide' the Priest, Aaron son of Zōhar.

16 THE EIGHTH

His name was Lā'el son of Bekher. He gave him a permanent possession from the border, east of the vineyards, to the town of 'Akkōh. He appointed as his 'aide' the priest Joseph son of Ṣ^{e}nînāh.

17 THE NINTH

His name was Bekher son of 'Ôr. His border was established from the hill country of Naqôrāh until Tyre. The latter was (re-)built by our leader Yered son of Mahal'ălēl, who lived there until he died (in Kwfr M^{e}rû'an). He appointed as his 'aide' the Priest Aaron son of Zebhed.

18 THE TENTH

His name was Šafaṭ son of Ẓ^{e}bhû, son of Makhîr. He gave him a permanent possession from the brook of Lîṭāh — which is said to be the River Tiberias — as far as Sidon and its environs. He appointed as his 'aide' a priest, Zārîz son of Mānîr, who was endowed with great wisdom, knowledge and understanding.

19 THE ELEVENTH

His name was Bārād son of Š^{e}rî'ān, son of 'Ămād. He gave him a permanent possession from the hill country of Gālîl unto the valley, and as far as Lebanon and all the villages around it, from the mountains and the lowland. He appointed as his 'aide' a priest, Zayyith son of Lēvî, a distinguished man, whose renown was heard everywhere, in all priestly circles. For he was paramount in all branches of wisdom, understanding, knowledge and exegesis. The favour and forgiveness of the Lord be upon him, Amen.

§10

1 These are the heads of the community of Samaritan-Israelites whom the honourable Priest Baba Rabbah selected, and among whom he apportioned all the cities of the land of Canaan where all the Samaritan-Israelite communities resided.

2 The said Baba Rabbah appeared among his people to
perform all these deeds in the year 4600 of the creation,
corresponding to the year 1806 after the entry of the Israelites
3 into the land of Canaan; corresponding to the year 1545 after
the concealment of the holy Sanctuary which they had made in
the desert, as the Lord had commanded Moses. This, in turn,
4 corresponds to the year 1326 since Solomon son of David, the
king, built the Temple in the city of Jerusalem on the site which
his father had acquired from the Jebusite, namely, the place of
5 the threshing floor. This corresponds to the year 1050 from
the exile of the Israelites to Assyria in the days of the
pontificate of the High Priest Ăqabhyāh, and it corresponds
6 with the year 1005 since the arrival of the Samaritan-Israelites
from the first exile in the days of the pontificate of the High
Priest Ś^{e}rāyāh. This was the exile of Nebuchadnezzar. This, in
7 turn, corresponds to the year 795 after the arrival of the
Samaritan-Israelites from the second exile, the exile by the
king of the Greeks. Their arrival was in the days of the
pontificate of the High Priest 'Abd'ēl son of the High Priest
'Ăzaryah, in the thirty-fifth year of his pontificate. It also
8 corresponds to the year 755 from the time the Israelite
community established their Temple for a second time in the
city of Jerusalem, through the instrument of Zerubbabel,
Nehemiah and Ezra the Priest who brought with them
authority from the king of Babylon in order to establish the
9 Temple and the city. It corresponds, likewise, to the year 655
after the King 'Askander who ruled over all the nations, and to
10 the year 308 after the appearance of Jesus son of Miriam, wife
of Joseph the Carpenter, a descendant of King David, against
whom some Judaeans arose, and they crucified him.
11 It was at that date, in those happy days, that the Lord,
may His name be sanctified, revealed this great man who
ruled over all the community of the Samaritan-Israelites in
12 the land of Canaan for forty years. Even the Judaean
community was subject to his authority. He spread abroad
the faith of Israel, he built the Synagogues and directed all
his energies to teaching the Samaritan-Israelite community
the exact reading of the holy Law, a reading based upon the
true version as transmitted through the generations of Israel
from the seventy Elders, the Elders of Israel who lived in the
generation of the Master of the Prophets, Moses son of
13 'Amram, peace be upon him. He also established well-ap-
pointed Assembly Halls and he restored all the Israelites to

14 their (rightful) places. He appointed Aaronite priests (peace be
upon Aaron) over all the cities belonging to the Samaritan-
Israelite community, among whom were the Ḥavtawi priests,
descendants of our master Ithamar, peace be upon him.
15 These are their names: The firstborn was 'Abdî, the second
was Melekh, the third was Ṣidqī'ēl, the fourth was Śābhē'a, the
16 fifth was 'Or, the sixth was 'Āz. Numerically they grew
abundantly and spread all over the land of Canaan.
17 When the honourable Priest, Baba Rabbah, apportioned
the land of Canaan according to the families of the
Samaritan-Israelite community and allotted the priests over
them, he addressed them thus: 'Go in peace, be strong and
of good courage. Do not fear or stand in awe of any man as
18 long as I live. May the Lord your God put the fear and
dread of you upon all the peoples round about you. But you
shall fear none but the Lord your God and the God of your
19 fathers, who delivered you from the iron furnace. Direct all
your energies to keep His charge, His statutes, His
commandments and His judgements all your days, in order
that you may live.
20 The Sages of the Israelites and their leaders and priests
went forth from the presence of the honourable Priest Baba
Rabbah as a Samaritan-Israelite community which possessed
21 great strength and abundant happiness. At that time the
community of Samaritan-Israelites found favour in the sight
of the Lord their God; He increased happiness in their
ranks, the iron yoke He broke from off their necks, the bars
of their yoke He snapped and He led them enduringly.
22 Now when the Sages arrived at the cities which the
honourable Priest Baba Rabbah had allotted to them, the
inhabitants of the cities surged forward to express their joy
and to lift up their voices with songs, praises and adorations
of their God and the God of their fathers, who had chosen
them from among all the nations and had delivered them
23 from this affliction. The Samaritan Israelites performed all
this activity in accordance with the instructions of the Sages
and Elders and the honourable king, the Priest Baba
Rabbah, may the favour and forgiveness of the Lord be
24 upon him, Amen. They went on joyously celebrating and
demonstrating their faith in the Law of Moses son of 'Amram,
peace be upon him.

§11

1 Now the chiefs, who had been appointed over them by
authority of the kings of the foreign nations, arrived to
prevent them from carrying out the statutes of the holy Law,
2 just as they used to prevent them previously. However, all
the men of the Samaritan-Israelite community rose up
against them and quickly slew them and burnt them in fire.
3 Simultaneously, in every city, in every town and in every
place this act was committed against the honoured chiefs of
the nations in all the cities of the Israelite community. It
took place on the night before the New Moon of the seventh
(month), and the Samaritan-Israelites established a commemoration to that event.

4 After the men of the Samaritan-Israelite community had
slain the chiefs appointed over them by the king of Edom,
and had burned them in fire, emissaries and officers of the
5 king got to hear of this matter. They therefore sent some
messengers to apprehend all the representatives of the
Israelite community in order that they should accompany
6 them to the king of Edom. When the honourable king, the
Priest Baba Rabbah, heard of this he went to meet them,
with the men who were stationed with him, and they slew
7 innumerable men. Those that were left fell back and fled
before them to their own kings, in dejection of woe. They
recounted to them everything that had happened to them,
and how the honourable priest, King Baba Rabbah, whom
the Samaritan-Israelite community had appointed over them
as their new king, had slain a great number of them.

8 The honourable Priest Baba Rabbah realised (the
consequences of) all that he had done to the emissaries of
the kings, and he knew what he could expect from the kings
— that they would amass together a great army to come and
9 wage war against him. He therefore chose men from among
the youth of his people, the Samaritan-Israelite community,
men of war, whom he had trained to confront and to do
battle against the kings of the nations.

10 When the kings of the nations heard about the act
perpetrated by King Baba Rabbah against the emissaries,
they amassed many men from their armies and sent them
into battle against King Baba Rabbah, with a strong force.
11 Baba Rabbah went out to meet them with great determination,
and the Lord gave over into the hand of King Baba Rabbah all

12 their army. He smote innumerable of their men and totally
crushed them, filling the whole mountain of ʿAsqōr — which is
opposite the Holy Mountain, the Mount of Blessing, Mount
13 Gerizim Beth-El — with their corpses. The remainder fled and,
hurrying to their kins, they told them what the honourable
King Baba Rabbah had done to them, how they had
slaughtered the majority of their men, and how the Lord had
given them over into his hand and into the hand of the
community of Samaritan-Israelites with him.

14 Now when the kings heard this report they were very
angry and incensed against the honourable king Baba
15 Rabbah and against all the Samaritans with him. The king of
Constantinople thereupon arose and assembled a vast
number of men, in their thousands and tens of thousands, to
send into battle against Baba Rabbah and all his people.
16 When the matter was reported to Baba Rabbah he sent to all
the places of the Samaritan-Israelites, summoning all their
17 warriors. They came to him from every quarter, from the
entire hill country, lowland, coastal area or plain, ten thousand
warriors, bearing their own weapons — swords, spears and
arrows — and fully equipped to meet their enemies with a stout
heart.

18 When the honourable King Baba Rabbah realised how
large was the number of his warriors and how much
19 sustenance would be required, he set out, heavily armed and
with great determination, and drove out all the foreigners
from round about him — for they were enemies of the
Samaritan-Israelite community — and dispossessed them.
20 Now when the report arrived, of how the righteous King
Baba Rabbah had slain so many of their men, the remainder
fled from before Baba Rabbah. He then quartered troops in
those cities, took possession of them and settled in them his
warriors who had quickly come to him in the battles against
21 his enemy. He also appropriated from the community of
Samaritan-Israelites a tax which they were accustomed to pay
to the kings of Edom, and he purchased with it .... and
weapons for his warriors. He provided his warriors with all
22 their daily requirements. He also issued a command that it
should be proclaimed throughout all the cities of the
Samaritan-Israelite community that they should no longer
pay taxes to the kings of Edom, neither ... nor food to the
kings of Edom, as they had been (obl)iged to provide for
23 (the upkeep of) their armies. He made them give an under-

taking that from that (day) onwards they would contribute
24 only to the Samaritan-Israelite arm(y). Then the righteous
King Baba Rabbah established his residence in the town of
'Amartah (where are buried) our masters, the ancestors
of the High Priests, Eleazar, Ithamar and Pinḥas, peace be
25 upon them forever. There are also there many graves of
prophets, elders and many pure and righteous people. It
26 was because of this that its name was called the town of
'Amartah; for it was *established ('Ith'ămart)* by the graves of
these honourable righteous ones. The righteous King Baba
Rabbah set up his camp in it.

§12

1 After this, a herald came to the righteous King Baba
2 Rabbah and informed him thus: 'Your enemies have come
3 with a host so vast that it cannot be numbered.' Then Baba
Rabbah and all the sages of the Samritan people presented
themselves before the Lord their God and, prostrating
themselves upon their faces to the ground, they spoke thus:
4 'O our God, the Lord, do not keep Your presence (f)ar off
from us; do not hide Yourself in time of distress. With
pri(de) .... the children of .... shall serve .... You
will .... among the poor .... your God
.... in his heart You will not inquire, for You .... Have
regard to our provocation, to take into Your own hands
5 ..... whose words are wearisome. You have been a shield
and help to Your people. Break the arm of the wicked; let
6 them seek without avail. The Lord is King for ever and ever.
The foreign nations perish from their land. The desire of
the humble You hear, O Lord. Sustain their spirit and
incline Your ear to hear their request. Let no man on earth
7 ever terrify them again. Save, O Lord, Your people, for the
pious are destroyed, and the faithful have disappeared from
8 among the children of men. How long, O Lord, will You
forget us? For how long will You remove Your presence
from among us? For how long must we rely upon ourselves
for counsel, and must grief dwell daily in our hearts? For
9 how long must our enemies prevail over us? See and answer
us, O Lord our God. Enlighten our eyes lest we fall into the
sleep of death, lest our enemies say, "we can prevail over
them," lest they say that we shall stumble. Yet, we trust in

Your lovingkindness and we sing of Your name, so that it
may go well for us.'
10 When Baba Rabbah and all the elders of the people had
completed this prayer they sounded a note upon the
trumpet, in commemoration of their obligation to fulfil the
commands of the Lord which He commanded through the
Master of the Prophets, His servant Moses son of 'Amram,
peace be upon him forever.
11 'When you enter into battle in your land against an enemy
that oppresses you, you shall sound an alarm upon the
trumpets, and this will serve as a reminder of you before the
Lord your God, and you will be delivered from your enemies.'
12 They therefore cried out with a mighty cry, saying in
unison, 'Look down from Your holy habitation, from heaven,
and deliver Your people Israel from the hand of their
enemies.'
13 The Lord heard the sound of their cry on that day and
He gave their enemies into their hands; so that the
Samaritan-Israelite community smote a large number from
among their enemies. This battle raged on the mountain
country opposite the holy city of Shechem. The Israelites
14 splattered the blood of their enemy all over the place. The
blood flowed down from that mount like water, and the
name of that place has been called "the route of the unclean
blood" until this day.

§13

1 After this, the righteous King Baba Rabbah and all the
elders of the people came and prostrated themselves to the
ground before the Lord their God, and prayed thus:
2 'We will give thanks unto you, O Lord, with all our
strength. In praise we will proclaim the Lord as the Rock of
3 our Salvation, our shield, our Deliverer. From our enemies
4 we were delivered. The death pangs surrounded us as the
5 torrents of destruction overwhelmed us. The bonds of Sheol
tightened about us and the snares of death were set to catch
6 us. In our anguish we called to the Lord, and cried out to
our God; and the Lord heard our voice and the sound of
7 our cries. The earth shook and the foundations of the
8 mountains quaked and shook by reason of His anger. A
burning fire was kindled in His nostrils as He swept aside
the heavens and descended. He let loose His arrows against

our adversaries and scattered them, many lightning shafts
9 with which He terrified them. He saved us from our enemies
and adversaries when they were too strong for us; He
brought us out into an open place and delivered us, for He
10 delighted in us. The Lord will bestow lovingkindness upon
us according to the abundance of His own lovingkindness,
and we will be wholehearted towards Him and preserve
11 ourselves from iniquity. For, with the loyal He shows Himself
loyal and with the blameless man blameless; with the pure He
shows Himself pure and with the perverse He shows Himself
tortuous. With the humble He is a saviour, but the haughty-
12 eyed He casts down. He will light our lamps and banish
13 our darkness. For by You we have crushed an army and leaped
14 over a wall. The ways of the Lord are perfect and His word is
15 righteous. He is a shield to all who trust in Him. What God is
there but the Lord? What Rock is there but our God?

16 We will disperse our enemies and overtake them, and we
will not return until we will have made an end of them.
17 Though they cry, no saviour will save them. We will pound
them finer than dust before the wind; we will cast them out
18 like the earthenware sherd. You will deliver us from the
clamour of the peoples, and will make us masters of the
19 nations. Nations we never knew shall be our subjects; as soon
as they hear the report of us they shall obey us. Foreigners
shall come cringing to us, strangers shall fall and emerge
20 from their chambers. Our God, the Lord, lives and our Rock
21 is blessed. The God who saves us is exalted. The Lord, who
grants us vengeance and makes the peoples to wilt away
22 before us so that we tread upon their backs, grants us deliverance from our enemies, even from all who rise up against
23 us. He redeems us from violent men. Therefore we will praise
You among the nations, O Lord, and sing to Your name with all
24 our strength, even to the One who gives us victory and keeps
faith with the son of His beloved ones.'

§14

1 At that time, the Chaldean king decided to wage war against King Alexander. In the ensuing battle between them, the Chaldean king took cities from the King (Alexander). For this reason he was prevented from fighting against the righteous King Baba Rabbah.

2 At that time, the Arabs, sons of Ishmael, came to the city
3 of (Da'riah), plundered it and destroyed it. This was a large
city in which many of the Samaritan-Israelite community lived.
4 The righteous King Baba Rabbah heard of their coming and
he went to meet them. He smote them, disintegrated them and
pursued them to the other side of the Jordan, slaying
5 innumerable of their men. The Samaritan-Israelites plundered
the Arabs of their flocks of sheep and cattle as well as their
garments, silver, gold, and weapons too numerous to count.
6 Then the kings got to hear that the righteous king, the
Priest Baba Rabbah, had gone forth to meet the Arabs, sons
of Ishmael, in battle and had smote them, disintegrated
them and pursued them beyond the Jordan. Those very
Arabs had acted as thieves, highway robbers and bandits,
waylaying horses, conducting themselves with arrogance,
doing anything they pleased, their dominion being so strong
at that time. For that reason, all the kings were glad and
7 rejoiced. They sent to the righteous King Baba Rabbah food
and provisions, enough for ten thousand of his army. They
also sent him silver, gold and robes. They communicated
with him, praising him for the act that he had performed
against the Arabs.
8 Then the righteous King Baba Rabbah sang this song to
9 the Lord, saying thus: 'I will sing to You, O Lord my God,
10 my strength and my song. I will glorify and exalt You. The
11 Lord is mighty in war; Lord is His name. The king rejoices
in Your exaltedness, O Lord; how shall he not delight in
12 Your victory? Your right hand, O Lord, is glorious in
stength; Your right hand, O Lord, has shattered the enemy.
13 For You have given me my heart's desire, and You have not
14 refused me anything I asked. For You welcomed me with
goodly blessings, You have set upon my head a wreath of
15 lovingkindness. Who is like You among the mighty ones,
Lord? Who is like You, majestic in holiness, worthy of awe
16 and praise, who works wonders? Your salvation has brought
me great glory; You have invested me with majesty and
17 honour. The king puts his trust in the Lord; the loving care
18 of the Most High holds him unshaken. Your hand shall
19 reach all Your enemies; You will shatter all Your foes. Your
hand will exterminate their offspring from the earth, and rid
20 mankind of their posterity. Be exalted, Lord, in Your might;
we will sing, praise and exalt Your power.'
21 Then the righteous King Baba Rabbah summoned the elders

of the people, its leaders and officers. When they came to him,
he addressed them thus:
22 'Now we are obliged to offer song, praises and thanksgiving
in abundance to our God and the God of our fathers, who has
dealt righteously with us in His superabundant lovingkindness,
has saved us by this victory, has delivered our enemies into our
hand and has shattered those who came to take us and our
children and our wives into captivity. The Lord has given them
into our hand and we have taken all their cattle and all their
possessions.
23 Now our enemies know that it is from the Lord our God
that this victory of ours has come. For we have crushed
them, and by reason of this they have sent us fine gifts and
24 have honoured us in this splendid way. This came about
only by reason of the lovingkindness of our God, our Shelter
and our Lord, towards us. He who made our enemies fail
before us and endowed us with this great glory. For,
although we were too weary to rise up against them, fearful
25 of their violence and overcome by their might, now God has
fulfilled for us what He expressly stated through the Master
of the Prophets, the son of 'Amram our teacher, in our
books of the Holy Law: 'Though your enemies dwindle away
before you, you shall tread upon their backs.'

§15

1 After this, the honourable king, the Priest Baba Rabbah
2 assembled all his people before him, and spoke thus: 'Return
now in peace, every man to his city and to his place. If, at
any time, I shall have need of your services, I shall send and
3 call you. However, let there remain with me three thousand
4 men from among you. Let them be stationed near me, at all
times let me find them standing by me. Let them dwell in
the villages around the city of 'Amartah where I live; let
them not be distant from me.
5 This pleased the elders of the Samaritan-Israelites, their
chiefs and officers, and they answered thus: 'The thing
6 which you have suggested to do is good.' They therefore did
as he had commanded them, and stationed three thousand
warriors in the villages which were around the city of
7 'Amartah. The righteous king, the Priest Baba Rabbah, then
blessed all his people, and each man returned to his place

with great rejoicing and peace of mind, praising the Lord their God, may His great name be blessed, with songs.

8 The Elders of the Samaritan-Israelite community would come in from the towns near to the holy city of Shechem every night of 'Ḥadah' — at the beginning of every week — and assemble with the Elders of that city and go together to the city of 'Amartah in order to congregate with the righteous King Baba Rabbah, may the favour and forgiveness of the Lord be upon him, Amen.

9 It was at that time, when the whole Samaritan-Israelite community enjoyed honour, glory and abundant strength, that they would rejoice and be glad in the revelation of their faith; for the Lord — may His name be blessed — had removed from them the violence of the enemy. At that time, when each man camped side by side with his neighbour, the Samaritan-Israelite community would assemble at the Hall of Assembly every night of 'Ḥadah' with abundant rejoicing. This custom has remained operative among them to this day.

10 The righteous King Baba Rabbah, may the favour of the Lord be upon him, Amen, — as for the place which bore his name, it was not customary to open it except by permission of the priests. It then remained (open) for just one day.

11 Some time later King Alexander died. That king, in his
latter days, had not been able to wage war against the
Samaritan-Israelite community, for the Lord, may His name
be blessed, had imposed upon him the dread, fear and awe
12 of them. The kings at that time were too feeble to levy a tax
upon the Samaritan-Israelite community, neither could they
wage war against them. They sent a message to summon the
13 elders and leaders of the Judaean community, as follows: 'If
you succeed in smiting the righteous King Baba Rabbah and
defeating him, we will give you authority to build your
14 Temple which is in the city of Jerusalem. The Elders of the
Judaean community then assembled and discussed with each
other the following question: 'How shall we proceed against
King Baba Rabbah so that we may be able to defeat him and
15 build our Temple?' Some men of them took the view thus:
'Why should we requite Baba Rabbah evil for good? For,
since the kingdom of Baba Rabbah has flourished, all the
burdens and troubles imposed by those kings has been
16 removed from us, and they were unable to do us harm. Now, if
we proceed against King Baba Rabbah and do not achieve our
objective, we will have been responsible for bringing upon

ourselves much harm from Baba Rabbah and all his people, the community of Samaritan-Israelites. We will then become the enemies of King Baba Rabbah, as well as of all the kings of the nations.'

17 Others among them took this view: 'Indeed, we shall succeed in inflicting harm upon King Baba Rabbah and smiting him. Let us attack him and not desist, perchance we may build our Temple. Do you not know, brethren, that King Baba Rabbah and all his people of the Samaritan-Israelite community will prevent us from bulding our Temple, and will tell us that the city of Jerusalem is neither the holy city nor the chosen place. On the contrary, they will say that the chosen place is Mount Gerizim Beth-El.'

18 However, the thoughts of the righteous King Baba Rabbah were not these. His sole intention was to manifest the faith in the holy law of Moses, to multiply hymns and praise to the God of heaven and earth — may His holy name be blessed — to base everything upon the reading of the holy Law and to carry out its precepts and laws with faithfulness.

19 At that time there were a number of men of the Judaean community, living in the town of Nemarah. Some of the Judaean Elders came to that town and took secret counsel among themselves in order to direct their attention to the slaying of the righteous King Baba Rabbah, in reward for which they would obtain from the foreign kings permission to build their Temple in the city of Jerusalem.

§16

1 At that time, the righteous king, the Priest Baba Rabbah went to the town of Nemarah. His visit took place on the sixth day of the week, so that he could observe the Sabbath
2 at that town, as was his custom, spending the whole of the Sabbath day in the Synagogue. For, whatever place Baba Rabbah came to he would enter the Synagogue on Sabbath eve and would not depart from it until the conclusion of the Sabbath.

3 Now the plan of the Judaeans was to attack the righteous King Baba Rabbah and all his men on the Sabbath eve; for at that time the Samaritan-Israelite community would be unable to take up arms. They would then attack them inside the Synagogue while they were standing in prayer, and destroy them there.

4 But the Lord, may his name be blessed, did not want them
to achieve their purpose, for in His wisdom He disclosed their
secret plot on the fifth day of the week, before the arrival of
5 King Baba Rabbah to the town of Nemarah, which was on the
(eve of the) seventh day of the week. The Lord, sanctified be
His name, disclosed the secret plot of the Judaean community
on the fifth day of the week to the community of Samaritan-
Israelites.

6 Its revelation took place in this manner: A Judaean
woman had a friend among the Samaritan-Israelite women.
Because of the great love that existed between the Israelite
women and the Judaean woman, on the fifth day of that
week the Judaean woman said to her sister, the Israelite, 'My
sister, I beg of you not to go on Sabbath eve to the synagogue.'

7 The Israelite woman replied thus to her Judaean sister:
'Why, my sister, would you hold me back from attending the
8 Synagogue? What is your motive?' The Judaean woman
replied, 'Why do you urge me to tell you the reason now? I
am greatly afraid, for as soon as I reveal to you the reason,
you will disclose all that I have uttered, and I will bring great
suffering and punishment upon myself.'

9 The Israelite woman answered thus: 'If you will tell me
the reason, I will not disclose it to anyone, as you command,
my sister.'

10 So the Judaean woman spoke up, saying, 'Be aware, my
11 sister, that the Judaeans have plotted to strike King Baba
Rabbah and all his men on the eve of the Sabbath. While
they are standing in prayer they will come upon them
12 stealthily and smite them there. Now that I have told you, I
beg you to keep it a secret and not to speak of it.'

13 Now when the Israelite woman of the Samaritan-Israelite
community heard this report from her Judaean friend, her
14 face became tense with zeal. She went quickly to the
righteous King Baba Rabbah and told him of the matter. She
did not mention, however, the name of the Judaean woman,
as she had promised her.

15 When the righteous King Baba Rabbah heard these things
16 he was most angry with the Judaean community. He had it
disclosed to them that he would spend the night of the
17 Sabbath in the Synagogue, from Friday. In the evening King
Baba Rabbah arrived at the Synagogue, dressed in linen
garments. When, at sunset, it grew dark, the righteous King
Baba Rabbah took off the linen garments which were the

dress for the holy Sabbath, and slipped out of the Synagogue
without anyone knowing that he had left.
18 At sunrise, an innumerable crowd of Judaeans assembled
and came to the Synagogue. They searched thoroughly there
for the righteous King Baba Rabbah, for he was the one they
19 wanted. They shut the doors and set it on fire, for they were
sure that the King Baba Rabbah was in the Synagogue.
20 When the King Baba Rabbah, may the favour of the Lord
and His forgiveness be upon him, Amen, observed this deed
of the Judaeans, he cried out against them in a loud voice.
All his men also cried out in unison, 'What have you been up
to, and what is your intention?'
21 The Judaeans were terrified at the sound of their shouting,
for it was very great. Fear and trembling overcame them, they
were in trepidation, terror overtook them and all their hearts
melted. They threw away their weapons from their hands and
fled before the righteous King Baba Rabbah and his men. Baba
22 Rabbah and his men went out. His men pursued them,
overtook them and brought them back to the righteous king,
the Priest Baba Rabbah. Some of the men drew near and,
23 falling before him to the ground, they addressed him thus: 'We
beg you, our lord, let us be your servants. We have sinned
against the Lord your God and against you in seeking your life,
though you did us no evil; only good you have done for us.
Indeed, you are the cause of the removal of the iron yoke from
upon us, which was imposed by the foreign kings.'
24 The righteous King Baba Rabbah issued a command to his
men, and they seized them all. He said to them, 'Why have
you requited good with evil? Did you not know that my sole
intention was to strengthen the faith of the religion of Israel
and to remove the violence of all the kings from upon you
25 — those with whom you have waged many wars. Now the
Lord has given them all into my hands and I have taken all
the tribes of Israel from beneath their grasp, so that they
might manifest the faith of Israel, sing praises and songs to
the Lord their God, pray and read in the book of the Holy
Law of Moses in a loud voice, with none to prevent them,
26 having been hitherto unable to do so. Notwithstanding this,
you have come against me to shed my blood and to burn me
27 and all my brethren in fire. Woe to you; woe to you. Did you
not know that the Lord would give you into my hand? Now
you shall have no deliverance.'
28 King Baba Rabbah issued the command and they removed

the Judaeans from his presence and put them under guard
until after the Sabbath. They then set them before him so
that he might pass a just sentence upon them.
29 Baba Rabbah said, 'I have no obligation to spare you alive
after you have sought my life and the lives of my men, to kill
us on the night of the holy Sabbath when we were standing
in prayer, singing praises, magnifying and extolling the Lord
our God and the God of our fathers.'
30 Thereupon he slew them and burned them in fire, doing
just as the Lord had commanded in His Holy Law, (as it
says), "And you shall do unto him as he had intended to do
to his brother." He also confiscated from the Judaeans the
31 hill opposite the tower. He slew the inhabitants of it. No one
remained, neither man or woman, except the woman who
had disclosed the matter to her Israelite friend. For she had
sought the protection of her Israelite friend and entered the
Samaritan-Israelite community. For she feared for her life
32 from the Judaean Community. The righteous king, the Priest
Baba Rabbah, sent a message to her friend, summoning that
woman, and he dealt well with her.

§17

1 After this, all the Judaeans heard what the righteous King
Baba Rabbah had done to their Judaean brethren, inhabitants
of the town of Nemarah. Some of them went and burned all
2 the crops of the Samaritan-Israelites' fields. When King Baba
Rabbah heard, he went out after them with all his men and
smote them, leaving but a small remnant of them.
3 When King Gordianus heard of the action that they had
taken against the Samaritan-Israelite community and against
the Priest Baba Rabbah, he issued an edict that their Temple
should be built in the city of Jerusalem. He sought, thereby,
to foster enmity between the Judaean and the Samaritan-
Israelite communities, so that strife should exist between
them.
4 Now the righteous King Baba Rabbah had not prevented
the Judaeans from building their Temple in the city of Jerusalem; but when the Judaean community assembled together
all the materials of the house that were required for the
building, at the very moment that they wanted to begin it, the
5 Lord produced a great sign from heaven. This was the sign: a

very great whirlwind carried away all that the Judaeans had
prepared and gathered together, and scattered it over the
6 surface of the whole land. The Judaean community consequently ceased to build their Temple. Afterwards, (the site of) this
house left the possession of the Judaeans, until this day, so that
they were unable to build it.

7 Then Baba Rabbah and the Samaritan-Israelites sang this
8 song to the Lord: 'To You, Lord, do we lift up our hands.
9 In You we trust, O our God, therefore let us not be ashamed,
neither let our enemies exult over us. Those that wait for You
shall not be rent, but those that deal treacherously with us
10 shall be rent. Make known to us Your ways, O our God.
11 Make us to understand Your paths. Guide us by Your truth
12 and teach us, for You are the God of our salvation. Your
mercy and lovingkindness are of old; the rememberance of
13 them is with us now. Turn not to our stubbornness and
wickedness; for the sake of Your goodness, O Lord, remember
14 us according to Your lovingkindness. You are righteous and
15 upright, but we are perpetrators of sin. All the ways of the Lord
are lovingkindness and truth for those who observe His statutes
16 and commandments. For the sake of the holiness of Your holy
name, O Lord, make expiation for our iniquity. Who is that man
17 who fears the Lord? He will guide him to the way of His
18 choosing. His soul shall abide in goodness and his seed shall
19 inherit the earth. The Lord's counsel is with them that fear Him,
and His covenant is with them that preserve the truth and
declare His holiness.

20 Sing unto the Lord, you who are the Lord's children.
Ascribe glory and strength to the Lord, our God; ascribe
21 greatness to the Lord our God. Worship the Lord on Mount
Gerizim, his holy Mountain. To any other than it you may
22 not turn. The Lord will grant strength to His Samaritan
people with peace'.

§18

1 When the hand of the Edomite kings came down heavily
against the righteous Priest Baba Rabbah, may the favour of
the Lord and His forgiveness be upon Him, Amen, he
summoned to him all the elders of his people, members of
the Samaritan-Israelite community, and spoke to them thus:
2 'I have well determined to do this thing which I shall now

tell you, that it may be well. It is my desire to send Levi, the
son of my brother, to the cities of the Romans, to work
among them. He should present himself as one of them, and
3 acquaint himself with every custom of their Faith. Let him
repair to some place and pose as an Elder — since they
know not his origin nor what he is about. The purpose of
this is that he might ascend Mount Gerizim Beth-El, the
Chosen Place, and direct all his effort to breaking down the
4 bird that is situated there. If he does so, we will be able to go up
to Mount Gerizim Beth-El and seek the Lord our God, whose
name is sancified upon it. Perhaps He will accept us and deliver
5 our enemies into our hands'. (For there was situated on that
holy Mountain, Mount Gerizim Beth-El, a bird, like a dove,
used for the performance of divination and sorcery by the
6 Roman sorcerers. That bird was made of brass, but to any
Israelite coming up to Mount Gerizim Beth-El the bird which
they had made would call out *'Ibrîyôs.* When the Romans used
to hear the call of this bird they would arise, search for the
Israelite person until they apprehended him with a view to
slaying him, which they invariably did. For this reason the
Samaritan-Israelite community was unable to ascend Mount
Gerizim Beth-El.)

7 Now when the Elders of the people and its officers heard
this from the righteous king, the Priest Baba Rabbah, they
replied together, 'Our lord, do according to what is right in
your sight; for whatever you command us we will hear and
obey.'

8 Baba Rabbah answered them thus, 'If you desire to do this
thing, deliver to me the signatures of your hand, so that
after the son of my brother is brought back from there, you
will not deal abhorrently by refusing to accept him back to
9 the religion which he has today.' They did as he commanded
them, and gave him the signature of their hands.

10 After this, Baba Rabbah had Levi, the son of his brother,
brought to him. He assembled all the Elders of the people,
its leaders and officers, commanding the son of his brother
11 in their presence, in these words: 'Nephew, know that it is
necessary for us to send you to the cities of the Romans,
those heretical Baal worshippers and perpetrators of abomina-
tions, who walk on the evil path. Be on your guard lest you be
ensnared into following them; and direct your mind to
studying every single aspect of their belief.

12 Nephew, take heed to observe the practice of your own

Faith, and do not deviate from this good way, that through it
you may live out your full life and your after-life.
13 Nephew, take heed lest you neglect the regular daily and
14 nightly reading of the holy Law. Nephew, rouse yourself to
observe all the statutes and commandments of this Law.
15 Nephew, be on your guard lest that which proceeds from
your own desire entices you. At all times remember all that
the Lord your God created you for, and the abundant
goodness that you receive thereby throughout your life and
16 after-life. May the Lord, His name be sanctified, be your
support in all the deeds that we will require you to perform'.
17 He then disclosed to him what he must do there and Baba
Rabbah sent away his nephew Levi and many Elders of the
people. They returned to their places, and Levi set out,
making for the city of Constantina.
18 Now Levi was a man of perception and wise knowledge, a
19 righteous spokesman among his contemporaries. Whatsoever
he undertook the Lord made to prosper. It was for that
reason that his uncle, the righteous King Baba Rabbah, sent
him to the country of the Edomites, the land of the Romans,
20 with no one to accompany him. Levi was seventeen years old
at the time that he left for the city of Constantina.
21 On arrival at that city he concealed his identity, applied
himself to study and directed all his energy to learning all
Roman customs. He attained his objective within ten years,
so much so that he became unique among the Romans.
There was not to be found among them any man as
knowledgeable as he in the practices and general affairs of the
22 Romans. His rank gradually rose among them until he attained
the highest rank. They accorded him a high station, waited
upon him, invoked him for a blessing, kissed his hand at all
23 times and, because of the volume of wisdom he revealed to
them, they called his name 'Great Skopos'. He was given the
highest rank, so that not one Roman king could ascend his
royal throne except on his authority. It was he who invested
them with their kingly crown and robes.

§19

1 Thirteen years after Levi had departed — he was now
thirty years of age — he said to the chief Roman king, 'It is
my desire to go to the land of Palestine, to the city of
Shechem which is in that country, in order to see the

2 Synagogues there.' The king thereupon directed all the
soldiers in the province of Constantina to accompany Levi.
3 He set out, leaving the province of Constantina. There went
with him all the leaders of the Roman people, their officers,
some of the kings and all the army, in order to wait upon
him and do whatever he would command them.

4 He set out with an innumerable entourage. When Levi
and all who were with him approached the holy city of
Shechem, the senior king who was with him isued an order
to all nations, saying, 'Arise and come forth, all of you, to
meet the great 'Skopos' who is with me.'

5 When the righteous King Baba Rabbah heard this he was
very afraid and distressed. He summoned to him all the
Elders of the Samaritan-Israelite community, and all their
6 heads and officers, and spoke to them thus: 'We did not act
sensibly in sending Levi, my nephew, to the land of the
Edomites; for, during these thirteen years, since he left until
this day, we have heard no report of him or what he has
been doing in that land. Will not my heart fail if that
7 nephew of mine dies in the Edomite land? Furthermore, I
have heard a report of this 'Skopos' that he is a man of
violence, and that he has come to our land in order to slay
us all. We have no alternative now but to go out and meet
him. We must fear for our lives because of him, lest he
becomes angry with us. With such a large number of Roman
soldiers around him, if he orders them to strike us they will
8 smite the lot of us. Moreover, what can we do about him,
seeing that we are unprepared for battle or for any offensive
action, having no weapons with which to smite the enemy or
defend ourselves against them? Furthermore, with such a
large force at his disposal, if he gives the command to smite
us, they will smite us until we are completely destroyed, for
they are unnumerable.'

9 When all the Elders, leaders and officers heard this they
feared greatly, and spoke thus to the righteous King Baba
Rabbah: 'We trust in the Lord our God, may His name be
sanctified. He will cleave to us and support us, and deliver us
from these wicked people.'

10 Then Levi, Baba Rabbah's nephew, who was called
'Skopos', arrived at the gate of the holy city of Shechem. All
the Samaritan community went out to meet him, with the
11 righteous king, the Priest Baba Rabbah, leading them. When
they approached him he looked closely and saw that it was

his uncle, the Priest Baba Rabbah, with all the Israelite
community with him. Fear was visible on their faces and,
with Phylacteries between their eyes, they were crying out
and addressing goodly greetings to him in a very loud voice.
12 When he heard the sound of their cries, he had compassion
for them.

13 The righteous King Baba Rabbah and all his people did
not recognize him, though he recognized them. For, when
he had departed from them for the land of the Edomites, he
was a lad whose face was hairless and unworn. Having settled
there, he was now thirty years of age, with a very long beard
14 and dressed in garments all of black. Quite apart from this, he
became invested with the highest rank, a rank which no
member of his community ever expected him to attain.

15 Levi turned to the king who was accompanying him and
spoke thus: 'Who are these men, the like of whom I have not
16 seen before in all my travels?' The king answered, saying,
'My lord, these are a rebellious people who call themselves
Samaritan-Israelites. Those are the representatives of the
17 Samaritan community.' He asked further, 'Whom do they
worship?' The answer was given, 'They serve a God whom
no man can see. Regarding Him, they assert that He is the
God of gods, Lord of lords, God of heaven and earth and all
created things.'

18 The 'Skopos' then demanded, 'Why do they not worship
the idols and Baals and forsake their own belief which we
have not authorised?'

19 The king answered, 'Indeed, my lord, we have already
spoken to you at great length abouth this matter. Regularly,
up to the present day, we have demanded that they do this,
but they have not listened to us, neither have they worshipped
the Baals or idols. They have not desisted from calling upon
their own God as the supreme God and Lord, Creator of all
beings.'

20 The 'Skopos' answered the king thus, 'If they will not
listen to us or do as we command them, and if they will not
forsake their own Faith and serve the Baals as we do, none
21 of them shall remain alive.' (This statement, concerning the
Samaritan-Israelite community, was heard by all — it being
about them that the 'Skopos' had made his statement.)

22 Then the 'Skopos' — who was Levi, nephew of the righteous
King Baba Rabbah — made his way to the Chosen Place,
Mount Gerizim Beth-El, accompanied by the king's ministers.

23 As they approached the top of the mountain the brazen bird,
the object used for divination, cried out *'Ibrîyôs,* as he always
did whenever a member of the Israelite community chanced to
be on that mountain. (This cry of *'Ibrîyôs* is translated into the
holy language as *'Ibhrî bî 'ădônî* ('There is a Hebrew around
me, my lord').)
24 The great 'Skopos', that is Levi, said, 'What is this?' They
answered, 'This bird is of copper; it is an object of divination
which our brethren, the Roman chiefs, have left in this
place, on account of the Samaritan-Israelite community. For
whenever anyone of them comes on to this mountain, it cries
25 out *'Ibrîyôs.* The 'Skopos' replied, 'I see now that it is not
ceasing its cries. Go, look out and search the whole of this
mountain, and if you find a member of the Samaritan-Israelite
community, strike him down so that we may have some rest
from the noise of the cries of this bird.'
26 They sent many men to search out the whole mount for
any Samaritan-Israelites. They went and searched every
27 corner of that mountain but found no Hebrew there. They
came back and told the king and his men, 'We have searched
the whole mountain and found no Hebrew on it.'
28 The 'Skopos' then came to the Synagogue on top of the
mountain and sat down there, with all the Elders and leaders
standing before him. Still, the brazen bird was crying out
'Ibrîyôs in a loud and raucous voice. It did not cease its
crying for one moment during the whole of that night, until
29 the morning. Levi turned to the servants who had searched
the whole mountain and said, 'Have you searched every
corner of this mountain and really not discovered any
Samaritan-Hebrew there?'
30 They answered, 'By God, we have searched every corner
of the mountain, as you commanded us, and we have discovered
no Hebrew child or adult of the Samaritan-Israelite community.'
31 Levi replied, 'Surely this bird has gone mad because its
master is missing. It can no longer serve any purpose other
than to depress our spirit and give us a headache from the
32 noise of its cries. Yesterday we were deprived of sleep.' The
king said to him, 'My lord, what do you wish us to do with
33 it?' 'Break it up,' he replied, 'and throw it away.' They
hurriedly broke up the bird and threw it away as he had
commanded.
34 This happened on the night of the seventh New Moon.

Around the (first) third of the night, about four hours after
the beginning of night, all the officers, elders and leaders, as
well as the king and the men who were with him, all fell
asleep; for he had made them drunk with wine and strong
drink. He (Levi) had, in fact, urged them to drink so much
that they had become drunk and had fallen asleep.

35 When Levi saw that the drinking had taken control of
them, so much so that none of them could distinguish right
from left, and that when he commanded them either to lie
down or rise up, they remained lying down in a very deep
36 sleep, he immediately rose up, sword in hand, and went down
from Mount Gerizim Beth-El to seek out his uncle, the
righteous king, the Priest Baba Rabbah, at the town of
'Amartah, for he knew that his uncle's residence was there.

37 When the righteous King Baba Rabbah got to hear of the
instruction issued by the 'Great Skopos', his nephew, Levi, he
assembled all the heads and Elders of the Samaritan-Israelite
38 community at the town of 'Amartah. They were all faint-
hearted, fearful and confused, not knowing how they should
act towards this man, the 'Skopos', so that he might desist
from attacking them and find a way to obtain his sympathy,
and thereby escape his punishment.

39 In the moment of their confusion over this matter, Levi
stood at the door and knocked lightly. Their fear increased
and their trembling became so intense that not one of them
was able to open the door in order to see who was knocking.

40 The righteous King Baba Rabbah himself rose up, where-
upon all the princes rose with him, and they went to see who
41 was at the door. When they opened the door they took fright,
for the 'Great Skopos' himself was standing at the door. They
were unable to talk to him, so terrified were they the moment
42 they saw him. Levi hurried, however, and fell at the feet of his
uncle, the righteous king, the Priest Baba Rabbah, and kissed
them. He took his hands in his own and kissed them; and,
falling about his neck, he wept, saying, in the holy language of
43 the Hebrew tongue, 'Now I can die, having seen you again, that
44 you are still alive.' The righteous King Baba Rabbah was now
sure that the 'Great Skopos' was Levi, his nephew.

45 At that time there was the sound of great celebration in
that place, among Baba Rabbah and all those assembled there
46 of the Samaritan-Israelite community. Baba Rabbah then took
his nephew's hand and led him into an inner place. Seating him
47 at his right hand, Baba Rabbah started to ask his nephew about

all that he had done during the period of his exile in the land
48 of the Romans. Levi, the 'Great Skopos,' related to Baba
Rabbah all the things which he had done, in the hearing of all
who were gathered there. Their rejoicing knew no bounds,
and they sang praises and songs of thanksgiving in a great and
loud voice to the Lord who had delivered them from every
49 disaster and retribution.

When Levi had finished addressing his uncle Baba Rabbah,
he added the following: 'Tomorrow night, in the middle of the
50 night, mobilise sword-bearing men. Let them stay close to me
and observe my orders. For, when the enemy falls asleep, I will
quickly rise up and strike their necks with the sword, in
revenge for the Lord, may His name be sanctified. We will
smite them, destroy them and blot out their name from under
the heaven. May help from the Lord our God attend us, and
may He deliver us from their evil.'

51 Thus it happened that Levi rose up and ascended the
mountain quickly, discovering all the Romans asleep and
quite unaware that he had ever left the mountain or returned
52 to its summit. (Now this took place on the night of the
termination of the festival of the seventh month, or, to be more
exact, the night of the termination of the festival of the Eighth
Day of Solemn Assembly.)

53 The righteous King Baba Rabbah then sent a message to
all the cities round about him, wherein men of the
54 community of Samaritan-Israelites lived, in which he said,
'Be equipped and armed for war, and be ready at midnight.
When you see the flame of fire on the top of the hill which is
on top of the Chosen Place, Mount Gerizim Beth-El, then
smite the leaders and officials appointed over you by the
55 Romans. Leave no remnant of them, but destroy every one
of their officials, as well as all those who might prevent you
from consolidating your Faith. Smite with the sword all those
around you until they are destroyed, so that you may reach
your brethren and assemble, all of you together, in the plain
of Moreh, which is next to the Chosen Place, Mount Gerizim
Beth-El.'

56 So it was that about midnight the whole army of the
righteous King Baba Rabbah, may the favour and forgiveness
of God be upon him, assembled in their hosts. They all
57 ascended the holy Mountain, Mount Gerizim Beth-El, with the
righteous King, the Priest Baba Rabbah leading them. There
was but a spear's throw between them and the summit of the

Mount of Blessing, Mount Gerizim Beth-El, when Levi realised
58 how close they were to him. He rose up with great zeal, sword
in hand, armed with divine aid, sanctified be His name, and he
pierced with his sword the king, his men and all the Elders who
were to be found on that mountain.

59 Then Levi cried out in a loud voice: 'The Lord is mighty
60 in war; Lord is His name.' When the Samaritan-Israelite
community heard their cries, they also cried out in unison,
'The Lord is mighty in war; Lord is His name.'

61 The whole earth trembled at the sound of their shouting.
At that moment not a beast in the field remained crouching
in its lair. On hearing the noise of the people, they all fled at
the sound, saying, 'Such sounds we have never ever heard
before.'

62 After that, Levi and his uncle, the righteous King Baba
Rabbah, and all the men who were with him, arose and
kindled a fire on the top of the hill which was the summit of
the Mountain of Inheritance, Mount Gerizim Beth-El, so that
the whole community of Samaritan-Israelites, who dwelt in
the cities, might see it and do all that the rightous King Baba
63 Rabbah had commanded them. When all the people living in
the cities, the settlements and other places saw the flames of
fire, they arose and smote all the leaders and officers who had
been appointed over them by the Roman community, allowing
none to remain.

64 The Israelite community arose that night and overthrew
all the Roman meeting-houses and all their posts, blotting
out their name from the Mountain of the Divine Presence,
65 Mount Gerizim Beth-El. From the day the Samaritan-Israelite
community did this to the Romans, Samaritan children have
set fire to the wood of their Succah-booths on the night of the
termination of the festival of the Eighth Day of Solemn
Assembly, which concludes the festivals of the Lord. This
episode has thus remained a memorial among them unto this
day.

Lord. This episode has thus remained a memorial among
them unto this day.

66 Then the righteous King Baba Rabbah and all the Elders
of the people sang this song:

67/68 'The Lord our God is our shepherd, we shall not want. To
the Lord is the earth and the fullness thereof, the Divine
69 Presence and all that dwell therein. For he founded it upon
70 the seas and established it upon the rivers. To You, O Lord

71 our God, will we lift up our face; in You we have trusted,
and You did not let us down. Therefore our enemies have
72 not derided us. All who wait for You will suffer no violence;
but they that deal treacherously without cause will suffer
73 violence. The Lord is our salvation, whom shall we fear? In
the Lord's hand is the life of our souls, of what shall we be
74 afraid? For when the wicked approached to devour our
flesh, our adversaries and enemies all stumbled and fell.
75 Though a great host should encamp against us, our heart
will not fear. Though war should arise against us, we will not
tremble; for He is our deliverer.

76 One request of the Lord we have — that will we seek after:
that we may dwell in His place, the Mountain of Blessing, the
Mount of Holiness, the Mount of Inheritance and Divine
Presence, the Chosen Place, Mount Gerizim Beth-El.

77 May our heads be raised high above our enemies around
us, may His will be efficacious and may His habitation be
disclosed to us, that we may offer our sacrifices upon His
78 altar. Then will we see it established, though not yet; then
we will behold it, though not soon. A star shall come forth
out of Jacob, a comet shall arise from Israel. He shall smite
the heads of Moab and beat down all the sons of strife.
79 Edom shall be his conquest, after which Israel will do valiant
80 deeds. Blessed be our God forever, and blessed be His name
forever and ever.'

§20

1 After these events, when the Roman inhabitants of the cities
that had been saved got to hear of all that the Samaritan-
Israelite community had perpetrated against their men, they
2 became inflamed with a great fury. They assembled together
innumerable men to seek out the righteous King Baba Rabbah
3 and all his Samaritan people. When Baba Rabbah was
informed about them he did not flee from his place until they
4 had reached the neighbourhood of the holy city of Shechem.
Then Baba Rabbah made haste and went to meet them at that
5 place, engaging them in war. The Lord gave them into his
hand, and he smote many of their men. The rest fled before
6 him. He pursued after them a day's journey before returning
to his place, singing and praising the Lord his God, may His
name be blessed forever and ever.

7 When this was later related to the king of Rome and to all
his people, the Roman inhabitants of the cities which were
saved, they waged war against the righteous King Baba
Rabbah. The latter and all his people defeated them, and those
that were left fled before them. They pursued after them a
day's journey, and they could not count how many Romans
8 they slew, for there were so many. When the Roman king got
to hear of it, and what the righteous King Baba Rabbah and his
people had done to the men who had been saved, he grew very
9 furious and full of rage. He sent word that an innumerable
body of men be gathered together and he sent them into battle
against the righteous King Baba Rabbah and his Samaritan
people.
10 When Baba Rabbah heard of their coming, he went out to
11 meet them and war broke out between them. He prayed to
the Lord thus:
'Lord God, as You have previously dealt with me, so now
give these wicked men into my hands.'
12 And the Lord accepted his entreaty and gave them over into
his hand. The war between the army of the righteous King
Baba Rabbah and the Roman army took place in the city of
'Askor. The Lord gave them over into the power of the
Samaritan army and they trounced them, only a small number
13 being spared. These hastily fled before the Samaritan-Israelite
community and went straight to their own kings, telling them
all that the righteous King Baba Rabbah and his Samaritan
14 people had done to them. They said to them, 'They gave us a
good trouncing, but we saw no one slain among them.'
15 The Roman kings were enraged against the righteous
king, the Priest Baba Rabbah, and against all his Samaritan
16 people. They hastily assembled a vast army, so vast that it
17 could not be numbered. It was reported to the King Baba
Rabbah thus: 'Know that a vast army of Roman kings is
marching against you in their thousands and tens of
18 thousands. King Baba Rabbah assembled all the Elders,
heads and leaders of his people and disclosed this to them.
19 They wrote letters, which they issued to all the cities of the
Samaritan-Israelite community, telling them of the approach
of a Roman army of innumerable proportions to fight against
20 the Samaritan-Israelite community. They therefore sent all
their warriors to them, and they all assembled in the city of
King Baba Rabbah, the city of 'Amartah. They numbered ten
thousand men, all bearing arms, between twenty and forty

21 years of age. Baba Rabbah billeted them in the cities around
the city of ʻAmartah.
22 A herald then came and told King Baba Rabbah: ʻKnow
that your enemies are upon you in innumerable strength.'
23 The righteous King Baba Rabbah was frightened and sorely
distressed. He entreated the Lord in this prayer, facing the
Chosen Place, Mount Gerizim Beth-El, saying:
24 ʻO Lord God, in You we have trusted; fail us not, but in
25 Your righteousness deliver us. O Existing One, deliver me
speedily from this oppression, and be to me and to all my
congregation as a Rock. Deliver them and deliver me, for
26 You are my Rock, my proud sword and my shield. Lead me
in the counsel of Your holy name and guide me. O my God,
extricate me and all my people from the net which our
27 enemies have laid for us. For You are a Rock, and into Your
hand do we commit our spirits. You have redeemed us, O
God, compassionate and gracious, long-suffering, abundantly
28 constant and true, our God, from our enemies who observe
what is sheer vanity. But we have trusted in You; we rejoice
29 in your constancy. For You take notice of our lowliness, and
30 do not surrender us into the hand of an enemy. You, who
have established us, take pity on us. Take pity on us, You
who have established us. For we are in distress, for the days
of our life, and that of our fathers before us, have ended in
31 grief. By reason of our sins our strength has failed and our
32 bones melt away. We have become a reproach to all our
enemies. We are forgotten out of mind, like the dead, and
33 have become like a worthless vessel. Yet in You do we put
our trust, for You are our God and the God of our fathers.
34 In Your hand is our spirit; O deliver us from the hand of
35 our enemies and persecutors. Cause Your face to shine
36 towards us and save us with kindness. O Lord, we will not be
ashamed, for we have prayed to You, and, according to
37 Your will, our enemies shall lie down in Sheol. O how great
is Your goodness, Lord, which You have stored up for those
38 that fear You. This You will do to confirm Your salvation.
You will hide them in Your secret place; You will hide them
from the wrath of the wicked, even in booths, from the
39 enmity of sinners. Blessed is the Lord, who has made us
40 pre-eminent over all peoples. Love the Lord, you sons of His
loved ones, the faithful whom the Lord preserves because
41 they walked in His ways. Let your hearts be strong and
courageous, all you who walk on the path of His laws.'

§21

1 When King Baba Rabbah had completed his prayer and
his convocation, he went to a spot near the battlefield —
knowing that the battle between him and his enemies would
be there — and he concealed there some of his soldiers in
2 some tombs. He commanded them thus, 'When you see war
break out between us and our enemies at the site of the
battle, and I cry out to you in a loud voice, saying, 'O you
who dwell in the tombs, they have routed me and are close
on my trail,' then you shall emerge from the tombs and say,
'Do not fear, we have come to your aid; do not fear.' Then
3 use your swords on all the enemy.' The number of men
whom Baba Rabbah had concealed in the tombs was five
thousand.
4 When King Baba Rabbah and the men of his army
approached the enemy, the priests blew on the trumpets and
all the people raised their voices and cried out in unison,
with a loud voice, 'The Lord is mighty in war; Lord is His
5 name.' The earth shook at the noise of their cry, and the
battle broke out between them and their enemies. It was a
great battle on that day, the like of which had never taken
6 place in those times. Then King Baba Rabbah cried out in a
loud voice from the thick of the battle, saying, 'O you who
dwell in the tombs, they have routed me and are close on my
7 trail.' The Romans fell silent at the sound of the shouting.
The men whom he had hidden among the tombs hurriedly
emerged and said in a loud voice, 'Do not fear Baba Rabbah,
we have come to your aid, all of us. Do not fear Baba
Rabbah, for all the dead will follow us from every side'.
8 When the men of the Roman army saw this, they thought
that it was real. Fear and dread befell them, and they
trembled and fled before King Baba Rabbah and before the
9 men of his army who were with him. The Lord gave them
over on that day into the hand of King Baba Rabbah and he
smote them and pursued them as far as the border of the
territory of the Samaritan-Israelite community.
10 These battles, to which we have previously referred, as
well as this present battle, took place after Levi, nephew of
King Baba Rabbah, had returned from the Roman cities.
11 There were no battles between the Samaritan-Israelite
community and the kings of the Romans prior to Levi's
12 departure to the Roman cities. For Baba Rabbah had sent his

nephew, Levi, to the Roman cities before his purpose was
13 made known. For it was that Levi who broke down the brazen
bird, brought into being by sorcery, as a result of which no
Samaritan-Israelite was able to ascend to the summit of Mount
Gerizim Beth-El, Mountain of Blessing, Chosen Place. For that
bird was perched on the top of that mountain, and if it
detected any Samaritan within the border of the mountain, the
bird would cry out *'Ibrîyôs.*
15 All the battles between Baba Rabbah and the Roman kings
were as a result of the deeds of the righteous King Baba
Rabbah and his nephew, Levi. For they demolished the Roman
meeting-house which was at the summit of the Holy Mountain,
the Mountain of Blessing, the Chosen Place, Mount Gerizim
Beth-El. They smote all the Elders who were there, and all the
Roman leaders who were lording it over the Samaritan-Israelite community, as well as the king who came with Levi
from the city of Costantina.

REST OF FOLIO 438 IS ILLEGIBLE

.... by the hand of the faithful one of his house, the
Master of the Prophets, Moses son of 'Amram, peace be unto
him forever. So that all the Roman kings knew that the King
Baba Rabbah would prevail in war against them, being
strong-hearted and courageous, ready for any battle and
18 unperturbed by their confederacy. For many years he had
waged wars against them, and the Lord had given them all
into his hand.

§22

1 After these events, the king of Costantina saw fit to sue for
peace with the righteous King Baba Rabbah. He besought
him to come to him to the city of Costantina, his royal city.
2 This policy conformed to a plan of the Roman king of the
3 city of Costantina and all the men of his kingdom. It had
three aims: first, they sought to ascertain the strength of
King Baba Rabbah, whether he possessed the ability to wage
greater wars than this (they, themselves, were weary because
of him, and, furthermore, they had heard how he had
driven out the Arab Ishmaelites, pursued them and taken
spoil of all they possessed — their sheep, cattle, camels, asses,
silver, gold and innumerable flocks), or was he, indeed,
unable to wage any more war because he was also tired out?

4 Secondly, they wanted to terminate the enmity between
themselves and the righteous King Baba Rabbah and his
people, the Samaritan-Israelites; for they could no longer
muster men for war at any time against King Baba Rabbah,
for they had many enemies quite apart from the Samaritan
5 community. Thirdly, they said, 'Perhaps we may have
dominion over King Baba Rabbah, who is the cause of all
these wars taking place and the killing of many men in the
ranks of the battle, men who are sent against him.'

6 The name of the king of Costantina at that time was
7 Philip. He and all his men wrote to King Baba Rabbah and
sent emissaries from among the leaders of his kingdom,
carrying in their hands a letter in the King Philip's
8 handwriting. This is what he wrote in that letter: 'Peace be unto
you, my lord, King Baba Rabbah. I request my lord, the great
and honourable King Baba Rabbah, to grant the request of his
servant, the king of Costantina, at this time, and do him the
honour of coming to him to that city to stay with us for a while
that we might see his glory, after which he may return in peace
to his place.'

9 When King Philip's letter, and the heads appointed by the
king, arrived, they delivered it into the hand of King Baba
Rabbah. He read the letter and was cognisant of all these
10 things. King Baba Rabbah then said to the emissaries of
King Philip, 'I am well able to wage war against the king of
Costantina for the whole duration of my life. Also my
Samaritan-Israelite people are innumerable and the men of
11 the army at my disposal are stout-hearted.' The emissaries
were afraid at what they saw of Baba Rabbah's achievements.

12 Then Baba Rabbah assembled all the Elders and heads of
his people, also his father, his son and all his family, and
13 read before them the letter of the king of Costantina. He
related to them his plan, saying, 'It is my intention to go to
14 King Philip, the king of Costantina.' His father, the High Priest
Nethan'ēl, the Elders of the people, its heads and leaders and
all who were assembled, replied, 'For what reason do you
intend to do this? How can you wish to go at this time, leaving
your people behind, like tender children whose father has left
them and forsaken them in a state of confusion, not knowing
what to do; particularly since the Lord, may His name be
sanctified, has made us prosper through you?'

15 The Elders of the people and its leaders approached and
said to him, 'Our master, we beseech your honour not to do

this thing which you have told us, for we are afraid that
after your going we will revert to our former lowly estate,
our oppression, weariness, poverty, distress and incapacitation.
16 For you know that the enmity and hatred between us and the
Romans is now very keen because of the wars in which we have
17 engaged with you, and because of the defeat of their men. We
beseech you, our lord, to stay and not to go far from us or to
cause yourself to leave and abandon us, lest our enemies mock
us?'

18 King Baba Rabbah answered thus, 'No. Listen to me, for I
19 must go now to the city of Costantina. You know full well
that I fulfil my obligations to the Lord alone, may His name
20 be sanctified. Perhaps my journey to the king of Costantina
will be instrumental in removing the hatred that exists
between us and these nations, so that the fire that has raged
between them and us unto this day may be quenched.

21 Now, therefore, do I wish to go to King Philip to make
22 peace with him and to enter into an alliance. My brethren,
do not be oblivious of the fact that this matter has been a
protracted one for us and we are left with no strength to
wage any further war against our enemies; and that, though
the great kings are weary of these wars, we, quite apart from
23 our small number, are unable to withstand these wars. By
the will of God, may His name be blessed, I will soon return
to you. If, however, it transpires that something unforeseen
happens to me, or they sentence me in order to prevent my
return to my home and my land, or they slay me, I will
therefore now give you instructions concerning my son,
24 Levi.' (This refers to Levi, his own son, as distinct from his
nephew, Levi.)

25 They answered him in unison, 'If you desire now to go to
the city of Costantina, as you have said, take with you some
men from among the people to minister to you and serve
you in the land of your enemy, so that they may know your
glory and honour your high status.'

26 King Baba Rabbah answered the leaders of the people
thus, 'I will not do so, for I fear to do something without us
knowing whether its outcome for us will be happy. Rather
that I should alone be involved than many men of our
people.

27 Now, therefore, I give you a command in order that you
may rejoice greatly in this world and live forever in the next
world: You shall observe the commandments of the Lord,

sanctified be His name, that are in His Holy Law, and shall
not cease reading His Holy Law at any time, but shall teach
it to your sons and daughers and to your children's children.
28 Furthermore do I command you that if you will be
courageous and strong, and will not fear, be dismayed or
frightened, then the Lord your God, sanctified be His name,
will not forsake you, fail you or rebuke you; neither will He
break the covenant which He made with your forefathers
and with your great Prophet Moses, son of 'Amram, peace
29 be unto him forever. Also, be on your guard lest your hearts
turn aside from His ways and from observing His statutes
30 and commandments. Know that all that the Lord does to His
people, the Samaritan-Israelites, is but a trial by Him, in
31 order to give them a happy outcome. Happy is he that
observes, and woe to the one who departs from the way of
truth.'

§23

1 When the righteous King Baba Rabbah had finished
commanding his Samaritan people, he took hold of the hand
of Levi, his son — with tears rolling down his cheeks like
2 rain — and brought him right up to his father, the High
Priest Nethan'el. He kissed the hands of his father, saying,
'If it please you, my lord, here is my son Levi; receive him
3 from my hands, for I give you charge of him.' He fell again
before him and kissed his feet, saying, 'I pray you, sir, you
whom the Lord, sanctified be His name, has made the cause
of my very being, look after my son, the fruit of my body,
and be favourable to him at all times.'

4 He then turned to his brother, the priest 'Aqbon, and said
to him, 'My brother, I command you this day concerning my
5 son Levi: Teach him the upright way.' He then turned to all
the Elders of the people and said to them, 'Look after this,
6 my son, until good fortune will attend you.' His statement to
them was along the lines referred to above.

7 The righteous King Baba Rabbah rose early and went with
the emissaries of King Philip, the king of Costantina. All his
brothers, cousins, relatives, members of his family, Elders of
the people, its leaders and chiefs, as well as a large number
of the people, rose and went to the outskirts of the city to
8 send him on his way, before returning to their place. His son
Levi and his brothers, the Priest 'Aqbon and the Priest

Pinḥās, wept. They then sent him on his way, returning to
the city broken-hearted.
9 The righteous King Baba Rabbah travelled until he
reached the border of the environs of the city of Costantina.
One of the emissaries ran hastily and told King Philip of the
arrival of the righteous king, the king of the Samaritan-
10 Israelites, Baba Rabbah. King Philip issued a command,
which they announced publicly among the Roman people:
that they should all come out together to meet the King
11 Baba Rabbah. Shortly afterwards there assembled all the
men of the king's army and all the leaders of the people, all
the Elders and all the people, carrying crucifixes and Baals
in their hands. They came out to meet King Baba Rabbah to
the outskirts of the city, singing their prayers.
12 At that time, all the Roman kings who were his subjects
were present in the city of Costantina. They all went out
13 with King Philip to meet King Baba Rabbah. Now, when
they saw King Baba Rabbah they all alighted from their
chariots, so that not one rider remained in his chariot, apart
14 from King Baba Rabbah. When he made to do as they had
done, and descended from his chariot, they prevented him,
saying, 'No, my lord, we are your servants. We have done
this in order to honour you, for it is fitting that we do so.'
15 That day, of the arrival of the righteous King Baba Rabbah
to the city of Costantina, was a great day for the Romans,
the like of which none of the Roman kings had ever
experienced.

§24

1 Now, when King Baba Rabbah entered the city of
Costantina, having passed the hill, King Philip said to the
heads of his realm, 'Now King Baba Rabbah is in our hands
and under our rule, advise me please what we should do.'
2 Those men were divided into two groups. One group said,
'Let us set upon him and kill him.' The other group said,
3 'That is not a good plan; we should not smite him.' The
latter approached the king, saying, 'You know that Baba
Rabbah is a great king. Before he came to you you knew
this, and you also knew all that he had done, how he had
4 smitten many times the men of our army. Notwithstanding
all this, we swore to him that we would do him no harm.
5 Indeed, he could have succeeded against us. He was not
incapable of withstanding us in battle, but trusted in our firm

promises to him, and therefore did not attack us. He would not
have let himself fall into our hand if he had not known that no
6 mishap would befall him because of us. Now that he has
trusted in our promise and entered under the aegis of our
7 protection, it is not good that we should kill him. If the king
treats him wrongly, it will be a reproach to the king and all his
people. Men will relate this throughout every generation and
will record it in their histories. It will thus remain a bad
8 reproach unto us for all time. However, if the king commands
it, let us have him to remain with us all the days of his life,
never to leave this city. There is no difference between killing
him and shutting him up for the rest of his life in this city, until
9 the day of his death. The king will not be unmindful of the fact
that King Baba Rabbah would prefer us to set upon him and
kill him rather than that he should remain imprisoned among
us in this city.'

10 This plan pleased King Philip, and he summoned the
righteous King Baba Rabbah, may the divine favour and
forgiveness be upon him, Amen, and spoke kindly to him.
He gave him silver and gold, vessels of silver and vessels of
11 gold, vessels of brass and many robes. Then he said to him,
'My lord Baba Rabbah, all my people will wait upon your
every word.'

12 King Philip gave these instructions to all who were in
charge of the gates of the city: 'If King Baba Rabbah seeks
to go outside the city, you shall restrain him and tell him that
no one can go outside the city except with King Philip's
13 permission.' There were officers over the gates of the city of
Costantina, and no one could enter or leave that city unless
by the authority of the king's men.

14 After a long time the righteous King Baba Rabbah approached King Philip saying, 'I heartily desire to return to
my land and birthplace. I therefore now beseech the king to
grant that I may return to my land and my father's house; for I
pine greatly for my father, who is awaiting my return to him and
to my brothers, my son and all my relatives.'

15 King Philip answered the righteous King Baba Rabbah,
saying, 'You will remain with us all the days of your life.'
16 The righteous King Baba Rabbah then realised that King
Philip was indeed imprisoning him, and that he would
subsequently be unable to leave the city of Costantina. The
righteous King Baba Rabbah held his peace and spoke no
more of this matter to the king.

§25

1 When the High Priest Nethan'el got to know that King
Philip had imprisoned his son, the righteous Baba Rabbah,
in the city of Constantina, he sent for his son 'Aqbon and
said to him, 'Give your daughter, Rebecca, in marriage to
2 Levi, your brother Baba Rabbah's son.' He gave her to him
in marriage, as his father had commanded, and he made
festivity in his honour for seven days, according to the
practice of Israelite bridegrooms.
3 After this, the High Priest Nethan'el died and was
gathered unto his people at a ripe old age. May the favour
and forgiveness of the Lord be upon him, Amen.
4 After the death of the High Priest Nethan'el, Levi, the son
of the righteous King Baba Rabbah, pined for his father. So
he went to the city of Costantina and lived with his father
5 for a few days. At that time, the righteous King Baba Rabbah
contracted a serious illness. Baba Rabbah realised that his death
6 was approaching. Now he had a friend, a Jew from among the
Jewish community. So the righteous King Baba Rabbah sent for
him and said to him, 'My brother, place your hand under my
thigh; for I adjure you by the God of heaven and earth, that you
take this, my son, back to my land and birthplace, and hand him
over to his relatives, and that you will not suffer him to become
polluted through uncleanness.'
7 His Jewish friend placed his hand under the thigh of the
righteous King Baba Rabbah and swore to him about this
8 matter. Then Baba Rabbah took the hand of his son Levi, and
handed him into the care of his Jewish friend, saying, 'My
friend, take care not to depart from my instructions which I
9 have commanded you. His Jewish friend replied, 'I will act
according to all the instructions which you have given me.'
The righteous King Baba Rabbah then responded, 'God is
witness between me and you.'
11 After this, the righteous King Baba Rabbah died and was
gathered unto his people, may the favour of the Lord and
12 His forgiveness be upon him, Amen. His son Levi and his
friend, the Jewish man, arose and bathed him, after the law
of the Israelites, and clothed him in shrouds — white
13 garments. The righteous king died in the city of Costantina,
and the day of his death was a special occasion for the
14 inhabitants of the city of Costantina. The king of Costantina
and all his people wept for him, and they went, young and

15 old, after him to bury him. They treated him on that day
exactly as they had done on the day of his arrival at the city
16 of Costantina. They buried him in a spacious and fine
sepulchre, and the Romans later built a Synagogue over his
grave.

IV. COMMENTARY

Note: Phrases followed by an asterisk (after the colon) are from the H2 text.

§1

1. נתן ... שלשה בנים: The employment of this verb, as well as H2's שת, to denote the begetting of children (in contradistinction to the Niph'al /yld) is significant. These verbs are especially employed when it is a *divine* bestowal of offspring that is being emphasized. As examples we may cite Gn 4:25 (šāth zera') and Gn 17:16 (nāthan bēn), where the transitive verbs with divine subject connote the formal conferment of an offspring that is to serve a special divine purpose. (The birth of Seth is stated to be as compensation for the slain Abel, and that of Isaac in order 'to establish my covenant with him, an everlasting covenant, and to his seed after him.'). The employment of these verbs, to describe the gift of three sons to Netan'el, thus assumes an added significance, serving to highlight the specially ordained destiny to which God was calling them as restorers of Samaritan fortunes.

לכהן הגדול נתנאל: This syntactical order, wherein the name of the person follows the defining noun, or the 'noun of nearer definition' (G.K. §131g), is extremely rare in *B.H*, and then 'only in certain combinations' *(Ibid)*, e.g. *ha-melekh š^e^lōmōh; ha-melekh dāvid.*

2 וזאת שמותם:* The fem. demonstrative pronoun *(zō'th)* is preferred, for general use, with either masc. or fem., sing. or pl., nouns (see on 22:22). With masc. nouns it invariably preceeds the noun.

הראש:* 'The first' (H1: *hā'eḥād*). The form *hārō'š* occurs frequently as the ordinal number. *B.H.* added to this basic form the termination *ôn.* The vowel dissimilation which followed the addition of the termination, resulting in the form *ri'šôn,* was preserved in *SH* as *ri'yšôn* (see 9:8*). The ordinal employed by H1 — *hā'eḥād* — is rare in *BH.* 'In such cases as Gn 1:5, 2:11, the meaning of *first* is derived solely from the context' (G.K. §98a).

עקבון: The semantic development of the name *'Aqbôn* is clearly delineated in the genealogical lists of the *Tolidah.* The primitive form of the name appears in a list of twelve princes who accompanied one Ṣaddîq ben Tobhiyyah when he fled to 'Aqrabith after an Arab raid on Mount Gerizim *(Tol.,* ed. Neubauer, 400). The name of the prince was *'Qb,* which is probably a hypocoristicon (for a discussion of biblical hypocoristica, see M. Noth, *Personennanem,* 36–41) for *Ya'ăqōbh.*

The form *'Qb,* appearing there for the first time in Samaritan records, is expanded, about a century later, into the name *'Aqqûbh* (b. 'Amram), whose son was called — by further theophoric expansion — *'Ăqabhyāh.* The latter is said (*Tol.,* 401) to have been taken captive to Babylon by Nebuchadnezzar. It is not without significance, therefore, that the name *'Aqqûbh* appears for the first time in Judaist biblical sources only in the post-exilic period, being restricted to the books of Ezra (2:42), Nehemiah (7:45, 8:7, 11:19) and Chronicles (I Chr. 3:24, 9:17). It is tempting, therefore, to detect Samaritan influence here, in the adoption of the name *'Aqqûbh* by the Judaean community. The same may be said for the name *'Ăqabhyāh*: This 6th cent. B.C. Samaritan name does not occur in Judaistic sources until rabbinic times, with *'Ăqabhyāh b. Mahălal'ēl,* a contemporary of Jesus.

The name *'Aqbôn,* which appears for the first time as the name of a 2nd cent. A.D. Sam. High Priest (Neubauer, *op. cit.,* 403), is a variation of *'Ăqabhyāh,* the theophoric termination being replaced by the common nominal termination *ôn.* The choice of this termination was possibly conditioned by its diminutive function (see *GK* 86g), suggesting an underlying meaning of 'little heel' *('Āqēbh).* This termination is represented in Syriac as *ûn,* thus providing a vocalization of either *'Aqbôn* or *'Aqbûn.* From the first appearance of this name it completely displaced the earlier forms and remained one of the most popular Samaritan priestly names for many centuries. No fewer than eleven High Priests in the genealogical lists of the Tolidah (Neubauer, 403–417) bear the name *'Aqbôn.*

נתנאל: Our Netan'el is the third High Priest to bear this name *(Tol.* 401, 402, 403). It appears predominantly as a post-Exilic levitical or priestly name (see ***BDB. Lexicon,*** 682).

פינחס: He was the father of Levi, who features prominently in our Chronicle as the saviour of the community (see §18–19). Nothing of any significance is reported, however, about Pinḥās.

3. קרית מחנה: Bibl. *Maḥănayim,* 20 mls. E. of Shechem.

.. אשר היא בקצה: Used here not in biblical sense of 'adjoining,' but rather 'in the region of.' The geographical identification is omitted in Abu'l Fatḥ.

4. היה איה: Delete איה as dittography.

איש מוסר: *AF*: 'A man of awe (هَيبَة) and authority.'

ויהי איש מצליח ... בידו: Gn 39:2,3.

5. ותהי עליו רוח: Common idiom, especially in book of Judges (3:10, 11:29, 14:6, 19, 15:14 *et al.*), for imparting warlike energy and executive, or administrative, power (***BDB*, *Lexicon, sub*** **רוח** c. (1).

ומלא אתו .. רוח:* Cf. Ex 28:3, 31:3, 35:31.

ואציל עליו מן רוח:* Cf. Nu 11:17.

6. ויהי בימים ההם ויגדל: Heavy influence of phraseology culled from 'Call' of Moses. Cf. Ex 2:11.

וירא בסבלותם וירא: See previous note. None of this biblical phraseology is represented in H2.

בעל אימה ומשלה:* Hendiadys. This phrase probably inspired *AF*'s rendering 'awe and authority' in v 4.

צפר:* 'Became' (H1: *hāyāh*). Cf. *v*ᵉ*ha-qōšṭ ṣ*ᵉ*phar mithk*ᵉ*bî* (v12).

איש מורם:* 'Distinguished person'. Lit. 'elevated'; cf. Is 2:11, 17.

שנאה אימנותו הכפור':* 'Enemies of His Faith, deniers ..' H2 adopts a more militant attitude toward pagan (and other) enemies of the community. This sentiment is not represented in H1.

7. צרעה: 'Hornet'. Used figuratively of ferocious and destructive forces; cf. Ex 23:28, Josh 24:12. The word is also found in Sam. Theology as the name of an evil spirit or demon, together with *'Ăza'zēl* and *B*ᵉ*liyya'al* (See Ben-Zevi, *Sepher Ha-Šōmrônîm,* 142; Bowman, *Samaritanische Probleme,* 52). This usage is not found, however, in the Midrashic literature. B.Z. Luria (Beth Miqra' 47, 494) connects the noun *ṣir'āh* with /*'rṣ*.
Heavy influence of phraseology culled from 'Call' of Moses; cf. ויתחכם (Ex 1:10); שרי מסים (Ex 1:11); למען ענותם (Ex 1:14); וימררו את חייהם (*Ibid.*).

8. ויעבר בענינו ... ביצרו: *'Inyān* and *Yēṣer* are popular in Marqah's vocabulary of psychologcial terms; the former meaning 'idea,' 'imagination,' the latter meaning 'desire,' 'inclination,' 'thought.'

ואתור:* 'He cogitated.' The verb *tûr* occurs in this sense in Syriac. The word *yaḥšōbh* (Is 10:7) is rendered *tār* in the Syr. version.

מדעותו:* 'intelligence,' 'mind.' Abstract noun endings in *ûth* are a particular characteristic of H2.

9. מחשבו: Sam. mas. form *(maḥšābh)*

יגלי קנאה: The translation *'because* he revealed' follows the H2 rendering. Alternately we may understand the phrase as, '(his plan) *to* reveal.' A characteristic of the Samaritan style of the Chronicle is to substitute the infinitive of intention, or obligation (*GK* §114:1), by a simple imperfect (cf. 8:26, 17:4, 19:1 *et al.*).

להראות את פני יי': 'Appearing, or presenting oneself, before

God' for pilgrimage is expressed in *BH* (at least according to the masoretic vocalization) through the Niph'al conjugation (Ex 23:17, 34:23). Construing our phrase as a Niph'al would provide the sense of a personal intention on Baba's part to 'appear before the Lord.' The context, however, suggests a much wider, national mission, as reflected in the Arabic (A1) rendering: 'Causing the presence of God to be seen (sensed).' We may therefore regard our infinitive as Hiph'il rather than Niph'al, and render as A1.

10. ואחל בראש:* A1: 'And he showed that (zeal) first.' The verse is omitted in *AF*.

מתיסרים:* 'Obedient to him.' (lit. 'with him.'). Verb unattested in *BH* in Hithpa'el conjugation.

11. האזינו .. לאמרתי: Cf. Dt 32:1,2.

רוח הקנאה: Cf. Nu 5:14,30.

12. לנגלא: Possibly a contraction of the noun *niglā'ûth* (10:10), or read as Pa'el Inf., equivalent of *l^e gallē'*. We conjecture that the *l^e* might be an example of the 'emphatic *lamedh,'* known to us from Ugaritic, and attested to in *BH*.

וימחו .. דגליו: An alternate translation might also be proposed: 'that all their *heresies* be blotted out.' This rendering construes the *Daleth* of *d^e gālāyv* as a relative particle, and the form *gālāyv* as derived from the noun *gēl*, 'dung' (*BDB Lexicon*, 165) — a derogatory play on the noun *gillûl*, 'idol.'

כי חלשו הכפור:* *AF* renders, 'For infidelity has prevailed (غلب الكفر). The verb *ḥlš* is unattested in *BH* in Pi'el conjugation, in sense of 'to weaken.' Render: 'For denial has weakened it (sc. the observance of the law).

כפור:* Tal. Ar: *k^e phîrāh*.

ומבקש לו יגויע:* 'And seeks to annul it.' In *BH* the vb. is intransitive, appearing only in Qal.

והקשט:* — A term of gnostic significance.
AF: 'And solid truth has become annulled, namely the memory of the *body* ('corpus', الجسم) of sincere doctrine.' Did *AF* confuse the meaning of the Heb. text before him, construing our verb as the noun *g^e viyyāh*, a body?

13. וידיק .. את חניכו: Aph'el /*dûq*, 'look attentively at.' However, the preposition *'al* would be required for this meaning (see *Cowley*, II (Glos.), liii). The mark of the accusative *('eth)* rather suggests the sense of 'to muster.' Indeed, for the *MT*'s *vayyāreq 'eth ḥănîkhāyv*, 'And he mustered his trained men' (Gn 14:14), the *SP* has *vayyādek* (as Akk. *diku*, to call up troops).

יצרו: In *BH* the term *yēṣer* generally has a pejorative sense. Only twice (I Chr. 29:18; Is 26:3) does it occur in a sense favourable to man. The Sam. usage is clearly in the latter category. Its particular nuance of 'determination, resoluteness' is also found in the *DSS Hôdayôth* (1QH 1:35, 2:9, 36).

14. **ויקרא את**: Vb *qr'*, in sense of 'calling *to*', normally takes the preposition *'el.*

ונדב:* Arabic نَدَبَ , 'to convey a message.' However, the appearance of this root in a Zinjerli inscription, in the sense of 'inciting,' 'urging,' 'instigating' (a sense which *BDB* regards as underlying Ex 35:29, *ăšer nādabh libbām* — 'whose heart impelled them'), provides an excellent meaning for our phrase: 'And he roused his companions.' This sense of /*ndb* also occurs in Mandaic (see Drower and Macuch, *A Mandaic Dictionary,* 290) and in Jewish-Aramaic (Jastrow, *Dictionary,* 877).

15. **דלא בהם .. הנמל את בשר ערלתו**:* This gloss was probably inserted into H2 (it does not appear in H1) in order to clarify the sense in which the term *hā'ărēlîm* ('the uncircumcised') is being used. Since the word is also employed in the sense of 'uncircumcised of heart' (Lv 26:41), which would also suit our context, it might have appeared necessary to add this clarification.

אלהינו ואלהי אבותינו: This phrase is omitted in H2, in conformity with its general tendency towards economy in religious terminology and sentiment.

הצרים לתורת מ': There is no doubt that this Qal ptc. /*ṣûr* is here employed in the sense of 'to show hostility toward' (Arabic ضَارَ ; *BDB*: צור III), rather than 'besiege,' 'confine.' There is no occurrence of this sense of *ṣûr* (in Qal) in Jewish Aramaic. The preposition l^e is on analogy of *ṣrr* (employed by H2), though also with *ṣûr* in Mandaic (e.g. *lbar anašia ṣarna,* 'I show hostility to people,' Drower and Macuch, 388).

מצררים:* Possibly Pō'lēl / *ṣûr*; see previous note.

ימררו את חיינו: Exodus terminology (Ex 1:14); see on v 6 above.

16. **עד מתי לעדה הרעה הזאת**: Nu 14:27.

ינכרו צרינו .. רמה: Dt 32:27.

עד מתי .. למוקש: Ex 10:7.

17. **תשקע ... אש**: Nu 11:2.

ימנעו לנו: Vb *mn'* usually takes preposition *min;* but see Ps 84:12.

מבקשים ישמידו:* Infinitive replaced by imperfect; see on v 9 above.

ישמידו לנו:* *BH* takes simple accusative with vb.

וימיתו:* Gloss, or misplaced from before *lānû.*

וימאנו:* Confusion with *mn',* as in next verse.

18. **מן המקרא ...**: This verse, not represented in H2, might

serve the purpose of clarifying, or emphasizing, the most acute of the restrictions imposed by the enemy.

20. שמענו אדני: Cf. Gn 23:6.

מנעת: (H2: *temā'ēn).* Sing. vb with pl. subject; perhaps in partitive sense, though generally a stylistic characteristic of the Chronicle.

וכי נלאים: Subj. pronoun omitted with participle.

בזאת הימים: See on v 2 above.

הזינו: This additional demonstrative might convey the nuance of 'at this *particular* time.' The form *hāzênû* is close to the common Mandaic fem. demonstrative, *hā'zên* (the *û* termination being a contraction of *hû*) and the Tal. Aram. *hādên* (though the latter is a masculine pronoun). This is the sole occurrence of this form in our section of the Chronicle.

במה מדרשו יעפלו:* 'From achieving their desire.' Perhaps metathesis of /*P'l* (lit. *'doing* what they desired'). The biblical /*'pl* has the sense of 'swelling up,' (Arabic عَفَلٌ 'tumour') as in the noun *'Ōphel,* 'a mound' (II Kings 5:24). As a vb the root occurs but once in the *OT* (Hb 2:4), with the suggested meaning of 'puffed up with pride'. Its usage here may also be related to this basic sense of *rising,* reaching toward, attaining (their desire). The vb is found again, in the perfect tense, in 10:22.

שפלו:* The object *(lāhem)* suggests that the Pi'el is here being employed, with the causitive sense of 'to make (or bring) low.'

21. אזלת ידינו: Dt 32:36.

ותקומה .. שנאינו: Lv 26:37.

בין ידי:* Common idiom, 'before' (= *liphnê*); cf. *bên yādāyv* (3:6*), 'before him;' *min bên y^edê* (10:20*), 'from before' (= *milliphnê).*

§2

1. יעקב: Gloss (not in H2); for clarification that Israel here refers to Jacob and not, generically, to his offspring.

קנאו ליי׳: Emotive phrase, borrowed from context of *zeal* of Pinḥās (Nu 25:13), here apparently with apologetic motive, in order to mitigate, if not idealize, the action of the two sons of Jacob.

בתורותו: Orthographic variant of *b^etôrāthô.* The second vowel is not to be confused with a plural form. It is merely an orthographic representation of the long vowel *ā,* which is closely related, in Samaritan, to the vowel *ō* (or *ô).* The long *ā* was apparently pronounced in a manner corresponding to the sound of the vowel *û,* which would explain the orthography of the *singular* noun *tôrāh*, with 3rd person possessive suffix, as *Tôrûthô*. To give but one example of this: In the Sam. lexicon, *ha-mēlîṣ*, which gives the Samaritan Hebrew word followed by the Arabic and Aramaic equivalent, we have the singular noun, 'our body' (we know that the singular is intended because of the form of the Arabic and Aramaic equivalents) written as גביותנו. Ben-Hayyim, in his edition (*LOTS* II, 440), comments that the pronunciation of this word was clearly *gibyūtīnū*.

2. ויקחו שני בני יעקב..: Gn 34:25, 26.

הרג לפי רחב: *BT*: *hārgû*.

ואתכוננו:* Vb used in H2 with special meaning of 'preparing for battle' (cf. 11:9).

והתחתנו אתנו:* Gn 34:9.

חרבו בימינו:* Gn 34:25.

4. ויאספו .. לוי: Ex 32:26.

והרגו .. קריבו: Ex 32:27. BT: *k*^{e}*rôbhô*.

העגל הקב:* 'The accursed Calf,' *cum* A1.

5. יי׳ יתקדש שמו: A comparison of the renderings of H1 and H2 on this verse discloses the secularist bent of the latter, which makes no reference to God as the bestower of the blessing.

6. אז: Employed here in a simple relative sense; the equivalent of *ka'ăšer*.

מלבין: *AF*: مِن دُون . Idiomatically equivalent to בין ידי (see on 1:21).

יתר שאת .. עז: Gn 49:3.

לאלה:* Common Sam. designation of God; also occurs in biblical Aramaic, vocalized אֱלָהּ.

בל:* 'Without (the help of) his people.' In *BH*, however, the negative *bal* is never joined to a noun (see G.K. 152 (f)). The occurrence of the phrase *bal 'ittî* ('before my time') in a Phoenician inscription (see *BDB sub* בל) provides, however, a precedent for our expression. It is possible, however, that we should read *bên*, *cum* H1.

7. ופינחס .. הכהן: Nu 25:11.

הנני .. על בני ישראל: *Ibid.*, vv. 12–13.

יכפר: *Waw* omitted by haplography from previous word *lē'lōhāyv*.

8. This verse is omitted in *AF*. It appears to have been transposed from after v 2.

חתת: 'Terror', see Jb 6:21 (*hapax* in absolute form, though construct occurs in Gn 35:5).

אשקח: Aph'el *šqḥ* (= *šq'*), 'cause to sink, descend upon.'

9. ונקנה: Orthog. variant of *ûn^{e}qannē'.*

פגענו: Read: *pāg'û.*

להם: Equivalent of biblical preposition *b^{e} (bāhem).*

השותפים ביהוה:* See on 1:15.

10. קוממית: Either abstract noun *qôm^{e}mîth,* or construct form of *qôm^{e}miyyāh.*

לעם סגולה: Dt 7:6.

11. שובה: Equivalent of *BH m^{e}šûbhāh* (Je 3:6).

ולעמל לפני גדלו בצלות: *AF*: 'To resort to His gate in Prayer.' The vb. *'ml* is frequently associated, in Samaritan and Rabbinic literature, with the connotation of spiritual endeavour, to express *intensity* of activity. Cf. *ûbhatôrāh 'attāh 'āmēl* (Aboth, 6:4).

גדלו: This noun has a gnostic flavour. Seventy six of the Piyyutim published by Cowley commence with the word *b^{e}gādlô.* It is used in the sense of a creative (or created) force, akin to Shekhinah or the Rescuing Power of *Soter,* Saviour, a central figure in gnosticism. Cf. *Marqah*: 'When he said GODEL (greatness) he sought to strengthen the words by holiness' (Macdonald ed., II, 140).

והציאם: Variant of *ṣôm.* The *î*-sound developed through the influence of the extension of media-*waw* verbs to media-*'ayin* forms, in order to preserve the consonantal character. Forms like *qûm* and *ṣûr* thus became *qā'ēm* and *ṣā'er.* Samaritan *i* and *e* being mere variants, the form *ṣî'am* evolved naturally, though the word was probably pronounced *ṣeyyam,* (See Z. Ben-Hayyim, "A Samaritan Piyyut from Amoraic Times," *EI* 4 (1956), 119, where the word *dy'n,* from */dûn,* is transliterated *deyyan).*

12. ולהדבקה: Niph'al */dbq,* unattested in *BH.*

עד ישים: 'So that,' 'in order that.' Frequently employed in our Chronicle to introduce a purpose clause, though unattested in *BH* in this function.

נתקוי:* 'Prevail over(?)' Arabic قَوِي 'to be strong.' Unattested in *BH* in this conjugation.

שבעדותו:* Metathesis for *Ši'bdûthô.*

13. השובים: Equivalent of *ha-šābhîm;* for relationship of *ū* and *ā* vowels in Sam. Hebrew, see on v 11.

14. ונקים את דגלי: A lacuna has occurred here after *dgly.* Either read *d^{e}gāleyhā* (as our tanslation), or add H2's continuation '(banners of) truth which have been erased.' The latter is supported by *AF* (بنود الحق). For *degel* in symbolic sense of *prestige,* cf. Ct 5:10.

15. ודרסה: Read *v^{e}nidr^{e}sāh.*

ירכי האימן: 'The base (basis) of the Faith.' While such a sense may be derived from the phrase, it is likely that the reading owes its form to a scribal misunderstanding of the term *'arkhônê* in H2 (see below).

ונשיד:* 'We will bolster (lit. 'plaster'); cf. Dt 27:2,4. This follows the reading *v^e^nāšîd.* More probably we should read *v^e^nāšîd,* the */šîd* being a derivative of the Aram. *šdy, šd',* 'to lay a foundation.' Targumic rendering of *mî yārāh* (Jb 38:6) is *man š^e^dā'.*

ארכוני הדת: 'The authority of the law.' Gr. *ἀρχεῖον.*

לדרגי אשר: Unusual construct noun before relative pronoun. Perhaps orthog. error for *lidrāgîm.*

מימינו אשדת: Dt 33:2.

16. **ולא נטה משפט .. נכיר פנים**: Dt 16:19.

ונשוב שובה בלא שובה: Possibly a proverbial expression: 'We shall return in repentance, with no going back (to our former ways).

מסה ומריבה: Ex 17:7.

17. **עשוי**: Passive form for active participle; common in Aramaic.

עונים: Masc. termination for usual *'ăvōnôth* (see previous verse). The masc. termination serves to substantiate the forms *'ăvōneykhā* (Ez 28:18), *'ăvōnênû* (Is 64:6) *et al.,* which have been impugned by some scholars (see C. Siegfried and B. Stade, *Hebräisches Wörterbuch,* 87).

18. **לא פג**: Aramaic extended the semantic reach of the biblical */pûg,* 'to grow numb,' to encompass the idea of *faintness, lethargy, refraining.* The noun *pûgāh* is very common among Karaite auhors, in the sense of 'doubt,' with a vb *hithpôgēg* (see J. Gottlober, *Bikkoret Le-Toledot Ha-Keraim,* 216).

נקעתנו: Sam. variant of *na'ăqāh;* see Cowley, II, lxiii.

במצור ובמצוק: Dt 28:53, 55, 57.

ובכוח והמצליח יעננו: Read: *ûbh^e^khôḥô ha-maṣlîaḥ,* 'And by His strength, the Prosperer will answer us.'

19. *AF,* in line with H2, condenses vv. 18–19: 'He will help us and give us success, to defeat those uncircumcised and impure ones.'

ועבוטה יעביטנו: Dt 15:8.

עבודי הנכרים: Elyptical for *'ĕlōhê ha-nākhrîm.*

מן חסר: A philosophical term for the non-existence before Creation. See Macdonald, *The Theology of the Samaritans,* and, especially, our discussion of this phrase, *CESC,* 487 ff.

הארץ אחזתנו:* Construct noun with definite article! Perhaps intended as in appositional relationship.

ותשאר ראשם מתנדחים:* 'Their leaders shall remain banished.' Lack of agreement between verb *(v^e^tišā'ēr)* and masculine subject (rō'š). Perhaps read *v^e^tišā'ēr).* The singular subject (rō'š) is possibly construed collectively, hence pl. *mithnadḥîm.*

20. **ארץ האחרים**: Eschatological term for hereafter, future life, nether world.

וראשם יקדית: Our translation follows the A1 rendering: 'Their heads shall be bowed.' */qdh = /qdd.* The eschatological context would favour a reference here to (Hell-) burning, from */yqd.* Render: 'where their chiefs shall be consumed in fire.'

21. **בנו**: Scribal error for *bānay.*

נרגף: Read *nirdōph,* cum H2.

ונחלשם: Unattested Pi'el usage of verb.

שם:* 'Then,' as Arabic ثُمَّ (cf. Ho 6:7, Dt 33:21).

האלות המרירה:* Sing. participle with plural subject, cf. 17:5*, 22:17.

§3

1. **מעיני**: 'Leaders,' as supervisors of the community, Pa'ēl */'yn,* 'to watch over,' Arabic عَيَّنَ , 'appoint.'

דהוכיח עם:* Unattested preposition with Hiph'îl */ykḥ.*

2. **לחץ**: Read *rāḥaṣ.* Ritual washing of hands, face and feet before Prayer recalls Islamic prescription. *AF* تَوَضَّأ .

3. **לחם לא אכל ... שתה**: Ex 34:28. Sinaitic Revelation terminology.

הצליח את דרכו: Gn 24:21.

5. **ויחן שם ... ההר**: Ex 19:2.

6. **ויחל את פני יי'**: Ex 32:11. The attributes of God, enumerated in this verse, — *šiltān, gôdel* and *kābhôd* — all have gnostic significance and figure prominently in Marqan thought.

ויצליח את צלותו: The subject being Baba, it could hardly have the usual sense of 'making (his prayer) to prosper' *(BDB.* **צלח** II). We propose a reading *vayaṣlî* (*ṣlûthô* being the cognate accusative), 'He framed his own (personal) prayer.' However, the occurrence of */ṣlḥ* in the sense of 'to rush', 'to do (or come upon) powerfully' (Ju 14:6, 15:14 *et al.*), suggests a rendering, 'he put great effort into his prayer.' This sense of */ṣlḥ* suits admirably the context of the phrase *vatiṣl^e^ḥî limlûkhāh* (Ez 16:13) for which we propose the rendering: 'You rushed (i.e. prematurely) into kingship.'

7. **אם נא מצאתי חן**: Cf. Ex 34:9.

8. **אחר חסול צלותו**:* An explanatory gloss.

9. **שיאלי**: See on *ṣî'am* (2:12).

10. **אה**: = *hē';* pronounced *ē* by the Samaritans.

אה מן המצא: Infinitive Absolute */mṣ',* 'to exist' (cf. 15:10*). The detachment of the relative pronoun *d^e^,* after *min,* has been noted as a characteristic of very early texts (E. Munk, *Des Samaritaners Marqah Erzahlung uber den Tod Moses,* 1890, 40); it is, indeed, a characteristic of our Chronicle (see the continuation of our verse, also 4:19 *et al.*).

נוע הנועות: 'The Prime Mover' — a philosophic doctrine which, according to Maimonides, was rejected by the Muslim Mutakallemim thinkers. In the course of his critique of the "twelve propositions common to all Mutakallemim" (*Guide for the Perplexed,* Friedlander ed. (1904), 120) he observes that 'most of the Mutakallemim believed that it must never be said that one thing is the *cause* of another' (p. 125).

The term *nû'a ha-nû'ôth,* 'Mover of all movement,' would approximate, therefore, to the views of the Asha'ariyah, who assumed that 'when a pen is set in motion *God creates four accidents*: man's will to move it; man's power to do so; the motion of the hand; the motion of the pen, *none of which* is the cause of any of the rest' (*ibid.*).

והשכן השכינות: A1: 'And made to be still that which is still.' This rendering presents an apposite contrast to the previous phrase, *nû'a ha-nû'ôth.*

בחר .. סגולה: Dt 7:6. The reference to the 'Chosen People' is missing in H2 and in Arabic MSS.

שב על: 'To return to.' cf. Mi 5:2; Ne 4:6.

מאחטאו:* The first *'Aliph* does not represent the def. art., which would be anomalous with suffix, but rather the trace of the helping vowel which the Sams. append to the beginning of words commencing with sounded *š^{e}va'.* The simple form *ḥ^{e}ṭā'ô* (Masoretic *ḥaṭā'ô*) would necessitate this.

שמור הברית והחסד:* Dt 7:9, 12.

ופלטו מחזק דלותו ידעיו: Alternate rendering: 'And delivers those who know Him from the intensity of *their poverty.'* This understands the noun as abstract *dallûth,* rather than the Sam. form of the *d^{e}lāthô* (from *deleth,* 'door'). The adoption of this rendering would provide a subtle play on the words *d^{e}lûthô* (preceeding phrase) and *dallûthô.*

אה דבוק למן בך מדבק:* Cowley *(TSL,* II, liii) explains *cleave* in the sense of 'help;' likewise Ben-Hayyim, in his "Pîyyut Shômerôni Miymey Hā-'amôrā'îm" *(EI* 4), consistently renders */dbq* in the sense of 'help.' It is obvious, however, that in our context such a sense would provide a totally irreverent sentiment — 'O Thou who helpest them that help Thee.' It is clear, therfore, that */dbq* is here, quite literally, 'to cleave.' Render: 'O Thou who cleavest to them that cleave to thee.'

11. בני עבדיך: A1 omits, *cum* H2.

כבודיך: In anticipation of the nouns *raḥămeykhā* and *ḥăsādeykhā*, *kābhôd* is treated (or vocalized, at least,) as a plural.

ולא בטח: Occurs only once in *BH* as a noun ('security'); cf. Is 32:17.

12. מה רבו צרינו: Ps 3:2. The quotations from the Psalms, when singular in form, are here converted into the plural to give them a communal relevance.

אשר כחשו .. אשר חשכו: Play on words by metathesis.

אשר כחשו את שמעך: 'Who have denied the report of You.' Alternate rendering: 'Who have denied Your name.' The *'ayin* would then represent the sounded *e* according to Samaritan pronunciation.

אשר חשכו: 'Who are in such darkness,' reading *ḥāškhû*. Alternately, 'Who have desisted from observing,' reading *ḥāśkhû*.

הכפורים ... ובנביך ובכתבך:* Possibly an anti-Christian polemic, denouncing the elevation of Jesus in place of Moses and the rejection of the Old Testament *(k^ethābhkhā)* in favour of the New.

מתשבצים:* For *mithšaqqṣîm*. No transposition of *th* before sibilant.

דיעבדו לבעלים:* Here Baba refers back to the pagan rulers who preceded the era of Christian ascendancy in the reign of Constantine.

13. The Psalm verses that follow are omitted by *AF* and other Arabic versions, as they are by H2. Only significant variations from the *BT* are referred to in the notes that follow.

במקראנו עננו: Cf Ps 4:2.

14. עד מתי: Cf Ps 4:3.

התפשות: Abstract noun. For the phrase *tpś Tôrāh,* see Je 2:8.

ולמיח: Cf. 3:32. *Myḥ=mḥh.*

16. לאמירתי האזינה: Cf. Ps 5:2.

הקשיבה ... אתפללתי: Cf. Ps 5:3.

17. כי לא תחפץ: Cf. Ps 5:5.

ההלכים בדרך בישתה: Condemnatory gloss.

18. הן ... עונינו גדולים מנשא: Cf. Gn 4:13.

באלה: *Bêth pretii.*

פן: Used here in the unusual sense of 'rather than.'

ישמידו לנו: *Dative incommodi.*

19. שגבו:* 'Make inaccessible,' 'cut off,' 'block.' Only in Imperfect tense in *BH*.

The Psalm verses may also have been employed to smooth over a lacuna in H2 between vv 19–22.

20. אדני יי׳: Cf. Ps 6:2.

חננו יי׳: Cf. Ps 6:3.

כי חלים אנחנו: *BT*: *kî ’umlal ’ānî.*

נבהלה נפשנו: Cf. Ps 6:4.

21. שובה יי׳ והצלינו: Cf. Ps 6:5.

22. אדני יי׳ ... אלה הרשעים בנו: This represents a conflation of vv 18–19, to provide a suitable context for the continuation (or post-lacuna) material of H2. The point of continuation in H1 is the phrase commencing *v*[e]*lō’ tiśā’ ‘ālēnû* (= H1’s *lō’ tisbōl*).

ולזכרון ..... ימנעו: Repeated from v 14.

לן:* Contraction of lĕnān (= lêth ’ănān).

23. מכל הרדפים לנו: Cf. Ps 7:2.

פרק כי אין מציל: Cf. Ps 7:3.

בלעדיך לנו: Gloss for elucidation, and in order to avoid a sentiment betraying lack of belief in God’s redemptive power.

24. אם עשינו מום: Cf. Ps 7:4. *BT*: *’im ‘āśîthî zō’th.*

אם גמלנו רעה: Cf. Ps 7:5. *BT*: *’im gāmaltî šōlmî rā‘.*

25. לא תשים אויב: Cf. Ps 7:6.

ולא ירמס כארץ כבודינו: *BT*: *vayyirmōs lā’āreṣ ḥayyay ukh*[e]*bhôdî.*

26. לא ירפך ולא יעזבך: Dt 31:6.

27. בצר לך: Dt 4:30.

ובקשת משם ... ומצאתו: *Ibid.* v 29.

28. יי׳ אלהינו: Cf. Ps 8:2.

29. מפי עוללים ... עז: *Ibid.* v 3.

להשבית אויב וצורר מתנקם: *BT*: *l*[e]*ma‘an ṣôr*[e]*reykhā l*[e]*hašbîth ’ôyēbh ûmithnaqqēm.*

30. כי נראה: *Ibid.* v 4. *BT*: *kî ’er’eh.*

גאיך: *BT*: *’eṣb*[e]*‘ōtheykhā.*

מה אנוש: *Ibid.* v 5.

רשע: Explanatory gloss.

This Psalm is employed by the Chronicler in a spirit the very opposite of that intended by the Psalmist. The latter expressed it in the form of a tribute to human worth, whereas the Chronicler extracts from it a damnation of the wicked foes of the community.

כי תמשילהו: *Ibid.* v 7.

במעשה גאיך: *BT*: *b*[e]*m‘aśê yādeykhā.* See above, where the Chronicler rendered the *BH* ‘fingers’ by ‘pride’ *(gē’eykhā).* Here he renders the *BH* ‘hands’ in the same way.

31. נודך יי׳: Cf. Ps 9:2.

ונתפא: Read *v*[e]*nithpā’ēr.*

ונזמרה עליון שמך: *Ibid.* v 3.

בשוב: *Ibid.* v 4.

32. כי ... תגער גויים: *Ibid.* v 6.

הסכנתך: Gloss.

מפני עמך: Gloss.

משגב ... לעתות בצרה: *Ibid.* v 10.

33. ויבטח ... שמך: Cf. Ps 9:11.

כי אל רחום וחנון שמך: Cf. Ex 34:6.

ולא תעזב דרושיך: Cf. Ps 9:11.

ולא תרף: Cf. Jo 10:6.

34. בעמל משה: Cowley *(TSL* II, lxv) renders *ba'ămal,* 'for the sake of' (but see on 2:11). Possibly *'ămal* is intended to convey the notion of *intercession* (lit. 'toiling' on behalf of the rights and needs of others).

כפי בצענו בקנאתך:* Render: 'Now help us in accordance with our resolve (to walk) zealously before You.' The vb. 'to walk' (= 'to be') is either understood or omitted in transmission. Arabic versions understand H2's *qin'āh* in the sense of 'Unity,' *cum* H1 (*AF*: توحيد).

35. מבור ... אריצנו: Cf. Gn 41:14.

המחלש: Cf. 1:12*. H1: 'The mighty conqueror,' perhaps in the sense of 'the weakener (of the enemy).'

חבש:* 'Imprisoned.' All biblical references have opposite sense of 'binding up', 'comforting.'

36. אגאלת הם: Unusual preposition with *g'l.*

37. ואמרת על גדלך: Text dubious.

38. צרר: 'Distress'.

39. והים שמת לחרבה: Cf. Ex 14:21.

הלכים ביבשה: Cf. Ex 14:29, 15:19.

טבעו בתוך הים: Cf. Ex 15:4.

נבקעת מימי הים:* Cf. Ex 14:21.

וכעופרת במים צללו: Cf. Ex 15:10.

40. ערי הגבורים להם נחלת: A1: 'And gave to them the land of the stiff-necked giants (Amalekites)'. Vb. */nḥl* apparently Pi'el, cf. Nu 34:29; Jo 13:32.

ירשת אתם:* 'You made them to possess.' Transitive sense suggests a Pi'el form of vb. Elsewhere only Dt 28:42 *(y^eyārēš).*

§4

1. לפניו ... הקהלו: Tendency to place preposition before vb.; cf. *lô y^esaprû* (1:19), *'ālāyv yiṣb^e'û* (11:8).

מעיני:* See on 3:1. Always in construct form. The parallel with *nādîv* (H1) suggests that *m^e'aynê* is to be understood in the very broadest sense of leadership, encompassing influential men in all areas of religious, social and military endeavour. This is further underlined in 20:19 where *mᵉʿaynê* is paralleled in H1 by *ziqnê vᵉrāʾšê vᵉšōṭrê ʿammô.*

2. עין לבבכם: H2: *maddāʿēkhem.* For a discussion on the distinction between *lēv* and *maddaʿ* in early Samaritan thought, cf. A. Broadie, *An Investigation into the Cultural Ethos of the Samaritan Memar Marqah* (Unpublished Ph.D. Thesis, Glasgow, 1975), 341–343. The phrase *ʿēn lᵉbhabhkhem* is rare, and possibly suggestive of special insight and gift of prediction.

ומה מדעיכם לכם אורו:* The significance of this phrase is underlined by a passage in Marqah which speaks of knowledge as a *'light* that shines in the heart' *(Memar Marqah,* I, 136; II, 222). 'Heart' and *maddāʿ* are, of course, related terms (see previous note).

3. כל אשר תאמר ... ונעשה: Ex 24:7. This verse places the role of Baba, and his relationship to his community, as parallel with that of Moses as instruments of divine redemption (see on 1:6, 3:34).

מצוך: Unattested noun *mᵉṣāv;* perhaps read *miṣvāthkhā.*

ויענו:* Sole example of *Waw Consecutive* in H2; perhaps read *vᵉʿānû.*

4. ולא נמרי את פיך: Dt 1:26, 43; 9:13; Josh 1:18.

ולא נעזב לקולך: Unattested usage of *ʿzb* with prepostion *lᵉ* in the sense of 'forsaking.'

6. תצוה לנו: Vb */ṣvh* usually takes Direct Object with *'eth.*

7. שמועים: 'Obedient.' Passive in form, active in meaning.

והרוחים: Note masculine termination; but in v 10 *ruḥôth.* Such variation is not uncommon in our Chronicle (e.g. *gᵉlālim* and *gᵉlālôth,** 1:20; *nimṣa'ôth* and *nimṣā'îm,** 3:10).

8. לשמע ולעשות את כל קולך: Pregnant construction; perhaps for *'eth kol qôl miṣvāthᵉkhā.*

9. וילכו הכהן: In cases of a single subject with extra subjects appended with *waw copula* H1 anticipates by employing a plural verb *(vayyēlᵉkhu),* whereas H2 maintains the initial singular requirement *(yāṣā').*

מושבי: *Masc.* construct occurs only once in *BH,* Ez 34:13.

הסגירו להם: For the use of *lᵉ* to introduce object of */sgr,* see Amos 1:9.

מסגרים אתם:* */sgr* in Pi'el conjugation occurs only in book of Samuel (— and then not in participle!), where its sense is 'to surrender up', not 'to close.'

10. ויקרא את ספר התור': This first act is in accordance with the priority given to Torah in Baba's programme of reform (see 1:18, 15:18).

לאלהי הרוחות יי': Nu 16:22, 27:16.

אל צבאות: As a designation of God — 'God of the battle array of Israel' — this is not a Pentateuchal phrase. It would be a mistake, however, to conclude that it has precisely the same sense as in the later books of the Bible. Bearing in mind the view of Ben-Zevi *(Se.H.* 24) that *śar ha-ṣābhā'* was the title given to Baba Rabbah, as well as the covert allusion to this title in a 4th cent. amulet — as suggested by J. Caplan ("A Second Samaritan Amulet from Tel Aviv", *EI* 10, 255–257) — it is possible that the sense of the phrase *'ēl ṣ^ebhā'ôth* in our passage is 'God of *Baba's* hosts.'

לאלהי השמים וארעות:* Unusual plural form when referring to the earth. Cf. v 11 where we have the usual phraseology, *'ĕlōhê ha-šāmayim v^ehā'āreṣ.* The plural termination *ôth* probably entered under the influence of the many plural nouns which follow in succession to each other in this verse.

11. זידונים האדומים: 'Tyrannical Ones,' cf. Targ. Ps 86:14, Pr 21:24, Job 31:3. The term *zêdîm* occurs in the *'Amîdāh* (daily liturgical) composition of the Jewish Synagogue: *v^eha-zēdîm th^e'aqēr ûth^ešabbēr.* A variant of the word *v^eha-zēdîm,* found in other rites, is *ûmalkhûth zādôn* — the term *malkhûth* being, in rabbinic literature, a specific appellation of the Roman dominion. Significantly, both Jewish and Samaritan-Palestinian traditions employed the term *zēdîm* (or *zēdônîm)* to describe the hated conqueror.

חכמי התורה: H2: *Šimmûrê ha-Tôràh.* The identity and status of this group is fully discussed by us in a chapter on "The Administrative Reforms of Baba Rabbah" (*CESC* 405–459).

חמישים:* The poor syntax created by the insertion of this numeral into the context suggests that it was a later gloss, disclosing the number of *Šimmûrê ha-Tôrāh* whom Baba managed to summon. It is not to be dismissed, however, on that score, since it appears again in 5:1,* where it is endemic to the context. H1, rather surprisingly, does not include this important piece of information in its version.

12. הכהן: H2 consistently omits this epithet from Baba's title, in consonance with its general tendency to economy in religious terminology or personal attributes (see on 1:15).

לאמר: Omitted in H2 which, unlike H1, does not model itself on biblical style or terminology.

מאדכם: The noun *m^e'ōd* (Dt 6:5, 'might') is employed in the Chronicle in the sense of 'full attention,' 'mind,' 'concentration.'

אנשים נשים וכל הטף: A total programme of school and adult education is here envisaged, with no dicrimination between the sexes. The intensity of the course instituted by Baba is referred to in v 20.

מקרת: Orthographic variant of *miqrā'ath* (see next verse). The shorter form occurs again in v 20.

13. אתקדשו:* A secular nuance of the verb *qdš,* in the Hithpa'ēl conjugation, with the sense of 'devoting attention.' A1: 'And expend the utmost of your effort.'

14. ולא תפלו בתרדימה: Cf. Gn 2:21, 15:12.

דרך תמימה: Cf. Ps 101:2; Prov 11:20.

ולא תהונו מן השלים:* Uncertain phrase. Arabic هَانَ, 'to be light.' Perhaps: 'Do not be lethargic (= H1's, *vᵉlō' tipplû bᵉtardēmāh)* in the pursuit of perfection (= H1's, *derekh tᵉmîmāh).*

16. לכו נא הגברים: Ex 10:11.

17. יי' אלהי אבותיכם ... לכם: Dt 1:11.

18. ויכחשו לכם אויביכם: Dt 33:29.

ואתם על במתם תדרכו: *Ibid.*

אמן תמשלו: 'You may rule faithfully.' Either read *'ōmen,* '(in) faithfulness' (cf. Is 25:1), or as adverb, *'āmēn* ('truly,' Dt 27:15–26).

19. כל איש מכם לא: Omission of relative pronoun.

הכה:* Infinitive Absolute (cf. Dt 3:16), or read *'akkeh* (cf. H1), or *hakkû* (Imperative).

אשר אנכי מצוה אתכם היום: Dt 11:27.

20. טרחה: The exacting standards of proficiency in the reading of the Law and the mastery of the scholarly writings, demanded by Baba, were clearly resented at first by the people. This is reflected in the use of such terms as *ṭirḥāh* and *'āqāh**.

כי הוא אבם:* Text corrupt? Possibly parenthetical ('For he was their father'), with *'ăbhām* a contraction of *'ăbhîhem,* though comparison with H1 suggests that a verb has dropped out.

21. המגיפים: *BH*: *maggēphôth.*

אתבסרו: Orthog. variant of *'ithbaśrû,* 'to receive good tidings.' *AF*: تَبَاشَّرُوا .

§5

The general import of this section is fully analyzed in our chapter on "The Administrative Reforms of Baba Rabbah,' *CESC* 405–459.

1. כמו האנשים אשר צוה ... את משה: — Another Moses motif.

אנשי חיל ... שנאי בצע: Ex 18:21.

ואתה תחזה: *Ibid.*

יראה אלהים: *BT*: *yir'ê.*

2. חכמים: See our discussion of this term, *CESC* 418–423.

3. שלשה מן הכהנים ... משבט יוסף הצדיק: To this day the Samaritans maintain a tri-partite tribal division into the tribes of Levi, Menasseh and Ephraim.

והכהנים היו: Delete as gloss.

4. ישתמה ... בישראל:* Echo of Dt 25:10.

5. נקראו חכמים: H2: *šôf*[e]*ṭîm*. For a discussion of the relationship between the titles *šôf*[e]*ṭîm* and *ḥăkhāmîn,* see *CESC loc. cit.*

ויחלף: Used here in the sense of 'to deprive of,' 'withdraw (a title)'. The required, causative sense suggests either Pi'ēl (see Gn 41:14) or Hiph'îl (see Gn 31:41). In both instances the biblical usage suggests the sense of 'exchange,' 'substitute,' rather than merely 'withdraw.'

6. ויסר לאנשים: The verb *sûr* usually takes the preposition *min.* See, however, Job 12:20, *mēsîr śāphāh l*[e]*ne'ĕmānîm,* 'He removes the speech of the faithful.'

7. והגלל לדבר הז': For detailed discussion of the succeeding episode, see *CESC* 423–426.

בשן: 'Stretching from the stream Jabbok (thus including northern Gilead) northward to Hermon, between Gennesaret (W) and the mountains of Hauran (E)' (B.D.B., 143). In the *Onomasticon* of Eusebius (ed. Klostermann, 112) there is a reference to a Samaritan community in Bashan (Eus: 'Batanaia'). See M. Aviyonah, "'Al M[e]rîdôth Ha-Šômrônîm B[e]biza'ntiyyum" *EI* 4 (1956), 129.

חייב: Pi'el usage.

8. העיר: With reference to a geographical location such as Bashan, the H2 rendering, *m*[e]*dînāh* seems far more accurate. The reference in the *Onomasticon* of Eusebius (see previous note) to the Samaritan settlement of *a place in Bashan* called Tarsila (Tasīl), provides us with the likeliest identification. (On the question of its identification, see E.Z. Melamed, "The Onomasticon of Eusebius," *Tarbiz,* 3, 260 note 107.)

אשר הנכון לו: Double relative!

בא שמה: Read *bā'û, cum* H2.

וישלמו עליו: 'They came to greet him.' Unattested in this sense in *BH.* The Hiph'îl occurs, with the preposition *'el,* in Josh 11:19, in the sense of 'to submit to.' It occurs in this sense in Arabic, form IV: 'to submit oneself,' esp. to God (whence participle *Muslīm,* and Infinitive *Islām).* It occurs again, in 25:8, in the related sense of 'to hand over, 'entrust to the care of.'

9. בגלל הדבר הזה: Dt 15:10.

מקום חנותיהם: Both words have the technical meaning of 'rank,' 'position,' 'seniority' (see 5:21, 22, 31). See, further, on v 17.

כי לא יצאו הם: Subject pronoun following verb; perhaps for additional emphasis (cf. *hāyû hēm,* 5:11).

למחוץ לעיר: Prefixed Lammed; variation of biblical construction *'el miḥûṣ l^e* (Lv 6:4, 10:4).

11. היו יעשו: Past frequentative action is expressed by finite verb in imperfect with auxiliary verb 'to be' in perfect tense. See, however, on v 12.

נמלה: 'Cicumcision.' Noun derived from Niph'al formation. H2's *n^emîlāh* appears to be a hybrid of Niph'al and Hiph'îl forms.

ימילו: Hiph'îl /*mûl*? Only one occurrence of Hiph'îl, in Ps 118:10.

12. יהיו ... אמרים: Frequentative action in the future is expressed by employing the imperfect of *hāyāh* with participial form of main verb.

14. היה איננו: Read *hû' 'ênennû.*

והסוכילים:* The H1 version, 'neither a sage nor a scholar,' is more refined than that of H2.

15. רק היה משתמר: Delete *raq* as dittography from first word of sentence.

The statement made here, that only the names of the priests were preserved in a genealogical list (Tôlîdāh), is founded on the tradition that during the Bar Cochba revolt the Romans destroyed all the literature of the community. The latter succeeded in rescuing only the scroll of the Torah and a scroll giving the genealogical chain of the priests (Ben-Zevi, *Se.H.* 22).

16. כנות: 'Pedestal,' 'office,' cf. Gn 45:22.

17. עד ידע כל אחד מהם את מקומו: This phrase is remarkably close to the rabbinic adage that a scholar is one — *ha-makkîr 'eth m^eqômô* — 'who knows his own *rank'* (— and, in consequence, defers to seniority). See Aboth 6:6.

19. ויצגם: The root *nṣg* does not appear in *BH*. It is also rare in Sam. Hebrew. H2 has the more common /*'md.*

20. תטלל: Lit. 'drop dew,' *Cowley,* 11, lvii.

ומפתרו: The elucidation of the name, provided by H1, is not given by H2. There are many such indications that H1 is a polished version of H2.

חבתה: Alternately *'abhtāh* or *habhtāh* (الحفتاوى), 'the second priest, usually at Damascus' (Cowley, II, lv).

21. ראש הפתורים לפניו: Chronicle Adler renders *'ad yih^eyeh sôphîr rō'š bēn yādāyv*; translated: 'Il devint le premier secrétaire devant le grand-prêtre.' The *Pater* seems to have been a rather more senior administrator, however, than that conveyed by Adler's 'secrétaire.' One feels that Adler's literal rendering of

sôphîr has misled him here. The title *sôphēr,* in Judaistic tradition, has a far more comprehensive and juridical significance than is conveyed by the literal sense of the title. Indeed, it was the title assumed by the early Pharisaic legislators themselves!

The term *Pater* occurs among the titles of communal officers in the ancient Synagogue of Rome, as, for example, the *Pater Synagogae* (U. Kaploun, *The Synagogue,* Popular Judaica Library, 4).

23. **ולו המקראה השנית**: Adler renders: *v*^{e}*lô ha-q*^{e}*rî'āh ha-šēnîth;* translated: 'C'était le second lecteur.'

The term *miqrā'āh,* we suggest, refers to the specific duty or function of acting as precentor for the reading of the Law, or of teaching the correct method of reading. Verse 19 points out that an important part of Baba's hierarchic reform was the appointment of people to act as guardians of the neglected traditions appertaining to the correct method of Scripture reading. The *pater* would then have been the "expounder" of Scripture, as opposed to the teacher of the skill of *reading* the law, a function referred to by the term *miqrā'āh.*

The Chronicler would then be asserting that p^{e}rûba'î (v 20) was the Chief Expounder, followed by 'Amram (v 26). Third and fourth in the rank of Expounders are not preserved. The fifth Expounder was Yiśrā'ēlî (thereby accounting for the fact that he is placed fifth in the arbitrary order). The sixth in rank is not preserved. The lowest in the order of seniority was Yoṣbî (v 22).

The term *māqôm,* used in the context of this list, refers exclusively to geographic situation, or administrative area, in relation to Mount Gerizim, not to rank (even though the term does also have this connotation; see on 5:17). This is made clear in v 21, where the leader whose administrative area was in closest proximity is described as having the first *māqôm,* and also in v 22, where Yoṣbî, although last in the rank of Expounders, yet occupies the second *māqôm.* The town of Yislāh (Silāh), associated with him, is a mere 12 km. N.W. of Mt. Gerizim, which would suit the designation *māqôm ha-šēnî,* in geo-administrative terms.

24. **ויזכר**: Probably Hiph'îl, 'He recorded,' reading *vayazkēr.*

הרימו תרומות: Cf. Nu 15:19.

25. **ישראלי**: Adler adds: *v*^{e}*hû' sôphēr ḥămîšî.*

26. **כופר ספאסה**: Viz. Sebaste.

27. **עמרם דרה**: 'Amrām Dārāh is referred to again in 9:12. Bearing in mind the great contribution of this man, it is surprising that the Chronicles are the only source of information, or tradition, regarding his date and activity. As a contemporary of Baba Rabbah, and a member of his hierarchic 'inner circle,' we

may assume that the main stimulation and encouragement which ʻAmrām and his son, Marqah, required in order to foster their pioneering literary activity, came from Baba, and the hopes he raised for a comprehensive Samaritan renaissance.

On the slender basis of a reference to ʻAmrām as *Kāhănāh rabbāh ʻamrām dārāh*, in a Vatican Ms. of a *piyyut*, Ben-Hayyim *(LOTS* III, pt. 2, 12) opined that ʻAmrām was a High Priest. It is obvious that, from the *sitz im leben* of our Chronicle, wherein Nethan'el is the High Priest, Baba the effective leader of the community and ʻAmrām but one of the seven members of the ruling praesidium (no more than *sixth* in the list of such leaders, and occupying only the *second Miqrā'āh)*, that Ben-Hayyim's contention cannot be substantiated.

הלף: Aph'el /Alp.

בתי הדראן: Lit. 'Stanzas of (strung) pearls.' Arabic درّان . Hebrew poetry of the Jews also adopted this metaphor, by employing the term *ḥārûz* for 'rhyming verse.'

28. בתים מרקה: Read *bāttê marqāh*, the final *Mem* intruding by dittography (in anticipation of the first letter of *marqāh)*.

תמונו:* 'Appointment,' 'rank.' Rare noun, related to /*mnh*, 'to appoint.' Tal. Aram. *m^{e}mûneh*, 'superintendent.'

§6

1. יתוב: 'Degree,' 'status,' 'position.' The noun usually employed is *mêthûbhāh* (see v. 9) or *mêthûbhîs* (ibid.*). The Hebrew form occurs in 5:31, *môšābhô.*

2. תחשכו ל: 'Discipline them,' (H2: *tikhl^e'û)*. This is a slight semantic shift from the shade of meaning that the /*ḥśk* suggests in *BH*, viz. 'to spare,' 'hold back.'

והייתם פנים ל: 'Lit. 'You shall be a face (front) to,' i.e., 'go before.'

3. לא תכירו פנים ... לאלהים הוא: Dt 1:17. Chronicle Adler inserts the continuation of the biblical verse.

4. אנכי אדרש מעמו: Dt 23:22.

5. ארבע אנשים:* H1 has the expected masculine form *'arbā'āh* of the numeral. The H2 orthography was probably influenced by the elision of the first of the three succeeding vowel sounds.

מראים:* 'Overseers'(?) H1: *Pôq^{e}dîm.*

6. מתוך את: Curious intrusion of *'eth* after preposition.

8. תשוב את: Read *tāšûbh 'el.*

מלא ידו לכהן: Ex 28:41 *et. al.*

המתמשיח:* *Forma mixta;* noun *māšîaḥ* in verbal setting. Perhaps read *hammithmāšaḥ.*

§7

For a full discusion of the identity and role of the *Mišpaḥath Haššibh'îm,* as described in this section, see *CESC* 460–473.

1. ובקהל ישראל ... עמה יתקרו:* The H2 rendering is complex, and it is probable that a lacuna has occurred. The term *yisrā'ēl haššᵉmārîm* may refer to the *Samarians* (as opposed to 'Samaritans'); and the import of the verse is that among the Israelite *Samarians* were some who called themselves (reading šᵉmēh for 'ammāh) *Samaritans.*

2. יתבו: Pᵉ'al form of */ytb* here used in transitive sense, 'to appoint,' 'set up.' Indeed, M. Dahood, commenting on the phrase *yāšᵉbhû kissᵉ'ôth* (Ps 122:5), concludes, amid evidence from Ugaritic usage, 'that the verb *yašabh* can govern the accusative case' (M. Dahood, *The Anchor Bible,* Psalms III, 206).

אשר הפקידם ... הכהן בבא רבה הזוכ': The subject is awkwardly separated from the verb it governs; but cf. 11:9, 15:3, 22:15*.

שמיע:* 'Discipline.'

3. במקומותם: H1, characteristically, simplifies the rare word *mᵉkhōrôthêhem* in H2.

מכרתיהם:* Noun *mᵉkhôrāh,* only in Ezekiel (Ez 16:3, 21:35, 29:14). It has the sense of 'origin' (lit. place of *digging out.* See *BDB. sub* 11 כור).

Baba's inability to dislodge the *Mišpahath Haššibh'îm* from their position of influence and autonomous independence is explained by the term *mᵉkhōrôthêhem.* They were well 'dug in', their forebears having been associates with those areas from earliest times.

4. עריהם ... היא: Sing. pronoun with plural subject. Perhaps used collectively.

5. בבא רבה הזוכירים מטרם: The plural *ha-zôkhîrîm* actually qualifies 'the seven sages' mentioned at the beginning of the verse. The intervening phrase might be a gloss (but see on v 2 above).

6. מסעדים: Pi'ēl. *BH* has only Qal form. It is conceivable, however, that we have here a plural form of the *hapax legomenon mis'ād* (I Kings 10:12), 'support.' The sense of the phrase would then be, 'These seventy were supporters of (lit. 'supports with') the priest Baba Rabbah.'

טמונים:* Josh. 7:21. The vagueness of this term is removed in H1 by use of the term *mašbîr.*

משביר: Irregular form of the noun *šebher,* 'grain' (Gn 42:1). In *BH* the term *mašbîr* means 'the seller of grain.'

וישיגו אתו ב:* Lit. 'they overtook him with,' i.e. 'to lavish upon.' Clarified by H1's *vayyitnû lô.*

במתנות הפחרות:* Curious expression. Aram. */pḥr,* 'to hollow out, scrape' (= *ḥpr*). The parallel with *ṭ^{e}mûnîm* (lit. 'buried,' 'concealed') is inescapable, suggesting that *paḥărôth* may have the sense of 'rare.' Alternately, the Aramaic noun *paḥra'* means 'earthenware,' and the phrase may mean that they gave 'earthenware gifts' to Baba. According to one report, Samaritans only ate and drank from earthen vessels on the Sabbath, not from metal ones. If a metal vessel became unclean, one might inadvertently purify it on the Sabbath. To prevent this, earthen vessels — which cannot be purified — were used (see K. Kohler, "Dositheus, the Samaritan Heresiarch," *AJTh,* xv (1911), 413–14.). Does this suggest a Dosithean identity for the *Mišpaḥath Haššibh'îm?*

It is unlikely that *paḥărôth* means, merely, 'beautiful' (*/pḥr* being an orthog. variant of */p'r*).

§8

1. ויפקדו: Qal or Niph'al. If Qal, in an active sense ('whom he had appointed'), we have the problem of a singular suffix qualifying a plural subject *(ha-ḥăkhāmîm).* This is solved by reading *vayyiph-q^{e}dēm,* the 3rd pers. pl. suffix being supported by H2's rendering, *y^{e}ṣavveh 'ōthām.*

A Niph'al sense (reading *vayyippāqdû*) would be doubtful, however, since the basic structure and import of the sentence is active in sense, with Baba as subject.

מגרעות:* *Hapax* in *BH* (I Kings 6:6), where it is used in the unequivocal sense of 'ledge, recess'. Here it is synonymous with *š^{e}gāgôth,* in the sense of 'deficiencies.'

2. חפצותי: Noun *hephṣāh* unattested in *BH.*

הדבר הראש הגדול: Baba's emphasis on the importance of Torah reading was certainly a reaction to the lengthy period when such public readings were proscribed by the Romans, with serious consequences for religious knowledge and observance (see 1:18).

ומן כלילה: 'Scrupulously,' lit. 'out of whole (-heartedness).'

על מקרת העשרה: 'According to the reading of the ten.' This abstruse phrase might suggest an attempt by Baba to introduce the prerequisite of a quorum of ten for the Reading of the Law, as in Jewish tradition. We would accordingly render the phrase as 'in the *assembly* of ten'. Cf. *miqrā' qōdeš* ('a holy *convocation*'), Ex 12:16.

Alternately, the reference in H2 to *ha'esrôth hā-'iqqārîm,* 'the ten principles' might point to some system of cantillation or accentuation signs, on the Judaistic pattern of *n^e^gînôth.* Coincidentally, the invention of these signs is attributed to the first half of the 4th cent. *(Encycl. Jud.,* 16, 1413).

הגדול: A gloss, clarifying that by *ha-dābhār hā-rō'š* Baba meant 'the chief matter,' rather than 'the first topic.'

3. **שימו זכרון ... המלמדים**: A1: 'Remind the teachers.' The prescription to make a *zikkārôn* 'between you and between the teachers' suggests more than merely 'reminding them.' It appears to call for a regular *(b^e^khol 'ēth)* revision course *(zikkārôn)* in which the appointed leaders are to instruct and 'refresh the memories' of the teachers.

ונסיתם את התלמודים: 'And search the learned literature.' It is possible that a scribal error had occurred here, and we should read *talmîdîm,* 'disciples.' The nouns *talmûd* and *talmîd* are, occasionally, interchanged in Samaritan literature (see Cowley, II, lix). The verse would then call upon the scholars to conduct regular 'tests of the students' (for *nassôth,* 'tests,' see 9:4).

4. **מקוה מים לטהרה**: For a discussion of Baba's *Miqveh,* and especially the expression in our verse, *l^e^'ēth 'ittôth kol ṣ^e^lôth,* see our chapter on "The Administrative Reforms of Baba Rabbah," *CESC* 443–453.

5. This verse has the hallmark of being a gloss.

6. **בית כנשה**: Adler: *k^e^nîšāh.*

7. **הפרנג**: 'The Franks.' The singular is used in a collective sense.

בית המעבד: 'Place of Worship.'

הריפתים:* A curious nomenclature for the Franks (H1). It might be connected with the name *rîphath* (Gn 10:3), son of Gomer, firstborn of Japhet. *BDB* (*Lexicon,* 937) quotes Josephus' identification of Riphath with Paphlagonians.

More probably, however, our Riphtim is a transliteration of 'Ripuarians,' one of the three main branches of the Franks. The Ripuarians were the most successful of the Frankish tribes, reaching their zenith in the Rhineland conquests of the 5th cent. H2 preserves a tradition that the *Riphtim* sent officials to prevent the Samaritans from observing their religion (see 11:1, 4).

מדד:* 'Dimension.' *BH*: *mad, mēmad, middāh.*

בצרה: Boṣra in Edom. The name 'Albāṣrah appears in the Asatir (ed. Ben Hayyim, ch. 2, 1.21) as a city built by Tubal Cain as a centre for his tool-making industry. The original name was *s^ekhîphāh,* or, according to another version, *s^ekhîphas.* This is suggestive of the name Scopus, and, conceivably, it was for that reason that it was identified with Albāṣrah, the Citadel.

We cannot rule out the possibility that Boṣra is identical with Bostra, the birthplace of Philip the Arab, who figures prominently in our Chronicle. Bostra is identified with Philippopolis in the Trachonitis (Victor, *De Caesaribus,* 28, 1). For discussion of this name, see I. Sonne, "Historical Sources," *JQR* (N.S.), 26, 150–1; S. Lieberman, "The Martyrs of Caesarea," *op. cit.,* 249–251.

8. מאבנים ההיכל: Scribe notes his own error by dotting the last letter of *mē'ăbhānîm.* Read *mē'abhnê.*

אנשי שאול: For the account of the hostility between Saul and the Samaritans, see J. Macdonald, *The Samaritan Chronicle No. II,* 123–128.

10. בתי כנשיות שבעה: Adler and H2 have 'eight Synagogues.' The H1 version was undoubtedly motivated by the uncertainty surrounding the eighth Synagogue (see v. 18).

Vv. 11–19 are treated in detail in our chapter, "The Location of Baba's Synagogues According to the Account of the Chronicler," *CESC* 490–504.

§9

2. המקום המב׳, הר הב׳ מקום, הק׳ הר הנח׳ והש׳ הר גר׳: We have here a classical example of H1's predilection for pious attributions, as contrasted with H2's simple reference to *hā-hār ha-kōdeš.*

ויעלים:* Arabic 'Alima, 'to make known,' or, perhaps, read *v^eya'ălî,* 'he shall submit (his request)'.

3. ויגידו לו על דבר משפטה: Cf. Dt 17:9.

4. נקיבו: 'His designation,' cf. Nu 1:17.

5. והגלל: *BH* employs only the construct case of *gālāl* with prefixed *b^e,* as in *biglal.*

לא פנה פניו: Cf. Jer 2:27, 32:33.

ישמו את עצמם: Cf. I Kings 19:2.

במלאכות תרחקם: Note detached relative pronoun (cf. 4:19); also singular verb after plural subject (cf. 12:1*, 14:3*).

יי׳ הקדוש יתקדש שמו: Pious epithets of H1 omitted in H2.

יתורו:* Verb *tûr* or *tā'ēr* occurs in Sam. Aramaic in sense of 'to pay attention to,' 'consider,' 'think;' see on 1:8, also Ben-Hayyim, *LOTS* II, 507.

העודות עלמה:* Read *'ôdôth* (construct), 'existing things,' 'affairs.' Syr. ܥܝܕ (pa.) 'accustom;' ܥܝܕܐ 'usage.'

והודות:* Contraction of *v^ehā'ôdôth.*

6. על עמו דמצא אתם:* This cannot mean that Baba appointed priests over the people 'whom he had found,' which would give no sense. We suggest that this phrase has become transposed, and that it should qualify 'the priests.' The verb */mṣ'* is here used in the sense of 'gather together,' 'assemble' (cf. *ûmāṣāh lāhem // yē'āsēph lāhem,* Nu 11:22).

The sense of the phrase would then be that 'Baba allotted the priests, *whom he had assembled,* over his people.' This interpretation is also supported by the use of this verb in 10:1*.

7. כרני הדת:* The noun *kōren* occurs in the *Ha-mēliṣ,* the Hebrew/Arabic/Sam. Aramaic lexicon, as the equivalent of the Heb. *mišpāḥāh,* 'family.' The sense of our passage would then be: 'Who were appointed over the religious and pious families.'

8. הראש: H1 always employs the term *rō'š,* 'head,' in place of H2's ordinal *ri'yšôn.* (cf. 8:2).

לוזה: Identified with Bethel in Bible (Gn 28:19), and with Mount Gerizim — and especially with a spot east of the lower ridge — in Samaritan tradition. It is there, at an area still called *Luz* by the Samaritans, that Passover is celebrated (J. Bowman, "Pilgrimage to Mount Gerizim," *EI* VII, 17). In the *Tolidah* it is again mentioned: lûzāh 'ăšer hî' šōmrōn (ed. Bowman, 12א).

עד מקום הגליל: The continuation — *'ăser 'al ha-yām* — supports the H2 reading, *'el ha-gilgāl.*

The reference is clearly to Gilgal, by the brook of Kānāh (Josh 16:8), on the Sharon plain. See Josh 12:23.

נערה: Adler supports the H2 reading, *na'ănāh* (perhaps Gr. *neanis*).

9. מעסכר ... לטבריה: The variation in geographical identification of boundaries between H1 and H2, coupled with the H1 corrective gloss (*v^ehā'ĕmeth* ...), indicates a confused tradition. On 'Askōr, see Montgomery, 20.

טרבלוס: This was the medieval orthography for Tiberias (Ben-Zevi, 117).

אחזת מחנים:* A lacuna has occurred; read, *'ăḥùzath* (*naḥălāh mi-*) *maḥănayim.*

10. בן תהם: Tolidah: tēhôm (— a common priestly name; see *Tolidah,* ed. Bowman, 12א, 13ב). *AF*: *nēhām.*

11. כפר חלול: Probably identified with k^efar qallîl, well-known Samaritan agricultural village, 3 km. N.W. of Ma'ăbhartāh.

בית השבט: Also called *bēth šōphēṭ. AF* (translating, rather than transliterating, the name) renders بيت الكرم . It is identified by Conder with the Talmudic *k^ephar šōbhthî* in lower Galilee (see *Ber. Rabb.* 85, 7).

לביט:* Read *l^ebhêth.*

סרד: This name, of Marqah's grandfather, is variously transmitted. *AF* renders برد (133) and صريد (130). The latter is possibly an error for صريد (see Ben-Hayyim, "Piyyuṭ Šômrônî Miymê Hā-'ămôrā'îm," *EI* 4, 119, n. 11).

טוטה: Probably originates in Roman name Titus.

12. אבי הכהן מרקה: Chronicle Adler adds supplementary detail regarding Marqah: 'Ce fut le père de Marca, le grand savant, qui etait instruit dans toutes les sciences. Il avait fait un commentaire sur le Pentateuque, dont il nous reste un fragment sur les miracles que Dieu fit en Egypte, un fragment sur le cantique de Moise et un autre sur le second cantique de Moise.'

Adler makes the identification of our 'Amrām with 'Amrām, father of Marqah, a certainty — as does H2's comment: *v^ehû' b^eqōšṭ* ... H1 is more reserved, however, in its judgment, stating it merely as 'a tradition.'

13. שמעלעימה: H2's reading *šimt^e'îmāh* is supported by Adler. The name is omitted, however, in *AF.* It should be noted that the letters *ṭ* and *'* are easily confused in Samaritan script. The name is curious, and might mean, "pleasant name."

מגבול ים וין לפלשתים: Read, with H2, *migg^ebhûl yām dēn.*

14. עד נהר מצרים: Adler reads *naḥal miṣrāyim.* The Samaritan settlement in Egypt began with Alexander the Great's conscription of Samaritan troops to guard the district of Thebes (Josephus, *Ant.* xi, 340–346).

15. קיסריה: Caesarea was an important Samaritan centre from the 1st to the 6th cents. A.D. (see Ben-Zevi, *Se.H.* 99–100).

אהרן בן זהר: Adler and *AF* read *'ahărōn ben 'ōhar.* The latter form may have originated through the influence of the name *'ahărōn,* which the scribe had just written.

16. לאל: Adler reads *zā'ēl.* The name *lā'ēl* is known from Nu 3:24, which is rendered by the LXX as *Δαήλ.* This may explain the Adler version.

מגבול מקדם הכרמים: Read, with H2 and Adler, *migg^ebhûl ha-karmel.*

תהוות:* Perhaps connected with *ta'ăvvôth* (Gn 49:26), in the sense of 'boundaries.'

צנינה: H2: *ṣ^ephînāh. AF* and Tolidah read *ṣ^enînāh* with H1; Adler reads *ṣ^ephînāh,* with H2.

17. הר נקורה: H2: *'Alna'qôrāh.* Perhaps identical with the

village of *al-Nā'ūra,* N. of Jezreel Valley and E. of the Hill of Moreh (see *Encycl. Jud.,* 2, 917).

כופר מרואן: *AF*s rendering helps us to identify this site. He reads *mā'rôth.* The town of Meroth, in Upper Galilee, is listed by Josephus as having been fortified by him in the year 66 A.D. *(Vita,* 188; *Wars,* 2, 573). It is probably to be identified with the well-known town of Meron, burial-place of R. Simeon bar Yohai (see J. Aharoni, *Hitnaḥaluth Shivte Yisrael ba-Galil ha-Elyon* (1957), 95 ff.).

The rendering of the Tolidah, *k^ephar m^erôn,* supports this identification.

18. בן צפו: H2: *ṣ^ephô; AF*: *ṣābhôr.*

נחלת ליטה: The identification is suggested by reference to the other boundary, Sidon. Clearly we are dealing here with the area of Mt. Hermon, the larger part of which belongs to Lebanon. *Naḥal Lîṭāh* is probably the Litani (Leontes) Valley, to the West of the mountain.

בן מניר: H2 and *AF* render *mākhîr; khaph* and *nûn* being easily confused in Samaritan script.

19. בן שריאן: H2, *cum* Tolidah and Adler, renders *šîrā'n.* The fact that this leader's possession stretched as far as Lebanon prompts the suggestion that there may be a connection between his name and Siryon, mentioned together with Lebanon in Ps 29:6. It is thus conceivable that this leader inherited (or was confirmed in) his family holding by Baba Rabbah.

§10

1. מצא אתם: See on 9:6.

ויחלק עליהם את כל ארץ כנען: A *Joshua-Dositheean* tradition. See our discussion, pp. 180–183.

2. ארבע אלפים: Both H1 and H2 are characterized by a looseness in gender-agreement between adjectives and nouns, especially in the case where numerals are employed (cf. *šiššāh mē'ôth**, *'eḥād 'eleph* (v 4) and *'aḥath 'eleph* (v 5)).

ושמנה מאות ושש שנים: This is clearly a correction of H2's erroneous version which states that Baba appeared one thousand, eight hundred and *sixty-six* years after the entry into Canaan. The date of the entry into Canaan is consistently given in Samaritan sources as 2794 A.M. If Baba appeared, as stated, in the year 4600 A.M., then this must have been 1806 years after the entry into Canaan, in accordance with the H1 version.

Vv. 4–5 are omitted in H2, whose chronology, as we have noted above, seems to have suffered in textual transmission.

4. לבנות את שלמה ... בית מקדש: The date of Solomon's Temple, according to Sam. tradition, was 3274 A.M., which accords with the statement that Baba appeared 1326 years after that event, viz. in 4600 A.M.

את שלמה: A charateristic of H1 is its employment of the preposition *'eth* with *subject* clause. It occurs again later in this verse, in the phrase, *'ăšer qānāhû 'eth 'abhîv.* See J. Macdonald, "The Particle *'eth* in Classical Hebrew: Some New Data on its Use with the Nominative," *VT* XIV, 3 (1966), 264–275.

והוא מקום הגרן: See II Sam. 24:16; I Chr. ch. 21.

5. אלף וחמשים שנה לגלות ...: The first exile, according to Samaritan tradition, was in the year 3550 A.M. (lower chronology).

כהנת הכ׳ הגדול עקביה: See the chronological list of High Priests, conveniently arranged by J. Macdonald (The Samaritan Chronicle No. II, Appendix V, 222).

6. למובא מן הגלות: The first Return, according to the Samaritan tradition, was in the year 3595 A.M.

נסחת הראישונה:* /*nsḥ* occurs in Dt 28:63 in the sense of being 'torn away from one's land;' hence the development of a nominal form, *nāshāh,* denoting 'exile.'

גלות נבוך דנצר: Both versions are erroneous as regards this statement; for the exile of Nebuchadnezzar was, of course, the *second* exile, not, as stated herein, the first. The same error occurs in Chronicle Adler. The reference in H1 to the Pontificate of the High Priest Seriah is, however, correct. He ministered at the return from the *first* Exile (see Macdonald, *loc cit.*).

7. גלות השנית ... היא גלות מלך היונים: The second exile is popularly referred to in Samaritan sources as the 'Greek Exile,' possibly because of the dominating personality of Alexander the Great, and the traditions concerning his relationship with the community and their Temple (see Montgomery, 68), as opposed to the obscure period until the fall of the Persian empire.

It was probably this popular, though chronologically confusing, tradition that was responsible for the erroneous identification of the first Exile with Nebuchadnezzar.

8. לעמיר: 'Restoration,' 'rebuilding;' Arabic عمّر.

9. לגלות המלך אסכנדר:* The expression *l^egālûth,* which is omitted in H1, is erroneous, having crept in as a result of the many previous references to 'Exiles.' There was, of course, no exile by Alexander.

10. ויצלבו אתו: The Samaritans were eager to dissociate themselves from any complicity in the death of Jesus, and, at the same time, to throw the guilt squarely upon the Judaeans. The discourtesy shown by the Samaritans to Jesus (see Montgomery, 157–164), and the latter's apparent contempt for their beliefs (*op. cit.*, 161–2), may have thrown some degree of suspicion upon the community. This is indeed confirmed when we read the section of our Chronicle which covers the period of Jesus' activity. The apologetic note which characterizes the account is most marked, as the following passage will illustrate:

> Now Jesus the Nazarene did not consult the community of the Samaritan-Israelites at any time in his life. He did not stand in their way, nor did they stand in his. They did not impose upon him, nor he on them, in any way. He was, however, the subject of vengeance on the part of his own people, his own community, from whom he rose, that is, the Judaist community. They hated him wholeheartedly; so much so that they were the cause of his execution, his crucifixion (J. Macdonald and A.J.B. Higgins, "The Beginnings of Christianity according to the Samaritans," *NTSt* 17, 11. See especially, sections 81–85.).

Vv. 11–20 appear to have come from a separate source. It is a self-contained unit, which fits uneasily into the context and seems to be more like a summary of Baba's achievements rather than a personal history. Its original purpose might have been to trace the origin of the *Ḥavtawi* priests of Damascus. (Do we have here a clue to the original provenance of the Chronicle?)

11. בימי הטובים: Read *bayāmîm ha-ṭôbhîm.*

הארץ כנען: Read *bᵉ'ereṣ kᵉnā'an.*

הספר:* The context suggests the meaning 'period,' /*spr* 'to count.' In Mishna Nazir vii, 3 there occurs the phrase *yᵉmê sᵉphērô*, 'the period of his counting.' Our noun would then be *sāphēr.*

12. גם עדת בני יהודה: There is no basis for the claim that the Judaean *community* was under Baba's authority. Individual Jews, inhabiting border areas or villages with a preponderance of Samaritans, might, however, have regarded it as politic to acknowledge him.

המתעתקת ... שבעים הזקנים: Underlying this statement is an unmistakable polemical claim for the accuracy of the Samaritan transmitted text. The Judaists also made the same claim; and, to this day, in the Jewish Synagogue, the verse, 'And this is the Law which Moses placed before the Children of Israel, according to the word of the Lord, by the hand of Moses,' is recited as the scroll is raised aloft after reading. For the Samaritans to have made such a claim, in this context, is understandable, bearing in mind that Baba's reform regarding accurate reading of the Law followed on after a period of acute neglect, prevention of such reading and observance, execution of the religious leaders and teachers, and destruction of the Torah scrolls, during the persecution of Severus. It was thus imperative for the Samaritans to stress that they, nonetheless, still possessed an authentic tradition going back to the seventy Elders who disseminated the Law in the time of Moses.

בימי אדון הראישונים והאחרונים:* From the H1 version, *'ădôn ha-n^e bhî'îm,* it would seem that the word *ha-n^e bhî'îm* has been omitted from H2. Moses is most commonly described as *'ădôn ha-n^e bhî'îm.* This would be rather mystifying, however, since it would provide us with a rendering: 'in the days of the Master of the Former and Later Prophets.' We know, however, that the Samaritans have never accepted any prophets other than Moses, and would certainly take no recognition of the Judaistic distinction between Former and Later Prophets!

It is conceivable, therefore, that the original version of H2 was not *'ădôn,* but *dārê,* 'generations,' thereby providing the rendering, '(from the priests who functioned) in the early and later generations.'

The word *dārê* occurs earlier in the verse, and might well have been repeated. Alternately, *'ădôn hā-ri'yšônîm* might mean 'lord of the *first-mentioned* (sc. in this verse)' — namely, the Elders — 'and the *last-mentioned'* — namely, the priests. Such a sentiment, upholding Moses' authority even over the priests (notwithstanding the influence of Aaron), would most likely have emanated from a 'Moses-Dositheán' tradition.

15. עבדי: Old Levitical name; see I Chr 6:29, II Chr 29:12, Ezr 10:26. Also in Nabatean Palm. *(see Cook, North Semitic Inscriptions,* 87).

שבע: Benjaminite name, e.g. *Šebha' ben Bikhrî* (II Sam 20:1, I Chr 5:13); also in placename, *B^e'ēr Šebha'.*

אור: I Chr 11:35; also in name 'Ûr kaśdîm, and as kernel of 'ûrî (Ex 31:2), *'Ûrîy'ēl* (I Chr 6:9), *'Ûrîyāh* (II Sam 11:3) and *'Ûrîyāhû* (Jer 26:20).

עז: Variation of Levitical name *'Uzzāh* (I Chr 6:14) or *'Uzzî* (I Chr 5:31, 32).

16. פרו וישרצו וירבו ויעצמו: Ex 1:7.

17. חזקו ואמצו אל תיראו ואל תערצו: Dt 31:6.

18. פחדכם ומראכם: Dt 11:25.

אשר הוציא .. מכור הברזל: Dt 4:20.

19. **דהסגיל**: * /*sgl* only in nominal form in *BH*, as *s^e^gûllāh*, 'a possession.' Perhaps derived here as denominative.

נפשותיכם: A gloss, to clarify that it is a spiritual, not corporeal, existence that is conceived of in the Hereafter.

20. **האנשיאים**: The *'Aliph* in the definite article serves a similar purpose to that of *'Aliph Tawila* in Arabic. Here, especially, to avoid the sharp sound of the Masoretic *dāgesh* in the *Nun*.

בהעם ישראל: Definite article with a noun in construct case!

21. **ויפרק עול הברזל מעל צוארך**: Dt 28:48.

וישבר מטות ... קוממית: Lv 26:13.

22. **עפלו**: /*'pl* 'to swell up,' 'surge forward', see on 1:20. The H2 rendering, *'āphlû ... biśmāḥôth*, elucidates the sense of 'swelling, or erupting, with joy.'

§11

1. **הרפתים**: * See on 8:7.

2. **וחליצו להם**: * 'Equipped themselves for war,' cf. Nu 32:21. It may also carry the sense of 'plundered them (sc. the enemy),' denominative of *ḥălîṣāh* (II Sam 2:21). See *BDB, Lexicon*, 322, col. II.

ומחו צרבותם: Either, 'they swept away their ashes,' /*ṣrb*, 'to burn, scorch,' or, 'they blotted out their existence,' see 19:50* (= H1's *šēm*), 19:64*, 22:10*.

עת אחד: As in later *BH*, *'ēth* is occasionally construed as masculine (see *BDB*, Lexicon, 773).

3. **זכרון למודע**: For a full discussion of the practice referred to in this verse, see chapter VIII.

עודה: * 'Occupation,' variation of noun *'iddān*.

טף: * Apparently a variation of noun *daph*, 'board, timber.'

3. **יעבירו מן אש**: * *ya'ăbhîrû min* = *yabh'îrû b^e^*, 'to burn in fire,' cf. Nu 11:1, 3.

חיב עשותה: * The exhortation contained in this verse, to observe the custom of burning the Succah boards, 'at the right time; fathers, sons and little ones, according to the correct procedure of the community,' has a polemical ring, suggesting that the ritual was, in fact, in danger of falling into desuetude, probably as a result of its origin and significance having been long forgotten. Hence the need to prop its importance by means of the solemn exhortation contained in the verse.

דהלכים על טף אימנותה: * 'Who walk upon the path (lit. boards) of their faith.' A play on the word *taph* is detectable. Perhaps burning the *boards* of the Succah booths was to be construed, in a figurative sense, as walking the *board,* or path, of faith.

Alternately, the phrase *'al taph* may be idiomatic for 'eagerly,' /*tpp* 'to take a quick step.' Render: 'Who walk eagerly in their faith.'

4. רפיתים:* Orthog. variant of *rîphtîm* (11:1).

5. יתפשו על: In *BH* /*tpś* takes the preposition b^e.

יקמצו על נגישי:* /*qmṣ* in the sense of 'to seize *people*' is an extension of the biblical usage, 'to take a handful (of flour),' Lv 2:2, 5:12, Nu 5:26.

6. והנים:* Cf. Ex 9:20.

7. ברע דבר: 'In an evil condition,' cf. Ex 32:12. Preposition b^e as *Beth essentiae.*

אשר הקימו: Delete as dittography.

הקים מלך חדש: Cf. Ex 1:8.

עדפה:* 'Intense,' variant of *'ădîphā'.*

8. יתשפע:* Lit. 'would flow (in abundance) from' = 'result from' = 'be the consequence of.'

9. רגלאים:* Adj. *riglâ'î* (N.H. rāgîl), 'accustomed.'

חמישים:* *BH*: *ḥămûšîm* (Ex 13:18, Nu 32:17), 'in battle array.'

מלכי התרפים:* Perhaps, 'idolatrous kings' (see Gn 31:19, 34:35), but, more likely, metathesis for *riphtîm* (see v 4 above).

10. ביד חזקה ובזרוע נטויה: Dt 4:34.

11. דכה אתם במדכה: Nu 11:8.

12. ומלא את כל הר עסכר מן נבילותם: In Akkadian, 'to fill a mountain with corpses' is a common idiom.

13. וכחשם:* In *BH* /*kḥš* is always intransitive.

14. Note the succession of Hithpa'ēl forms in this sentence. An extreme example of H2's predilection in this direction.

ואתפוררו:* 'They quaked with fear,' Cf. Is 24:19, 'to split.' Arabic فَرفَرَ 'to shake.'

ואתחילו:* Synonym of previous verb. /*ḥûl,* /*ḥîl,* 'to writhe in anguish,' Dt 2:25. There is no Hithpa'ēl form in *BH.*

15. ויסף: Assimilation of *'Aliph;* read *vayye'ĕsōph.*

אלפים ורבבות: Idealistic hyperbole.

עסכרים: 'Troops,' 'camp.' Arabic عسكرى.

The verses which follow, until the end of the section, have suffered much in textual transmission.

17. פא: Read *pē'āh.*

בחרחים: Read *baḥărābhîm.*

וברחמים: Read *ûbhirmāḥîm.*

נכנונים: Read *n^ekhônîm.*

שפעת:* Orthog. variant of *s^ephath,* representing the peculiar Samaritan pronunciation of the *pataḥ* vowel.

18. **הצוה**: Read *ha-ṣābhā'.*

19. **ויכרש אכתל**: Text corrupt; read, *vayy^{e}gāreš 'eth kōl.*

כי אובי ... השמרים: A verb has been omitted after *ha-š^{e}mārîm;* probably *hāyû.*

20. **בה**: Read *bā'.*

ויהי כי בה המגיד למלך הצדיק בבא רבה: This phrase should be deleted as a textual intrusion, probably from 12:1.

נצו: The context requires the sense of 'fled.' This, indeed, provides confirmation of the reliability of the *MT*'s reading *nāṣû* (— *hapax, //nā'û*) in Lam. 4:15. *BDB* (*Lexicon* 663, col. I) observes that 'the text is very dubious,' and suggests the meaning of 'to fly (?).'

Our text clarifies the exact nuance in which this verb was employed in Palestine, namely, 'to flee' (= *nûs*). It is more likely, then, that the root is */nûs,* rather than *BDB*'s */nṣh. /Nûṣ* would then be a rare variant of */nûs,* possibly conveying a more urgent sense of (flight in) panic.

וידגד: The translation, 'he quartered,' is based upon a reading *vayyidgōr* (cf. Jer 17:11). Alternately, read *vayyidgōd,* a denominative of *g^{e}dûd,* 'troop,' in the same meaning, 'to station troops.'

ויורשים: The second *yodh* is merely an orthographic representation of the *ṣērê* vowel in a lengthened form.

צבה: Read *ṣābhā'.*

אשר הקהלו אליו: 'Who had quickly come to him.' Alternately, 'whom he had assembled,' reading *hiqhîlû* (for defective spelling of Hiph'îl, see Nu 20:10). In pronunciation, the soft breathing of the second *hey* is barely audible, which would explain its omission here.

21. **יביאו ל**:* Lacuna. Restore with *l^{e}malkhê 'edôm.*

22. **ויעבירו ...**: For the lacuna, insert *qôl.* Cf. 23:10.

מומס: Read *môsām.*

מית ...: Read *mithpaqqdîm,* 'commanded,' on basis of 19:55*.

23. **ויכרת**: Elyptic for *vayyikhrōth b^{e}rîth.*

למן ... הזה: Read *l^{e}min ha-yôm ha-zeh.*

יקחו: For */lqḥ* in sense of 'donate,' see Ex 25:2.

לצב.: Read *laṣṣābha'.*

24. **הצי ... ב.**: Read *ha-ṣaddîq bābhā'.*

עמרתה ... בה אדונ': Read *d^{e}niqb^{e}rû bāh 'ădôn ...*

ארשי: 'Ancestors.' The noun is a contraction of the words *'al rēš,* 'in the beginning.'

26. **אתעמרת**: Syr. ܥܡܪ 'to indwell,' 'inhabit,' 'colonize.' Also

found in Ethtaph. form ܐܬܬܥܡܪ, 'to be made to dwell, to be settled (Payne Smith, Syriac-English Dictionary, p. 418).'

§12

2. עד כי חדל ... מספר: Gn 41:49.
The lacunae in this verse were originally filled by quotations from Ps 10: 1–14.
אל ... חק: Read *'al tirḥaq*; cf. Ps 10:1.
אל תעלים: *Ibid.*
4. בגאו ...: Read *b*ᵉ*ga'ăvath;* cf. Ps 10:2.
בלבו לא תדרש: Cf. Ps 10:13.
כעסנו: Cf. Ps 10:14.
5. אתה ההית: Read *hāyîthā; Ibid.* Second *hey* dittog.
שבר זרוע: Cf. Ps 10:15.
6. יי' מלך עולם: Ps 10:16.
נכרים: Gloss, not in *BT.*
תאות: Ps 10:17.
תתן אזנך לשמע את שיאלם: *BT*: *taqšîbh 'āzn*ᵉ*khā.*
לא יוסף עוד: Cf. Ps 10:18. BT: *bal yôsîph.*
7. הושיע יי': Ps 12:2.
כי נשמדו: *BT*: *kî gāmar.*
כי ספו אמונים: *BT*: *kî phassû.*
8. עד אנה: Ps 13:2.
עד מתי תסיר: *BT*: *'ānāh tastîr.*
עד אנה נשית עצות: Ps 13:3.
כל יום: *BT*: *yômām.*
9. ראה ועננו: Cf Ps 13:4; B.T: *habbîtāh va'ănēnû.*
אניר: *BT*: *hā'îrāh.*
נישון למות: *BT*: *pen 'îšan ha-māveth.*
פן יאמרו אויבינו: *Ps 13:5.*
ואנחנו בחסדך: Ps 13:6.
נשיר לשמך לטוב לנו: *BT*: *'āšîrāh layhōvāh kî gāmal 'ālāy.*
10. משה בן עמרם: H2 has no mention of Moses; cf. 3:26.
שופרים:* *BH* always has the *ôth*-termination for the plural of *šôphār.*
11. וכי תבואו: Cf. Nu 10:9.
לפני יי': Delete as dittog.
ונועשתם: Read *v*ᵉ*nôša'tem, cum SP.*
12. השקף ...: Cf. Dt 26:15. *BT*: *hašqîphāh.*
והצל: *BT*: *û-bhārēkh*
13. ויזרקו: Departure from Biblical sense of 'sprinkling blood (of sacrifice). Here, 'to shed' — in a purely secular sense.

ויהי:* Single occurrence of *Waw-Consecutive* in H2; possibly under influence of biblical quotation in previous verse.

נפש:* 'Gave them release (refreshment)'. Syr. ܢܦܫ, 'refresh.' In *BH* only in Niph'al.

ההו: Read *hahû'.*

14. דרך דם הטמאה: H2 attributes a different commemorative appellation to the place — *'ebhen ha-ṭāmē'.* The noun *'ebhen* might refer to the city of Shechem itself, which is known by the name *'ebhen,* after the stone of Jacob; see 8:18, and *CESC,* pp. 449 ff.

§13

The present section, comprising the Thanksgiving Prayer of Baba Rabbah, is an almost *verbatim* rendering of the Judaistic Song of David, found in both Ps 18 and II Sam ch. 22. The main difference is that the Chronicler converts expressions into the plural in order for the song to represent a communal vehicle of expression.

It is beyond doubt that the Chronicler was basing himself upon the version contained in the Psalter, not that of II Samuel. Evidence is marshalled in the notes which follow to prove this point (a point whose ramifications are analyzed in chapter VI) by drawing attention to many instances of differences between the Samuel and Psalms versions, and where the version of our Chronicler coincides with the latter.

A characteristic of the Chronicler's treatment of his material is that of simplifying biblical phraseology which is difficult or unfamiliar (see on vv. 11, 14, 18 and 19).

2. A variation of Ps 18:3 (II Sam 22:2, 3).

3. Cf. Ps 18:4 (II Sam 22:4).

מהללים: Since this ptc. (Pu'al) qualifies 'God,' the conversion into the plural is unnecessary.

נקרא את יי׳: *BT* omits *'eth.*

4. Cf. Ps 18:5 (II Sam 22:5).

אפפו אתנו: *BT*: *'ăphāphûnî.*

חבלי מות: With Ps 18. The Samuel version has *mišb^e rê māveth.*

5. Cf. Ps 18:6 (II Sam 22:6).

סבבו לנו: The full form of */sbb* accords with the Psalms version. The Samuel version has *sabbūnî.*

תפשו בנו: *BT*: *qidmûnî.*

6. Cf. Ps 18:7 (II Sam 22:7).

קראנו ליי׳: *BT*: *'eqrā' yhwh.*

צעקנו: Under the influence of the Psalm version our Chronicler varies the verb in this stich. (The Psalmist actually employs the verb */šv'*.) The version of II Samuel, however, merely repeats *'eqrā'*.

7. Cf. Ps 18:8 (II Sam 22:8).

ומוסדי: With Ps 18. The Samuel version has *môsdôth*.

8. Cf Ps 18:9 (II Sam 22:9).

אוקדת: Explanatory gloss; */yqd* being more common in Samaritan literature than */qdḥ*.

ויט שמים וירד: Ps 18:10 (II Sam 22:10).

וישלח חציו ... ויחרדם: Cf. Ps 18:15 (II Sam 22:15).

על צרינו: Suppl. gloss.

9. **מאיבינו הצילנו**: Cf Ps 18:18 (II Sam 22:18).

ומשנאינו: With Ps 18. The Samuel version has no *Waw Copula*.

ואל מרחב הוציאנו: Cf. Ps 18:20 (II Sam 22:20).

הוציאנו: With Ps 18. The Samuel version detaches the object pronoun, reading: *vayyōṣi' lammerḥabh 'ōthî.*

10. **יגמלנו**: Cf. Ps 18:21 (II Sam 22:21).

ונהיה תמים ... מעונינו: Cf. Ps 18:24 (II Sam 22:24).

עמו: With Ps 18. The Samuel version has *lô*.

11. **עם חסיד ...**: Cf. Ps 18:26 (II Sam 22:26).

התמים: *BT*: *gebher* (II Sam: *gibbôr)*.

עם טהור יתטהר: The Chronicler has here simplified the biblical version, which has *'im nābhār tithbārār* (II Sam: *tittābhār)*.

יתפתל: The Hithpa'el form is clearly based upon the version of Ps 18:27 (*tithpattāl*), */ptl*. The Samuel version *(tittappāl)*, assumes a */tpl*.

It may be supposed that it is out of deference to deity that the Chronicler places his verbs in the third person.

ועם עני יושיע: Cf. Ps 18:28 (II Sam 22:28).

רמות: With Ps 18. Samuel version has *'al rāmîm*.

12. **הוא יאיר**: Cf. Ps 18:29 (II Sam 22:29).

יאיר: With Ps 18. The Samuel version omits vb.

13. **כי בך**: Cf. Ps 18:30 (II Sam 22:30).

בך: With Ps 18. The Samuel version has *b^{e}khāh*.

14. **דרכי יי' תמימה**: Cf. Ps 18:31 (II Sam 22:31).

תמימה: The *BT* construes *derekh* as masculine: *hā'ēl tāmîm darkô.*

צדיקה: Simplification of *BT*: *ṣ^{e}rûphāh.*

הבטחים: Simplification of *BT*: *ha-ḥōsîm.*

15. Cf. Ps 18:32 (II Sam 22:32).

זולתי אל': With Psalm version. The Samuel version repeats *mibbal'ădê.*

16. Cf. Ps 18:38 (II Sam 22:38).

נפרד: Read *nirdōph.*

17. יצעקו ואין מ׳: Cf. Ps 18:42 (II Sam 22:42).

יצעקו: With Psalm version. The Samuel version has *yiš'û.*

ונשחקם: Cf Ps 18:43 (II Sam 22:43).

על פני רוח: With Psalm version. The Samuel version has *ka'ăphar 'ereṣ.*

כחרש: 'Like a (broken) potsherd,' see Lv 6:21, Nu 5:17. *BT*: *k^e ṭîṭ.*

נשליכם: Simplification of *'ărîqēm* (Ps), *'ădîqēm* (Sam).

18. תפלטנו: Cf. Ps 18:44 (II Sam 22:44).

תשימנו: With Psalm version. II Sam. has *tišm^e rēnî.*

עליונים לכל הגוים: *BT: l^e rō'š gôyim.*

גוים לא ידענו: *BT*: *'Am lō' yāda'tî.*

19. This entire verse follows the version of Ps 18. The Samuel version transposes the two stichoi.

יכחשו: with Ps 18. The Samuel version has *yithkaḥăšû.*

בני זרים: Cf Ps 18:46 (II Sam 22:46). *BT*: *b^e nê nēkhār.*

יפלו: *BT*: *yibbōlû.*

מחדריהם: *BT*: *mimmisg^e rôthēhem.*

20. Cf. Ps 18:47 (II Sam 22:47).

יי׳: Not in *BT.*

ורם אל ישענו: With Psalm version. The Samuel version repeats *ṣûr* before final word.

21. ... האל הנותן: Cf. Ps 18:48 (II Sam 22:48).

בגללנו: *BT*: *lî.*

ויכחשו ... נדרך: An intrusion from Dt 33:29.

22. מפלתנו מאבינו: Cf. Ps 18:49 (II Sam 22:49). This phrase follows the Psalm version. II Sam. has *umôṣî'î mē'ôybhay.*

מאבינו: Read *mē'ōybhēnû.*

מגאלנו: *BT*: *taṣîlēnî.*

23. Cf. Ps 18:50 (II Sam 22:50).

נרנן: *BT*: *'ăzamēr.*

בכל כוחינו: Not in *BT.*

24. Cf. Ps 18:51 (II Sam 22:51).

מגדל: With Psalm version. II Sam. has *magdîl.*

לנו: *BT*: *malkô.*

לבן אהביו: *BT*: *lim^e šiḥô.* The latter two adjustments to the biblical text would have been made by the Chronicler in order to remove the personal (and theological) reference to King David before employing it as a communal song of thanksgiving.

התשבחן והמודאה ... והתהללות:* Cf 4:10.

והורמת:* 'It was intensified' (lit. 'lifted up), see 14:1.

§14

1. קם בפני: Lit. 'It arose before,' i.e. 'It occurred to.'

ביניהם: Delete; superfluous gloss.

כי ילחם אלאסכ׳:* Preposition omitted after */lḥm.*

ולחמו:* */lḥm* taking direct object (see previous note).

מנו:* Dialectal variation of *minnêh,* or read *mimmenû,* the first letter having been omitted by haplography from previous *he'ārîm.*

והורמת:* See on 13:24.

2. (דאריה) עיר: The town of *Dō'r* (or *Dôr*), S. of Carmel, on the Mediterranean, is mentioned in the Bible (Josh 12:23, 17:11; Ju 1:27). This town was inhabited by Samaritans in the 4th cent. A.D. (see *Ben-Zevi, Se.H.* 99, and *M. Avi-Yonah, GRP.,* 52).

H2's omission of the name of any particular town plundered by these marauding Arabs seems to suggest that this was a general invasion of 'the cities of Canaan,' or at least of the area of Samaria.

3. ערים מתכוננה:* Sing. verb after plural subject. Cf. 9:5, 12:1.

4. ערבת הירדן:* The term *'ărābhāh* is regularly applied in the Bible to the Jordan-Valley, 'either W. of River + adjacent plain; near ford (opp. Jericho),' or, 'to the Jordan valley, E. of the River' (***BDB*** *Lexicon,* 787).

H2's designation is most suitable in this context, pointing out, as it does, the direction in which the Arabs would have taken flight in order to reach their homes.

It is also conceivable that metathesis has occurred here, and we should read *'ebhrath ha-yardēn (= 'ēbher ha-yardēn).*

6. גונבים נחשים ... שפיפון: Cf. Gn 49:17.

ועלי ארח: Read without *Waw Copula, cum* Gn 49:17.

ממשלם היתה: *Mimšāl* construed as fem., but possibly read *memšaltām.*

7. בהערבים: Non-elision of definite article with preposition b^e; cf. *b*^{e}*hā'ām* (10:20).

מדל:* Contraction of *mdlh* (= *mah d*^{e}*lêh*), following the same semantic development as *NH*: *māmôn.*

8. אז ישר ...: Vocabulary from the Song of the Sea (Ex 15), serving to cast Baba in the role of a second Moses (see on 1:6, 7).

9. אשירך: Dative tacked on to the verb, without the (biblical) prepostion l^e.

עזי וזמרתי: Ex 15:2.

אנוהיך וארוממך: *Ibid.* The form *'anvehykhā* represents the appendage of the object pronoun to the full form of the verb with final radical *hey.* The same phenomenon occurs in our

Chronicle in the case of nouns (ending in *eh*) with pronominal suffixes; hence the forms *qāṣehhû* (21:14), *qāṣehnû* (17:13), *miqvāhyv* (22:15). These are due to the appending of the suffix to the absolute form, rather than to the construct ending.

10. גיבור במלחמה: This is the reading of the *SP*. The *MT* has *gibbôr milḥāmāh*.

11. יי׳ בגאותך ישמח מלך: Cf. Ps 21:2. M.T: *b^{e}ʻāz^{e}khā*.

ואיך בישועתך לא יחד: *MT*: *ubhîšû'āth^{e}khā mah yāgîl m^{e}'ōd*.

12. ימינך יי׳: Ex 15:6.

13. תאות לבי: Cf. Ps 21:3.

כל מבטא שפ׳: *MT*: *va'ărešeth ś^{e}phāthāy*. Chronicler simplifies uncommon vocabulary. See introductory note to §13.

14. כי תקדמני: Cf. Ps 21:4.

נצר חסד: *MT*: *'ăṭereth pāz*.

15. מי כמוך: Cf. Ex 15:11.

נאדרי בקדש: *Cum SP*. The *MT*. has *ne'dār*.

עשה פלאה: *Cum SP*. The *MT*. has *phele'*.

16. גדול כבודי: Cf. Ps 21:6.

שמת עלי: Chronicler simplifies biblical *t^{e}šavveh*.

17. כי המלך: Cf. Ps 21:8.

לא ימוט: *MT*: *bal yimmôṭ*.

18. תמצא ידך: Cf. Ps 21:9.

תרעץ לכל שנאיך: *MT*: *timṣā' śōn'eykhā*.

19. פריהם: Ps 21:11. *MT*: *piryāmô*.

20. רומה: Ps 21:14.

21. לקרת: Defective orthography.

22. נתן: Probably Inf. absolute, *n^{e}thōn*.

צדק ... עלינו: Unusual prepostion with /*ṣdq*. The H2 version, *hēṭîbh* suggests that the context requires a causative meaning, 'to *show* justice towards.' Perhaps, therefore, we should read *hiṣdîq 'ālēnû*. In Talmudic literature, the phrase *hiṣdîq 'ālāyv 'eth ha-dîn* ('He vindicated divine justice') is very common. Viewed in this light, we have an explanation for our, otherwise problematic, preposition.

לקחות ... לשביות: Quasi-Infinitives, with *ùth*-termination, in verbal-noun sense.

23. מאת יי׳ ... היתה זה: Cf. Ps 118:23.

המצליח: This appears to be a noun, 'prosperity' (= H2's *niṣ'ănû*). Alternately, the *Hey* might have arisen through dittography from previous word *zeh*. *Maṣlîaḥ* would then be a participle: 'made us prosper.'

24. ומכוננו: Possibly a euphemism for *māqôm* as a reference to the Deity — 'His Omnipresence' (as common in Rabbinic

literature); or, perhaps, 'His steadfastness,' from the same basic meaning of /*kûn*.

אשר כחשו את שנאינו: Cf. Dt 33:29.

וישילחו: Read *vayyišlaḥ*.

פניהם: In sense of preposition *liphnēhem*.

25. ויכחשו ... תדרך: *Ibid.*

§15

1. ואיטיב: The context suggests the sense of 'blessed them,' lit. 'He invoked *goodness* upon them.'

2. עתה הלכו: Dittog. Read *'attāh* l^e*khû*.

אתצריך: No transposition before sibilant. See on 3:12, 15:2, 24:5.

3. לי ... קרוב: Unusual word order, with preposition well before adjective.

4. חצרים: 'Villages.' Cf. Lv 25:31; Josh 19:8.

לבר:* Read l^e*bhal*.

יחדש:* Pu'al; 'be changed,' 'renewed.'

5. חסיד:* A rather strong word to convey the sense of 'acceptable.' Assuming that /*ḥsd*, in Palestinian tradition, also possessed this less benign connotation (than 'kindness'), might not the phrase *šômēr ha-b*^{e}*rîth v*^{e}*haḥesed* (Dt 7:9, 12) mean, more plausibly, 'who keeps his covenant and *agreement*?'

7. שלשים:* Perhaps read *śāśîm*, 'rejoicing.'

זהו: Form /*zhh* = /*zhr*, 'joy,' (see Ben-Hayyim, *Tarbiz*, 10, 354, n. 6).

8. ראש כל שבוע: Explanatory gloss.

9. היה וכל: Delete *Waw* of *v*^{e}*khōl*.

ששונים: Stange participial form, from noun *śāśôn*.

וישאר זה המעשה: This custom appears to be similar to the Judaean institutions of *Mišmārôth* and *Ma'ămādôth*. Here, the priests went to Shechem while the laymen prayed in their own towns.

זהים:* See on v. 7.

האבדת:* 'Removed;' lit. 'lost.'

10. המקום אשר על שמו: We are not told *which* place 'bore his name.' If the reference is to Baba's Synagogue which remained standing until the 14th cent., it would be mystifying why it should have been kept closed at times other than when he was visiting. It might refer, however, to the specific residences assigned to him for use in each town when paying a pastoral visit, as H2 especially seems to suggest. The fact that only priests were permitted to

open it might have been merely a security measure in order to avoid defilement by impure persons.

The verse appears to have been transposed from another context. It fits uneasily into the present material.

11. יהוה:* Delete as gloss. The glossator seemed unaware that there was already a subject — 'fear' — of the sentence.

12. אז: Unusual as a relative of time. H2: *kad.*

למלחמותם: See on 14:22.

13. נטשנו:* Occurs only once in *BH* in this sense of 'permit.' See Gn 31:28.

לבנות את בית מקדשכם: This echoes the tradition that the Emperor Julian granted permission to the Judaeans to build their Temple. See J. Juster, *Les Juifs dans L'empire Romain,* II (1914), 247.

14. נוכל על: In *BH* /*ykl* takes the preposition l^e in the sense of 'to prevail *over,*' see Gn 32:26, Nu 13:30.

Vv. 15–17 are not represented in H2. They constitute an extraneous tradition, and were probably inserted by the H1 compiler either for dramatic quality or to fill a lacuna in the original — a problem we frequently encounter with composite writing.

15. ... למה נשלם: Cf. Gn 44:4.

משאי וטרחי המלכ׳: Characteristic employment of a succession of construct nouns.

18. ולרב: Qal (Infinitive) in causative sense of 'to multiply.'

19. כסות: Adjective *kas* or *kēs,* 'covered,' hence 'secret.'

ויתנו לו ... להמיתו: 'They gave (their attention) to him ... to slay him.' Apparently ellyptical for *nāthan lēbh.*

נכליה:* Noun *nēkhel* only in Nu 25:18.

ונכלו:* Pi'el; *ibid.*

§16

1. פרט הימים:* Perhaps, 'At this *particular* time.' Tal. Aram. *p^erāṭ,* 'singled out,' 'specification,' 'explicit' (Jastrow, *Dictionary,* 1224).

2. ולא יצא ממנו: The custom of not moving out of one's residence on the Sabbath was based upon a literal understanding of Ex 16:29. The modern Samaritans 'stay strictly within doors on the Sabath, except to go to the Synagogue' *(Montgomery,* 33).

3. קעצים: Read *qā'ēmîm.*

ואתנכלו:* Gn 37:18.

על שאת:* Variation of *lāśē'th.*

שם לא יכלו ... כלי מלחמה:* If we understand *šām* in its usual sense of 'there,' the verse would appear to be suggesting a prohibition against wearing weapons in the Synagogue. However, *šām* also has the sense of 'then' in our Chronicle (see on 2:21; cf. 19:40); in which case, the emphasis would be on *time* rather than *place*, viz. 'At that time (sc. the Sabbath) they would be unable to take up arms.'

4. כסות עיצתם: See 15:19. Here as abstract noun *kassûth* 'secrecy'.

מפני: Used here in the sense of *liphnê*, 'before' (in temporal sense). However, note the comment of ***BDB*** (*Lexicon*, 818) on the form *mipp^{e}nê:* 'Frequently rendered *before* in A.V. R.V., and so confused with *liphnê*; but the *min* retains always its full force in the Heb.'

As far as Samaritan Hebrew is concerned ***BDB*** is incorrect, as the present sense of *mipp^{e}nê* makes patently clear. If this Samaritan usage was current throughout Palestinian spoken tradition, then ***BDB*** is incorrect in its limitation of the scope of this preposition.

מיום הששי ... ואתאמר מיום החמישי:* The confusion over the exact day of Baba's arrival, and the revelation of the Judaean plan to him, is aggravated by H1's reference to 'the *seventh* day' (v 5), a reference which is itself contradicted in the same verse by the mention of the *fifth* day of the week. Mention of 'the fifth day of the week' is actually made in vv. 4, 5 and 6 of the H1 version, which suggests its legitimacy.

It is therefore the opening statement of v 5 ('Now it was on the seventh day of the week that the Lord ... revealed the hidden plan ...') that must be regarded as suspicious. We suggest that it actually qualifies the statement made at the end of v 4 — 'before the arrival of the King Baba Rabbah to the town of Nemarah.' A glossator then inserted the note, *'it* was on the seventh day of the week,' meaning the *arrival of Baba Rabbah.* Unfortunately, the glossator's introductory word, *hāyāh,* was ill chosen as a conjunction (he should have written, with *Waw Copula, v^{e}hû' hāyāh,* 'and that was (to be) on the Seventh day.' The absence of the conjunction was responsible for the tacking on of the phrase to the following verse, with the attendant confusion that this causes.

התלתם:* 'Deception.' Denominative of */tll,* 'to deceive,' Gn 31:7.

6. ומאהבה גדלה היתה: Detached relative pronoun; see on 9:5.

ממניך: Dittog. Read *minnêkh* ('from you') *cum* H2.

אחמד:* Samaritan usage is semantically weaker than the Biblical sense of 'desire,' 'take pleasure in,' 'delight,' with strong emotional overtone. Here it simply means, 'request,' 'wish,' 'demand' (see 18:8, 19:1*).

8. **אז אגלי ליך**: Rare use of *'āz* to introduce a relative clause of time, in the sense of 'when.' See, however, 15:12. Perhaps *'āz* is used here for *mē'āz* (cf. Gn 39:5, Ex 5:23).

תגידי ... על לשני: Lit. 'You will disclose it upon my tongue.' Either, idiomatic for 'in my name' = '(as having emanated) from my tongue,' or read *'al lešônēkh,* '(You will disclose it) upon *your* tongue.'

The phrase *'al pîykh* (16:9) would appear to support our first suggestion, however.

לנפל את נפשי: The context seems to require a transitive and causative sense, as *'to cast* my soul down.' The problem is avoided if the verb */npl* is here construed as Pi'el *(lenappēl),* though this is unattested in *BH.*

Alternately, the Qal usage may also be retained, with *'eth* as introducing the *subject* (see on 10:4; also, 8:19, 13:1, 17:6) — a common characteristic in our Chronicle. The sense would then be, 'for my soul to fall ...'

9. **אדברו**:* Rarely with *accusative* pronominal suffix; but cf. Gn 37:4.

במוצא שפתי:* Dt 23:24.

11. **ותאמר אליה**: Delete as dittog.

נכמרת:* Cf. Gn 43:30. Subject: *śenē'ûth* ('hatred was intensified'). In this sense, see also 16:23,* *vaḥăṭā'ēnû nikhmereth* ('Our sins were intensified'). In *BH* it is rather employed in the sense of 'to grow warm and tender' *(BDB., Lexicon,* 485 col. I).

וחרוצים:* 'Will break in.' A semantic extension of the basic meaning 'to cut.' Here, 'to cut one's way in.'

וכרת:* Read *yikkārēth* ('That their memory should be destroyed.').

12. **תמושני חרדה**:* Lit. 'that trembling does not *feel* me,' i.e., 'take hold of me.'

13. **ויקם גיד הקנאה בפניה**: Adler reads *qām gîd ha-qin'āh vayyakh bāh,* 'la veine du zèle se mit à battre en elle.' Our reading seems preferable.

The phrase *qām gîd ha-qin'āh,* to denote intense indignation, occurs in a *Tašqîl* of a Torah scroll in the Gaster collection. Quoted by Ben-Zevi, *Se.H.* 291 n. 57.

14. **לא זכרת לו**: Lit. 'she did not remember to him.' A causative sense ('mention') seems rather to be required here, but Qal may also serve this purpose (see on v 8 above).

בצררה:* *Ṣerārāh* is apparently a variant of *ṣārāh.*

15. אתבצר:* Uncommon usage. H1's rendering *yiḥar 'appô* provides the clue to the sense in which it is employed, although the exact nuance is unclear.

משנתן:* Text corrupt, perhaps through lacuna. Read *yiqqaḥ šᵉnāthô.*

17. לבוש בגדים בדים: Adler adds: 'And he was dressed in his Sabbath clothes, white garments, with a *Ṭallîth* over his head.'

The modern-day priest wears a *Ṭallîth* during the reading of the Law, though it contains no fringes (*Montgomery,* 32). The wearing of the *Ṭallîth* during Prayer seems, however, to have been common practice in the medieval period, for laymen as well as priests. This is evident from a reference in *Abu'l Fatḥ* (see quotation in *Ben-Zevi,* pp. 177–8) to the building of the *Kinša* at Shechem by 'Aqbon b. Eliezer (V), who 'took his *Ṭallîth* from off his head·(See Adler's reference, above, to the *Ṭallîth* being worn 'over his head.') and heaped earth from the pile beneath him into his *Ṭallîth'* — building the edifice, thereby, with his own hands.

ויהי השמש ... ועלטה: Gn 15:17.

במחשכת העין: Either, 'in the twinkling of the eye,' as from /*ḥśk,* 'to hold back;' or, 'in a concealed spot,' lit. 'in (a place of) darkness to the eye,' i.e. hidden from view, /*ḥšk,* 'to be dark.' cf. 3:12.

18. השמש לאביו: Read *ha-šemeš lābhô',* Gn 15:12.

וימששו: 'They searched for,' cf. Gn 31:34; also below, 18:6.

דלקדשות השבת מחלל:* Not in H1. As has been observed (see on 1:6), H2 adopts a more militant approach toward the enèmies of the community.

עפלון:* 'Their eagerness, passionate desire,' see on 1:20.

20. רצון ... וסליחתו: H2 omits all such epithets of praise and reverence.

אוי מזה באתו: Read *'ê mizzeh bā'them,* cf. Gn 16:8.

21. ותפל ... אימה ופחד: Ex 15:16.

וירגזו: Ex 15:14.

ויאחזם רעד ונמגו: Ex 15:15.

אתשברת:* No transposition of *taw* and sibilant.

אתשברת צלעם: 'Their rib was broken.' See on 21:8*.

22. ותכו לרגליו: Dt 33:3.

23. ויאמרו לו: Chronicle Adler attributes this confession to a small group of Judaeans who did not flee with the rest in panic and fear at their defeat, but who immediately surrendered and acknowledged their error. It is not clear from Adler whether the latter suffered the same violent end as their brethren who were brought back as prisoners after their abortive attempt to flee.

נכמרת:* 'Intensified,' see on 16:11.

24. ועשית עמם: Read v^e*'āśîthî.*

25. ויקרו: Orthographic variant; contracted form of *vayyiqr*^{e}*'û.* For an example of elision of the *'Aliph* as final radical, cf. *mēḥăṭô* (Gn 20:6) for *mēḥăṭ*^{e}*'ô.*

28. מעלי: Read *mē'ālāyv.*

29. עתי: Read, either *'ittî* or *'ālay.*

השיר:* Infin. Absolute: *hāšēr,* 'to leave over.'

30. ... עשית לו כאשר: *BT* has verse in plural.

§17

1. תבואתים:* Apparently based upon the Masoretic *K*^{e}*thibh* form *tābhô'thāh* (Dt 33:16).

2. וצא:* Common form of perfect */yṣ'*

3/4. קבצו כלים הבניאן:* Read *qibb*^{e}*ṣû k*^{e}*lē ha-b*^{e}*nî'ān.*

וארשו: Common Sam. verb, 'to begin.'

יעפלו: See on 16:18.

5. סופה גדלה: The legend of the whirlwind is related by the traveller Benjamin of Tudela (see M. Adler, "The Itinerary of Benjamin of Tudela," *J.Q.R.*, xvii (1904), 148).

לניאן: Read *libhnî'ān.*

ותזרע: Variant of */zrh,* 'to scatter, fan, winnow,' Ex 32:20. This might, however, be a semantic expansion of the idea of *scattering* seed *(zera'),* applied also, in the Sam. dialect, to scattering or dispersing people.

רוחות מנשבה: Singular participle with plural subject; see on 2:21.

6. יצא את הבית הזה: See on 16:8.

אורשלים:* As in original form, *Urusalim.*

7. ... אז ישר לאמר: Ex 15:1. Samaritan orthography omits a second *yodh* in *yāšîr;* see *SP* (ed. *Von Gall) ad loc.*

8. The rest of this section, comprising Baba's Song of Thanksgiving at having frustrated the plan of the Judaeans to rebuild their Temple, is mainly based upon Psalm 25.

נרים את ידינו: Cf. Ps 25:2. *BT*: *naphšî 'eśśā'.*

9. קויך לא יטרף: Cf. Ps 25:3. *BT*: *qōveykhā lô' yébhōšû.*

יטרפו הבוגדים: *BT*: *yēbhōšû ha-bôg*^{e}*dîm.*

10. ארחיך חכמנו: *BT*: *'orḥôtheykha lamm*^{e}*dēnî.*

11. הדריכנו: Cf. Ps 25:5.

12. רחמיך: Cf. Ps 25:6.

13. אל תפן: Cf. Ps 25:7.

14. צדיק וישר: Cf. Ps 25:8. *BT*: *ṭôbh v*^{e}*yāšār.*

15. כל ארחות: Cf. Ps 25:10.

לשמרי חקותיו ומצותיו: *BT*: *l^e^nōṣrê b^e^rîthô v^e^'ēdôthāyv.*

16. למען קדוש: Cf. Ps 25:11.

17. מי הוא אנש: Cf. Ps 25:12.

18. נפשו תלין בטוב: Cf. Ps 25:13.

19. סוד יי׳: Cf. Ps 25:14.

ובריתו לשמורי אמת ספר קדשו: *BT*: *ûbh^e^rîthô l^e^hôdî'ām.* The Chronicler has here varied the biblical text in order to incorporate a specific reference to his community.

20. שירו ליי׳: Cf. Ps 96:1, 98:1 *et. al.*

בנים אתם ליי׳: Dt 14:1.

והבו כבוד ועז ליי׳: Cf Ps 29:2.

21. השתחוו ... בהר גריזי: *Ibid.*, with typical Samaritan insertion of reference to Gerizim.

22. יי׳ יתן עז לשמרים ... השמרים בשלום: Cf. Ps 29:11, with insertion of Gerizim motif.

§18

For a full discussion of the episode of the talking bird on Mount Gerizim, as described in this section, see our chapter VII: "The legend of the speaking Bird in the Light of Rabbinic Polemic."

1. חזקת יד: Cf. Ju 9:24.

ונמצא בספר הימים ... בכיר העברי:* This reference, to a Hebrew source underlying our Chronicle, is of crucial importance for countering any suggestion that our Chronicle may be a Hebrew *translation* of an Arabic original, such as were made, for example, of *Abu'l Fatḥ*'s Chronicle.

This introductory source-reference, totally unexpected in the middle of a Chronicle (and omitted in H1), might well indicate a different source for the material which follows. There are, indeed, minor variations in style and approach to the material (see on vv. 7, 12).

בכיר: 'Script,' (see v 8: *b^e^khîr y^e^dêkhem*); perhaps originally designating specifically the Majuscule Script; *b^e^khîr* in the sense of 'primary, major one.'

3. וישוב לאנה: 'To some place,' cf. I Kings 2:36.

כמו (קסיס): Text dubious. The H1 rendering, 'such as *qasîs*' is improbable, a place by that name not being known. A possible rendering is, 'he shall return *as* a *Qasis* (= *Qašîš*, 'Elder'), though this does no justice to the high office of *Episcopos* attained by Levi;

nor, had he been merely a *Qašîš,* would he have been enabled to turn the table on the Romans in the manner he did.

The H2 rendering — *bid^{e}mûth qesem,* 'as if by magic' (lit. 'divination') is far more plausible. Levi's sudden appearance among the Romans could be construed as a miraculous act.

4. לעלות הר: The preposition *'el* is omitted after Infinitive in both H1 and H2 (see also v 6). The verb */'lh* is possibly construed in the sense of 'to go up *to.*'

ננטש:* Niph'al; 'we will be enabled,' lit. 'left alone.' See on 15:13.

5. והמחשפים: Read *v^{e}ha-m^{e}khašphîm* (as in continuation: *min kôšphê).*

6. הר גרזים בית יקרא: Read *bēth 'ēl yiqqārē'.*

וימששו על: 'Search for,' see on 16:18.

ויגוהו: Elision of *hey* of vayyahargûhû; see on 16:25.

מטלסם: Read *m^{e}ṭōlmās,* 'formed;' *Cowley* (Gloss.), lvii.

7. כל הישר בעיניך עשה: Cf. Ex 15:26.

נשמע ונעשה: Ex 24:7, *cum SP.* (the M.T. inverts the verbs; see on 4:3.)

ונשוב למה ההינו בו:* This suggests that vv. 1–6 were quoted from an extraneous source, being the *dibrā' 'ôdāh* referred to in v 1.

ודמעינן ומצנפת ראשינן:* Uncharacteristic multiplication of complimentary attributes, more associated with the style of H1 than with H2.

דמעינן:* 'Our Supremo.' For a discussion of the origin of the title *dema',* see Ben-Hayyim, *LOTS,* III, pt. II, 148 n. 12.

אעשה:* Read *na'ăśeh.*

8. לא תגעל נפשכם: Cf. Lv 26:30.

עמין:* Variation of *ḥāmîn, /ḥmh,* 'see,' 'perceive.'

בכיר ידיכם:* See on v 1.

אשמרו אשמרו: Delete one as dittog.

מקוהי: 'His place.' *Miqveh* ("gathering *place*") and *māqôm* are interchangeable in the Chronicle.

לא תחמד נפשותיכם: 'You should not make (unjust) demands (lit. requests, *desires*) of him.' See on 16:6.

The H2 rendering is, uncharacteristically, verbose.

10. בני אחיו: Read *ben 'āḥîv.*

מתקוי: 'Accompanying,' 'gathering (together with);' cf. noun *miqveh.*

11. הכופרים עבודי הבעלים: A common form of denuciation; see 1:15.

עשוי התועבות: Cf. 2:17.

על רע דרך: *Ibid.*

פן תנקש אחריהם: Cf. Dt 12:30.

ושים בלך: Read *śîm libbᵉkhā.*

ושים תורותך:* Read, with H1, *vᵉśîm libbᵉkhā.*

12. ביהוה ובמשה:* Uncharacteristic inclusion of reference to Moses. H2 usually omits these, possibly as a reaction to the "Moses-Dosithean" manifesto. see 12:10.

וביום נקמה:* Is there an attempt here to avoid alluding to the theological doctrine of Future Life, as in H1's *'aḥărîth.* Another circumlocution, apparently to avoid such a predicament, occurs in v 15 (see below).

15. את אשר הלך: Read *'ēth 'ăšer hālakhtā,* or *'ēth 'ăšer 'attāh hōlēkh.*

וביום דבר ... נפשו:* H2 avoids using the term *'aḥărîth,* and its description of 'the day when all creatures will receive the recompense for what their soul attained' neatly side-steps the crucial issue of whether this recompense will be in *this* world or in the *future* world *('aḥărîth).*

18. ריטור: 'Spokesman,' Gr. *ῥήτωρ,* title of honour; a public speaker, pleader or orator.

וכל אשר הוא ... מצליח בידו: Gn 30:3.

19. ממלא:* Tal. Aram. *mimmêlā',* 'of itself,' 'for that reason alone' (see Jastrow, *Dictionary,* 773); exactly parallel to H1's *ûbhiglal ha-dābhār ha-zeh.*

20. ללקסטנ': Contraction of *lᵉ'alqôsṭanṭînāh.*

שבע עשר:* Loosening of gender-agreement, especially in numerals, cf. 10:2, 3; 18:21.

21. הסכנת: Noun *haskānāh,* 'custom,' /skn 'to be of service, wont, accustomed,' see Nu 22:30.

22. ויתברכו ממנו: Cf Gn 22:18.

העדה ואתעלי:* Lacuna after *hā'ēdāh* (?). We propose *'enāš kᵉvvāthêh,* 'a man like him.'

23. אסקף: Gr. *Skopos,* 'leader' (Supervisor). The verb */sqp* occurs frequently in the sense of 'being high,' whence *sᵉqûphāh,* 'The Most High (God). The noun *'asqōph* occurs only once, however, in Cowley (— and was overlooked in his Glossary) in a hymn of Pinḥas b. Isaac, the father of the scribe of our Chronicle (see Cowley, I, 109).

The noun *Squpana* occurs in Mandaic. Drower and Macuch conjecture 'smiter? entangler? (*A Mandaic Dictionary,* 335) in the phrase *qramtẖ Isqupana ḏ-'l dilan hambaga hua (Das Johannisbuch der Mandaer,* ed. M. Lidzbarski, 143:12) — 'I covered (entangled?) the entangler? (or smiter?) who was our enemy.'

It is possible, however, that *squpana* is also a derivative (like *'asqōph)* of the Greek *Skopos,* and the meaning of the above crux would then be, simply, 'I trapped the commander (or 'leader', *Skopos*) who was our enemy.'

בחנות: 'Rank, position,' cf. 5:6; also in Yadin, *War Scroll,* pp. 46—7.

§19

1. **מדרשי אלך**: 'It is my desire *to go.*' Imperfect replaces Infinitive; cf. 17:4.

להראות: Read *lir'ôth.*

מהלכותו:* Abstract noun, *mahalkhûth.*

אחמד:* See on 16:6.

אנשק הכנשנות: H2 alters this to the inoquous verb 'to see.' Levi would hardly have disclosed to the Romans his spiritual affinity and reverence for the Synagogues!

2. **עסכרים**:* See on 11:15.

3. **הנביאם**:* Read *hann^{e}bhî'îm;* used here rather loosely in the sense of 'leaders,' prps. religious leaders.

בשרתו: Read *l^{e}śārthô.*

4. **כקרב ... מעיר שכם**: Read *l^e'îr š^{e}khem.*

להקרוב מן:* Non-elision of definite article after preposition *l^e;* cf. 10:20, 14:7.

נעריו: These were, clearly, military attendants or knights of the king's retinue. See J. Macdonald, "The Status and Role of the *Na'ar* in Israelite Society,' *JNES,* 35 (3), 147–170.

5. **ויירא מאד ויצר לו**: Gn 32:8.

6. **מגידו**: 'Report, fame,' cf. 9:19.

מגידו ועוד: Dittog. of *waw;* read *maggîdô 'ôd.*

7. **להכיתנו**: Orthographic variant of *l^{e}hakkôthēnû,* see v 8 (*l^{e}hakkôth*).

ויתל בנו:* */tll,* cf. Gn 31:7.

8. **מה נוכל נעשה**: See on v 1.

כלי מלחמה נדקר בה: The noun *kēlîm* is here construed as fem. See H2's *kēlîm t^{e}mîmāh.*

9. **להמלך**: See on v 4.

מזאת הרשעי: Read *hār^{e}šā'îm.*

מזאת הר' האלה: Double demonstrative; cf. on *hāzēnû* (1:20).

אירא:* Noun, 'fear.' Orthographic variant of *yiyrā'* (= *yir'āh*).

יהובה:* 'The Giver,' */yhb,* designation of Deity.

וירא את ענינו ... עמלנו ואת לחצנו:* Dt 26:7.

10. בסקוף הרה:* Read harām; see v 7.

אל שכמה: Preposition *'el* with noun bearing *locative hey.*

11. וטטפות בין עיניהם: Ex 13:16; Dt 6:8, 11:18.

This rendering is far from revealing. It cannot mean that the Samaritans appeared wearing their Phylacteries, since the Samaritans do not observe this ritual *(Montgomery,* 32; *Ben-Zevi,* 148), but rather interpret the biblical injunction in a figurative sense. They did, however, at one time, wear *qame'as* *(qᵉmî'îm)* or amulets containing *qᵉṭāphîm,* or brief digests of Torah passages. See J. Bowman, "Phylacteries," *TrGUOS* XV (1953–4), 170.

It is apparent that the H1 chronicler has made an attempt here to correct, or at least make some sense of, H2's most abstruse expression, *ubhᵉ'ên 'ênāyv ṭ'tāph ha-yir'āh mᵉṭaphtēph,* which seems to mean 'fear flowed deep in their eyes.' It is strange, however, that H1 should have used such a well-known Pentateuchal expression! Read, Perhaps, *kᵉṭōṭāphoth, 'as* frontlets between the eyes,' to convey the idea of fear, on the faces of the Samaritans, as conspicuous as phylacteries. (Was he, indeed, suggesting that on this particular occasion, if not in common practice, they actually donned *ṭōṭāphôth,* by which he meant the Samaritan equivalent of the Judaistic phylacteries, namely the *qᵉmî'āh*? It would not be inconceivable that, in a life and death situation, they would have resorted to the wearing of amulets to ward off the impending disaster.)

מתרקף: The */rqp* remains unattested, read *mithraḥēph,* 'quaking,' cf. Je 23:9.

טוטף היראה מטפטף:* A noun *ṭōṭāph* occurs in a poem published by Ben-Hayyim, "Piyyûṭ Šōmrônî liśᵉmāḥôth," *Tarbiz,* 10 (1938–9), 351: *Tōṭāph rad min ṣidqāthôn.* On the basis of Ben-Hayyim's conclusion that this phrase means *'bounty,* came down because of their righteousness,' we may understand our problematic rendering of H2 as, 'an *abundance* of fear was manifested between their eyes.'

12. מן עיניו על גבות פניו: Read *min gabbôth 'ênāyv 'al pānāyv,* cf. Lv 14:9.

13. כרניו:* On */krn,* see Ben-Hayyim, *Tarbiz,* 10, 366.

14. כי לא הביטו: Lit. 'They did not see;' used here in the sense of 'expect' ('For they had not expected that ...'). A similar semantic development occurs with */ṣph* 'to look' > 'expect'.

משיגותה:* Abstract noun, *mᵉśîgûth,* 'attainment,' */nśg.*

העינינה:* Noun *'inyānāh,* 'state'.

15. למלך אשא אתו: Read *lammelekh 'ăšer.*

18. אשר לא נאמר בה אנחנו: Text problematic. Lacuna?

גלולות:* Always with masc. termination in *BH.*

תמונות:* Ex 20:4.

עינות:* Read *hā'ēnayîm,* 'eyes.' The termination has been confused with that of *'ayyîn* in the meaning of 'a well' (pl. *'ăyānōth,* Dt 8:7).

19. ויענו: Read *vayya'an.*

אגיבו: * See *Ha-mēliṣ* (ed. Ben-Hayyim, *LOTS,* II) 551.

ענינו נפשותינו:* Cf. Lv 16:29.

20. וינדחו:* Turned aside,' Dt 4:19, 30:17.

פן ... יכעסו אתנו: Cf. Dt 32:21.

22. עוף הנחשת אשר ההוא: Words transposed. Read *'ôph ha-n^{e}ḥōšeth hahû' 'ăšer ...*

24. ואתא מר: Read as one word, *v^e'ith'ămar.*

26. ושלחו ... יחפשו: Imperfect for infinitive, see vv. 1, 8, above.

28. ועוד הנח': Read *v^e'ôph ha-n^{e}ḥ ...*

רגע אחת: *BH* always construes *rega'* as masculine.

זאת הלילה: There is a preference for *zō'th* as the demonstrative pronoun with *both* genders. However, it is generally only employed with masculine nouns when it preceeds them in the sentence; see 1:20, 2:9, 19:9.

29. אל הנערים: See on v 4 above.

אצליו:* Noun *'āṣîl,* cf. Ex 24:11 ('leaders'). Only in Is 41:9 does it have the sense of 'borders' as required here.

31. שגיעון: *BH*: *šiggā'ôn,* Dt 28:28.

רעות רוח: Eccl. 1:14.

נושן: 'Sleep' (*BH*: *šēnāh, šēna', š^{e}nāth*), cf. Lv 26:10, *yāšān nôšan,* but only in derived sense of 'inactive or stationary through *age* (= *yšn* to sleep).'

ולא יתרון בו: Cf. Eccl. 1:2, 2:11.

יגר לראשינו: Lit. 'it will assail our heads,' /*gûr,* 'to stir up strife, attack.' It is possible, however, that we are dealing here with a noun, *y^{e}gar* (= *makh'ôbh* in H1). *BDB* relates *y^{e}gar,* 'heap' (Gn 31:47), to a verb with a basic meaning of 'to throw (stones together).' This would provide a suitable semantic sense here to a noun *y^{e}gar,* presenting a (literal) rendering: 'an assailment for our heads.'

טוב השנתן: 'The best (part) of our sleep.' Note the definite article with a noun with possessive suffix.

32. והשליכו את בחוץ: For *'eth* read *'ōthô.*

33. ההעוף: Read *hā-'ôph.*

34. הלילה ההיא: *BH* construes *laylāh* as masculine.

ונגע יאכל:* Read *v^{e}rega' ...,* 'at the moment they had eaten.'

והגמי אתם: /*gmy = gm'* (*BH*), Gn 24:17.

35. לא ידע הימין מן השמאל: Dn 12;7, Jon 4:11.

ואסתולל: * 'Prevailed over,' cf. Ex 9:17 (and below, 20:12).

37. הדבר אשר דבר: The reference here is to the speech of Levi in v 20 above.

28. אשר נחם בהכותם: Lit. 'that he might be moved to pity in the matter of smiting them.'

איך ישיגו לפאתו: Lit. 'how they might attain to his side.' Perhaps, however, read *l^ephatōthô,* 'to persuade him,' cf Ex 22:15.

עובדם: * 'Their work, doing, fate,' noun *'ăbhād,* Eccl. 9:1.

40. שם: * See on 16:3.

41. ולא יוכלו ... כי נבהלו מפניו: Gn 45:3.

42. ועקד: 'He knelt.' *BH* 'to bind,' whence 'to bind limbs together,' > 'to kneel.' Syr. ܟܒܫ 'bend.'

43. אמותה הפעם ... כי עודך חי: Gn 46:30. Rare example of H2 quoting *verbatim* a biblical verse.

47. גירתו: 'His exile,' from *gēr,* 'stranger.' Alternately, 'his lodging,' cf *gērûth,* Je 41:17.

48. תונף ותורם: Ex 29:27.

בקול גדול רם: Read *gādôl vārām.*

לבב ... מרך: Cf. Dt 20:3.

50. קרובים ממני: 'Near *to' (BH qārôbh 'el).*

ונמחה את שמם מתחת השמים: Dt 9:14.

והכה צואר הנכ': Cf. Ez 21:34.

54. חלוצים: Nu 32:30.

חמישים: = *ḥămûšîm,* Ex 13:18.

לא תשירו ... שריד: Nu 21:35.

תשירו: Contraction of *taš'îrû;* see v 63.

55. דגלי אימנותיכם: 'Ensigns of the faith,' see 1:12.

The reference is probably to its fundamentals or outward signs.

על פי חרב כבסו אתם: Interesting usage of */kbs,* 'to tread,' in sense of 'to tread down, subjugate.' *BH* employs verb exclusively in the sense of 'to wash' (lit. 'tread the clothes in water').

56. כחצית הל': Orthog. variant of *kaḥăṣôth.*

ויצבאו: Nu 31:7.

57. כמטחוי קשת: Gn 21:16.

קרובים ... ממנו: 'Near *to'* (H2: *qārbhû min*); see on v 50.

59. יי' גיבור במלחמה יי' שמו: Ex 15:3. The reading accords with the *SP.* The *MT* reads *'îš milḥāmāh.*

This battle-cry was used on other occasions by Baba Rabbah (see 21:4). The verse was regarded as efficacious in warding off evil, and was popular, therefore, as an inscription on Samaritan amulets (see J. Kaplan, "A Second Samaritan Amulet from Tel Aviv," *IEJ* 25 (1975), 25.

61. אתחרקו ברחוקה: * Read *'ithrāḥaqû* ..., 'They fled far off.'

(H1: 'They fled at their voice.') This reaction of *flight* in the face of a terrifying experience is paralleled by Ex 20:15.

ולא נשאר ... עוף והחיה:* The direct influence upon the animal world of such unique moments is stated in Ex 11:7.

ובבקע:* Masculine form (?) of *biq'āh;* see on 20:25.

62. האיש: Read *hā-'ēš.*

64. מחוץ ומבית:* Unusual transposition of popular biblical idiom; cf. Gn 6:14; Ex 25:11.

צרבת:* See v 50. The biblical sense of 'scab,' 'burning' (Lv 13:23), is hardly appropriate. Contextually its sense seems to be 'life,' 'existence,' 'presence.'

65. יוקדו את עץ הסכות: For a discussion of this practice, see chapter VIII: "Samaritan Fire-Practices in the Light of a Mishnaic Accusation."

67. יי׳ רעינו לא נחסר: Cf. Ps 23;1.

ליי׳ הארץ ומלואה: Cf. Ps 24:1.

השכינה וכל היושבים בה: *BT*: *tēbhēl* v^e*yōš*^{e}*bhê bhāhh.*

69. כי הוא על ימים: Ps 24:2.

ועל נהרים כוננה: *BT*: v^e*'al* n^e*hārôth* y^e*khôn*^{e}*nehā.*

70. אליך ... נשא את פנינו: Variation of Ps 25:1. *BT*: *naphšî 'eśśā'.*

71. אלהינו בך בטחנו: Ps 25:2.

ולא תרפנו: *BT*: *'al 'ēbhôšāh.* The identical substitution occurs in Baba's next prayer, 20:24.

ולא יצחקו אויבינו: Simplification of *MT*'s *'al ya'alṣû.* See introduction to §13; also v 74 below for further examples of H1 simplifying uncommon words and phrases from the Bible (and also from H2).

72. כי כל קויך: Ps 25:3.

לא יטרפו: *BT*: *lō' yēbhōšû.*

יטרפו הבוגדים חנם: *BT*: *yēbhōšû ha-bôg*^{e}*dîm rêqām.*

73. יי׳ ישועינו ממה נירה: Cf. Ps 27:1. *BT*: ... v^e*yiš'î mimmî 'îrā'.*

יי׳ בידו חיות נפשותינו: *BT*: *Yahweh mā'ôz ḥayyay.*

74. כי קרבו הרשעים: Cf. Ps 27:2. Simplification of *BT*'s, *biqrôbh 'ālay* m^e*rē'îm.*

75. כי יחן עלינו מחנה רב: Cf Ps 27:3. *BT*: *'im taḥăneh 'ālay maḥăneh.*

76. שאלה מאת יי׳: Cf. Ps 27:4. *BT*: *'aḥath šā'altî ....*

שובתינו ... הר הברכה: A neat alteration of the *BT*'s *šibhtî* b^e*bhêth yahweh.* The biblical */yšb* is transformed into */šûb,* to conform with the Samaritan aspiration of *returning* to the sacred site.

77. וירום את ראשינו: Cf. Ps 27:6.

78. ונראה ... ולא עתה: Cf. Nu 24:17.

נשורנו ולא קרוב: *Ibid.*

דרך כוכב ... וקם שבט ... ומחץ ... בני שת: *Ibid.*

וקדקד: *Cum SP.* The *MT* reads v^e*qarqar.*

79. והיה אדום ... חיל: Nu 24:18.

80. וברוך אלהינו ... לעולם ועד: Characteristic doxology of books of Psalms; cf. Ps 41:14, 72:19.

§20

1. ערי (המוצל): 'The cities which had been saved.' However, the H2 rendering of b^e*'aššûrāh,* 'in Assyria,' coupled with the fact that the word *ha-mûṣāl* is bracketed — normally suggesting a place-name — both indicate that indeed *mûṣāl* is the name of a town. No town of this name, however, is preserved in Roman sources, though we do have a reference to a village, near Jerusalem, by the name of *Môṣāh* ('*Αμμους κολωνία*), which was established as a military colony by Vespasian (Mishnah *Sukkah* 4:5; *M. Avi-Yonah, GRP* 82). Should this identification be correct, then the H1 reference would be far more plausible than H2's 'Assyria.' It would, indeed, have been far more likely for a local Roman garrison to have attempted to take revenge than for a far-off 'Assyrian' force.

2. על כספר: Read *'al ha-mispār.*

3. פג לבו: Cf. Gn 45:26.

5. ושבר אספם: Lit. 'He broke their gathering,' noun *'ōseph.* Perhaps the sense here is that of splitting their military *formation.*

מנוסת חרב: Lv 26:36.

6. עלת התמיד הקריב: Whether this represents an authentic tradition or not, we have no means of determining. The Passover sacrifice is, as we know, the only one offered by the community; and the H2 Chronicle, in referring to the 4th cent. period, makes no reference to any other sacrifice.

Is it conceivable that Baba was inspired by his victory to re-introduce the daily sacrifices which had long passed into desuetude? The phrase *'ōlath ha-tāmîd* (Ex 29:42) is too specific for it to be construed merely as a synonym for 'thanksgiving offering.' H1 wisely omitted this reference.

7. ערי (המוצל): H2 renders here 'Alexandria,' and on v 1 (where the identical phrase occurs), 'Assyria.'

10. ואפיל החרב בהם:* Cf. Ez 30:22, II Chr 32:21 (= 'to overthrow').

11. כהסכנתם: Read k^e*haskānāth*^{e}*khā,* 'As is Your wont,' see on 18:21.

12. ויעתר לו יי׳: Gn 25:21.

נקעתו:* Noun *niq'āh;* metathesis for *na'ăqāh.*

ואסתולל:* See 19:35, 22:17.

14. וחולל: Variation of *ḥālāl,* Dt 21:1.

לא נפקד איש מהם:* Cf. I Sam. 25:7.

16. עד כי חדל לספר כי אין מספר: Gn 41:49.

מתכמרים:* We propose the reading *mithkāmnîm,* 'lying in wait (ambush),' see Jastrow, *Dictionary* 646 col. II.

כחול הים ... יספרו הספרים:* Prosaic variation of Gn 32:13.

18. זקני וראשי ושטרי עמו: Succession of nouns in construct.

21. מכרתים:* Hoph'al; 'Cut off' (detached from aid and protection), cf. Jo 1:9.

22. אתשיג הדבר ... כי שנאיך:* Unusual example of abrupt intrusion of direct speech into a reported context. This does occur (after *kî*), however, in Gn 21:30, 29:33.

נעותים:* Perhaps, 'oppressors,' Aram. /*'ûth.* Jastrow quotes the phrase *malkā' m*^{e}*'avv*^{e}*thā'* 'a tyrannous king' *(Dictionary,* 1060). It might, however, be related to Hebrew /*'ûth,* 'to give aid, help,' cf. Is 50:4 (see comment of ***BDB Lexicon,*** 736 col II.). The Niph'al would here provide a plausible sense of 'in league.'

24. ויירא ... ויצר לו: Gn 32:8.

The prayer which follows is an adaptation of Ps 31.

24. עליך בטחתי ... פלטני: Cf. Ps 31:1.

לא תרפני: *BT*: *'al 'ēbhōšāh;* see on 19:71.

25. הצילני והיה לי ... לצור: Cf. Ps 31:3.

במהר: Equivalent of *BH*'s *bimhērāh.* There is a tendency in the orthography of the Chronicle to omit the final *āh* from feminine nouns (cf. *biq*^{e}*'ā,* 19:61; *n*^{e}*ḥām,* 23:5; *śemaḥ,* 25:2).

כי צור לי אתה: A simplification of *BT*: *kî ṣal'î um*^{e}*ṣûdāthî 'attāh* (Ps 31:4).

26. הוציאני ... טמנו לנו: Cf. Ps 31:5.

וגם כל עמי: Supplementation, for adapting the Psalm to the context of the community's particular struggle.

אשר טמנו: *BT*: *zû ṭāmnû.* Here the Chronicler renders biblical poetic vocabulary (*zû*) into a more colloquial idiom.

כי אתה צור לנו: Simplification of *BT*s *kî 'attāh mā'ûzî.*

27. בידך ... ואמת: Cf. Ps 31:6.

פדי אתנו: Read as one word, *p*^{e}*dî'thānû.*

רחום וחנון ... ורב חסד ואמת: Expansion of divine epithets (*BT*: *'ēl ĕmeth*) on basis of Ex 34:6.

28. שנאנו ... בטחנו: Cf. Ps 31:7.

29. כי תראה את דלותינו: Cf. Ps 31:8. *BT*: *'ăšer rā'îthā 'eth 'ānyî.*

וביד אויב: Ps 31;9.

30. מכוננו רחמנו רחמנו מכוננו: Cf. Ps 31:10. *BT*: *ḥānnēnû Yhwh.* The term *mākhôn* is an epithet of divinity, in the sense of 'Omnipresent,' as *māqôm* in Rabbinic literature. See on 14:24.

כי כלו ביגון: Cf. Ps 31:11.

31. כשל בעונינו: *Ibid.*

ונמסו את עצמינו: Simplification of *BT*: *va'ǎṣāmay 'āš^e šû.*

32. חרפה ... היינו: Ps 31:12.

נשכחנו כמת מלב: Ps 31:13.

ככלי ריק: *BT*: *kikhlî 'ōbhēd.*

33. עליך בטחנו: Ps 31:15.

34. בידך רוחינו: Ps 31:16. Simplification of BT: *b^e yād^e khā 'ittōthay.*

35. האירה ... אושיענו: Ps 31:17.

36. אדני לא נבוש: Ps 31:18.

כי אליך אתפללנו: *BT*: *kî q^e rā'thîkhā.*

37. מה רב טובך: Cf. Ps 31:20.

הצפנת: *BT*: *ṣāphantā.*

38. ועשית אתו לקוים את ישועתך: *BT*: *pā'altā laḥôsîm bākh.*

תסתירם: Ps 31:21.

בנסתרתך: *BT*: *b^e sēther pāneykhā.*

מכעסות הרשעים: Simplification of *BT*s *mērūkhsê 'îš.*

מקנאת החטאים: *BT*: *mērîbh l^e šōnôth.*

39. ברוך יי' ... הפלאנו: Ps 31:22.

40. אהבו את יי': Ps 31:24.

41. חזקו ואמצו: Ps 31:25.

§21

2. ישבי הקברות עקרוני: For *'iqrûnî* read *'izrûnî, cum* H2; see also v 6. *Kôph* and *zayyin* are easily confused in Samaritan script.

בעלאות קולי: 'At the top of my voice.' Aram. noun *'êlā'*, 'height,' cf. 23:14*.

4. צבאים: *BH* always construes this noun with fem. termination (cf. *rûḥîm* for *rûḥôth*, 2:19).

בחציצרות: Orthog. variant of *ḥaṣôṣ^e rôth* (cf. *l^e hakîthānû*, 19:7).

יי' גיבור במלחמה: See on 19:59.

ותחרד הארץ ... צעקותם: See 19:61.

5. כמוה לא נהיתה: Ex 11:6.

6. דלית שמעו כמו: Final syllable (*hû*) omitted; cf. 19:61, 20:25.

8. ותפל ... אימה ופחד: Cf. Ex 15:16.

אתשברת:* No transposition of *taw* and sibilant; cf. *'ithṣ^e rîkh* (15:2).

8. אתשברת צלעם: 'Their rib was broken' — a striking idiom to denote the physical manifestation of intense emotional fear. This idiom occurs again in 16:21*. Cf. the English idiom, 'he was shattered (by what he saw).'

לחצרות: 'Villages,' cf. 15:4 *(ḥăṣērîm).*

9. ויתנם יי׳ ביום ההוא ביד: Cf. Ju 6:1.

10. הנפילה:* 'War' (= H1's *milḥāmôth*). The noun is apparently a denominative of the verb */nfl,* which verb is used consistently by the Chronicler with *milḥāmāh* to convey the sense of '(war) *breaking out;'* cf. 21:2, 5, 15.

12. בן אחי: Read *ben 'āḥîv.*

13. אשר ה׳ בכלי הכשף: Lacuna. We propose the reading *'ăšer hāyāh na'ăśāh.*

14. קצההו: Several examples occur in our Chronicle of the possessive suffix being appended to the full (absolute) form of a noun ending in *hey.* Cf. *q^e^šehnû* (17:13), *miqv^e^hāyv* (22:15).

15. כי הרסו את בית כנשת הרומים: Both H1 and H2 refer here to one specific *kinšāh* which was destroyed by Baba. In the account of the battle (19:64), however, reference is made to *'all* the Roman *kinšāhs!'*

אתמכה:* The verb 'to smite' is construed as */mkh,* rather than *nkh.* In *BH* there is no Hithpa'el form of this root.

16. ... דהוו מסים על:* Pregnant construction, for *d^e^hăvû śārê missîm* (cf. Ex 1:10), 'who behaved as taskmasters toward them.'

ואגדיל אסונו: 'His distress was intensified'. *BH* employs the noun *'āsôn* in the sense of 'mishap, evil, harm,' especially with */qr'* (*qrh* in Gn 44:29), 'to occur' (see *BDB Lexicon,* 62 col. I). The context here suggests rather an emotion (or state of mind) which, in fact, approximates closer to the suggested Arabic root underlying the biblical noun *'āsôn,* namely, أسِن , 'to be sorrowful, distressed.'

17. מלכי (הרומים) יעו: Read *yād'û* for *yā'û.*

בבא רבה יעשה עשות מן מכר נפשו ואבד כל עמו בשביל אלה: The rendering of A1 helps to elucidate this perplexing verse: 'And Baba Rabbah continued to labour as one who had sold his soul (= *k^e^man mākhar naphšô*) and the souls of his people for God.' Significantly, the H1 Chronicler probably had difficulty in elucidating the Aramaic version before him, and therefore omitted the entire phrase.

אתקשטו:* 'They realised' (lit. 'they knew the truth').

אסונו חזק:* 'In his intense distress' (see on previous verse).

מתנכון:* Rare Hithpa'el. Derivative of *nākhôn,* 'ready, prepared.'

§22

1. ידרש ... שלום: Dt 23:7.

אתחסד:* 'It seemed agreeable, pleasing.' The noun *ḥesed* and the adjective *ḥāsîd* both have a non-pietistic sense in the Chronicle. See 15:5.

יעלים על: Arabic *'alima,* 'to be strong,' hence, here, 'to pressurize,' 'forcefully persuade.'

2. מאומים: 'Aims, objectives, reasons.' Noun *mā'ûm.* In ***BH*** employed only as indefinite pronoun.

החזי ... החזות:* /*ḥzy*, /*ḥzh*. The sense of *'deceitful* plan' occurs in Je 14:14, *ḥăzôn šeqer* (// *tarmîth libbām,* 'craftiness of their intention.'

תדבירות:* 'Persuasion(?)' The Hiph'îl form of *dbr* (from which the noun appears to derive) occurs in the sense of 'to make submissive, persuade,' cf. Ps 18:48, 47:4; Jastrow, *Dictionary,* 278.

נביאתו:* The noun has the general sense of '(religious) leader,' with no overtone of prophetic calling.

3. כי הם נלאה: Read *kî hēm nil^e'îm, cum* H2.

הל הוא:* Interrogative particle (Arabic هَل); cf. Dt. 32:6, *hal^{e}yahweh tigm^{e}lû zō'th,* and ***BDB*** note (*Lexicon,* 210).

5. חמות האף:* Abstract noun *ḥammûth,* 'heat of (anger.)'

6. אנשי משפטו: Lit. 'the men of his judgement,' viz. his advisers' ('îš 'ēṣāh, Is 40:13).

8. יתן את שיאלך: 'Will grant the request of.' Read *šî'ălath.* For the construction *nāthan š^e'ēlāh,* cf. I Sam 1:17, 27.

תחמדותי: Abstract noun, 'my desire.' The noun *taḥmādāh* occurs in a hymn of Marqah *(Mārāh d^e'ĕlāhûthāh, Cowley,* 846; *Ben-Hayyim, LOTS* II, 258).

בחזותה: See on v 2 above. Here the noun occurs in its literal sense of 'his presence' (lit. 'the sight of him').

9. וזה היה בכנע מן מלך האדום: The expression *b^{e}khāna'* is perplexing. Either the sense is, 'this was (written) *with humility,'* in the ordinary sense of /*kn'.* 'to be humble,' but postulating a noun *kenā'* ('humility'); or, alternately, we may render, 'this (sc. the letter) was (wrapped or folded) *in a bundle,'* cf. Je 10:17 (*'ispî mē'ereṣ kin'āthēkh*). The point of the comment would then be that it was sent as a confidential document (see v 12: *rāzô,* 'its confidential import'), *well-wrapped* and sealed.

12. המלך (קסטנטנה): The place-name was clearly added by a glossator, as the construct relationship, created by the addition of a place-name, would not permit the addition of a definite article with the *Nomen Regens.*

סדר משפחתו:* See on 23:7.

14. **אשר זממת לעשות**: Cf. Dt 19:19.

כילדים רכים: Gn 33:13.

הרף מהם: Ex 4:26.

ויצפרו נביכים:* 'They will swiftly be(come) confused.' /*ṣpr* is a denominative of *ṣippôr,* 'a bird,' see Jastrow, *Dictionary* 1298, col. II.

15. **דלותינו**: See on 3:10.

מסכינותנו: Abstract noun *maskînûth;* orthog. variant of *miskēnûth* (Dt 8:9).

מצוקנו: 'Our straits,' cf. Dt 28:53, 55, 57.

מוצרנו: Variant of noun *māṣôr,* which forms a common biblical couplet with *māṣôq* (see previous note).

במקוהיו:* See on 21:14.

וחרקותך:* Read *v^e^raḥăqûth^e^khā.*

נבקש ... בחסר מהלכך:* 'We petition that you do not go away;' lit. '... the desisting from your going away.' The noun *ḥōser* (or *ḥeser* or *ḥăsar*) is employed as a negative particle (= *l^e^bhiltî*). See also 22:17, 23 (*ḥisrôn*).

16. **אויבה**: Variant of *'êbhāh,* 'enmity' (Dt 3:15).

ומכות אנשיהם: *Makkôth* employed here as Infinitive Construct, according to Samaritan usage of /*mkh* for /*nkh;* see on 21:15.

17. **חסר מפומך**: Read *mippûqākh* ('that you desist from going away'), /*pûq.*

לבבותינו תרך:* Sing. verb with pl. subject; see on 2:21.

הפרך: Cf. Ex 1:14.

18. **הלך**: Either Inf. Absolute (— which would be a stylistic rarity for H2) or read *'ēlēkh, cum* H1.

20. **ותכבי האש**: For figure of quenching fire of contention, cf. II Kings 22:17.

ותשקע ... אש: Nu 11:2.

21. **אחפץ הלכת**: Read *lālekheth.*

ונצפר בבטח מתקשר:* 'That we may *speedily* make an alliance in security.' On /*ṣpr,* see v 14.

22. **וזה דבר ילא ... על פיהם הבוראות**:* In contrast to the prosaic rendering of H1 on this verse, the H2 rendering is unusually descriptive and colourful: 'This situation would weary even kings in whose treasuries lie hidden and visible riches, and who are obeyed by many subjects.'

דישקו על פיהם: Cf. Gn 41:40.

23. **קרוב**: The preposition *qārôbh* ('near') is here employed adverbially, in the sense of 'soon'. It is thus the equivalent of *b^e^qārôbh.* This is attested to by both H1 and H2 usage.

בחסרון שובתי: For *ḥesrôn* as negative, see on v 15 above.

הזמן:* Hebrew equivalent of Aram. idiom *hā'îdnā'*, 'this time, now.'

24. This verse, not represented in H2, is an elucidatory gloss, to avoid confusion over identity of Levi.

25. אנשים מן העם: H1 has it that the request was for '*some* of the people' to accompany Baba. H2, rather improbably, states it as a request for the whole community to be permitted to accompany their leader into exile (*kūllānû nēlēkh* ...)

ויק מיתוביך: Read *viyqar.*

27. ולמדתם אתה אל בניכם: Cf. Dt 11:19. *BT*: ... *'ōthām 'eth* ...

חצר עלמה:* 'Wordly dwelling' (Arabic *ḥadara*, 'to dwell'); or, 'wordly confines' (Arabic *ḥazara*, 'to fence in'). For discussion of these roots, see *JAOS* (1939), 22–37; *AJBA* 11, 1 (1972), 102–3.

28. לא יעזבכם ולא ירפ': Dt 4:31.

ולא ינזפכם: *BT*: *v^elō' yašḥîthekhā.*

ינזפכם: Aram. /*nzp* 'to chastize' (cf. *z'p* 'to be angry'). More appositely, Arabic *nazapha* 'to weaken (by loss of blood)'.

אל תיראו ואל תערצו ואל תחפזו:* Dt 20:3.

29. והשמרו פן יסורו לבבכם: Cf. Dt 11:16; *BT*: *pen yiphteh l^ebhabh^ekhem.*

30. הוא נסות מאתו להטיבם באחריתם: Cf. Dt 8:16.

דבחר בכם וחשק ...:* Cf. Dt 7:6, 7.

§23

1. כאשר כלה ... ממצות את הש': Infinitive Construct here replaced by simple noun, used in verbal sense (verbal noun), 'from the commanding (lit. 'commandment') of his Samaritan people.'

על לוחו: 'Upon his cheek.' Aram. *lôḥa'*, 'jaw, cheek' (Heb. *l^eḥî;* Dt 18:3).

2. פקדנותי: 'My deposit.' Abstract noun *piqdānûth.*

5. ומאהבים:* *BH* only preserves Pi'el participial forms with suffixed possessives; cf. Ho 2:7, 9; Je 22:20.

והנחם:* 'Comfort,' 'relief'; masculine form of *neḥāmāh,* cf. 19:61, 20:25.

6. שביל הרז:* Read *hārômez, cum* H1. The Sam. *kôtēl* is a passive form. Heb. *rāmûz,* 'hinted at, referred to' (= *hazzôkhîr*).

7. סדר קריביו:* Lit. 'family *order*' (or 'arrangement'); perhaps in the sense of 'order of succession' (cf. Tal. Aram. *k^esîdrān*). This meaning is supported by the family *order* as enumerated: '... his brothers, his cousins, his near relatives and all the members of his

family.' In 22:12 it is used, however, in the sense of the entire familial *assembly.'*

11. ויהי כמעט: In *BH kimm^{e}'āṭ* has the sense of 'almost' (cf. Gn 26:10), 'hardly' (Ct. 3:4). Here, however, the sense is 'shortly,' 'in a *little* while.' H2 makes this clear in its rendering *b^{e}rega' 'āḥath. BDB* (*Lexicon* 590), indeed, read this sense into II Chr 12:7 (*v^{e}nāthattî lāhem kimm^{e}'āt liphlēṭāh*), though this is not followed by modern translations (see *NEB*: 'I will let them *barely* escape').

כל אנשי צוה: For *ṣābhā'*. The variation in the orthography of this particular word is suprising; cf. 11:20 (*ṣābhāh*), 24:3 (*ṣ^{e}bhā'ênû*).

12. פוקידת:* 'The command of' (= *p^{e}qûdath;* see on v 6).

13. נשאר תארו מזרח הך צהר:* 'His face (lit. 'form') was shining with brightness.' This description of Baba is omitted in H1. This is possibly another attempt to depict Baba in the image of Moses, 'the skin of whose face was shining' (Ex 34:29).

15. ערשיו:* 'His thrones.' Arabic عرش .

§24

1. ויבא בתוך הגבעה: 'He came *to* the hill;' a ballast construction.

אעיצו נא אלי: Cf. Nu 24:14. Here in 'Aph'el, though no Hiph'il form in *BH.*

שוה בבא רבה:* Read *š^{e}rāh,* 'Baba Rabbah is (lit. 'lies') in our power.

בקמצת ידינו:* 'In our grasp,' cf. Lv 2:2, 5:12. Fem. form of biblical *qōmeṣ.*

מן החזי:* 'Fitting;' *N.H*: *min hārā'ûy.*

נעשהבו:* Read as two words: *na'ăśeh bô.*

2. ובו יסיתו:* Read *ubhô y^{e}mîthô,* 'or to kill him.'

3. אנשי צבעינו: See on v 11 above.

פחרו:* 'His glory,' Variant of *p^{e}'ērô.*

בעדרו בחרב עסכר': 'When he uprooted the troops with the sword,' cf. I Chr 12:35, 38 ('ōdrê *ha-ma'ărākhāh*) for military association of */'dr.* One meaning of the verb *'dr* is 'to cast out, reject, banish.' In Tal. Aramaic it occurs, however, only in the derived conjugations.

עסכרו: Read *'askārîm.*

4. ועם זה וזה: Colloquial idiom, 'quite apart from that.'

5. ולא הוא ילאו נגיפותינו:* 'Our attacks did not weary him.' Strange use of subject pronoun (hû') for object *'ōthô.* This might have been under the influence of the opening word of the sentence, where *v^{e}hû'* occupies a specially emphatic position.

ואצתדק אתו שבועתינו: 'Our oath was *regarded as* righteous

(reliable).' BH changes the *taw* to a more emphatic *ṭêth* after first radical *ṣādê* in Hithpa'ēl, whence *niṣṭaddāq* (Gn 44:16).

לא יקראנו אסון: Gn 44:29.

6. ויבא תחת צל קרורותינו: Gn 19:8.

איננו חסד:* 'It is not right' (= H1's *'ên tôbh*); see on 22:1.

7. איננה הדירה: 'Dishonourable,' cf. *hādûr* (Is 63:1). The form *hādîr* appears in a poetic composition by Abraham Al'ayye: *v^ezāraḥ* ... *v^ehôphî'a v^ehādîr* (see *Ben-Hayyim, LOTS* 3, II, 339).

בספירה: 'At times,' 'regularly.' See on 10:11*.

8. נעזבו אתנו: Read *na'aṣrô 'ōthô*, 'let us imprison him,' a reading supported by the continuation of our verse — *ûbhēn 'ăṣārô kol y^emê ḥayyāv* — as well as by v 9, *'āṣûr.*

אש הדבות:* 'The fire of enmity,' Aram. */dbb*, 'to speak evil, be hostile.'

10. ואתנאשת: Read *v^e'ithnaṭṭēšt*, 'wrath was removed.'

11. על פיך ישק כל עמי: Gn 41:40.

12. לציאתו אתו:* Delete *'ōthô* as dittog.

למען לא ירף:* 'That he should not fail.' It is strange that Philip should have needed to offer such a feeble excuse — or any excuse — in order to justify his actions to the guards! Significantly H1 omits this phrase.

13. כי פקידים היו: An explanatory gloss, not in H2, describing the permanent guard which was stationed at all times around the walls of Constantinople in order to control access to, and exit from, the city.

14. אלכה ואשובה אל ארצי: Ex 4:18.

כי נכסף נכספת אל אבי: Cf. Gn 31:30. In quoting the biblical verse *verbatim*, the Chronicler omitted to adjust the person of the verb. Read: *nikhsaphtî.*

16. מסגיר עליו:* 'Was imprisoning him,' cf. Lv 13:54 (where verb takes a direct object).

לחצרו ולקהליו:* Read *ûl^e'āhālāyv*, 'to his own confines *and tents.*'

הצור והתמים בפעליו: Cf. Dt 32:4.

§25

1. זבג:* Usual Sam. variation of */zbg* or *zûg* (Tal. Aram.), 'to marry.

2. ויעשו לו שמח: 'They made for him a festivity.' Masc. form of *śimḥāh;* see on 19:61, 20:25; 23:5, *et al.*

3. ויגוע ... ויאסף אל עמו זקן ושבע ימים: Cf. Gn 35:29.

5. מחץ: 'Illness' (H2: *v^e'ithmāḥēṣ*, 'he succumbed to illness'). *BH* invests this root with the more violent and militaristic

connotation of 'smite through, wound, severely shatter' (BDB *Lexicon,* 563).

ויגע בבא ר׳ כי קרבו ימיו למות: 'And Baba Rabbah *sensed* that his death was near.' A slight semantic shift occurs in the usage of /*ng*': 'to touch the mind = to realise, to sense.

6. The phraseology of this entire verse is culled from Gn 24:2–4.

7. Phraseology culled from Gn 24:9.

10. אלהים עד ביני ובינך: Gn 31:50.

11. אתעתק ... במות:* A refined reference to *dying;* 'was removed into death.'

12. בנו לוי ... איש היהודי: That only Baba's son, assisted by a non-member of the community, should have been delegated the sacred task of preparing the corpse for burial, is not to be construed as a slight to a beloved leader. Samaritan tradition recommends the avoidance of defilement through contact with the dead. Ben-Zevi records that the modern Samaritans frequently leave to outsiders the preparing of the corpse for burial, and any other contact with it (Ben-Zevi, *Se. Ha.* 149). Levi, being the next of kin, was the only exception in this instance, aided by an outsider, Baba's trusted Judaean friend.

14/15 מחנה:* Used here as 'a gathering (of mourners).'

V. THE CHRONICLE

H1 AND H2 VERSIONS, AND THE PROBLEM OF DATING THE CHRONICLE

The text which forms the basis of our study is a section of a Samaritan Chronicle, or *Sēpher ha-Yāmîm*. The Chronicle, in its H1 version, is MS. 1142 in the Gaster collection of the John Rylands library, Manchester. Another version, H2, almost parallel, though employing a totally independent, Aramaic-orientated, literary style — as opposed to H1's usually pure classical Hebrew orientation — was found in the same collection, and is numbered MS. 1168. We have used the latter version as our major secondary source, and have reproduced it in the left-hand column of our text of the Baba Rabbah section of Chronicle II. We have also made constant reference to the other Hebrew Chronicles, to *Abu'l Fatḥ's* Arabic Chronicle and to other, more modern, Arabic versions, such as MSS. Al, 2 *(at-Ta'rikh),* even though their contribution is inevitably circumscribed.

J. Macdonald, who also utilised H2 as a secondary text for his critical edition of the biblical texts,[1] was inclined to the view that H2 was a later version of H1.[2] He states that 'it seems likely that this Chronicle II version was possessed by a lesser known family, possibly not living in the Nablus area *but certainly under the influence of Arabic,* though at a time when that language had not yet been totally assimilated by the Samaritans.[3]

The present writer has been unable, however, to detect any traces at all of Arabic influence on H2, and Macdonald himself subsequently expressed oral reservations to the present writer regarding his previous conclusions relating to the comparative lateness of H2 and its dependence upon H1. There are, indeed, stronger indications that H1 might represent a later revision, or version, of the H2 genre, in a form based upon the classical Hebrew style of the Bible — even to the extent of employing *Waw-consective* — and interspersed with Biblical, even non-Hexateuchal, quotations.

---

[1] J. Macdonald, *The Samaritan Chronicle No. II* (B.Z.A.W.), 1969.

[2] *Op. cit.* 10–11.

[3] *Ibid.*

A fuller discussion on the characteristics of the two versions is given below.[4] At this point we would merely note the intriguing classical style of H1, and offer a speculative suggestion as to its motivation.

We must not forget that a move away from the Aramaic or Arabic vernacular and a return to pure Hebrew literary forms and structures would not be a phenomenon. A Hebrew renaissance along these lines took place in the ninth century A.D., in the case of the Midrashic literature of Palestine. A notable example is that of the *P^e^siqtā' cycle,* especially the *P^e^siqtā' Rabbāthî.* 'The date of its compilation is stated in the book to be 845 C.E. It is distinguished especially by the use of Hebrew words and expressions, instead of the Aramaic employed by the earlier Midrashim, by its poetic style ... which shows an acquaintance with the school of neo-Hebrew poetry which began to flourish in Palestine in the seventh century'.[5]

It is conceivable, therefore, that H1 is the residual legacy of a parallel movement among Samaritan writers. The fact that only one MS. is extant to testify to the existence of such a trend does not suprise us, knowing the great losses of Samaritan manuscripts sustained during the Middle Ages.[6] On the other hand, H2, although replete with Aramaisms, still contains a sufficient admixture of (non Waw-consecutive) Hebrew for it to be assigned to the same provenance, as part of the same trend. In our next chapter[7] we will discuss the thorny problem of the appearance of Judaean Psalm-verses in a Samaritan Chronicle. If there was a medieval Samaritan renaissance of the Hebrew language it might explain their willingness to cast as wide a net as possible, from *early* — if not, in their opinion, *Biblical* — literature. The book of Psalms would have been an obvious choice as a literary and linguistic reservoir, since, apart from, and because of, its natural, devotional appeal, it had the unanimous acclaim of all discerning *literati,* so much so that both Karaites and Rabbanites united in regarding it as the most important source for liturgical creation.[8] The Samaritans would not have been ignorant of this development going on around them, which indeed might have contributed to a Hebrew renaissance in

---

[4] See pp. 212–223.

[5] M. Waxman, *A History of Jewish Literature,* 1, p. 140.

[6] See *CESC* 471.

[7] See pp. 193–197.

[8] See L.I. Rabinowitz, "The Psalms in Jewish Liturgy," *Historia Judaica,* VI, 109–122.

their own community. Possibly the Samaritans, like the Jews, smarted under the Karaite charge that they were using 'the language of Assyrians and Arameans, which is the shameful language of the men of the dispersion. For its sake the Hebrews have neglected their own tongue, and in it they laid down the fruits of their wisdom and thought in a jargon, which caused them to misunderstand Scripture, to weaken its interpretation, and to abandon its ordinary meaning.'[9]

If the above trends and attitudes did influence the Samaritans to essay a return to purer, Hebrew, expression,[10] then our two versions of H1 and H2 might represent different stages in the development and perfection of such a Hebrew style. H2, with its evenly-balanced synthesis of Hebrew and Aramaic, would reflect an early stage of the literary renaissance, when the influence of the *Defter, Marqah* and other Aramaic sources was still dominant. H1, on the other hand, with its flowing, classical style — though still betraying signs of being an artificial Hebrew creation, with some Aramaic forms being retained — would represent a later stage of the process. This accords with our general view that H1 appears to be a later, revised and supplemented, version of H2.

Any attempt to assign a date to the composition of our Chronicle is a hazardous exercise. The colophon, which we shall discuss below, is no help in this instance. However, the mixture of Classical Hebrew together with Aramaic words and grammatical forms readily suggests a 14th century composition, the period in which the revival of Hebrew among the Samaritans found its most prominent expression.

Among the writers of that period the ones who became the most accomplished in developing this new literary style were Pinḥās ben Yusuf of Shechem and his two sons, Eleazar and Abisha. Their poems were widely incorporated into the liturgy. Significantly, they took as their model and exemplar the poetry of 'Amram Darah and, especially, his son Marqah. Pinḥās ben Yusuf and Eleazar retained Aramaic in order to give an authentic flavour to the poetry they wrote in imitation of the style of Marqah. They regarded the "Verses of Marqah" as the purest

---

[9] Ibn Quraish, *Risala,* Intoduction. Quoted in S.W. Baron, *A Social and Religious History of the Jews,* VII, p. 6.

[10] On the ancient opposition to vernacular Aramaic, see S. Pinsker, *Liqqûtê Qadmôniyyôth,* II, p. 146.

expression of the spirit of Samaritanism; hence the appellation "The Samaritan Poet" when referring to Marqah.

This reverence for Marqah finds an unexpected echo in our Chronicle, in the list of the seven leaders appointed by Baba Rabbah to constitute his supreme council. The name of the sixth leader was 'Amram. Having stated this fact, our chronicler then refers to a tradition that this was none other than the famous "Amram, father of Marqah who was the master of scholars and scholarship'.[11] There then follows a reference to some compositions of 'Amram, which leads the Chronicler to a lengthy note on the liturgical poems of Marqah, the Daily, Sabbath and Festival services in which Marqah's poems are recited, and even a detailed note that 'where a fifth Sabbath occurs in the month, another of his compositions is recited before the Scriptural reading during the course of the Midday Service which replaces the Afternoon Service.'[12] This emphasis on the importance of Marqah and his compositions fits uneasily into the context of Baba's administrators, especially as no biographical details are given in the case of the other leaders, and, more to the point, the leader concerned was 'Amram, not Marqah!

The inference is that our Chronicler was here betraying a special admiration for the poet Marqah by creating an opportunity to make reference to him and to his special place in the liturgy. An admiration for Marqah, combined with the mixed Classical Hebrew and Aramaic style charateristic of the 14th century revivalist movement, would point toward the circle of Pinḥas ben Yusuf of Shechem (1308–1367 A.D.) and his sons Eleazar and Abisha as a likely provenance for our Chronicle.

The influence of Marqah upon our Chronicler is also evident in the Moses-orientation which characterizes both works. There is a tradition that Marqah's real name was Moses, but that 'since his people refused him the right to use the name, Marqah was substituted as having the same gematriac value.'[13] The *Memar Marqah* exudes glorification of Moses,[14] even commencing its theological treatment of Israel's history with the account of the Commission of Moses at the Burning Bush, rather than with the Creation.[15] There is nothing to equal Marqah's preoccupation

[11] 5:27.
[12] 5:28.
[13] Montgomery, p. 294.
[14] See especially *Memar Marqah* (Macdonald ed.) II, sec. 12.
[15] See Macdonald's discusion of this point, *Memar*, 1, p. xix.

with the uniqueness and greatness of Moses in either Samaritan or Judaistic literature.

This Moses-orientation clearly influenced our Chronicler who, in seeking to glorify Baba Rabbah, depicted him as a saviour repeating for his community the glorious deeds of salvation performed by Moses. The Chronicle depicts Baba as invoking 'the merit of Moses, the son of 'Amram'[16] in his petition for deliverance. He sees the oppression of his community as a counterpart to the Egyptian oppression:

> 'Grant us a new redemption ... for we are descended from Your righteous servants. As You dealt gloriously with our forefathers, the Israelites, deal with us in Your lovingkindness, and as You redeemed them, so redeem us.[17]

The veneration of Moses appears in another passage which speaks of the heinous sin of the oppressors of the community in that 'they deny You *and Your prophet,*'[18] — a sentiment that breathes Marqan theology.

The relationship of the community toward Baba Rabbah is depicted as being similar to that existing between Moses and Israel. The oath of allegiance taken by the people is expressed in the words used by Israel when swearing allegiance to Moses — *Kōl ’ăšer tō’mar ’ĕlênû nišma’ v^{e}na‘ăseh.*[19]

To further underscore his point, the Chronicler employs vocabulary from the 'Call' of Moses in order to represent Baba as a second Moses-figure. The following parallels may especially be noted:

ויהי בימים ההם ויגדל בבא	ויהי בימים ההם ויגדל משה
וירא בסבלותם וירא (H1, 1:6)	וירא בסבלותם וירא (Ex. 2:11)
ויתחכם (1:7)	נתחכמה (Ex. 1:10)
וירא את שרי המסים אשר שמו	וישימו עליו שרי מסים
עליהם למען ענותם (1:7)	למען ענותו (Ex. 1:11)
וימררו את חייהם (1:7)	וימררו את חייהם (Ex. 1:14)

The judicial relationship of Baba to his seven leaders is depicted as paralleling exactly the respective relationship of Moses

16 3:34.
17 3:35–36.
18 3:12 (H2).
19 4:3. Cf. Ex. 24:7.

towards his seventy Elders. This is most forcefully conveyed by Chronicle Adler,[20] which appends to 6:3 the instruction given by Moses to the Elders: 'And any matter that is too hard for you, you shall submit to me and I shall consider it' (Dt. 1:17).

Other parallels between Baba and Moses are reflected in the fact that Baba's activity is said to have lasted for forty years,[21] as did the ministry of Moses. Also, the employment of the epithet 'king' (*melekh)* to describe Baba may have been inspired by Dt. 33:5, where Moses is described as a 'king in Jeshurun'. Furthermore, as Moses retired to the seclusion of Sinai before receiving the Law, so Baba retires to the Chosen Mountain for a period of prayer and fasting before summoning his people to enter into a new spiritual covenant with God. Characteristically, when the Chronicler describes the joyous song of victory sung by Baba and his community, he introduces it with the formula of Exodus ch. 15: *'Āz yāšîr* (ha-melekh ha-Ṣaddîq Baba Rabbah) *'eth ha-šîrāh ha-zō'th.*

This portrayal of Baba as a second Moses is, as we have observed above, in consonance with the outlook of Marqah, and might have found such clear expression in our Chronicle because of the influence of Marqah upon the 14th century circle of Pinḥās ben Yusuf of Shechem. It is conceivable, though we have no clear evidence, that the Moses-motif was intended to be taken a stage further. Samaritan belief has it that, at the end of the present age, Moses will return in order to usher in the restoration of his people's fortunes and the kingdom of God on earth.[22] Furthermore, in the 14th century, with the reunion of the old priestly orthodox and the Dositheans, the new *Defter* which was created was permeated with a glorification of Moses — a doctrine directly inspired and influenced by the *Memar Marqah.* Moses becomes a messianic figure; his very name is sacred, like that of God. On Moses' account the world was brought into existence, and after his worldly existence he was taken up alive into heaven. J. Bowman has observed that 'there is no such doctrine of Moses, however, in the eleventh century writings of the priest Abu'l Hasan.'[23] This information might add some weight to our theory that our Chronicle emanates from the 14th century

[20] p. 90.

[21] 10:11.

[22] See Gaster, *The Samaritans,* p. 91; J. Macdonald, "The Samaritan doctrine of Moses", *Scot. Journal of Th.* 13, no. 2.

[23] J. Bowman, "Pilgrimage to Mount Gerizim", *EI* (1964), 7, 17.

circle, writing under the influence of Marqah's doctrine of Moses and, in consequence, casting Baba in the role of a second Moses.

The casting of Baba in that role throws up the possibility that the Chronicler conceived of Baba himself as a *Taheb* figure, the promised 'Prophet like unto Moses'[24], especially in terms of the eschatological role of *Taheb* which Moses fulfils in Samaritan thought. The *Taheb* inaugurates the period of *Raḥûtā,* when divine favour is restored to Israel. He is to be Prophet, Priest and King over the second kingdom. It is apparent that Baba's successes were interpreted by his contemporaries as being the result of a new *Raḥûtā* secured by Baba. This comes over clearly in the songs of praise contained in the Chronicle. Like the *Taheb,* Baba is also consistently described as priest and king.

We learn from Josephus[25] that the Samaritans of the 1st century A.D. were — like many other sects of the period — awaiting the arrival of their *Taheb,* and that one pretender to the office actually appeared during the period of Pilate's governorship. The yearning could only have increased over the succeeding two centuries; and the person of Baba must have been viewed as the fulfilment of the promise and the embodiment of the ideal. The parallels between Baba and Moses, however finely they are drawn by our Chronicler, might well have been influenced by that attitude, and enforced by the Moses-orientation of the 14th century provenance from which our Chronicle emerged.

Whether this Moses motif ought to be viewed against the backcloth of Dosithean polemic[26] is an open question, one which our present knowledge of that sect — notwithstanding the recent researches of J. Isser[27] — still makes it difficult to decide. A.D. Crown[28] has attempted to trace the development of a Dosithean group which, under the influence of the Patristic literature, glorified Joshua and, contasting him favourably with Moses, attempted to play down the role of Moses and develop a kind of 'Joshua Messianism'.[29]

Crown records a private suggestion of J. Bowman that Baba might have been regarded as a 'second Joshua'. His support for

---

[24] Dt. 18:15.

[25] *Ant.* xviii, iv, 1.

[26] For discussion on Baba's Dositheanism, see *CESC* 445 ff.

[27] J. Isser, *The Dositheans,* 1976.

[28] A.D. Crown, "Dositheans, Resurrection and a Messianic Joshua", *Antichthon,* 1, (1967), 71–85.

[29] *Op. cit.,* p. 80.

this theory is the slender fact of the abrupt end of the Juynboll 'Arabic Book of Joshua', which concludes after the time of Baba, thereby suggesting that 'the work may have been tailored to show Baba as Joshua's successor'.[30]

Crown himself finds other, equally loose, parallels between the activities of Baba and those of Joshua, in particular the division of the land of Canaan among the Samaritans. While such a division is indeed referred to, none of the Chronicles, however, make more than a passing reference to it,[31] and all describe the division as an arbitrary arrangement serving the more significant aim of allocating administrative areas to the six 'Priests of the sons of Aaron'. This was clearly a spiritual division, as the context makes clear,[32] and can in no way be compared to the great conquest of Canaan effected by Joshua, followed by his division of the land.

The reference to Baba's division of Canaan among the 'families of the Samaritan Israelites'[33] is itself suspect. Such a complex and important reorganisation deserves a much fuller description than the bald statement contained in the Chronicles. Not only is the 'division' linked to a priestly parish-structure — as we have mentioned above — but there are no references, as there are in Joshua, to the delineation of the various boundaries of the tribal, or 'family' possessions. More significantly, it is impossible to harmonise this tradition of a division of Canaan into family units, under the authority of six priests, with the other 'divisions' introduced by Baba as a fundamental part of his integrated reforms.[34] The latter, by contrast, are fully described, together with the names of the priestly and lay administrators of each 'division', as well as its location. The reference to another division, under six different priests, stands in total conflict.

The reference to a division of the whole land of Canaan is, in itself, suspect. The Samaritans only occupied a small part of the land, and nowhere in the Chronicle is it implied that they had designs upon the rest of the country. Chronicle II, in its full description of Baba's administrative reorganisation, confines the 'division' to the recognised areas of Samaritan habitation.[35]

---

30 *Op. cit.*, p. 85.

31 *Chr. II*, 10:14; *Adler*, p. 93 (not p. 95, as stated in Crown's note 97).

32 See *Chr. II*, 10:19–24.

33 *Adler*, p. 93.

34 See 5:16–31; 9:6–10:1.

35 See 10:1.

Crown's reference to a group of Joshua-Dositheans may explain the presence of such a conflicting tradition regarding the division of Canaan. It is conceivable that this tradition owes its genesis to a writer of the Joshua-Dosithean persuasion who, in an attempt to find points of contact between Baba and Joshua, described the former as following in the footsteps of the Biblical hero, Joshua, by apportioning the land to the Israelite families.

Granting the validity of the Crown-Bowman hypothesis, which detects a Joshua-Dosithean outlook in the account of the life of Baba Rabbah, and even allowing for the infiltration of one such Joshua tradition into the material which comprises Chronicle II, yet the overall Moses-orientation of this Chronicle suggests the possibility that it may have been written to serve the polemical aim of countering the Joshua-orientation of the other Chronicles by casting Baba in the role of a second Moses. Even if polemic was not, consciously, in the mind of the Chronicler, the Moses-orientation of Chronicle II does set it apart from the other Chronicles. It is unfortunate that Bowman and Crown had not been in a position to have read Chronicle II,[36] as then they would not have hastened to the conclusion that Baba may have been regarded as a second Joshua. The Moses-orientation of our Chronicle would have given them a wider perspective, and they would then have realised that the role of Baba is cast in accordance with the particular theological propensity — Dosithean or Orthodox Samaritan — of the Chronicler himself. The frequent refernces to Moses found in Chronicle II, and especially the glorification of him as the instrument of the giving of the Divine Law,[37] suggest that this Chronicle emanated from the period following on after the unification of the Dosithean and Orthodox groups, when Joshua 'Messianism' had finally been abandoned.

The non-Dosithean character of Chronicle II is, in fact, clear from the various references to festivals. Great play has been made, especially by Bowman and Crown, of the fact that Baba is said to have celebrated only the Sabbath and none of the other festivals — 'again suggestive of the apparent Dosithean nature of his ideas'.[38]

---

[36] See Crown's statement that 'our sources for examining Baba's career are Abu'l Fath, Chronicle Adler and Chronicle Neubauer.' (*Crown, op. cit.*, p. 84).

[37] See 3:26, 10:24, 12:10, 14:25, 21:17.

[38] *Crown*, op. cit., p. 84.

Significantly, Crown himself admits that 'the fact that only the Sabbath is mentioned could well be fortuitous'.[39] Furthermore, it cannot be over-emphasized that even if the other three Chronicles do lend themselves to such an inference, Chronicle II is sufficient to confound the suggestion. In this Chronicle we find references to the other festivals, and even to the minor Holyday of *Rōsh Ḥōdesh*. A significant reference occurs in the context of the regulations for the examination of a candidate for the title of *Ḥakham*. Baba's instruction was that the latter should submit himself 'either on the day of the New Moon or on *the days of the festivals*'.[40] References are also made to the festival of Tabernacles and the festival booths,[41] to *Shemînî 'Ăṣereth* — 'the conclusion of the festivals of the Lord',[42] to the Day of Atonement,[43] and to the festival of Revelation.[44] The suggesion that, in acordance with Dosithean practice, Baba only observed the Sabbath is thus patently without basis. These references to the festivals also prove that our Chronicle was not composed under Dosithean influence and that there is no evidence to present Baba as a Dosithean, and certainly not as a second Joshua. The only Dosithean strand we have uncovered is the tradition regarding Baba's division of the land of Canaan.[45]

* *
*

As will be clear from the foregoing discussion, our Chronicle II is not an isolated work, but must be viewed in relation to the other extant Chronicles of Samaritan history.

As a result of the extensive researches of Professor John Macdonald, a chronological classification of the Samaritan Chronicles was adopted,[46] according to which our Chronicle was designated as number II, preceeded chronologically by the *Asatir* and followed by the *Tolidah*.

---

39 *Ibid.*

40 9:3.

41 11:3(H2), 19:65.

42 19:52, 65.

43 5:27.

44 5:29.

45 See, however, A.D. Crown, "Some Traces of Heterodox Theology in the Samaritan Book of Joshua", *Bul, John Rylands Library,* 50, 1, 178–198.

46 J. Macdonald, *The Theology of the Samaritans,* New Text. Library (1964), 40–49. See also note 1, p. 290 above.

A re-assessment of the interrelationship of the Chronicles has been made by A.D. Crown,[47] who re-drafts Macdonald's table of Chronicles, though substantially retaining the same chronological arrangement. The contribution of Grown would lie in his demonstration of the processes by which Macdonald's seven (types of) Chronicles were enlarged or composed, as well as their interrelationship.

Crown differentiates between two types of Chronicle II: our own Chronicle — which he calls Chron. IIM (acdonald) — and IIA, which is postulated as the original *Sepher Ha-Yamim.* Chronicle VII (Adler and Seligsohn type, Rylands MS. 257 type and J Book of Joshua type) is established as an apocope of Chronicle IIA. Chronicle Adler and Rylands MS. 257 are admitted to be derivatives of an original *Sepher Ha-Yamim.*[48] Macdonald demonstrated, however, that Adler is not a derivative of our present Chronicle II; hence the enumeration by Crown of a Chronicle IIA, representing the original textual tradition upon which Chronicle VII type material was based.

The Chronicle II fills 281 folios. The first part, covering the Biblical books of Joshua, Judges, Samuel and Kings (II Chronicles). has been published, with full critical apparatus, by John Macdonald.[49] Together with A.J.B. Higgins, Macdonald also published a short section covering the period of the beginnings of Christianity.[50] No other sections have yet been published, and the present study, dealing with the period of Baba Rabbah, presents a critical treatment of folios 179–220.

The importance of Chronicle II has been highlighted by Macdonald, who, without reservation, regards it as 'the best and most accurate of all the Chronicles'.[51] This assessment is quoted, apparently with approbation, by H.G. Kippenberg.[52] R.J. Coggins, comparing Chronicle II with the other extant Chronicles, describes it as 'a more ancient and probably more reliable source'.[53]

---

[47] *Bul. John Rylands Library,* 54, 2 (Spring 1972) and 55, 1 (Autumn 1972).

[48] *Adler,* "Une Nouvelle Chronique Samaritaine," *REJ.* xiv, pt. ii, p. 98; Rylands Sam. MS. 257 fol. 116.

[49] *The Samaritan Chronicle II (BZAW),* 1969.

[50] "The Beginnings of Christianity According to the Samaritans," *New Testament Studies,* 18 (1971), 54–80.

[51] Macdonald, *Theology,* p. 44.

[52] H.G. Kippenberg, *Garizim und Synagoge,* Religionsgeschichtliche Versuche und Vorarbeiten, xxx (1971), p. 62 note 12.

[53] R.J. Coggins, *Samaritans and Jews,* (1975), p. 117.

A full general description of the nature of the Chronicle has been provided by Macdonald in the introduction to his edition. There is no need to duplicate this information here. We have also made some suggestions above regarding its provenance and theological inclination. One aspect of the Chronicle, however, still awaits clarification, namely the date when this sole surviving copy of the Chronicle was made, and the nature of its transmission.

No doubt, the high assessments of the value of Chronicle II, referred to above, were influenced not only by the quality of the published section, but also, in large measure, to the date attributed to our sole surviving copy of the Chronicle. Macdonald, basing himself upon the colophon, predicated the year 1616 A.D. The colophon reads as follows:

והוה הכלול מן כתב זה ספר הימים
בלילת חדה בחמשה ימים מן חדש
התשעי אשר היא שנת ששה ועשרים
ואלף לממלכת ישמעאל על יד העבד
המס׳ טביה בן פינחס שמש כנשת
שכם הקדשה אודי את יהוה

> 'Now the copy of this Chronicle was completed this night of the fifth day of the ninth month in the year 1,026 of the Kingdom of Ishmael, by the hand of the poor servant Tobhiah son of Pînehas, Minister to the Synagogue of Shechem. I thank the Lord.'[54]

The year 1,026 A.H., stated herein, corresponds to the year 1616 A.D., the year consequently taken by Macdonald as the date of our copy of Chronicle II.[55]

Doubt regarding the reliability of the date given in the colophon was expressed by Z. Ben-Hayyim in a review of Macdonald's edition of the Chronicle.[56] Ben-Hayyim expressed the opinion that the words ושלש מאות had been inadvertently omitted by the scribe before the word ואלף. The amended version would then provide a date 1326 A.H., corresponding to the year 1908.

---

[54] *Chron. II,* fol. 281 col. 2.

[55] Macdonald, *The Samaritan Chronicle No. II,* p. 69.

[56] Z. Ben-Hayyim, "A Samaritan Text of the Former Prophets?" *Lešonēnû,* 35 (1970–1), 294–302.

A reading of the last few folios of the Chronicle does, in fact, confirm the opinion of Ben-Hayyim. The Chronicler refers therein to a number of episodes connected with the High Priests and personalities who lived in the period leading up to his own day. He is particular to record the exact dates of their birth and death. All the dates specified are clearly 19th and 20th century dates. For convenience, and because the dating of our Chronicle is of such importance, we quote the final few entries:[57]

(i) ...וכן היה בשנת חמשה ושבעים ומאתים ואלף למלכת בני ישמעאל...

(ii) ...וכן היה בשנת אחד ותשעים ומאתים שנה ואלף...

(iii) ...ובשנת חמשה עשר ושלש מאות ואלף לממלכת ישמעאל...

These dates correspond to the years 1858, 1874 and 1897 respectively, thus making it abundantly clear that a scribal omission has, indeed, occurred in the colophon. Reference (iii), which includes the phrase ושלש מאות indicates, beyond any doubt, the nature of the omission, as suggested by Ben-Hayyim. Our copy may therefore be dated 1908.

Further evidence of this date is also furnished by the scribe's reference to his own ancestry. He informs us that he is the fourth son of the Priest Pinḥās ben Isaac ben Solomon. If we consult Cowley's genealogical tables[58] we see the scribe and his family listed at the foot of the Levitical family, thereby substantiating Ben-Hayyim's view that the MS. was produced at the beginning of this century.[59]

Ben-Hayyim, having established the comparative modernity of our MS., proceeded to write off Chronicle II as being, consequently, of little value. Ben-Hayyim even suggests that Chronicle II was produced 'probably by the same person who compiled the well-known "Joshua Book" published by M. Gaster in *ZDMG* 62 (1908).'

Ben-Hayyim's strictures, and lack of respect for Chronicle II, are reserved, however, for the Biblical material published by

[57] Fol. 281 col. 1.

[58] Cowley, *The Samaritan Liturgy,* II, xlvi.

[59] Cowley makes the priest Pinḥās ben Isaac even more prolific than does our colophon. Cowley attributes five sons to him (though he does not give their names), whereas our scribe claims to have been one of only *four* children (וימת על ארבעה בנים). Cowley's statement should be corrected accordingly.

Macdonald.[60] Ben-Hayyim would be the first to recognise, on the other hand the value of the later material contained in the Chronicle, its independent origin and the linguistic and historical value of a lengthy Hebrew Chronicle whose material is far richer than that of the existing Hebrew or Arabic Chronicles.

The quality and significance of the Biblical portions of Chronicle II are outside the purview of our study. One point that has to be made, however, — since it is relevant to both Macdonald's approach to his material as well as that of the present researcher — is that it displays a lack of critical acumen to confuse or lump together the date when a *copy* of a MS. was produced with the period when the literary and historical traditions underlying the Chronicle were first conceived and/or committed to writing.

The fact that we acknowledge, on the evidence of the colophon, that our copy was made in 1908, in no way forces us to the conclusion that it is a 'modern Chronicle' with no historical or literary value as an independent source. Obviously, the final folios, wherein the scribe has brought the Chronicle up-to-date, are circumscribed in importance; but the rest of the material — and especially the Baba Rabbah section, with its new insights into that period — is of great and abiding interest *no matter when a modern-day scribe discovered and copied his Chronicle.*

Cumulative internal evidence indicates, beyond doubt, that our section of the chronicle contains very old elements not found in any of the other Chronicles, and that it represents an authentic early expression of Samaritan historical tradition,[60a] couched in the medieval Samaritan Hebreo-Aramaic, familiar to us from other writings of the period.

Ben-Hayyim does, in fact, admit the possibility that the historical sections of our Chronicle might contain just such valuable source-material:

> 'Nevertheless, I say that even such a young source is worthy of close attention. Sometimes there may be hidden beneath a young Chronicle information pertaining to an unknown early source, or there may be found in it some material known from an early source but preserved in a more authentic form, because the MS. used by the compiler was more reliable.'[61]

---

60 Ben-Hayyim states: 'At any rate, *the Joshua part of the chronicle* (my italics). is identical with the "Joshua Book".'

60a See p. 196.

61 Z. Ben-Hayyim, *op. cit.*, 298.

Ben-Hayyim's reference to discovering 'information pertaining to an unknown early sorce' is, we believe, applicable in the case of our Chronicle. One particular reference could only have emanated from a very early source, since it reflects a ritual practice which was operative in the Chronicler's day, but which subsequently fell into desuetude, leaving no trace of its original existence — other than in Chronicle II.

The reference concerns the great victory won by the Samaritans with the help of Levi, nephew of Baba. Having routed the Romans, the memory of the victory was kept alive by a charming ritual practised by the Samaritan children. In commemoration of the beacons of fire, lit by Baba as a signal for attack, 'Samaritan children have set fire to the wood of their Succah-booths on the night of the termination of the festival of the Eighth Day of Solemn Assembly which concludes the festivals of the Lord. This episode has thus remained a memorial among them unto this day'.[62]

There is no trace of this practice in either the *Hillukh* or the *Masa'il al Khilāf.* Furthermore, John Mills, who visited the community in 1855 and 1860, spending a few months among them and having 'daily intercourse with 'Amram the priest,'[63] has left us a detailed description of the ritual associated with the festival of Succoth and the Eighth Day of Solemn Assembly. With reference to the latter, he states:

> The Eighth Day of Solemn Assembly is kept strictly as a day of rest, a peculiarly sacred day when they go down to the Synagogue, and the Service Book, adapted for the feast, is repeated by the priest.[64]

As Mills was careful to note any peculiar or unique custom practised by the Samaritans, it is certain that the ritual of setting fire to the Succah booths could not have been practised by the Samaritan children of those days.

I. Ben-Zvi was another scholar whose close relationship with the Samaritans extends over the past century. In his description of the community and their practices he makes no reference at all to the existence of such a custom.

---

62 *Chron. II,* 19:65. See pp. 205–208 below.

63 John Mills, *Nablus and the Modern Samaritans,* viii.

64 *Ibid,* 266.

The use of the phrase 'This episode has remained a memorial among them *unto this day,*' is, consequently, of supreme importance, pointing to an early date when this material was first chronicled. We have, naturally, no way of knowing when the practice was discontinued, but the fact that Chronicle II is the only source to refer to it is a significant pointer to its value as an early and independent source. Ben-Hayyim's description of it as 'a young Chronicle' is thus most misleading.

That our Chronicle is an abstract of an earlier Hebrew Chronicle is implied in a few passages. H2 introduces section 18 by referring to the source of the account which follows:

> And we have found in a Chronicle of our ancestors, written in the sacred Hebrew script, reference to further exploits of our great king and leader, Baba Rabbah, which we will relate in this book.[65]

The lengthy and detailed nature of the original Chronicle, from which our Chronicle II was abstracted, is expressly referred to in a later, unpublished part of the Chronicle:

> And this episode of the activity of the accursed Dusis, which we have described in this Chronicle, is but a part of a large work; but we have not elaborated upon the episode to provide all its details.[66]

These references to an original Hebrew Chronicle, of which Chronicle II is a digest, suggest that we may well have before us a substantial body of material that has been reproduced from the original source which was hitherto believed to have been lost. In his introduction to his own book, Abu'l Fatḥ lists among his sources a few Chronicles written in 'the Hebrew language' — خط عبرانى وافظ — which were obtained from the High Priestly circle in Damascus. He refers specifically to a Hebrew Chronicle containing a detailed description of the many deeds and exploits, some of them gilded with legendary material, associated with one of

---

[65] H2, 18:1 — ונמצא בספר הימים דלארשנו אשר הוא בכיר העברי הקדש יזכר בו דברא עודה על גדלות המלך בבא רבה ארשנו נספר אתו בזה הספר.

[66] וזה הדבר אשר בארנו אתו בזה ספר הימים ממעשי הארור דוסיס הוא חלק מרב כי לא ארכנו את הדבר בכל מעשיהם.

the greatest of the Samaritan leaders, Baba Rabbah.[67] The nature of our Chronicle, and especially the close relationship — in the Baba Rabbah section — between it and Abu'l Fatḥ's Arabic account, suggest the possibility that parts of our Chronicle may well have furnished Abu'l Fatḥ with the source material for his history.

In the context of this suggestion, the words of M. Gaster are apposite:

> 'From Baba Rabbah dates the renaissance, or better, the consolidation of the Samaritan commonwealth in the third or fourth century A.D. In his time lived their greatest poets and writers .... Such an elaborate Chronicle of the fourth century had evidently been preserved in Hebrew among the Samaritans down to the period of Abu'l Fatḥ (fourteenth cent.). Who knows whether it will not, sooner or later, come to light as so many other writings of the Samaritans hitherto unknown, and how much of it may be found in those already known.'[68]

Referring to the reliability of material or traditions emanating from the Baba Rabbah period, Montgomery avers that 'only for the period of the Samaritan revival in the IVth and Vth centuries does there appear to be any genuine native tradition.'[69]

Assuming then that Chronicle II achieved its present form as a result of a redaction of primary (Samaritan-Hebrew) material, can we be sure that the redactor treated his source with respect and transcribed it in its pristine form? The answer is, naturally, that we cannot be so sure. However, there are a number of indications that he regarded the text before him as inviolate. This explains the many difficult and complex phrases that occur in the Chronicle, and which would normally have lent themselves to simplification. This also explains the lacunae in the text, which no attempt has been made to fill.[70] Furthermore, in instances where the scribe was aware that an inaccuracy had occurred in the Chronicle's transmitted text, he did not presume to correct it, but rather added a corrective gloss. To give but one example: In the list of the administrative boundaries[71] we are told that Baba

[67] Abu'l Fatḥ, p. 139.
[68] M. Gaster, *Studies and Texts*, 1, p. 485.
[69] Montgomery, *The Samaritans*, p. 310.
[70] See 11:22, 23, 24; 12:4.
[71] 9:6–19.

Rabbah gave to the second leader a 'permanent possession from 'Askôr to Tarblos.'[72] The scribe or redactor — which scribe, of the many who must have copied the MS. down the ages, we do not know — adds the corrective gloss: 'This is actually from 'Askôr to *Tiberias.*' The fact that he did not just correct the original is clear evidence of his high respect for the Chronicle. It also serves to refute Ben Hayyim's description of this work as 'a modern Chronicle.' Another important factor militating against this assessment is the uniqueness of much of the vocabulary and grammatical forms — collected in our word-list[73] — which has no parallel in the 'modern' Samaritan-Hebrew idiom employed by writers during the past century in order to supply the requirement of scholars and libraries researching Samaritan literature, much of which was written in Arabic. The Hebrew of these *translators* inevitably betrayed the Arabic original, in the form of structures and phraseology which were clearly literal Hebrew translations of Arabic idiomatic expressions or characteristic forms. No translator, however competent, could completely disguise the Arabic provenance of his master-copy, especially when Arabic was, at the same time, his own native tongue. Yet, in our Chronicle, we have failed to uncover one clear example of an Arabic idiom underlying any Hebrew form. The conclusion is inescapable, that we are indeed dealing with an original Hebrew Chronicle, perhaps of the genre referred to by Abu'l Fatḥ as one of the sources for his own work.

The fact that our MS. is the sole extant copy of the Chronicle is indicative of its rarity. One would have expected that the original, used by the scribe Tobhiah ben Pinḥas, would still have been available. That this is not the case suggests that it must have been in a serious state of disrepair when Tobhiah undertook his task of copying it. Perhaps the sorry state of the original actually prompted him to devote his attention to it.

Had the original remained, for centuries, the property of the Shechem community it is still inconceivable that no further copies of it would have been made! A solution to this problem may be obtained, however, by consulting folio 280b, where the scribe, Tobhiah, speaks of his father's literary activities, and especially his devoted and indefatigable efforts to collect together from many sources the treasures of Samaritan literature. With reference to

---

[72] 9:9.

[73] See *CESC* 506–517.

our Chronicle II, Tobhiah states: הוא אשר קבץ את נדח זה ספר הימ׳ — 'It was he (i.e. his father, Pinḥas) who collected the copy of this Chronicle.' The use of the term 'collected' implies that the Chronicle had been obtained from an outside source, and had not been in the possession of the Shechem community. It might well have originated in either Damascus or Egypt, the other main centres of medieval Samaritanism.

Pinḥas himself had no opportunity to pay any attention to the Chronicle he had collected. The merit of doing so was that of his son, Tobhiah. It is possible that Tobhiah only became aware of the existence of the Chronicle when examining the large number of manuscripts left by his bibliophile father at his death. This is suggested by the fact that our Chronicle was completed in 1908, just ten years after the death of Pinḥas.

VI. JUDAIST PSALM-VERSES IN A SAMARITAN CHRONICLE

One of the most mystifying characteristics of the Baba Rabbah section of Chronicle II is the liberal use made of passages from the Biblical book of Psalms. This is surely one of the most glaring literary examples of the infiltration of Judaist influence into the stronghold of Samaritanism. The infiltration of Judaist ritual practices has been well attested,[1] but the Samaritans have zealously maintained a policy of exclusiveness in the domain of literature, and have resolutely refused to come to terms with the many winds of literary change that buffeted them from the direction of the Judaean centres of learning and culture. The classical example of this literary opposition to anything which smacked of Judaean influence was the translation of the Samaritan Pentateuch into Arabic, accredited to Abu al-Hasan of Tyre (11th cent.). His translation fell into disuse because it was felt to have become influenced by renderings of the Arabic translation of the Rabbanite scholar, Saadiah Gaon.[2]

The Psalm-verses are employed in our Chronicle in the context of Baba's prayers, petitions and praises of God. In this genre it would have been natural for the Chronicler to have employed passages from the Defter, or at least to have worked within its style and idiom. How then, do we explain the presence of these quotations from the Judaist Psalter in a Samaritan Chronicle?

Our starting-point will be a passage in the Midrash which refers to a discussion between a Samaritan and a Rabbanite theologian on the subject of the resurrection of the dead:

> The Patriarch of the Cutheans asked Rabbi Meir, 'I know that the dead will return to life, for it is written, AND THEY (sc. the righteous) SHALL BLOSSOM FORTH OUT OF THE CITY (sc Jerusalem) LIKE THE GRASS OF THE EARTH (Ps. 72:16). But when they arise, will they arise nude or in their garments?'[3]

---

[1] Samaritan observance of the festival of Purim, for example, is referred to by Mills (Three Months Residence, p. 266). On Samaritan wearing of fringes see A Spiro, "Samaritans, Tobiads and Judahites in Pseudo-Philo," *AAJR* XX, 289.

[2] *EJ* 14, 754b.

[3] *Mid. Ber. Rabb* 94, 6; *Qoh. Rabb.*, V, 12.

J. Isser, quoting this passage,[4] makes the following comment: 'A lay leader of the Samaritans during the second century A.D. knew that the dead would rise! And he quoted Psalms — a book not recognised as canonical by the Samaritans — as his reference! Surely we cannot be so naive.'[5]

The employment of Psalm-verses in our Chronicle[6] may, indeed, be viewed against the background of this passage, whose authenticity, unlike Isser, we have no reason to repudiate.

The topic under discussion in this instance is of crucial importance. Resurrection quite clearly had its place in mainstream Samaritan orthodox Theology.[7] The usual proof–text, marshalled from Gen. 3:19 ('To dust you shall return'), was decidedly unconvincing, and Samaritan theologians would obviously have been keenly interested to see how their Judaist counterparts derived the doctrine, knowing full-well that they were equally hamstrung by the lack of a clear statement on the concept in the pages of the Pentateuch. The 'Patriarch of the Cutheans' was quite clearly in sympathy with the sentiment expressed in the Psalm verse he quoted, and the fact that this did not come from a source recognised as Canonical by his community did not invalidate the truth of the doctrine in his eyes. There is thus nothing surprising about his demonstration of the fact that he was aware that *the Rabbis* had appealed to that Psalm verse as a support for the doctrine of Resurrection! He was merely addressing Rabbi Meir in the context of the latter's own theological exposition and probing it further.

It must also be noted that although the book of Psalms was not Canonical for the Samaritans, yet, as a book of hymns with few overt historical allusions and no theological or religious innovations, it contained nothing that was offensive to Samaritan belief. Quite the contrary; the Judaist Psalms might well have been accepted by some Samaritan groups as a useful devotional manual or source in the period preceding the Compilation of the *Defter* and rise and development of the Samaritan synagogue as a central institution.

---

[4] J. Isser, *op. cit.*, 145.

[5] Isser's quoted source for this passage — T.B. Sanhed. 90b — is incorrect. This passage does not, in fact, make any reference to Cutheans, but is introduced by the words, 'Queen Cleopatra asked Rabbi Meir.' See note (1) in Soncino Talmud, Sanhedrin, p. 607.

[6] See 3:12–14, 16–27, 20–21, 23–24, 29–33.

[7] For the Samaritan doctrine of Resurrection, see J. Macdonald, *The Theology of the Samaritans;* also *EJ* 14, 739a.

Our knowledge of this development is still limited, notwithstanding the contribution of Kippenberg,[8] though 'it is apparent that in Samaritanism, as in Judaism, the synagogue played an important part, undergoing a similar development even down to minor details.'[9] This being so, the Samaritans would clearly have had need of hymns or devotional songs along the same lines as those which developed into the Judaist Book of Psalms and the Qumran Covenanters' book of *Hôdayoth.* That we have nothing of this type of literature from the pre-Synagogual period in Samaritanism is surprising. It is just possible that some Samaritan communities — such as the one presided over by the 'Patriarch of the Cutheans' referred to in the Midrashic passage — actually used the Judaist Psalms in their own worship. It is also possible that certain of the Psalms, or individual verses from Psalms, were the common possession of both communities. These may have originated as northern Psalms, and come down as the common heritage of that part of Palestine, later to take their place as part of the Judaistic Psalter.

It would be contrary to all we have observed regarding the evolution of literary and liturgical genres to assume that the poetic and flowing 4th cent. compositions of Marqah and Amram Darah were inspired exclusively from within, with no borrowing or inspiration from a previously-existent, popular literary reservoir. It is quite conceivable that it was the Judaist (and, possibly, the northern) Psalms which fired the poetic spirit of the early Samaritan liturgical writers. Restricted to the few books regarded by their community as Canonical, they would have been unlikely to have possessed the inspiration and literary components to develop, as they did, a new and rich orchard of liturgical composition.

The problem of the final separation between Samaritans and Jews — a still hotly-debated issue — might also impinge upon this question of the use of the book of Psalms by the Samaritans. The observance of the festival of Purim by the Samaritans, as referred to by Mills,[10] is a clue to the lateness of the separation. Coggins avers that 'the decisive formative period for Samaritanism was the epoch from the third century B.C. to the beginning of the Christian

---

[8] H.G. Kippenberg, *Garizim und Synagoge* (1971). See, esp., pp. 145–171.

[9] Coggins, *Samaritans and Jews,* p. 137.

[10] Mills, *op. cit.,* p. 266. Cf. Montogomery, *The Samaritans,* p. 42; Coggins, *op. cit.,* p. 137.

era; it emerged from the matrix of Judaism during this time, *with some measure of communication continuing well into the Christian era between Samaritans and various Jewish groups* (my italics).'

This reconstruction of the situation would confirm our contention that the growing popularity of the Psalms and their absorption into Jewish liturgy would undoubtedly have had some repercussions in the Samaritan community. The Psalms would have been known to the latter, and probably rehearsed and recited in Samaritan Prayer-meetings and early Synagogues. It was only with the cultivation of their own unique *Defter* that the non-Samaritan elements were jettisoned. The Purim festival was able to survive, however, by a process of re-interpretation and a calendrical switch to a different month.[11] The Psalms, so closely identified by then with the spirit of Judaist Prayer, could not so easily be absorbed into the Samaritan ritual without incurring the charge of dependence upon Judaism. The Psalms or Psalm verses that had hitherto been regarded as northern, or common, tradition might well have been preserved by the Samaritans of the early centuries of the Christian era. Hence the Talmudic reference to a Samaritan 'Patriarch' quoting the Psalms, and hence the employment of passages from the Psalms — with some minor variations — by the author of our Chronicle. This consideration can but enhance the uniqueness of the Chronicle; for if these Psalm verses were indeed actually spoken by Baba Rabbah, then his generation would have probably been one of the last to use them; for before long the influence of the Defter, Marqah, etc., would totally have supplanted the use of the Psalms. This would be another indication that in our Chronicle II there have survived literary traditions and elements which were actually contemporaneous with the period being chronicled.

One final point may here be made regarding this meeting between Samaritanism and Judaism in the area of a common approach to, and use of, certain Biblical books. From the Tosephta we learn that in ancient Palestine there were Samaritans who were regarded as acceptable and suitably-qualified to teach the Pentateuch to Jewish children.[12] Such teachers could not have been ignorant of the other components of the Judaist Bible. Furthermore, if the suggestion that the Samaritan Targum is an adaptation of Onkelos

---

[11] Mills, *loc. cit.*

[12] *Tosephta 'Abhôdāh Zārāh*, 3, 1: ומוסרין לו תינוק ללמדו ספר.

rests on any valid foundation, this would also present a picture of educated Samaritan leaders, thorougly instructed in Jewish Biblical writings and Biblical tradition. This would certainly have included the Psalms, and may be a further explanation of the appearance of passages from this work in a Samaritan Chronicle.

VII. THE LEGEND OF THE SPEAKING BIRD IN THE CONTEXT OF RABBINIC POLEMIC

One of the most dramatic episodes in the account of the Baba Rabbah period is that of the legend of the speaking bird. This is woven into the account of the return of Baba's nephew, Levi, to Samaria after an absence of thirteen years, 'acquainting himself with every custom of Roman Faith' (18:2), in preparation for the longed-for day when the Samaritans would lead an insurrection against their hated oppressors.

The brazen bird is described as the main obstacle to Samaritan access to the Holy Mountain:

> 'For there was situated on that holy Mountain, Mount Gerizim Beth-El, a bird, like a dove, used for the performance of divination and sorcery by the Roman sorcerers. That bird was made of brass, and to any Israelite coming up to Mount Gerizim Beth-El the bird which they had made would call out *'Ibrîyôs.* When the Romans used to hear the call of the bird they would arise and search for the Israelite person .....'
>
> (18:5–6)

The sole motive behind Baba's decision to send Levi to the Romans was 'that he might ascend Mount Gerizim Beth-El, and direct all his efforts to breaking down the bird that is situated there.'[1] There follows an interesting and colourful account of Levi's fortunes among the Roman clerics, where he attained to the rank of 'Great Skopos'. From the account of his return to Samaria, accompanied by a great entourage comprising 'leaders of the Roman people, their officers, *some of the kings* and all the army,'[2] it would seem that Levi is being depicted by the Chronicler as an overseer with special responsibility for *kings.* Who these kings were is not stated, although the reference to Levi having set out 'from the province of Constantina'[3] provides the

---

[1] 18:3.
[2] 19:3.
[3] *Ibid.*

clue. Towards the end of the Baba Rabbah section it is related that Baba was imprisoned in Constantinople, where he was welcomed by all the *kings* who were resident there.[4]

Elsewhere we have analysed the Constantinople material[5] and found it to be unhistorical as regards the life of Baba Rabbah. Baba died before Constantinople became the prominent Roman administrative centre. The reference to 'kings' living there is, however, historical, as we have demonstrated.[6] Levi's association with the 'Roman kings' suggests that the Chronicler is depicting him in the role of supreme overseer of 'the nobles and many opulent senators of Rome and the Eastern provinces'[7] who were commanded by Constantine to take up residence in that city.

The conclusions that we have reached regarding the lack of historicity of the 'Constantinople period' in the life of Baba directly affect the Levi episode. Levi, likewise, could hardly have studied in Constantinople for thirteen years during the life of Baba, nor could he have become a city administrator. Baba died about 328 A.D.,[8] and Constantinople was not dedicated as the new capital of the Eastern Roman Empire until the year 330 A.D! It is thus apparent that the Chronicler has taken the legend of the brazen bird and woven it into a further legendary setting wherein the hero is Levi who returns from the Roman court of Constantinople and, with the help of Roman nobles and soldiers, is instrumental in destroying the brazen bird and restoring access to the holy Mountain.

In a later (unpublished) section of Chronicle II it is related how this same Levi became an adherent of the heresy propagated by Dosis.[9] It is conceivable therefore that this whole episode of Levi and the destruction of the brazen bird was fabricated in later Dosithean circles with a view to glorifying their most distinguished convert from Orthodox Samaritanism.

In the light of our foregoing remarks, we may separate two strands in the account of the brazen bird: first, the Levi-stand — which, as we have suggested, might have come from a Dosithean source — and, secondly, the legend of the bird, which, as a

4 23:12.
5 *CESC* 378–387.
6 *Op. cit.* 385.
7 Gibbon's phrase. *Ibid.*
8 *CESC* 373.
9 *Chron. 11,* fol. 475–479.

unified legend, challenges us to seek some explanation of its origin.

The description of the bird as 'like a dove' instinctively reminds us of the famous Talmudic charge that 'the Samaritans found a figure of a dove on the top of Mount Gerizim, and they worshipped it.'[10] This charge was levelled by a contemporary of Baba Rabbah, the Amorah Nachman bar Isaac (d. 356A.D.).[11]

The Talmudic report suggests that Nachman is giving his own, *ex cathedra,* interpretation of why social and religious intercourse with Samaritans is forbidden. The Talmud actually relates the proscription to an episode that is supposed to have occurred some two centuries earlier, in connection with a visit of R. Simeon b. Eleazar who was sent by Rabbi Meir to fetch wine from among the Cutheans:

> 'He was met by a certain old man[12] who said to him, PUT A KNIFE TO THY THROAT IF THOU BE A MAN GIVEN TO APPETITE (Pr. 23:2). Wherupon R. Simeon b. Eleazar returned and reported the matter to Rabbi Meir, who thereupon proscribed them. Why? — Rabbi Nachman b. Isaac explained: because the Samaritans found a figure of a dove ....'

It is significant that the dove-worship charge is not related by the Talmud in the name of any previous authority. Had that, indeed, been the true motive underlying the attitude of Meir, he would certainly have publicised the matter. Instead, we have a very abstruse warning of 'the old man' to keep apart from them. No reason, however, is given![13] Had there been any substance in the charge — had the charge even been made in the period of Rabbi Meir — it would hardly have been suppressed, to remain a mystery for two hundred years, requiring the elucidation of the 4th century Rabbi Nachman.

That the pre-4th century Rabbis knew nothing about dove-worshipping Samaritans is obvious from the fact that the slaughtering performed by a *Cuthi* was declared permitted by the

---

[10] Tal. Hullin 6a.

[11] See H. Strack, *Introduction to Talmud and Midrash,* p. 130.

[12] The 'old man', Montgomery rightly notes (p. 191), is a frequent Talmudic figure, 'a sort of oracle, probably representing popular opinion.'

[13] Indeed, the verse from Proverbs would suggest that the import of the warning was merely to discourage the scholars from imbibing too much wine!

distinguished authority Abbaye,[14] and from the fact that R. Johanan (d. 290 A.D.), and his pupil Rav Assi, had no compunction about eating of such meat.[15] The Talmud, in offering an explanation of Samaritan reliability, points out that the latter even go beyond the requirement of Biblical law; for, whereas Dt. 12:21 does not specifically include birds as requiring ritual slaughter, yet the Samaritans do accept its binding character, and are, in general, more scrupulous than the Jews regarding these laws.

The relevance of this seems to have been overlooked by Montgomery in his discussion of the alleged dove cult of the Samaritans.[16] Surely, had there existed such a cult it is inconceivable that they would have been regarded as suitable ritual slaughterers in the eyes of rabbinic law. Their slaughter would have been invalid for fear that the act was performed with idolatrous intention — whether or not they adhered to the details of practical halachic requirements.

The inescapable conclusion is that the Rabbis before R. Nachman's period were unaware of, or totally discounted, any calumnious charge that the Samaritans indulged in any idolatrous dove worship. It was only in the 4th century, when relations between the Jewish and Samaritan communities were especially strained[17] — exacerbated, perhaps, by the religous revivalism and military activities of Baba Rabbah, which threatened to upset the political stability of the whole region — that the Jews saw fit to make it abundantly clear to the Romans that the Samritans were a totally separate religious entity, and that they were acting unilaterally in their current enterprises under Baba Rabbah. The most effective way of demonstrating the separatist nature of the Samaritans was to charge them with idolatry.

For the origin of the charge a number of suggestions have been made. Especially fascinating are the theories of Selden and Ronzevalle, that Samaritan origins can be discerned in the primitive cult of Semiramis, practised under the form of a dove by the Hamathite colony in Samaria.[18] However, the fact that neither Mishnaic nor early Talmudic tradition knew anything of

---

[14] *Tal. Ḥullin* 3a.

[15] *Op. cit.* 5b.

[16] Montgomery, *The Samaritans*, pp. 169, 320.

[17] Echoes of this are heard in our Chronicle; see 15:12–19, 16, 17:1–6.

[18] See *Montgomery*, p. 321.

the existence of such a cult, which would hardly have sprouted suddenly in 4th century Palestine without any antecedents, coupled with the fact that Baba's reforms, on the evidence of the Chronicle, involved no sweeping changes in the spiritual direction of the Samaritan community other than an intensification of their trust and faith in God, suggests that the dove cult was not endemic to Samaritanism, but rather owed its calumnious reference to some event which had occurred *at the time when the charge was first recorded,* i.e. the 4th century period of Baba Rabbah and Rabbi Nachman b. Isaac.

The conclusion we draw is that Nachman was himself the author of the charge against the Samaritans, but that he bolstered his antipathy to them by attributing the charge of dove-worship to the 2nd cent. Tanna, Rabbi Meir.

But what inspired R. Nachman to level this particular charge against the Samaritans? Might not the idea have been implanted into his mind by a contemporary report of an effigy of a bird on Mount Gerizim, which bird had become a *cause célèbre* among the Samaritans?

Might not the legend of the brazen bird, as related in our Chronicle, have been the spark which fired Nachman's imagination? Whether or not he had received a garbled version of the events, or whether he deliberately distorted the facts as a plausible piece of anti-Samaritan propaganda, is immaterial. For our purpose, the 4th cent. tradition of the existence of an image of a dove on Mount Gerizim has highly significant points of contact with the legend as described in our Chronicle.

Might not the brazen bird, '*like* a dove,' have been, in fact, an emblem of the Roman eagle? This would have been erected to symbolise Roman occupation of the mountain, in the very same way that Herod had erected a large bronze representation of an eagle over the great gate of the Temple.[19]

The bronze eagle was probably posted at the main route up the mountain as a warning sign against Samaritan approach. It may or may not have had an inscription to that effect attached to it. We actually have a reference in our Chronicle to the practice of setting up a brass notice, especially when the purpose was to prevent access to an area. When the Samaritans had succeeded in driving out the Judaeans from the city of Shechem, during the reign of Ptolemaeus Claudius (ca. 140 A.D.), they 'made a brass

[19] Josephus, *Ant.*, XVII, 6 (151).

tablet in the holy city of Shechem, and inscribed upon it: NO JUDAEAN SHALL DWELL IN THE HOLY CITY OF SHECHEM.[20]

In the realm of the superstitions of the period, nothing could be more effective in warding off intruders than a bronze bird emblem. The two properties — it being a bird as well as cast in bronze — were both efficacious, it was believed, in repelling intruders. It must not be forgotten that our Chronicle does make it clear that the bronze bird, place on the mountain, was an object of divination and sorcery.[21] We are entitled, therfore, to seek out its significance in the realm of superstition.

Birds were used in Semitic magic to make an enemy become a fugitive.[22] This was wrought through transference of the birds' property of flight to the enemy. This also underlies the common Talmudic application of the metaphor of a bird with reference to the soul. Its *flight* from the body paralleled that of the bird in flight, the soul having been regarded as a fugitive from the corpse defiled by death.[23]

The position of bronze is also well attested in Semitic exorcism as an aid to *driving away* the undersirable. 'The suppliant would make a bronze image which would then be cast ceremoniously into a brazier. As with atonement, where the bird flies away with uncleanliness, so the bronze image of the bird was believed to possess, by transference, the properties essential to make sin or disease a fugitive.'[24]

To sum up our discussion: It is suggested that the legend of the speaking bird has to be separated from the account of Levi's glorious exploit, which we have attributed to a Dosithean source. We have highlighted a description of the bird in our Chronicle as being *'like* a dove,' but not actually that bird, and we have suggested that it was, in fact, the Roman eagle set up as a warning against trespassers on the occupied territory of Mount Gerizim. (This would, indeed, have been a choice site for a Roman garrison.) At the popular, superstitious, level, the symbol of the bronze eagle would have been regarded as possessing repellant properties, and would,

---

20 *Chron. 11* (unpubl.), fol. 345–6.

21 18:5.

22 R. Campbell Thompson, *Semitic Magic* (1908), 186. See, also, M. Gaster, *Folklore of Mossoul, PSBA* (1906), 106.

23 See, for example, *Lev. Rabbah,* IV, 5: 'God says to the soul, "Why have you sinned before me?" The soul replies, "It was the body which has sinned, not me; since I have come out of the body, *I have flown about like an innocent bird in the air*".'

24 R. Campbell Thompson, *Op. cit.,* 202.

therefore, have been viewed with great awe. This fact became embellished into the legend that it actually shouted *'Ibrîyôs* at the approach of any Samaritan. In hostile Jewish eyes the Samaritan predicament, aggravated by the presence of the hated Roman eagle upon their sacred Mountain, was turned to effective polemical advantage. The Samaritans were consequently charged, by Rabbi Nachman b. Isaac, with having worshipped the bird. Perhaps reticent to preach aloud any statement containing a reference to the eagle, in case it was misconstrued by the Roman informers, Nachman changed it to a dove.

Although we have described Nachman's charge as polemical, it may be objected that the presence of such a piece of sculpture at the central shrine, and the fact that it may well have accompanied the head of the emperor-divine, would have been regarded by the Rabbis as an infringement of the strict interpretation of the commandment against graven images.[25] There was thus some truth in the charge of idolatry, though this would have been totally discounted in any charitable assessment of the coercive situation — which the Judaeans were obviously not prepared to make!

---

[25] See M. Grant, *The Jews in the Roman World* (1973), 81.

VIII. SAMARITAN FIRE PRACTICES IN THE LIGHT OF A MISHNAIC ACCUSATION

According to ancient Jewish practice the New Moon was only officially declared after two witnesses had presented themselves to the Jerusalem Sanhedrin and testified that they had seen the first sign of the horns of the new moon in the skies. Since the diaspora communities, especially Babylon, recognised the prerogative of Jerusalem to determine the New Moon — and consequently the date of any fixed festival occurring within the forthcoming month — they obviously had to be informed without delay which day had been declared as the first day of the new month.

An early method of informing the far-flung diaspora communities had been to kindle beacons on the tops of hills. The message was then taken up by fire-stations positioned 'from the Mount of Olives to Sarteba, and from Sarteba to Agrippina, and from Agrippina to Hauran, and from Hauran to Beth Baltin. They did not go beyond Beth Baltin, but there the flare was waved to and fro and up and down until a man could see the whole exile before him like a sea of fire.'[1]

The Mishnah states that this practice of informing by beacons had to be abandoned:

> 'Beforetimes they used to kindle flares, but after the evil-doings of the Samaritans they enacted that messengers should be sent out.'[2]

This charge, that the Samaritans mischievously interfered with the process of Jewish observance, has always been accepted at face value. It was assumed that the bonfires that the Samaritans lit on the wrong day could only have been calculated to upset the Jews and create havoc with their attempts to convey to their fellow diaspora Jews the correct day of the new month.

The discussion that will follow is not an attempt to exonerate the Samaritans in any way. Its purpose is merely to refer to one

---

[1] *Mishnah Rosh Hashanah,* 2:5.

[2] *Mishnah, loc. cit.* 2:2.

or two fire-practices that are obliquely mentioned in the Baba Rabbah section of Chronicle II, to see these practices in the light of the part played by fire in Samaritan theology (and, *possibly*, practice) and to throw out the suggestion that the Samaritan bonfires, referred to with such odium by the Mishnah, just may have been part of a serious and authentic Samaritan purification ritual.

Our starting-point will be the faint traces of the concept of purification by fire among the Samaritans. This is referred to by Montgomery,[3] although nothing substantial has yet been brought to light on this subject. Montgomery relates the prohibition against burning anything, imposed upon the Samaritans by the emperor Zeno, to this religious fire-rite that is supposed to have been part of their ritual.

An obscure fire-rite is referred to in our section of Chronicle II. After Levi had dispatched the Roman force on Mount Gerizim, we are told that Baba lit a beacon on top of the mountain as a signal for his community to take revenge on the Roman administrators who had persecuted them hitherto. The victory and momentous slaughter that ensued was henceforth commemorated, we are told, by a fire ritual performed by Samaritan children; a ritual which, according to the Chronicler, had survived to his own day:

> 'From the day the Samaritan-Israelite community did this to the Romans, Samaritan children have set fire to the wood of their Succah-booths on the night of the termination of the festival of the Eighth Day of Solemn Assembly which concludes the festivals of the Lord. This episode has thus remained a memorial among them unto this day.'[4]

It does seem rather curious that the victory of Baba Rabbah should have been commemorated in such a manner, which can only be regarded as wilful destruction of a sacred ritual object!

The fact that this ritual was performed as a climax to the festival of Tabernacles — the last day of which is the 'festival of the Eighth Day of Solemn Assembly' — prompts an immediate association with the celebration of Tabernacles among the Jews. One of the highlights of this festival in Temple times was the lighting of torches and candelabra. These are graphically described

---

[3] Montgomery, *The Samaritans*, 112, 319.

[4] *Chron. II*, 19:65.

in the Mishnah,[5] which states that there were three golden candlesticks, of huge dimensions, in the Temple court which were lit on this occasion (called *Śimḥath Bêth Ha-Šô'ēbhāh,* the rejoicing of the place of water-drawing), 'and there was not a courtyard in Jerusalem which did not reflect the light of the *Beth Ha-Šô'ēbhāh.'* It is generally believed that this fire ritual was originally unconnected with the ceremony of water-drawing, and owed its origin to an ancient fire-festival, which, before it was Judaized, was possibly connected with worship of the sun or Baal-Adonis-Tammuz.[6]

It is possible that although the Samaritans, at an early period, had absorbed this fire ritual from Judaism, they were, however, at a loss to explain its origin and significance (In Judaism it remains unexplained, but, merged into the Water-drawing ritual, became regarded merely as a way of intensifying the gladness of the occasion.), not having the accompanying *Šô'ēbhāh* festivity to which to attribute it. Each generation probably had its own way of explaining the ritual, and our Chronicler has preserved a convenient explanation of the post-Baba period, which has related it to an event among the glorious exploits of that hero.

That the Samaritans should have absorbed a fire ritual from Judaism — there is the alternative possibility that the Tabernacles' fire-ritual was a common heritage from pre-Israelite, or early Israelite, days, before the schism — is not suprising bearing in mind their reverence for the spiritual properties of fire, as we shall presently demonstrate.

We must now turn to the second reference to a fire ritual in our Chronicle:

> 'Now the chiefs, who had been appointed over them by authority of the kings of the foreign nations, arrived to prevent them from carrying out the statutes of the Holy Law ... However, all the men of the Samaritan community rose up against them, quickly slew them and *burnt them in fire.* Simultaneously, in every city, in every town and in every place, this act was committed against the chiefs of the nations. ... It took place on the night before the New Moon of the seventh (month), *and the Samaritan-Israelites established a commemoration to that event.'* (11:1–3).

[5] *Mishnah Succah,* Ch. 5.

[6] See J. Hochman, *Jeruslaem Temple Festivities,* Ch. 4; H. Schauss, *Guide to Jewish Holy Days,* 305 note 226.

The exact nature of that 'commemoration' is related in 11:3[a]*, namely, by the custom of children making bonfires of Succah-booths to recall the burning of their enemies' corpses.

The most significant aspect of the passage is the hint given as to when this 'commemoration' would have been celebrated — 'On the night before the new Moon of the seventh month', in other words, on the eve of *Rosh Ḥodesh* and *Rosh Hashanah*! Is it just a coincidence that the Mishnah Rosh Hashanah charges the Samaritans with lighting bonfires on the eve of *Rosh Ḥodesh* in order to confuse the Jewish communities? Might it not have been that the Samaritans observed some fire ritual on that eve of the New Year (according to Samaritan calculation, which may have differed in a day from the Jewish designation, based, as it was, upon the testimony of witnesses) of which the Rabbis were unaware, and consequently interpreted the Samaritan action as deliberately hostile?

Again, it seems likely that the Samaritan Chronicler was linking a New Moon or New Year fire ritual to an event in the history of Baba's life. It is conceivable that the ritual was observed only on the eve of the New Moon of the seventh month, i.e. Rosh Hashanah, and that the Mishnah is inaccurate in implying that there was a Samaritan threat every *Rosh Ḥodesh;* or, alternately, it is possible that the Samaritans did observe such a fire ritual every eve of *Rosh Ḥodesh.* Either way, it is just conceivable that the Mishnaic Rabbis have done the Samaritans an injustice in claiming that they had deliberately sabotaged the Jewish communication system. We do not rule out the possibility, however, that our Chronicler may have deliberately attributed this commemorative ritual to the eve of *Rosh Ḥodesh / Rosh Hashanah* in order to parry the Rabbinic charge of harassment at that particular time of the year.

Without wishing to enter into the thorny arena of the critical theories regarding the origin of the Feast of Tabernacles, if the regnant theory, as developed by P. Voltz[7] and S. Mowinckel,[8] is correct, that its origin goes back to an old Israelite *New Year* festival, then it is possible that the fire rituals that are echoed in our Chronicle in relation to both Tabernacles ('The Day of Solemn Assembly') and the New Year might well have been a vestigial offshoot

[7] P. Voltz, *Das Neujahrfest Jahwes* (1912).

[8] S. Mowinckel, *The Psalms in Israel's Worship* (1962 tr.).

of the original parent festival of the New Year. In Judaism the fire element survived in the context of the Tabernacles' *Šô'ēbhāh* ritual, and in early Samaritanism in the lighting of beacons on both the eve of the New Year and the conclusion of Tabernacles. At a later period of Samaritanism, when the origin and significance of the fire ritual was no longer appreciated, it was temporarily saved from desuetude by a process of re-interpretation, of the kind we have noted in our Chronicle, which related it to the commemoration of victories won by Baba Rabbah.

The connection between *fire* and the New Moon or New Year need hardly be stated. We may merely quote the statement of Mowinckel, referring to the Temple festivity of *Šô'ēbhāh,* that 'like the *sunfires* all over the world it was originally meant to re-create and secure sun and light and warmth in the year to come.'[9] The first glow of the new light of the moon on the eve of *Rosh Ḥodesh* would, consequently, have been the appropriate occasion for a fire ritual, as obliquely referred to in our Chronicle.

Samaritanism shares with Judaism the identification and celebration of the days of the New Moon and the New Year as periods of Atonement. The fire ritual, traces of which, we have suggested, have been left in our Chronicle, may have had some special significance, therefore, as a purification rite.

The concept of purification by fire is mentioned, as stated above,[10] by Montgomery. His evidence is, however, sparse. A cursory reading of the *Memar Marqah* has convinced the present writer, however, that Marqah not only knew of the concept, but that it also wielded a considerable influence upon him.

One of the clearest references to the doctrine of purification by fire occurs in *Marqah* IV, 10:

> — *For a fire is kindled by my anger* (Dt. 32:22). Sodom and Gomorrah were evil, unclean places; the priest defiled, but the *fire purified* him.

Another reference makes it clear that Marqah believed that death by fire automatically expiated even the most grievous sin, leaving the sinner guiltless to receive recompense on the Day of Judgement:

---

[9] *S. Mowinckel, op. cit.,* 187.

[10] See above, p. 206.

— *I will heap evils upon them* (Dt. 32:23), in the world. They will be burnt and in the Day of Vengeance they will be justly recompensed.[11]

Marqah enumerates seven instances in the life of Moses where he was 'glorified by fire,' and one of the most frequently recurring attributes of Moses, referred to in Marqah, is that he 'trod the fire' of the burning Bush.[12] The purifying nature of that experience is akin to that of Isaiah, whose mouth was touched with burning coals, the consequence of which was to remove his guilt and pardon his sin.[13]

One would, indeed, have expected that the doctrine of purification by fire would have expressed itself in one form or another in Samaritanism, bearing in mind its established position in the sacred literature of early and late antiquity.

In the Old Testament fire is a familiar image for divine judgement,[14] and in the Apocalyptic literature we find frequent references to the destruction by fire of the whole physical universe, as well as fire being the instrument of judgment upon sinners.[15] In the New Testament the concept is developed of the refining fire which tests Christians,[16] and in post-New Testament apocalyptic we have the imagery of fiery trial, as well as the eschatological river of fire through which all men pass.[17] Trial by refining fire is similarly well attested in Qumran literature.[18]

The purifying and consecrating properties of the Temples were derived — it was believed by Jews and Samaritans alike — from the fact of heavenly *fire* having visited them. As regards the first Temple, this is expressly stated in II Chr. 7:1. The Samaritans taunted the Jews that Ezra-Nehemiah reported no such fire in the second Temple. The Samaritan smugness on this score was derived from their own sanctuary on Mount Gerizim having been visited by fire in the days of Joshua. The *Fanuta,* or hiding of the divine face, was ushered in, according to their belief, by the extinguishing of the fire.[19]

---

[11] *Marqah* (Ed. J. Macdonald), II, 174.

[12] *Marqah,* bk. iv, 12; vi, 2, 3, 11 *et. al.*

[13] Is. 6:7.

[14] Dan. 7:10, Is. 66:15, Mal. 4:1.

[15] 2 Bar. 44:15, 48:39, 59:2, 64:7; Ps. Sol. 15:16f. Sib. iii, 54, 689–691.

[16] 1 Cor. 3:13.

[17] Sib. ii, 252.

[18] 1Qh. iii, 29; 1QS. ii, 8; 1QH. v, 16; 1QM. xvi, 9.

[19] For further discussion on fire in the Temples, see A. Spiro, *Samaritans, Tobiads and Judahites in Pseudo-Philo,* 305–307.

The lighting of beacons by the Samaritans on *Rosh Ḥodesh* and the eve of the New Year may, consequently, have been part of a fire ritual whose origin may lie in pre-Israelite, or, at least, early Israelite, religion. It may have begun as a sun-festival ritual and developed as a purification-rite related to the themes of atonement, renewal and purification which are the basic motifs of those occasions. The Rabbis of the Mishnah may have been unaware of this Samaritan practice and its significance; and their charge that the Samaritans were purposely confusing their communities by lighting beacons on the wrong night may have been an unfortunate calumny.

IX. LINGUISTIC FEATURES OF H1 AND H2

(i) *General Considerations*

J. Macdonald, commenting on the distinctive Aramaic of the *Memar Marqah,* observes that 'in the first few centuries A.D. Aramaic was certainly the spoken and literary language of the Samaritans, and in this work (sc. *the Memar*) of that period there is revealed a form of that language, albeit through late MSS., possessing many interesting forms and loan-words, and many treasures of Aramaic syntax. Knowledge of the Aramaic of Central and Northern Palestine has never been as great as compared with that of Babylonia and Southern Palestine. Now the study of the Aramaic spoken by the large Samaritan population in Palestine can be further advanced.'[1]

This claim may equally be made for the H2 (Aramaic) version of our Chronicle, which presents us with a feast of idiomatic speech which has clearly differed little from the spoken Aramaic of the early centuries A.D. We will presently make the claim that the H1 version is either a revision of, or at least inspired by, the H2 original. Traces of the Aramaic substratum are clearly visible in many passages and forms.

If, as we have suggested,[2] H1's Hebrew orientation owes its origin to the medieval renaissance of Hebrew among the Samaritans, it may be assumed that the latter did not concoct a new and artificial form of that language, but that the Hebrew represented in their works represented an authentic literary tradition whch had been preserved by them, possibly in works that did not survive the ravages of time. The Samaritans would then have been paralleling the Karaite development of Hebrew, the style of which was largely biblical, but also containing freely derived verb forms.

When Samaritan Hebrew was first displaced by Aramaic it became a literary language. We would do well to take note, however, of what has been said regarding the fate of Judaean Hebrew in a similar situation: 'Although it became a written language, Hebrew did not remain petrified, limited to passages

---

[1] J. Macdonald, *Memar Marqah,* I, xxvii.

[2] See pp. 175–177.

quoted in their original form and meaning, but lived *an active life* in written texts. New topics necessitated an expansion of the language, especially in the coining of new terms for concepts and subjects not found in the Bible' (*Encycl. Judaica,* 16, 1608).

Because of the loss of the largest proportion of Samaritan MSS., over the centuries, as a result of persecution, we are unable to trace this development of the Hebrew language through its various stages. However, the H1 version of our Chronicle, with its close affinity to the classical style, is certainly of paramount importance for the history of Samaritan linguistics, as representing a purist trend — or even movement — among Samaritan writers, paralleling that movement in Jewish literary history which, from *Hayyuj* (12th cent.) onward, changed the whole complexion and direction of Hebrew philology and literature.[3] The scope of this study does not allow, however, for a discussion of such wider issues, and we must content ourselves, therefore, with an analysis of the general linguistic characteristics of the two extant versions — H1 and H2 — of our Chronicle.

The most striking and basic difference between these versions is that H1 is couched in a distinctive Classical Hebrew style, characterized by the use of *Waw Consecutive,* biblical phraseology and quotations. Elements of secondary Hebrew also occur, and are easily discernible. H2, on the other hand, is an Aramaic-orientated Chronicle, although inferior in quality to the Aramaic compositions with which we are familiar from the writings of Amram Darah, Marqah, Nanah and the Defter. Its phraseology is idiomatic, though often disjointed, ungrammatical and complex. This might well have been the result of a long and turbulent literary transmission.

(11) *The interrelationship of H1 and H2*

Notwithstanding the above-mentioned basic differences between the two versions, we incline to the opinion that H1, although a composite work, was compiled under the influence of the H2 version, which probably approximated closely to the *official* version of Samaritan history current in the medieval period.

H1's purpose seems to have been to present a new version, couched in the Hebrew idiom which reflected the outlook of the school of Hebrew renaissance writers of the previous period. A

[3] See S. Baron, *A Social and Religious History of the Jews,* VII, ch. xxx.

further purpose would have been to offer a revised version, supplemented with material gleaned from other sources, both oral and written. One of these sources, before the H1 redactor, probably contained the prayers which Baba is said to have recited on various occasions during his ministry, prayers which appear to have been culled from a version of the Psalter. These compositions do not appear in the H2 version, an omission which the H1 compiler was not prepared to tolerate. As a "Hebraist," he probably felt that the inclusion of these lengthy selections of Psalmody served the additional aim of fostering an appreciation of the finest quality of Hebrew literature.

The H1 compiler also addressed himself to the task of clarifying abstruse renderings in H2,[4] adding supplementary detail to H2's references[5] (even to the extent of providing explanations of the etymology of personal names[6]), correcting its errors,[7] filling in its lacunae[8] and heightening its dramatic effect by representing dialogue in direct speech where H2 has it in a reported form.[9] The H1 compiler also utilized the opportunity of including oral reports and traditions circulating within the community, but which did not possess the authority of literary substantiation.[10] H1's disclosure of the practice of Samaritan children to make a bonfire of the wood of their Sukkah booths in commemoration of one of Baba's great victories, is a notable example of H1's method of extending existing traditions.[11]

The H1 compiler seems to have been strongly influenced by the Moses-Dosithean movement, or, alternately, one of his sources might well have emanated from that school. This would explain the very strong Moses motif in that version, clearly setting out to cast Baba in the role of a 'second Moses.' References to Moses are introduced by him at every opportunity. Where, for example, he is about to quote a biblical passage he frequently introduces it by referring to 'the Law which He commanded by the hand of the Master of the Prophets, His servant, Moses ben 'Amram, peace be unto him forever.'[12]

---

[4] See on 7:3, 24:13.

[5] 5:27–29, 22:24.

[6] See 5:20.

[7] See 9:9, 10:2, 9, 19:11, 20:6.

[8] See 16:24–28.

[9] See 1:19/20, 5:13, 8:1–3, 22:10, 25:9, 24:14.

[10] See 8:18.

[11] See 19:65, the original source having been 11:3[a]*.

[12] 12:10.

The H2 version is a chronicle in the literal sense of the term. Its author had no other motive than to record events as they are supposed to have occurred, and traditions as they were handed down. It may thus be described as a secular account, as opposed to the H1 version which set out to present a type of *Heilsgeschichte,* especially nurtured by the inclusion of Baba's prayers and religious exhortations, which occupy a good deal of space in that version. This higher spiritual aim comes over forcefully in the H1 chronicler's lavish embellishments of pious sentiments and expressions of divine adoration.[13]

In line with this approach is the significant fact that whereas H2 always employs the *tetragrammaton,* H1, out of religious deference, never uses that sacred formula — even when quoting *verbatim* from the Bible.[14]

A difference of approach in the employment of epithets and attributes is also evident in respect of references to Baba Rabbah. H2 is comparatively sparing in its epithets, generally referring to him as, simply, Baba Rabbah. From §18 to the end of the Baba Rabbah section, however, the single epithet *gadlûth* occasionally occurs.[15] As we have observed in our commentary to 18;1, this end section is probably from a different source. The single extra epithet attached to Baba's name should not, therefore, be regarded as refuting the principle of H2's general niggardliness in reverential epithets.

H1, on the other hand, always appends an epithet of reverence to the name of Baba Rabbah. The simplest form of reference is *Ha-Kōhēn;*[16] the title *Ha-Melekh* is often added,[17] or *Ha-Melekh Ha-Ṣaddîq.*[18] H2 never refers to Baba as *Ha-Melekh,* and rarely as *Ha-Ṣaddîq.* Again, after the mention of Baba's name, H1 occasionally adds the invocation, 'May the goodwill and forgiveness of God be upon him, Amen'.[19] This is never included in H2, even though this must have been a common formula used by the Samaritans when referring to their revered departed leaders. This supports our contention that H2 is a 'secular' chronicle, whose purpose was merely to record history, without emotion or pious motivation.

---

13 See 9:2, 5.

14 See 3:20, 21.

15 See 18:7; 19:10, 13, *et al.*

16 See 5:1, 13, 16; 14:9,11. Cf. also *Ha-Kōhèn Ha-Gādôl* (7:6).

17 See 10:23.

18 See 14:1, 16:1, 19:5, 62.

19 See 19:43.

Wherever possible H1 utilizes a biblical quotation or turn of phrase. There is only one example, however, of H2 quoting a biblical verse.[20]

H1 is a more refined version, even toning down expressions which might appear irreverent. To give but one illustration: When referring to the various categories of people who would, or would not, qualify to use the title *Kōhēn* and *Ḥākhām,* H2 states 'the fools *(sokhîlîm)* among the priests ...' H1, on the other hand, refines this to, 'Any priest who is neither a sage nor a scholar.'[21]

H1 is also far less militant than H2 in its descriptions of the pagan enemies of the community. The latter adds derisory and condemnatory remarks, which H1 generally omits.[22]

H1 is totally independent of any of the Arabic versions, and is certainly not a translation of any such version. *Abu'l Fatḥ,* followed by other Arabic versions, approximates far more closely to the H2, Aramaic-orientated, version, even to the extent of rendering in reported speech those passages which H1 has converted into direct speech. Similarly, the Arabic versions do not have Baba's prayers.

In a number of instances, where H1 clearly could not make sense of the H2 rendering, it was forced to abandon the attempt and omit the phrase altogether.[23] Had the H1 chronicler had access to an Arabic version he would have frequently had no difficulty with such phrases which read smoothly according to the Arabic elucidation.

(iii) *A Linguistic Survey*

1. *Verbs*

(a) The verbal noun sense is not usually conveyed, as in biblical Hebrew, by an Infinitive construct with prefixed *b*^{e} *or k*^{e}. We have noted the propensity toward abstract nouns with *ûth* termination.[24] This is extended to an approach which transforms the simple verbal idea into a more complex verbal noun situation. Thus the phrase 'in order to take us and our children and our wives into captivity'[25] becomes, 'for the taking of our children, and the seizure of our wives' —

ובגלל לקחות את בנינו ולשביות את נשינו.

[20] 5:14.

[21] 5:14.

[22] See 1:6, 1:15, 16:18.

[23] See 21:17.

[24] See Word List (III), *CESC* 516–517.

[25] 14:22. See also 9:1, 10:2 *et al.*

Verbal nouns, with the power of governing like a verb, are not unknown in the Bible. Witness the form דעה את יי׳, where the secondary form of an infinitive acquires the value of a noun.[26] Its use in our Chronicle, however, is a distinctive feature.

(b) The simple infinitive is also commonly replaced — even where the ordinary verbal idea is intended — by a second verb in the *imperfect* tense. Hence the forms: אשאלך תרחם (3:11); דרשו יחלו (17:4). This also occurs after nouns; 'It is my desire *to go*' is expressed as מדרשי אלך (8:26, 19:1); 'It is my desire *to send,*' as מדרשי אשלח (18:2); 'It is good for us *to be,*' as טוב לנו נהיה (2:14). Also after participles: 'They are seeking to destroy' is expressed as, מבקשים ישמידו (1:17). Again, although this is not unknown in *BH*,[27] in our Chronicle it is a distictive feature.

(c) There is a strong tendency to place the main verb as late as possible in a clause — even after the object pronoun it governs. This occurs in both H1 and H2.

Examples:
(4:1) (אשר לפניו בעצם היום הזה הקהלו
(3:22) ולזכרון את שמך הקד׳ דרשים לנו ימנעו
(16:18)* דלקדשות השבת מחלל
(11:9) אשר להשמידו מבקשים

An awkward word order is often obtained in situations where the subject of a fairly lengthy clause is inserted at the very end, as in the following example:

(7:2). אשר הפקידם על כל קהל ישראל השמרים הכהן בבא רבה הזוכיר.

The same occurs in situations where adjectives are well separated from the nouns they qualify. Note the position of *ha-zôkhîrîm* in the following example:

(7:4). ושבעת החכמים אשר בחר בם הכהן בבא רבה הזוכירים

(d) There are many examples of both abstract and concrete *plural* nouns, whether they be masculine or feminine, being construed with the feminine singular of the verbal predicate. This construction is not unknown also in *BH*.[28]

---

26 See *G-K* (115d), 354.
27 *Op. cit.*, 385.
28 See *G-K* (145k), 464.

Examples: מלאכות תרחקם (9:5); אתת ... המגיעים (12:1)* ערים מתכוננה ורחבה (14:3); לבבותינו תרך (22:17).

(e) There is a particular predilection in H2 for using *Hithpa'el* forms. Where H1 has, for example, a past participle Qal, כתובים, H2 employs a *Hithpa'el* participle, מתכתבים (see 9:7). Where H1 has a *Niph'al,* נחסר, H2 employs a *Hithpa'el,* אתחסר (see 19:31). In 11:14 we have an extreme example of a succession of six *Hithpa'el* forms, where H1 has a simple *Qal* form:

H1: ... ויחר להם מאד ויקצפו
H2: ואתגדלו המלכים ואתגברו ואתחזקו ואתאמצו ואתפוררו ואתחילו.

Another aspect of the *Hithpa'el,* as employed in our Chronicle, is that, in verbs whose first radical is of the sibilant group, there is no transposition of the *taw* and the first sibilant, as occurs in *BH.* Hence such forms as מתשבצים (3:12), אתצריך (15:2) and אתשברת (16:21, 21:8). Furthermore, unlike *BH,* which changes the *taw* to the more emphatic *ṭêth,* after first-radical *ṣādê* (as *niṣṭaddāq,* Gn 44:16), our Chronicle makes no such adjustment. Hence the forms אצתדק (24:5) and אתצריך (15:2).

(f) There are examples in our Chronicle of verbs which in *BH* do not take a simple accusative, but only a dative, whereas in our Chronicle they appear as accusatives in the form of pronominal suffixes. Hence: אשירך, 'I will sing *unto* you' (14:9) and אדברו, 'I will speak *of* it' (16:9*).

(g) H1 employs a curious circumlocution in order to avoid a passive construction. The active sense is obtained by the employment of the preposition *'eth,* which in our Chronicle is used to signify the *subject* of the sentence.[29] Thus, in 17:6, the context suggests quite clearly a passive sense — 'The house *was taken* out of the possession of the Judaeans.' The Chronicler, however, expresses this as: יצא את הבית הזה מיד היהודים, lit. 'the house *went out* of the possession ...'

Again, in 16:8, to avoid having to say 'I will be the cause of my soul *having been cast* into great suffering,' the Chronicler creates an active situation by means of the preposition *'eth*: אני הגלל לנפול את נפשי בלחץ, lit. 'I will be the cause *for my soul to fall* into great suffering.'

[29] See on 10:4.

2. *Nouns*

(a) We have already noted the propensity for nouns with *ûth* terminations to convey an abstract sense. These occur more frequently in H2, though H1 is not unaffected by this usage, as Word List III demonstrates.[30]

(b) There are a few examples of nouns in the construct case taking a definite article. Hence the forms בהעם ישראל (10:20*) and הארץ אחזתנו (2:19–20*).

In the first of the above examples it will be observed that, in addition, there is no elision of the *hey* and the prefixed preposition *b^e^*. This is, in fact, quite common. Thus, בהערבים (14:7), להקרוב מן (19:4) and להמלך (19:9).

(c) The Chronicler's sense of style did not preclude him from expressing himself by a succession of nouns in the construct case — זקני וראשי ושוטרי עמו (20:18), where *BH* would have rendered: זקני עמו וראשיו ושוטריו, Another example occurs in 15:15, משאי וטרחי המ׳.

(d) A number of examples occur of words, ending normally in *āh,* loosing this final sound. The apocopated pronunciation is reflected in the orthography, as shown in the following forms:

בקע (for בקעה), 19:61
במהר (for במהרה), 20:25
נחם (for נחמה), 23:5
שמח[31] (for שמחה), 25:2
מצו (for מצוה), 4:3

(e) There are a number of examples of nouns which are construed in one passage as masculine and in another as feminine. Thus: בעת ההיא (19:45), but בזה עת (4:21). Also, nouns construed in different genders from those of the Bible. Thus, for example, רגע is construed as feminine (19:28) and כלי as femine (19:8). Regarding such variations in gender, we are advised to note the observation of M. Dahood that 'the frequent concurrence in Ugaritic and Hebrew of the same noun in both masculine and

[30] *CESC* 516–517.

[31] The occurrence of the phrase שמח גדול (14:6) suggests that the above forms may not be purely orthographic variants, but independent masculine alternatives.

femine gender cautions the Semitist against treating a noun as always masculine or always feminine.'[32]

There are also frequent variations in the gender of the plural suffix appended to a noun. Thus we find הרוחים (2:19) and הרוחות (4:10); מגפות (3:21) and מגיפים (4:21). The particular termination seems to be arbitrary, and does not convert the noun itself to the gender of the termination.

(f) We have already drawn attention[33] to forms which appear, anomalously, to be plurals (especially of feminine nouns) but which have singular possessive pronominal suffixes attached, e.g. חקותו (1:17) and תורותו (1:15). The long *ô* vowel, in the second syllable of these words, is, we have noted, nothing more than an orthographic variant of the long vowel *ā*, both being closely related, in the Samaritan pronunciation, to the sound *ū*, which is the sound actually represented in the orthography — not the long *ô* of the plural.

(g) As regards number, we find frequent examples of plural nouns with singular adjectives. Hence the forms: האלות המרירה (2:21*); ברחמיו היתרה (14:22); רוחות משנבה (17:5*) and כלים תמימה (19:8).

(h) There is an occasional freedom in the gender of adjectives. This is especially the case with numerals, as the following examples will illustrate:
ששה מאות (10:2); ארבע אלפים (10:3);
חמשה מאות*, שבע עשר (18:20, 21).

3. *Pronouns*

(a) *Relative Pronouns*

Very frequently the relative pronoun *'ăšer* (or Aramaic d^e) is omitted, and the attributive relation is expressed by simple co-ordination.[34] Hence:
כל איש מכם לא ישמר ויעשה (4:19);
אדרש אני ממניך לא תלכי (16:6).

Conversely, we also have an example of a *double* relative situation, as in אשר הנכון לו (5:8). This form may have arisen, however, through textual corruption.

---

[32] M. Dahood, *The Anchor Bible* (Psalms III), 43.

[33] See our note on 2:1.

[34] See *G-K* (155b), 486.

The normal relative pronoun *'ăšer,* when it stands as a relative of time, is frequently replaced by the word *'āz.* Thus:

כי אז אגלי ליך את הגלל (16:8);
והמלכים אז נלאו לקחת המוס (15:12).

In both these examples *'āz* stands for *ka'ăšer* (when).

(b) *Subject Pronouns*

Subject pronouns are occasionally omitted when serving as the subject of a participial clause, especially when the subject has once been described, or is obvious. Thus וכי נלאים בזאת הימים (1:20).

The subject pronoun is sometimes inserted after a verb in order to give extra emphasis. Thus:
כי לא יצאו הם (5:9).

(c) *Demonstrative Pronouns*

The demonstrative pronoun, as it occurs in our Chronicle, exhibits the familiar biblical characteristics, but also some that are unique and can only be explained as a suspension of the syntax, expecially governing the feminine demonstrative *zō'th.*

Thus, we find acceptable forms, such as הדבר הזה (18:8), זה המעשה (15:9), התורה הזאת (18:14), זאת האש (1:17), הערלים האלה (1:15) 'אהלין הערלי (1:15*), אלה שמותם (10:15).

Occasionally the definite article is omitted from the demonstrative pronoun where the normal rule of grammar would demand its appearance. Thus הדרך הטובה זאת (18:12).

The demonstrative *zō'th* is freely used without any consideration of its gender or number. Hence the biblically anomalous forms: בזאת הימים (1:20), זאת המלחמות (21:10).

In one instance the influence of the demonstrative pronoun *zō'th* is so strong that it influences the person and number of a following prepositional suffix; hence, זאת המוכחות והמגידות דהוכיח ... בָּהּ (3:1*). The third person sing. suffix of הָ is clearly the result of the influence of the demonstrative sing. *zō'th.*

Occasionally we have a double demonstrative. Again the lack of agreement between the two, in number or gender, does not seem to offend. Hence the forms בזאת הימים הזינו (1:20) and מזאת הרשעים האלה (19:9).

A most curious example of a double demonstrative occurs in the expression ואלה היא זאת הטרחה (4:20), with the addition of *hî'* as *copula.*

The demonstrative *zō'th* is clearly the favourite of our

chronicler, possibly since it was felt to convey a stronger emphasis than *zeh*. The importance of conveying emphasis outweighed even considerations of number and gender. It should be pointed out, however, that although *zō'th* occurs with masculine nouns, such licence is only extended where the demonstrative *precedes* the noun, as in *zō'th ha-ma'ăśîm* (2:9), *zō'th ha-laylāh* (19:28*).

An interesting demonstrative adverb occurs in the form הזמן, 'now' (22:23). This seems to be a hebraized form of the Aramaic האידנא.

4. *Negatives*

(a) Negatives are expressed in the usual manner. A negative sense is also conveyed, however, by employing the noun *ḥăsar* or *ḥisrón* (as constructs) before a verbal noun idea. The literal sense of the construction is then, 'lack of, absence of, desisting from,' as, for example, חסר מהלכך (22:15, see our note *ad loc.)*, 'that you should not go away' (lit. the *lack of* your going).

(b) To express the double negative 'neither ... nor,' we have the construction אין ... ולא in H1, and לית ... ולא in H2 (see 3:11).

(c) There is a penchant for placing the negative adverb as early as possible in the sentence, as וצוה לא אחד יתן המוס (11:22*). In this respect H2 reveals the tendency even more, as a comparison of their respective versions will demonstrate:

ולא היה זה היתוב בימי הרצון (6:6)*
וזה היתוב לא היה בימי הרצון (6:6).

5. *Glosses*

Attention is drawn in our commentary to the numerous glosses that have been inserted into our Chronicle. While the H1 redactor is particular about making his version as informative as possible by the aid of such glosses, he is not always too sensitive as to whether or not his gloss blends syntactically or stylistically into the context. A glaring example of this occurs in 7:4, where the insertion of the gloss makes for considerable awkwardness:

ושבעת החכמים אשר בחר בם הכהן בבא רבה הזוכירים

The gloss (*ăšer ...... rabbāh*) here separates the noun *ha-ḥăkhāmîm* from its adjective *ha-zôkhîrîm*, providing the awkward expression *Baba' Rabbāh ha-zôkhîrîm*.

6. *Purpose Clauses*

In addition to the usual ways of expressing purpose clauses our Chronicle frequently employs the particle *'ad* as introductory formula. In this respect it has the same sense as l^e*ma'an*, 'in order to.'

ויבן עוד ... בית כנשה עד יצלו בו העם (8:6)

ובאו פוקידי הרפתים עליהם עד ימנעו אתם (11:1*)

* *
*

It should be noted that the above account of the linguistic features of the Chronicle makes no claim to being comprehensive. The scope of this study has been limited to the Baba Rabbah section of Chronicle II. Any comprehensive treatment of the Chronicle's linguistic characteristics would, of necessity, have to consider the entire Chronicle. It is hoped, however, that our account will serve as a useful introduction through having highlighted some of the more general and significant aspects of the Chronicle's linguistic approach.

X. BABA RABBAH — HIS LIFE AND TIMES

To ascertain exactly when Baba Rabbah lived is well-nigh impossible as we are reliant exclusively upon our Chronicles, with no external references to him in any contemporary or later source.

The Chronicles — especially Chronicle II — are replete with rather loose points of contact with Roman history, especially in respect of the names of the Roman emperors with whom Baba is supposed to have had dealings. The chronology, however, is confusing, and a number of glaring contradictions must be admitted. A consequence of this is that we have to approach the Samaritan Chronicles judiciously and critically.

Internal Samaritan historical data are also very sketchily presented in the Chronicles; thus we do not even know the age of Baba when he assumed leadership. Montgomery is patently in error when he observes that 'his activity is said to have begun in his 40th year.'[1] No such statement is made in any of the Chronicles. Montgomery has clearly confused the age of Baba Rabbah at his call with the duration of his ministry, which is repeatedly given as 40 years.[2]

Even the convenient number of 40 years for the duration of Baba's reign is suspicious. Viewed in the context of the Moses-Baba motif — expressed nowhere so clearly as in our Chronicle, which even employs the biblical phraseology of the Call of Moses[3] in order to depict Baba as a Moses-Taheb figure[4] — the number 40 may be seen as a contrived attempt to parallel the duration of the ministry of Moses.

We have noted that, according to the evidence of our Chronicle,[5] Baba's father, Nethan'el, died only a short time before his son, who ended his days in Constantinople. The duration of Nethan'el's reign is given as 32 years. Thus there arises the additional, though related, problem of harmonising a figure of 40 years for the reign of Baba with a concurrent reign of 32 years for his father Nethan'el. Any attempt to allocate independent,

---

[1] Montgomery, *The Samaritans,* p. 102 n. 73.

[2] *Neubauer,* p. 404; *Adler,* p. 93; *Chr. II,* 10:11.

[3] See p. 177–180.

[4] See W.A. Meeks, "Moses as God and King", in *Religions in Antiquity* (Ed. J. Neusner), 1968, 354–371.

[5] 25:4,5.

successive reigns to these two leaders throws the carefully-wrought genealogical lists of the Chroniclers into total disarray.

In the light of these considerations, as well as of our discussion regarding the respective leadership roles of Baba and his father,[6] we can only conclude that the figure of 40 years for Baba's reign is an artificial attribution, paralleling the 40 years of Moses' ministry.

The truth is, rather, that Baba assumed leadership of the community *during the course of his father's ministry,* and the 32 years' activity attributed to Nethan'el must have overlapped quite considerably the period of Baba's leadership. It is conceivable that the total of 32 years was meant to comprise Nethan'el early period as High Priest, before Baba rose into prominence, as well as the final period as caretaker while Baba was incarcerated in Constantinople.[7] Baba's own rule probably covered a period of no more than 20 years, and he was little more than 40 years of age when he died.

A period of 20 years for Baba's ministry is in harmony with the Chronicler's tradition that Baba ministered during the reigns of the three Roman emperors, Severus, Gordianus and Philippus. The reigns of these three emperors spanned a period of 22 years, from 222 A.D. to 248 A.D. This figure allows for an overlap of the reign of Philippus who, on the evidence of our Chronicle, outlived Baba by a few years.

Baba's "appearance" (*niglā'ûth*) is said to have taken place in the year 4600 A.M.,[8] corresponding to the year 1050 since the first exile and the year 308 since the "appearance" of Jesus. Assuming the traditional date of 722 B.C. for the first exile, Baba's appearance would then correspond with the year 328 A.D. This accords with the figure of 308 years since Jesus, whose "appearance" was regarded as having taken place in the year 20 A.D.[9]

On the basis of our conclusion that the duration of Baba's ministry was no more than 20 years, we may state that, purely on the basis of the internal reckoning of our Chronicle, his ministry should be dated *circa* 308–328 A.D.[10] Assuming that Baba was

---

[6] See *CESC,* 411 ff.

[7] See, however, our discussion of the historicity of this tradition, below.

[8] *Chr. II,* 10:2; *Tolidah,* p. 404.

[9] Macdonald, *The Samaritan Chronicle No. II,* 221.

[10] The Chronicle's term "appearance" would not, therefore, have to be taken literally, coinciding, as it does, rather with the end of Baba's reign.

about 20 years of age when he assumed leadership — in order to do justice to the traditional '40 years' associated with him[11] — we may conjecture that he was born about 288 A.D. This date will be seen to fit the chronological data of the Chronicles admirably.

According to the Chronicles, 'Aqbon II ministered for 23 years, and Nethan'el (Baba's father), his successor, for 32 years. If 'Aqbon II's delegation to King Ardashir (Artaxerxes) of Persia — referred to by all the Chronicles — was sent about the year 230 A.D., near the commencement of 'Aqbon's reign and at the height of Ardashir's activity in the region, then, by adding together the stated years of the reigns of 'Aqbon and Nethan'el (total, 55 years), we come remarkably close to the date 288 A.D. which we have postulated for the birth of Baba Rabbah![12]

The most obvious difficulty is presented by the names of the Roman emperors with whom Baba is said to have had dealings. The emperors are named as Alexander, who was succeeded by Gordianus, who was succeeded by Philippus. These are, unmistakably, the emperors Alexander Severus (222–235), Antonius (Gordianus) III (328–244) and Julius Philippus (244–248). These reigns can obviously not be harmonised with a late third and early fourth cent. Baba Rabbah.

Furthermore, Philippus is referred to as 'the king of Constantinople,[13] and much space is taken up by the Chronicler with an episode describing how Philippus imprisoned Baba in that city until the end of his life. The anachronism is glaring: Philippus, a mid-3rd century emperor, could not have been 'king of Constantinople' when that city was neither founded until 324–326 A.D. nor dedicated by Constantine as the new capital of the Eastern Roman Empire until 330 A.D. Conversely, a Baba who lived out his years in Constantinople could not have had dealings with any of the emperors mentioned in the Chronicle, the latest of whom died some eighty years before its inauguration as capital city.

The visit of Baba to Constantinople is certainly one of the most mystifying episodes of the whole saga. No plausible reason is given as to why Baba should have totally ignored the earnest attempts of his father and community to dissuade him from

---

[11] An age of 20 years is also in line with our observation *(CESC* 410) that Baba's main support came from the younger generation, who were his own contemporaries.

[12] For further supportive evidence of Baba's dating, see *CESC* 377 ff.

[13] *Chr. II,* 22:6.

undertaking such a dangerous mission, especially as he did suspect that a trap was being laid for his life.[14] Furthermore, the Samaritans were strong and victorious at that juncture, and there was no military or political crisis confronting them, such as would have necessitated a personal meeting between Baba and the emperor.[15]

Another mystifying aspect of the episode is the fact that Baba steadfastly refused the request of the Samaritan leaders that he take with him an entourage 'so that they may know your glory and honour your high status.'[16] The stated motive of the Romans in extending the 'invitation' to Baba had been precisely that they 'might see Baba's glory'.[17] Baba's justification for going alone thus sounds in no way convincing or authentic.

These cumulative problems, both internal as well as chronological, point in a direction which would call into serious doubt the accuracy and credibility of the whole Constantinople episode. The options are either that it merely serves as *remplissage,* to round off the life of Baba Rabbah in the absence of any well-attested historical traditions regarding his last days, or there may have been a polemical motive underlying the legend. If the great and glorious hero of the Samaritan community had met with an inglorious end on the field of battle this fact would hardly have been admitted by a partisan and biased Chronicler seeking to inspire his co-religionists by depicting their history in the brightest of colours.

Assuming that the Chronicler belonged to that school of theological thought which sought to identify Baba as a *Moses-Taheb* personality, a divinely-sent deliverer, his motive in writing-in a 'Constantinople period' — in preference to admitting that the great man had ultimately led his people to defeat at the hands of the Romans — would be understandable and, possibly, even excusable. Similarly, someone writing from such a theological perspective as that of our Chronicler — who frequently employs a Moses/Baba association through the employment of Exodus terminology culled from the Call of Moses — would find points in common between Moses, 'whose burial place no man knoweth'[18]

---

[14] See 22:23.

[15] See 22:9, 10, where Baba even threatens the emperor's that he is 'in a position to wage war against the king of Constantinople for the whole of my life.'

[16] 22:25.

[17] 22:8.

[18] Dt. 34:6.

and Baba, who also left his brethren to live out his last days estranged from the community he had led and loved. We therefore relegate the Constantinople episode to the realm of legend, a legend whose creator was unwilling, and probably unable, to harmonise with his other sources which place Baba as contemporaneous with three emperors of the mid-third century A.D.

The chronological problem we have attempted above to unravel, as well as our Chronicler's anachronistic reference to the existence of the city of Constantinople as early as the period of the emperor Philippus, may also be explained on the assumption that he was misled by a tradition that had gained widespread credence, identifying Philippus as the first Christian emperor of Rome. This tradition is recorded by *Eusebius,*[19] and probably owes its origin to the fact that Philippus had displayed great friendship to Christians, that he had corresponded with Origen and had permitted the Pope Fabianus to convey the ashes of his predecessor from Sardinia to Rome.[20] This tradition may well have been responsible for the confusion in the mind of our Chronicler, who, having correctly associated Constantinople with the first Christian emperor, lumped both traditions together.

The period immediately preceeding Baba Rabbah was characterised by such repression and communal fragmentation that when Baba sought out men of scholarship to administer his religious and political reforms, he was able to muster but a few.

There did exist, however, some vestigial hierarchic structure. an upper class is referred to, by the name of *n^e^dîbhê haqqāhāl* or *m^e^'aynê hā'ēdāh* (4:1,9). These were probably men of localised prestige, heads of influential families, that had managed to hold on to their wealth in spite of the general decimation of their communal life. The latter never attempted to usurp spiritual or priestly leadership, and were in the vanguard of Baba's supporters, accompanying him on his mission around the communities, re-opening the Synagogues (4:9).

A more significant manifestation of a pre-Baba hierarchical structure was that of the *Mišpaḥath Haššibh'îm,* 'Family of Seventy'.[21] This was a rival oligarchic group, possibly of Dosithean origin,[22] whose name underscores their claim to descent from the

---

[19] Eusebius, *H.E.*, VI, 34.
[20] *Gesta Pontific. Rom.*, I, 25 (Ed. Mommsen).
[21] See §7.
[22] *CESC* 473.

seventy Elders of the classical Era of Favour.[23] It was this claim which had enabled them to wield power during the turbulent century preceeding Baba Rabbah, when the authority of the High Priesthood was at its lowest ebb.[24] That century had been characterised by a serious loss of communal cohesion, due to intensified Roman persecution as well as a spirit of decentralisation due to migration and the opening up of a new Samaritan diaspora.[25] In such circumstances, devolution of authority was probably forced upon the priestly leadership, thereby enabling this wealthy clan *(Mišpāḥāh)* to consolidate its influence and control over a number of cities — probably in the coastal region — where they had established important bases of trade and banking.[26]

The *Mišpāḥāh* maintained its own priestly ecclesiastical authority. The latter was constrained, however, to defer to the superiority of Baba's sages in matters of religious law; and, under the watchful eye of Baba's inspectorate,[27] they avoided any overt departure from Orthodox Samaritan tradition. Baba found it politic to tolerate their independence because of the enormous financial aid which they gave him to further the common national struggle.[28]

Baba attained leadership largely on the basis of his charismatic appeal — 'From his youth he was endowed with the holy spirit (1:4).' His chief support came from his own young contemporaries, the 'sons of his generation, who were obedient to his voice' (1:10, 14, 19). These young people were fired by Baba's nationalism, and shared his contempt for the apathy and lethargy of the priestly leadership presided over by Baba's father, Nethan'ēl. Such lethargy is not surprising, however, when we read the (unpublished) account of the fearful atrocities perpetrated, especially upon the leaders of the community, by Severus.[29]

Baba believed that the only way to guarantee the survival of the community was by intensifying its spiritual life and by a thorough-

---

23 Op. cit. 468.

24 *Ibid.* ff.

25 *Ibid.* 470 ff.

26 A. Crown, "The Samaritan Diaspora to the End of the Byzantine era," *AJBA* II, 1, 113.

27 7:4, 5.

28 7:6.

29 See *CESC* 407, 412–413.

going process of re-education under devoted and trained teachers and leaders.

He commenced his reform by weeding out those who paraded as sages (*Ḥakhāmîm*) without the requisite knowledge. He permitted only the distinguished doctors of the law to use that title, and particularly the seven who constituted Baba's supreme praesidum were to be known by that title. A distinctive apparel marked them apart from the lower ranking scholars who could also present themselves for examination in order to qualify for the title *Ḥākhām*.[30]

Baba also regularised the title *Kōhēn,* which was, at that time, assumed by any local leader or dignitary *whether or not he hailed from priestly descent.* The assumption of such a priestly title by the influential and wealthy classes may have been a ruse in order to qualify for exemption from personal taxation, especially the *Leitourgias.* Such exemptions were granted by the Romans to those in the category of priests, or *sacerdotes.*[31]

There is considerable confusion regarding the statement in our Chronicle that 'before the days of Baba Rabbah ... only the priests could circumcise the fōreskin of any Israelite child born to the people.' Bearing in mind how loosely the term *Kōhēn* was applied in the pre-Baba period, the statement might well be regarded as meaningless. Our conclusion is that, indeed, no reliability is to be placed on the statement, but rather is it to be regarded as a later gloss by a pietistic — possibly priestly — scribe. His motive, in adding that statement, was to change the import of the previous sentence which states that 'before the days of the priest Baba Rabbah no Samaritan-Israelite could circumcise the foreskin of any Israelite child' (5:11). This verse would seem to be testifying to the successful implementation of the total Roman prohibition of circumcision — as reflected in the famous episode of the Prefect Garman Ar-Rūmū.[32] The addition of the gloss ('It was only the priests ...') served to remove from the community that taint of having abandoned the most sacred rite. The polemical nature of the gloss becomes obvious if we consider the most unlikely event of a Roman decree forbidding circumcision on the one hand, yet permitting priests to undertake it.

---

30 9:3.

31 A. Jones, *The Greek City,* 228, 354 n. 33, and our full discussion, *CESC* 429–431.

32 T. Juynboll, *Commentarii in Historiam Gentes Samaritanae,* 151 ff.

Eager to regularise titular etiquette and exclude from the ranks of leadership those who were undeserving of it, Baba introduced the following regulations:

(i) The title *Kōhēn* was to be reserved for priests who were wise and scholarly, but who had not submitted themselves for formal examination.
(ii) Either of the titles *Kōhēn* or *Ḥākhām* could be used by priests who had successfully passed the formal examination. (In practice, they would probably have used both.)
(iii) The title *Šōfēṭ* was reserved for priests who, although ignorant, enjoyed some measure of communal importance.
(iv) No title was to be used by priests who were both ignorant and without influence or communal importance.[33]

In addition to the seven *Ḥăkhāmîm* of the ruling praesidium, Baba also appointed fifty men who bore the title *Šimmûrê ha-Tôrāh,* 'Bearers of the Tradition.'[34] These were men of advancing years, who could best be relied upon to recollect the authentic traditions of the community, as observed before its decline and disintegration in the era of persecution.[35]

From the instructions given by Baba to each of these respective groups[36] we learn that the 'Seven' had both a judicial role — deciding especially on matters of purity and impurity — as well as a supervisory role within the educational network. The 'Bearers of Tradition,' on the other hand, had no judicial authority. They were merely teachers of Torah and supervisors of the Synagogues.

Of the seven members of the praesidium, the four most distinguished *(ba'ălê šēm)* were given the rank of *pāqîd* (overseer),[37] with special responsibility for going on circuit, as controllers and overseers of the whole judicial system. Their itinerant function recalls the system of *Episcopacy* in the early Church, and especially that of the *Chorepiscopoi* — itinerant Bishops — in Syria and Asia Minor.

Baba also appointed eleven 'pairs' of priests — a system reminiscent of the *Zûgôth* in early rabbinic Judaism — to whom he

33 For a full treatment of the subject of Baba's titles, see *CESC* 420–425.

34 4:11*, 5:1*.

35 *CESC* 417.

36 4: 12–14, 5:8, 6:2.

37 6:5.

alloted areas of Samaritan territory as permanent possessions.[38] We are not told what specific tasks they performed, nor where exactly they fitted into the hierarchic system. They do not seem to have wielded any real authority, and their appointment may well have been merely a sop to the hurt feelings of the priestly families whose traditional authority Baba had replaced by his meritocracy of *Ḥăkhāmîm*. As local civic leaders (Mayors?), the members of the supreme praesidum would probably have consulted them when any measures affecting their particular territory were contemplated.

A relic of Baba's 'pairs' structure survived into the modern era, whereby the Levitical High Priest always had an associate to assist him in the Synagogue Service. The associate 'performs most of the service, though the High Priest is required for the blessing.'[39]

Meetings of the praesidium of 'The Seven' were held in the 'Hall of Meeting and Decision', which was specifically built by Baba as a place 'for hearing all petitions' (9:1). We are not told how fequently 'The Seven' had to make the journey to the supreme court. We may infer, however, from the fact that any candidate for the title of *Ḥākhām* could present himself for examination 'before the great king and before the *Ḥăkhāmîm* on a New Moon or a festival day' (9:3), that they were expected to be present at the Holy Mountain at the least on those occasions, in order to attend to judicial matters and other affairs of national interest.

Baba's reforms were particularly directed toward the reconstitution of the synagogue and the religious ritual as the primary source of inspiration in the life of the community. To that end he re-opened the synagogues closed by the Romans, built new ones — siting them in a strategic circle with Shechem at the epicentre[40] — and constructed a *Miqveh* at the foot of Mount Gerizim.[41]

Of great significance is this emphasis on ritual immersion and the construction by Baba of a number of ritual baths.[42] These are always referred to in a Synagogue context, implying the prerequisite of ritual purification for prayer. The necessity for ritual immersion, according to the Pentateuch, is restricted to instances of impurity,

---

[38] 9: 6–19.

[39] Montgomery, *The Samaritans,* 29.

[40] See *CESC* 490–504.

[41] 8:4.

[42] 9:1; 10:3.

such as defilement through contact with a corpse, reptile, or through nocturnal emission. According to rabbinic sources[43] it was only sectarians, such as the 'Morning Bathers' — probably the *'Ημεροβάπτισται* — who immersed themselves daily before morning prayers.

In 8:4, with reference to the *miqveh* built by Baba at the foot of Mount Gerizim, the Chronicle states that its purpose was that 'whosoever of the Samaritans wished to pray upon this mountain shall immerse himself *at the very time of every prayer'.* The Hebrew of the last phrase — *lᵉʻēth ʻittôth kol ṣᵉlôth* — is unnecessarily complicated, there being no reason for the word *ʻittôth.* Our rendering of this phrase — 'at the very time' — has, if correct, a sectarian ring about it. It is suggestive of a sectarian practice of reciting prayers while, *at the same time,* making ritual ablutions. Indeed, Abu'l Fatḥ tells us of the followers of Dusis ibn Fufily, who 'performed all their prayers in water'.[44]

In the context of the thorny problem of the relationship of Baba Rabbah to the Dosithean movement,[45] such a reference is obviously of crucial importance. It was precisely in the area of ritual purification that the *Dustan* sect introduced extra stringencies, surpassing even Pharisaic legislation.[46]

Although the context of the Dusis account would place him in the age of Baba Rabba,[47] chronological inaccuracies — such as bringing Simon Magus and Philo of Alexandria into the same period — make association of Baba and Dosithean apostles a rather tenuous assumption. The conclusion of S.J. Isser is that Dositheus was an early first century A.D. eschatological figure among the Samaritans, who became prominent through a particular sect of the Samaritans which had been formed a century earlier, and which was Pharisaistic, in contradistinction to the Sadducee-like "Orthodox" Samaritans. 'This sect, now called Dustan, or Dositheans, adopted him as their prophet, and created a Dositheus aretalogy'.[48]

There is, thus, no evidence for the appearance of a personality called Dustan, Dusus or Dositheus, in the period of Baba Rabbah. However, we may acknowledge that it would have been a not

---

[43] *Toseph. Yad.* 2:20; Tal. *Ber.* 22a.
[44] Abu'l. Fatḥ (e. Vilmar) p. 157.
[45] See S.J. Isser, *The Dositheans,* 1976.
[46] *Op. cit.,* pp. 84–95.
[47] Cf. Chron. Neubauer, *Journal Asiatique,* 6th series, 14 (1869) p. 404.
[48] S.J. Isser, *op. cit.,* 163.

unexpected socio-religious development that pre-existent eschatological or messianic ideas — couched in a sectarian mould — should have surfaced in the fourth century A.D., just at that cataclysmic period of decline, followed by sudden ascendency, of Samaritan fortunes.

References in *Epiphanius* and *Eulogius*, associating the Dositheans with extreme asceticism[49] and the eternity of the world, are assumed by Isser to 'have been reflections of secondary developments among the Dositheans or their daughter sects'.[50]

We may assume, therefore, that there was some Dosithean influence working among the Samaritan community of Baba's day, and that some expression of its 'Pharisaistic outlook' actually permeated the thinking of Baba Rabbah. A Dosithean 'daughter sect' might well have established a prayer-site upon Mount Gerizim, wherein immersion during prayer was practised, and this may well have been perpetuated by Baba *under the illusion that this was a traditional form of worship upon the Holy Mountain.*

J. Bowman would go even further. He asserts that 'there can be little doubt that Baba had become Dosithean; in fact the fourth century C.E. was the high water-mark of Dositheism, when the High Priest became such'.[51] It must be pointed out that Bowman's certainty on this score rests on no solid foundation of evidence from Samaritan sources, other than the unconvincing juxtaposition of both the Dusis episode and the history of Baba Rabbah. One or two observations on this are in place: first, as we have pointed out already,[52] Baba was never a High Priest. To this may be added the fact that he, consequently, did not personally supervise or, as far as we know from the Chronicles, even administer the Synagogue liturgical re-organization. He gave sole charge of this to the *Šimmûrê ha-Tôrāh.* Baba was, in fact, particular to point out that it was the "ancestral" traditions of the Synagogue that were to be perpetuated. There is not the slightest hint that Baba '*had become* Dosithean' or that he had espoused any tradition other than the one upon which he was nurtured.

On the question of the juxtaposition of the Dusis episode and that of Baba Rabbah we have noted above that no conclusions may be drawn from this, especially in the light of the fact that the

[49] For relevant texts see Isser, 39 (*Epiphanius*), 64 (*Eulogius*).
[50] *Op. cit.*, 162.
[51] John Bowman, "Pilgrimage to Mount Gerizim", *EI* 7 (1964), 21.
[52] See *CESC* 409.

Chronicle also places Simon Magus and Philo in that same period of Dusis. To this we may add that the *Tolidah*[53] actually places the arrival of Dositheus at Shechem in the period of *'Aqbôn,* the successor of Baba! It cannot be overstressed that, had Baba embraced a sectarian banch of Samaritanism, it is very unlikely that he would have built his entire, re-constituted administration upon the pillars of the old tradition. Baba sought out his *Ḥăkhāmîm,* his *Šimmûrîm* and his "pairs" of priests, from the body of the entire Samaritan community. He did not import any apostles of a new order.

We are prepared to admit the possibility, however, that Baba, in his effort to intensify spiritual awareness, absorbed something of the spirit of the Dosithean sectarians. The preservation of a Dosithean practice, such as immersion during prayer — on the Holy Mountain alone — indicates the direction of Baba's Dosithean tendencies. We do not rule out the possibility, however, as mentioned above, that Baba perpetuated the Dosithean practice, believing it to have been the "Orthodox" ritual associated with the Holy Mount.

At this point we may offer a suggestion which would account for the Chronicler's association of Baba Rabbah with the Dosithean apostles. The redactor of the Chronicle might well have been aware of the influence of Dositheanism in the Baba era, as suggested by the ritual of immersion during Prayer. He was also aware of the liturgical hymns attributed to one *ed-Dustan.* The hymns of *ed-Dustan* borrow liberally from the fourth century *Durrân,*[54] and were, therefore, probably regarded as emanating from that particular genre. If the redactor assumed that the liturgist *ed-Dustan* and the sectarian *Dusis* were one and the same person, and if he regarded the *ed-Dustan* hymns as being an original element in the fourth century *Defter,* then we can fully understand why he felt constrained to marshal his material relating to *Dusis* in the fourth century context of Baba Rabbah.

The reference to immersion during Prayer occurs, as we have noted, only in the context of the *miqveh* on the Holy Mountain. Baba did, however, construct ritual baths in other places, though it is not clear from the Chronicles whether these were for normal use or whether they also had a Synagogical usage, suggesting that immersion *before* Prayer was incumbent upon all.

---

[53] Ed. Neaubauer, p. 404–5.

[54] Cf. Cowley, vol. 11, xxii.

The problem is resolved, however, by a description of Samaritan worship written by the twelfth century traveller, Benjamin of Tudela. He writes:

> 'They remove their garments which they have worn before they go to the place of worship; and they bathe and put on fresh clothes. *This is their constant practice*'.[55]

This information, affirming that immersion was always a prerequisite for worship, owes its emphasis, if not its origin, to the reforms of Baba Rabbah and the ritual baths he built.

Surprisingly, our Chronicles give us no indication as to how long Baba's administrative reforms — and particularly his hierarchical structure — survived as the basis of Samaritan communal life. The solution to this problem is to be found, however, by paying attention to the circumstances of the post-Baba era, as described in the Chronicle. One of the most surprising features of the period is the assumption of leadership by Baba's brother, 'Aqbôn. 'Aqbôn had played no part in Baba's re-organization of the community, he had occupied no official position within the administration and had, consequently, no experience which might qualify him for the position of leader. Yet he assumes leadership, with the title of High Priest; and there is no reference which even betrays the continued existence of any vestige of Baba's appointees. Their titles do not recur, nor can their presence or authority be detected. It is as if, with the demise of Baba, there was a revolution which restored the old order of direct rule by the High Priest. So immediate and complete a reversion to the old order can really only be explained in the context of just such a revolution.

In our discussion of the date of Baba Rabbah we have referred to the difficulty of accepting the historicity of the tradition that he spent his last years incarcerated in the city of Constantinople. If that was, indeed, a legendary tradition, created in order to hide the fact of an anti-climactic defeat on the field of battle, it would explain why, in a mood of abject despair, and with all their unprecedented hopes of spiritual renascence and national independence dashed to the ground, Baba's administration — and administrators — would have been brusquely set aside and discredited. This would have been followed by a return to the only other form of government known to the community, that of High

---

[55] M. Adler, "*The Itinerary of Benjamin of Tudela*", *J.Q.R.*, xvii (1904), 135.

Priestly rule. If Baba did, in fact, fall in battle, then it would have been logical for the Roman authorities to have insisted on the removal of his devolved administration, with its complex power-structure, and the return to the old system, favoured by the Romans, of one leader who was solely responsible to the conquerors.

Our theory, of a post-Baba period of communal despair, is born out by most of the Chronicles, which speak of intensified persecution during that period. Our Chronicle[56] and Chronicle VII[57] both aver that the Samaritans were under tighter and firmer Roman control in the post-Baba period. Both these Chronicles place the Garman episode in that period, referring the circumcision to that of the son of 'Aqbon, who succeeded Baba.[58] These Chronicles also place the appearance of Dusis, and the expansion of his heresy, in this post-Baba period.[59] Psychologically, this would fit a period of spiritual disillusionment, as might be expected in the wake of the failure of Baba's movement to live up to its spiritual and national expectations.

A further pointer to a situation which might suggest the sudden removal of Baba's appointees is furnished by the account of a tragic error of judgement perpetrated by Baba's successor, the High Priest 'Aqbôn, at the cost of the life of his own daughter.

The episode is introduced by a harsh condemnation of 'Aqbôn's total lack of ability and suitability for judicial office:

> Now that 'Aqbôn was hasty in his judgement of all the people, so that many were wont to say of him: "The High Priest 'Aqbôn perpetrates injustice, and deals with cases expeditiously, before the truth has come to light. This is clearly because he is an incompetent judge. Had he been qualified to judge he would not have acted in this way, to rush the judicial process."[60]

The Chronicle then proceeds to relate how certain people, 'who hated the actions of the High priest 'Aqbôn,' proceeded to frame his daughter, bringing against her a false charge of immorality, with a view to demonstrating publicly the inability of the High Priest to evaluate true and false evidence. Acting in his usual

---

[56] See fol. 456.

[57] See Adler, *'Une Nouvelle Chronique Samaritaine"*, R.E.J. 45, 223.

[58] See, however, Montgomery, p. 101.

[59] *Chr. II,* fol. 467; Adler, p. 225.

[60] Fol. 452.

precipitous manner, 'Aqbôn had his daughter condemned and executed peremptorily.

The situation reflected in this story is one which fits exactly a transition period between the removal of Baba's judiciary and the emergence of one which had earned the confidence of the disillusioned community. The assessment of 'Aqbôn given in the Chronicle is precisely what we would have expected of a man suddenly thrown into the position of leader and judge in a period of great communal upheaval and with no previous experience. It does not stretch the imagination too far to suggest that the people 'who hated the High Priest', and attempted to demonstrate his incompetence, would have been the supporters — if not representatives — of the old order introduced by Baba.

Thus, although the resurgence of national pride engendered by Baba certainly survived many generations, and while his Synagogue buildings became the focal-point for Samaritan spiritual activity for centuries, and his intensification of the religious spirit paved the way for the great liturgists of the schools of Marqah and 'Amram Darah, yet it must be admitted that his detailed blueprint for a highly structured political and judicial system apparently did not long survive his own lifetime.

BIBLIOGRAPHY*

Abdel, D.M., A Comparative Study of the Unedited Work of Abu'l Hasan al-Suri and Yusuf ibn Salama. Univ. of Leeds Ph.D. Diss., 1957.

Adler, E.N. and Seligsohn, M., "Une Nouvelle Chronique Samaritaine," *REJ* 44 (Paris 1902), 188–222; *REJ* 45 (1902), 70–98, 223–255; *REJ* 46 (1903), 123 ff.

Adler, M., "The Itinerary of Benjamin of Tudela," *JQR* xvii (1904), 135.

Aharoni, Y., *Hitnaḥălûth Shivtê Yisrāēl ba-Gālîl há-Elyôn,* Jerusalem, 1957.

——, *The Land of the Bible,* London, 1967.

Appel, M., *Quaestiones de rebus Samaritanorum sub imperio Romanorum Peractis,* Breslau, 1874.

Avi-Yonah, M., "'Al Meridôth ha-Šomrônîm B^e^biza'ntium," *EI* 4 (1956), 127–132.

——, *Bîmê Rômā' Ubhîza'ntiyòn,* Jerusalem, 1946.

——, (Ed.) *Gazetteer of Roman Palestine* (GRP), in *Qedem* (Monographs of the Inst. of Archaeology, The Hebrew University), 5 (1976).

Baron, S.W., *A Social and Religious History of the Jews,* Columbia, 1958.

Barton, E.W. "The War and the Samaritan Colony," *BS* 63, 385; 64, 489; 65 43; 70 313; 78 1.

Ben-Hayyim, Z., *The Literary and Oral Tradition of Hebrew and Aramaic amongst the Samaritans,* 4 vols., Jerusalem, 1957–1967.

——, "A Samaritan Text of the Former Prophets?" *Lešônēnû* 35 (1970–1), 294–302.

——, "Piyyut Šômrônî Liś^e^māḥôth," *Tarbiz* 10 (1939), 351.

——, (Ed.) "The Asatir," *Tarbiz* 14 (1942–3), 2–3; 15 (1943–4), 2.

——, "A Samaritan Piyyut from Amoraic Times," *EI* 4 (1956), 119.

——, "Observations on the Hebrew and Aramaic Lexicon from the Samaritan Tradition," *Festschrift W. Baumgartner* (= S.V.T., 16), 1967, 12–24.

Benz, F.L. *Personal Names in the Phoenician and Punic Inscriptions,* Rome, 1972.

Ben-Zevi, I., "Ginzê Šômrôn," *Sinai* 10 (1942), 104–6, 215–222; 11 (1942–3), 156–162; 12 (1943), 410–417; 13 (1943–4), 245–250, 308–316; 14 (1944), 17–20.

——, *Sepher Ha-Šômrônîm* (3rd ed.), Jerusalem 1976.

Bowman, J., "The Exegesis of the Pentateuch among the Samaritans and among the Rabbis," *OTS* 8 (1950), 220–262.

——, "Phylacteries," *TrGUOS* XV (1953–4), 54.

——, *Transcript of the Original Text of the Samaritan Chronicle Tolidah,* University of Leeds, 1955.

——, "Early Samaritan Eschatology," *JJS* 6 (1955), 63–72.

——, "Faith in Samaritan Thought," (Samaritan Studies, II), *BJRL* 40 (1958), 308–315.

——, "Samaritan Law and Liturgy" (Samaritan Studies, III), *BJRL* 40 (1958), 315–325.

——, "Pilgrimage to Mount Gerizim," *EI* 7 (1964), 17.

——, *Samaritanische Probleme,* Stuttgart, 1967.

Bowring, J., *Samaria and Samaritans,* London, 1837.

Boyd, W.K. *The Ecclesiastical Edicts in the Theodosian Code.* New York, 1905.

* In the case of Hebrew titles, the original transliteration has been retained.

Broadie, A., *An Investigation into the Cultural Ethos of the Samaritan Memar Marqah, with Special Reference to the Works of Philo of Alexandria* (Unpublished Ph.D. Thesis, Glasgow University), 1975.

Brown, F., Driver, S.R., Briggs, C.A., *Hebrew and English Lexicon of the Old Testament,* Oxford, 1906.

Büchler, A., *Das Synedrion in Jerusalem,* Vienna, 1902.

Bull, R.J. "Newly Discovered Temples in Mount Gerizim in Jordan," *HTR* 58 (1965), 234–237.

Caplan, J., "A Second Samaritan Amulet from Tel Aviv," *EI* 10, 255–257.

Clair, G., "The Samaritans," *PEFQSt* (1888), 50.

Coggins, R.J., *Samaritans and Jews,* Oxford, 1975.

Cohen, J.M., "A Samaritan Authentication of the Rabbinic Interpretation of *Kephî Tahrā',*" *VT XXIV* 3 (1974), 361–366.

Conder, C.R., "Samaritan Customs," *PEFQSt* (1887), 233–236.

Cooke, G.A., *A Textbook of North-Semitic Inscriptions,* Oxford, 1903.

Cowley, A.E., "The Samaritan Liturgy and Reading of the Law," *JQR* 7 (1894), 121–140.

——, "Some Remarks on Samaritan Literature and Religion," *JQR* 8 (1896), 562–575.

——, "Samaritan Dealing with Jews," *JQR* 16 (1904), 474–483.

——, *The Samaritan Liturgy,* Oxford, 1909.

Crane, O.T., *The Samaritan Chronicle or the Book of Joshua,* New York, 1890.

Crowfoot, J., *The Objects from Samaria,* London, 1957.

Crown, A.D., "Some Traces of Heterodox Theology in the Samaritan Book of Joshua," *BJRL* 50 (1967), 178–198.

——, "Dositheans, Resurrection and a Messianic Joshua," *Antichthon* 1 (1967), 71–85.

——, "New Light on the Interrelationships of Samaritan Chronicles from Some Manuscripts in the John Rylands University Library of Manchester," *BJRL* 54, 2 (1972); 55, 1 (1972).

——, "The Samaritan Diaspora to the End of the Byzantine era," *AJBA* II, 1 (1972) 107–123.

Dahood, M., (Ed.) *Psalms* (The Anchor Bible), New York, 1970.

Dothan, M., "Archaeological Survey of the Rubin River," *IEJ* 2 (2) 1952, 115.

Drower, E.S. and Macuch, R., *A Mandaic Dictionary,* Oxford, 1963.

Eusebius, *Ecclesiastical History* (ed. Lake, K. and Oulton, J.E.L.) Loeb Series, 2 vols., 1926–32.

Gall, A.F. von., *Der Hebraische Pentateuch der Samaritaner,* Giessen, 1918.

Gaster, M., "Folklore of Mossoul," *PSBA* (1906), 106.

——, *The Samaritans; Their History, Doctrines and Literature,* London, 1925.

——, *Studies and Texts in Folklore, Magic, Medieval Romance, Hebrew Apocrypha and Samaritan Archaelogy,* London, 1925–1928.

——, The Asatir: The Samaritan Book of the Secrets of Moses (Oriental Translation Fund, N.S., 26), Royal Asiatic Society, 1927.

——, *"Samaritan Oral Law and Ancient Traditions,"* in *Samaritan Eschatology,* I, 1932.

——, "Samaritan Proverbs," in: *Studies and Essays in Honour of A.A. Neuman,* 1962, 228–242.

Gibbon, E., *Decline and Fall of the Roman Empire, London, 1854–1855.*

Gibson, J.C., *Textbook of Syrian Semitic Inscriptions,* 1, Oxford, 1971.

Ginsberg, H.A., "Aramaic Studies Today," *JAOS* 62 (1942), 233.

Gottlober, J., Bikkoret Le-Toledot Ha-Keraim, Vienna, 1865.

Grant, M., *The Jews in the Roman World,* London, 1973.
Gregoire, H., "Les Persecutions dans L'empire Romain," *MAB* 46 (1), 1951.
Halkin, A.S., "Samaritan Polemics Against the Jews," *PAAJR* 7 (1936), 13–59.
Heidenheim, M., "Die Samaritanische Chronik des Hohenpriesters Elasar aus dem II. Jahrhundert, übersetzt und erklart," in *Deutsche Vierteliahrschrift für English-theologische Forschung und Kritic,* 15 (1870), 347–389.
——, "Der Commentar Marqa's des Samaritaners,' *Bibliotheca Samaritana,* III, Weimar, 1896.
Higgins, A.J.B. (with J. Macdonald), "The Beginnings of Christianity According to the Samaritans," N.T.St. 18 (1971), 54–80.
Isser, J., *The Dositheans,* Leiden, 1976.
Jastrow, M., *Dictionary of the Targumim, Talmud Babli, Yerushalmi and Midrashic Literature,* Philadelphia, 1903.
Jones, A.M., *The Greek City,* Oxford, 1940.
——, *The Cities of the Eastern Roman Province* (2nd. ed.), Oxford 1971.
Juster, J., *Les Juifs dans L'Empire Romain,* Paris 1914.
Juynboll, T.G.J., *Chronicum Samaritanum, arabice conscriptum, cui titulus est Liber Josuae,* Leiden, 1848.
——, *Commentarii in Historiam Gentis Samaritanae,* Leiden, 1846.
Kahle, P., *Textkritische und Lexikalische Bemerkeingen zum Samaritansichen Pentateuchtargum,* 1898.
Kaploun, U., *The Synagogue,* (Popular Judaica Library), Jerusalem, 1973.
Kautzsch, E., (ed.) *Gesenius' Hebrew Grammar* (2nd English edition, revised by A.E. Cowley), Oxford, 1910.
Kenyon, K., *Archaeology in the Holy Land,* London, 1960.
Kippenberg, H.G., *Garizim und Synagoge,* Berlin, 1971.
Kirchheim, R., *Karme Shomron,* Frankf-o-M, 1851.
Klein, S., "'Eres Ha-Kuthim Bazz^{e}man Ha-Talmud," *Jerusalem* 10 (1914), 133–160.
Klostermann, E., (ed.) *The Onomasticon of Eusebius* in *GCS* (II, 1), 26, 86, 88, 92, 98, 108.
Kohler, K., "Dositheus, the Samaritan Heresiarch, and the relation to Jewish and Christian Doctrines and Sects," *AJTh* XV (1911), 404–435.
Leon, H.L., *The Jews of Ancient Rome,* Philad. 1960.
Lieberman, S., "The Martyrs of Caesarea," *JQR* (N.S.) 26, 249–251.
Loewenstamm, Ay. L., "Samaritan Chronology," *EJ* 14, 748–752.
——, "Samaritan Language and Literature," *EJ* 14, 752–757.
Low, A.P. *Aramaishe Pflanzennamen,*
Low, D.M., (ed.) *The Decline and Fall of the Roman Empire, by E. Gibbon,* London, 1960.
Lowy, A., "On the Samaritans in the Talmudic Writings," *PSBA* 2 (1879), 11–13.
Macdonald, J., "Comprehensive and Thematic Reading of the Law by the Samaritans," *JJS* 10 (1959), 67–74.
——, "The Tatragrammaton in Samaritan Liturgical Composition," *TrGUOS* 17 (1959), 37–47.
——, "Islamic Doctrines in Samaritan Theology," *Muslim World* 50 (1960), 279–290.
——, "The Samaritan Doctrine of Moses," *SJTh* 13 (1960), 149–162.
——, (Ed.) *Memar Marqah, The Teaching of Marqah,* 2 vols. (= *BZAW* 84), Berlin, 1963.
——, *The Theology of the Samaritans,* London, 1964.
——, "The Particle *'eth* in Classical Hebrew: Some New Data on its Use with the Nominative," *VT* XIV, 3 (1966), 264–275.

——, Articles under "Samaritan History," "Samaritan Religion and Customs," *EJ* 14, 727–737, 738–741.

——, (with A.J.B. Higgins), "The Beginnings of Christianity According to the Samaritans," N.T.St. 18 (1971), 54–80.

——, *The Samaritan Chronicle No. II* (= *BZAW* 107), Berlin, 1969.

Magie, D., *Roman Rule in Asia Minor,* Princeton, 1950.

Margoliouth, G., *Descriptive List of the Hebrew and Samaritan Manuscripts in the British Museum,* London, 1893.

——, Catalogue of the Hebrew and Samaritan Manuscripts in the British Museum, I–III, London, 1899–1935.

Meeks, W.A. "Moses as God and King," in *Religions in Antiquity* (ed. J. Neusner), Leiden, 1968, 354–371.

Melamed, E.Z., "The Onomasticon of Eusebius," *Tarbiz* 3, 260.

Mills, J., *Three Months Residence at Nablus and an Account of the Modern Samaritans,* London, 1864.

Mommsen, T., *The Provinces of the Roman Empire from Caesar to Diocletian,* London, 1886.

Montgomery, J.A., *The Samaritans,* Philad. 1907.

Montmolin, E. de., *Des Samaritains et de l'origine de leur secte,* Paris 1951.

Munk, E., *Des Samaritaners Marqah Erzählung über den Tod Moses',* Berlin, 1890.

Murtonen, A., An Etymological Vocabulary to the Samaritan Pentateuch. (Materials for a non-Masoretic Hebrew Grammar, II), Helsinki, 1958 (= Studia Orientalia, 24).

Neubauer, A., "Chronique Samaritaine, suivie d'un appendice contenant de courts notices sur quelques autres ouvrages Samaritaines," *JA* Extract No. 14, 1873.

Noth, M., *Die Israelitischen Personennamen,* Stuttgart, 1928.

Parker, H.M.D., A History of the Roman World, N.Y. 1939.

Payne Smith, R., *Thesaurus Syriacus,* Oxford, 1879–1901.

Petermann, J.H., Vollers, C., *Pentateuchus Samaritanorum ad Fidem Librorum Manuscriptorum apud Nablusianos Repertorum,* 1872–1891.

Pinsker, S., *Liqqute Qadmoniyyoth* II, Vienna, 1860.

Pritchard, J.B., *Ancient Near-Eastern Texts,* Princeton, 1950.

Purvis, J.D., "Ben Sira and the Foolish People of Shechem," JNES 24 (1965), 88–94.

——, *The Samaritan Pentateuch and the Origin of the Samaritan Sect,* Harvard, 1968.

Rabinowitz, L.I., "The Psalms in Jewish Liturgy," *Historia Judaica,* VI, 109–122.

Rapoport, S.J.L., Beer, B., "Der Berg des Ostens bei dem Samaritanern," ZDMG II (1857), 730–733.

Réville, J., *La Religion à Rome sous les Sévères,* Paris 1886.

Robertson, E., Catalogue of the Samaritan Manuscripts in the John Rylands Library, I–II, Manchester, 1938–1967.

Sassoon, D.S., *'Ohel Mo'ed; Descriptive Catalogue of the Hebrew and Samaritan Manuscripts in the Sasoon Library,* Oxford, 1932.

Scaliger, J., *Codex Scaliger;* as quoted in Junboll, T., *Commentarii in Historiam Gentis Samaritanae;* Leiden, 1846.

Schalit, A., *Roman Administration in Palestine* (Heb.), Jerusalem, 1937. English Summary in BJPES II (1–2), 1–8.

Schürer, E., *A History of the Jewish People in the Time of Jesus,* N.Y. 1961 (Abridged version by N.N. Glatzer).

Sidersky, D., "Note Sur la Chronologie Samaritaine," *JA* 10, 3–32.

Siegfried, C., Stade, B., *Hebraisches Worterbuch,* Leipzig, 1893.

Sonne, I., "Historical Sources," *JQR* 26 (N.S.), 150.
Spiro, A., "Samaritans, Tobiads and Judahites in Pseudo-Philo," *PAAJR* 20 (1951), 279–355.
Strack, H., *Introduction to Talmud and Midrash,* Philad. 1931.
Strugnell, J., "Quelques Inscriptions Samaritaines," *RB* 74 (1967), 555–580.
Swete, H.B., *Essays on the Early History of the Church and Ministry,* London, 1918.
Talmon, S., "The Samaritan Pentateuch," *JJS* 2 (151), 144–160.
Taylor, W.R., "A New Samaritan Inscription," *BASOR* 81 (1941), 1–6.
Thompson, R. Campbell, *Semitic Magic,* London, 1908.
Tsedaka, B., Articles under "Samaritan History", "Samaritan Holidays and Festivals," *EJ* 14, 733–738, 741–747.
Vilmar, E., *Abulfathi Annales Samaritani,* Gotha, 1865.
Vogt, J., *The Decline of Rome,* London, 1967.
Voltz, P., *Das Neujahrfest Jahwes,* Tubingen, 1912.
Wallace-Hadrill, D.S., *Eusebius of Caesarea,* London, 1960.
Waxman, M., *A History of Jewish Literature,* N.Y. 1960.
Wright, G.E., "The Samaritans at Shechem," *HThR* 55 (1962), 357–366.

INDEX